HISTORY OF THE GUARDS DIVISION
IN THE GREAT WAR
1915 – 1918

BY CUTHBERT HEADLAM D.S.O.

PUBLISHED BY
THE NAVAL & MILITARY PRESS

First Edition 1924

Printed and bound in Great Britain by
Antony Rowe Ltd, Eastbourne

DEDICATED

TO THE IMMORTAL MEMORY OF THE

OFFICERS, WARRANT OFFICERS, NON-COMMISSIONED OFFICERS AND MEN OF THE GUARDS DIVISION

WHO LAID DOWN THEIR LIVES FOR THEIR KING AND COUNTRY

IN THE GREAT WAR, 1915–1918

Ἄσβεστον κλέος οἵδε φίλῃ περὶ πατρίδι θέντες
Κυάνεον θανάτου ἀμφεβάλοντο νέφος.
Οὐ δὲ τεθνᾶσι θανόντες, ἐπεί σφ' ἀρετὴ καθύπερθεν
Κυδαίνουσ' ἀνάγει δώματος ἐξ Ἀΐδεω.*

* "On the Lacedæmonian dead at Platæa," Simonides:—"These men having set a crown of imperishable glory on their own land were folded in the dark cloud of death; yet being dead they have not died, since from on high their excellence raises them gloriously out of the house of Hades."—Translated by J. W. Mackail.

FOREWORD

I AM very glad to write a short Foreword to this History of the Guards Division. I served on Lord Cavan's staff during the first five months of the division's existence, and, as a Guardsman, I continued to watch its achievements throughout the remainder of the war with pride and admiration.

From its formation in August, 1915, to the Armistice in November, 1918, the division served on the Western Front and took part in all the great battles of the war with the exception of that of Arras. Its troops had a great tradition to maintain and very faithfully they maintained it. To the Guards Division attached the prestige that had been so gallantly won in the first year of the war by the battalions of Guards which formed part of the original Expeditionary Force. The high standard of discipline and the devotion to duty which had characterized those splendid troops were gloriously upheld by their successors. And the loyalty, patriotism and keen *esprit de corps* which inspired the infantry were fully shared by the other arms of the Service belonging to the Guards Division.

There was, I should imagine, no division in the British Army in which there existed so strong a family feeling, or one in which the moral was sounder, resting as it did upon a mutual confidence between officers and men. There was, of course, a wholesome rivalry between the various units in the division, but it was, as a keen and unprejudiced observer has remarked, "a rivalry towards a common ideal." The struggle against a skilful and courageous foe had to be won and all ranks in the Guards Division, from its commanders to the most recently joined recruits, were firmly convinced that victory could not be achieved without good discipline and hard work. On many a stricken field they proved the value of their training and gave an example of steadfastness and constancy to the whole Army.

The record of the Guards Division is very fully described by Colonel Headlam in the following pages. He has told his story dispassionately and without making any attempt to give undue prominence to the part played by the Guards in the Great War. He has thus succeeded, I think, in giving to those who may read his book a true picture of the life and work of the Guards Division, and has handed down to future generations of Guardsmen a record of military achievement which should be a guide and inspiration to them for all time.

Edward P.

PREFACE

IN the following pages I have endeavoured to give a clear and accurate account of the work of the Guards Division in the Great War. It is a strictly military record, based on the divisional, brigade and battalion War Diaries and supplemented, where necessary, by other official records, private diaries, personal narratives and various published works.

I have striven after no literary effects; I have interpolated no "purple passages." "Good wine needs no bush." The achievements of the Guards Division speak for themselves. My task has merely been that of the faithful chronicler, who, with a profound admiration for the heroes of whom he writes, sets down the events as they occurred throughout the campaign, and, by so doing, hopes to give to his readers a true picture of the great deeds that were performed and of the sufferings that were endured.

I have received the utmost assistance and encouragement in my work from **Major-General Sir Geoffrey Feilding**, without whose personal initiative this history of the formation with which he was so long and intimately connected would probably never have been written, as well as from Major-General Sir George Jeffreys and Major-General Lord Ruthven. I desire also to thank the various officers of the Guards Division who have helped me either by correcting my narrative or by allowing me to read their private papers and diaries.

I must acknowledge, too, my indebtedness to the Right Honble. Sir George Murray, who most kindly placed at my disposal the manuscript of the History of the Guards Division upon which his brother, Colonel Murray, was engaged at the time of his death. Colonel Murray had carried his history to the end of the first battle of the Somme and I have found useful guidance in his carefully prepared pages.

Like every other author who seeks their help, I have received much valuable advice from Brig.-General J. E. Edmonds and the Staff of the Historical Section (Military Branch) of the Committee of Imperial Defence, and have been given access to all the available documents and maps.

Finally, I must record the deep debt of gratitude which I owe to Captain Wilfrid Miles, who has helped me untiringly in the laborious work of research and who has kindly read through the proofs of this book, and made many valuable criticisms and suggestions. Major A. F. Becke and Captain Miles have supervised the preparation of the maps which have been drawn for me by Mr. H. Burge.

CUTHBERT HEADLAM.

CONTENTS

CHAPTER I

INTRODUCTORY.

(I) A preliminary note on the work of the Brigade of Guards before the formation of the Guards Division. (II) The formation and concentration of the Guards Division . . . (pp. 1-35)

CHAPTER II

THE BATTLE OF LOOS, SEPTEMBER, 1915.

(1) Reasons for the Allied Offensive in the Autumn of 1915. (2) Task of the First Army in the Allied Offensive. (3) Nature of the country on the British Front. (4) German defensive organization. (5) Preparations for the battle and the results of the first day's fighting. (6) Concentration of the XI Corps in the zone of operations—failure of the attack on the 26th of September. (7) The Guards Division takes over the line from the 21st and 24th Divisions. (8) Attack by the 2nd Guards Brigade on the Chalk Pit and Puits No. 14 bis. (9) Attack by the 3rd Guards Brigade on Hill 70. (10) Second attack by the 2nd Guards Brigade on Puits No. 14 bis. (11) Extension northward of the line held by the Guards Division and relief of the Division . . . . (pp. 36-69)

CHAPTER III

THE BATTLE OF LOOS (continued)—ACTIONS OF THE HOHENZOLLERN REDOUBT, OCTOBER, 1915.

(1) The Guards take over the line opposite the Quarries, 4th of October—alteration of their front owing to the loss of the Hohenzollern Redoubt. (2) German attack on the 2nd Guards Brigade, 8th of October. (3) Decision to continue the British advance—rôle assigned to the Guards—German attack on the 1st Guards Brigade repulsed—relief of the Guards Division completed, 13th of October—failure of the attack of the 46th Division—the Guards ordered to return to the line. (4) Relief of the

46th Division successfully carried out on the 15th–16th of October—attack by the 2nd and 3rd Guards Brigades on the Hohenzollern Redoubt and Dump trench. (5) Work of the Guards in the line—bombing attack by the 2nd Bn. Irish Guards on the west front of the Hohenzollern Redoubt —relief of the Guards, 26th–27th of October. (6) Some considerations on the Loos operations—share in them of the Guards Division . . . . . . (pp. 70–90)

CHAPTER IV

The Winter of 1915–1916.

(1) In rest billets in the Béthune area. (2) Relief of the Indian Corps by the XI Corps on the front east and south-east of Laventie. (3) The new line occupied by the XI Corps. (4) Move of the Guards Division into its new area. (5) Bad condition of the trenches—drainage difficulties. (6) Method of holding the line on the front of the XI Corps. (7) Arrangements for the well-being and comfort of the troops of the Guards Division during the winter. (8) The Divisional defence scheme. (9) Winter operations—raids and reconnaissances. (10) Winter Training— Schools and Courses of instruction. (11) Promotion of Lord Cavan—Brig.-General Feilding appointed G.O.C. the Guards Division—other changes in the commands. (12) The Guards Division leaves the XI and joins the XIV Corps (pp. 91–115)

CHAPTER V

In the Ypres Salient, March–July, 1916.

(1) The Guards join the XIV Corps in the Second Army area—in Corps reserve round Cassel and at Calais—relief of the 6th Division in the Ypres Salient, 16th–20th of March. (2) Work in the line—restoration and reconstruction of the trench system —activity of the German artillery. (3) Hostile raid on the 19th of April—death of Brig.-General Heyworth—the Guards relieved by the 20th Division—the 2nd Guards Brigade sent to relieve the Canadians opposite Hooge—the Guards Division takes over the left sector of the front of the XIV Corps, 16th–19th of June —work in the line. (4) Resumption of an aggressive policy on the front of the Second Army—raids by the Guards—departure of the Division to the Somme area, 27th of July. (5) Arrival of the Guards in the area of the Reserve Army—the Division goes into the line opposite Beaumont Hamel. (6) The social life of the Division—the "Daily Dump"—work of the chaplains . . . . (pp. 116–134)

CHAPTER VI

THE OPERATIONS ON THE SOMME — THE BATTLES OF FLERS-COURCELETTE AND MORVAL, SEPTEMBER, 1916.

(1) Objects of the Allies in the battle of the Somme—scope of the operations—nature of the terrain. (2) Opening of the Allied attack, 1st of July—progress of the advance to the middle of September. (3) The XIV Corps transferred to the Fourth Army front—preparations for the attack on the Morval—Lesbœufs—Gueudecourt line by the Guards Division. (4) The 3rd Guards Brigade relieves the 47th and 48th Infantry Bdes. in the line at Ginchy, 9th–10th of September—German counter-attacks in the neighbourhood of Ginchy—attempt to capture the " Quadrilateral "—inter-brigade relief on the Divisional front. (5) The 1st and 2nd Guards Brigades in the line—preparations and dispositions for the attack of the 15th of September. (6) Events of the 13th and 14th of September—assembly of the Guards battalions for the attack. (7) The attack by the 1st and 2nd Guards Brigades on the 15th of September. (8) The attack of the 3rd Guards Brigade on the 16th of September—relief of the Guards Division. (9) Return of the Guards to the line—preparations for the renewal of the offensive. (10) Capture of Lesbœufs by the 1st and 3rd Guards Brigades, 25th of September—the Guards Division withdrawn from the line for rest and training. (11) Work of the Guards Machine-Gun Companies during the fighting on the 15th and 25th of September. (12) Work of the Divisional R.E. and the 4th Bn. Coldstream Guards (Pioneers) during the course of the operations on the Somme. (13) Work of the Divisional Artillery on the Somme . . . . . . (pp. 135–186)

CHAPTER VII

THE WINTER ON THE SOMME, 1916–1917—THE GERMAN RETREAT TO THE HINDENBURG LINE, 14TH OF MARCH–5TH OF APRIL, 1917.

(1) The Guards in the training area—preparations for the winter—work of the Divisional R.E. and 4th Bn. Coldstream Guards (Pioneers) in the devastated area. (2) The Guards relieve the 17th Division in the line, 13th of November—method of holding the front—relief of the Guards by the 5th Australian Division, 21st of November. (3) The Guards relieve the French at Sailly-Saillisel, 4th of December—bad condition of the new front—their relief by the 20th Division, 1st of January, 1917. (4) Work of the Divisional Artillery during the months of October and November, 1916. (5) The Guards relieve the 8th Division between Rancourt and Saillisel, 11th of January, 1917—work in the new sector—severity of the weather—German

withdrawal on the Ancre. (6) Extension of the Divisional front—German withdrawal to the Hindenburg Line—pursuit by the Guards—difficulties of the advance—the Guards ordered to consolidate their new positions. (7) Reconstruction work done by the Division in the devastated area—concentration in the Heilly area preparatory to moving to Flanders, May, 1917 . . . . (pp. 187-214)

CHAPTER VIII

THE FLANDERS OFFENSIVE, 1917—THE BATTLE OF PILCKEM RIDGE, 31ST OF JULY.

(1) The Allied initiative on the Western Front—the spring offensive, 1917. (2) The opening of the summer campaign in Flanders— rôle of the Guards Divisional Artillery and other units of the Division in the battle of Messines, 7th of June. (3) The Guards take over the Boesinghe sector of the line preparatory to the British offensive on the Ypres front. (4) Preliminary preparations in the front area. (5) The problem of the crossing of the Yser Canal. (6) Reconnaissance work by the troops in the line. (7) Plan of attack by the Guards Division. (8) Work of the Divisional Artillery, Trench Mortars and Machine Guns on the Divisional front in the preliminary bombardments. (9) Postponement of the Ypres offensive—further raids by the Guards. (10) The crossing of the Yser Canal, 27th of July. (11) Artillery and machine-gun barrage, 31st of July. (12) Advance of the Guards to their first objective, 31st of July. (13) Advance to the second objective. (14) Advance to the third objective. (15) Advance to the fourth objective. (16) Organization of the new line, reliefs, etc. (17) Work of the Divisional R.E. and 4th Bn. Coldstream Guards (Pioneers), etc., 31st of July. (18) Advance of the Divisional Artillery, 31st of July. (19) Results of the day's fighting on the front of the Fifth Army—Share of the Guards Division in the general advance . (pp. 215-255)

CHAPTER IX

THE FLANDERS OFFENSIVE, 1917 (*continued*)—THE CROSSING OF THE BROEMBEEK, 9TH OF OCTOBER—SUMMARY OF THE WORK DONE BY THE GUARDS DIVISION IN THE BATTLES OF YPRES, 1917.

(1) Holding the line—relief of the Guards by the 29th Division, 7th of August. (2) In rest billets in the Proven—Herzeele area. (3) Work of the Divisional Artillery during the month of August. (4) Return of the Guards Division to the line, 27th of August. (5) Fighting on the Broembeek. (6) Relief of the Guards by the 29th Division, 21st of September. (7) Work of the Divisional

CONTENTS

Artillery during the month of September. (8) Preparations for the resumption of the offensive. (9) The Guards attack, 9th of October. (10) Work of the machine gunners, 9th of October. (11) Work of the Divisional R.E. and 4th Bn. Coldstream Guards (Pioneers), 9th of October. (12) Attack by the 3rd Guards Brigade, 12th of October. (13) Relief of the Guards by the 35th Division, 17th of October. (14) Work of the Divisional Artillery during the month of October. (15) Work of the R.A.M.C. on the Divisional front during the Ypres offensive. (16) Casualties suffered by the Guards during the offensive. (17) Summary of the work done by the Division in the Battles of Ypres, 1917. (18) Changes in the Commands and Staff of the Division during the course of the Ypres offensive . . . . (pp. 256–290)

CHAPTER X

THE CAMBRAI OPERATIONS, 1917—THE ATTACK ON FONTAINE-NOTRE-DAME, BY THE 2ND GUARDS BRIGADE, 27TH OF NOVEMBER.

(1) The reasons for the Cambrai offensive. (2) The Guards Division moves south—scope of the proposed operations in front of Cambrai explained to Major-General Feilding—opening of the attack, 20th of November—the Guards move into the battle zone—relief of the 51st Division in the line by the 1st and 3rd Guards Brigades. (3) Results of the fighting between the 21st and 24th of November. (4) The 3rd Guards Brigade sent to the assistance of the 40th Division—the 2nd Bn. Scots Guards and the 4th Bn. Grenadier Guards in action in Bourlon Wood and south-east of it, 25th of November. (5) The decision for the Guards to attack Fontaine-Notre-Dame—Major-General Feilding's objections to the attack overruled. (6) The 2nd Guards Brigade takes over the line preparatory to the attack on Fontaine-Notre-Dame. (7) Hurried arrangements for the attack. (8) Attack by the 2nd Guards Brigade upon Fontaine-Notre-Dame. (9) Withdrawal of the 2nd Guards Brigade to the British front line. (10) Work of the 2nd Guards Brigade Machine-Gun Company during the fighting, 27th of November. (11) Comments on the engagement of the 27th of November. (12) Relief of the Guards by the 59th Division. (pp. 291–322)

FRONTISPIECE: A Guardsman, 1914.
From a coloured sketch by OLIVE SNELL.

LIST OF MAPS

	FACING PAGE
Brigade of Guards: Operations, Aug., 1914, to Aug., 1915	24
The Battle of Loos, 1915. No. 1—Guards Division: Sept. 27th and 28th	68
The Battle of Loos, 1915. No. 2—Guards Division: October	90
Guards Division: Winter, 1915–16 (Neuve Chapelle front)	114
XIV Corps Sector: Ypres, 1916	134
Guards Division: Operations, Sept. 15th, 1916	164
Guards Division: Operations, Sept. 25th, 1916	186
Attack of Guards Division: July 31st, 1917	254
Guards Division: Operations, October, 1917	290
Guards Division: Operations at Bourlon Wood and Fontaine-Notre-Dame, Nov., 1917	322

HISTORY OF THE GUARDS DIVISION IN THE GREAT WAR, 1915—1918

CHAPTER I

INTRODUCTORY.

I. A PRELIMINARY NOTE ON THE WORK OF THE BRIGADE OF GUARDS BEFORE THE FORMATION OF THE GUARDS DIVISION.

IN the space available in this book, which really deals only with the history of the Guards Division, it is unfortunately impossible to give anything like an adequate description of the work of the Brigade of Guards in France before the formation of the division in August, 1915. At the same time any record of the Guards in the Great War which passed over in silence their doings during its opening year would clearly be open to criticism, for at no subsequent period in the titanic struggle did they ever excel their achievements in its first critical months. It is to be hoped that a full account of the share of the Guards in the campaign between August, 1914, and August, 1915, may some day be written; in the meantime, it is only possible to give a short summary of the engagements in which they took part before the Guards Division was formed.

* * * * * *

Six battalions of Guards went to France with the original British Expeditionary Force, which crossed the Channel between the 12th and 17th of August, 1914.

Of these battalions the 1st Bn. Coldstream Guards and the 1st Bn. Scots Guards belonged to the 1st (Guards) Bde., commanded by Brig.-General Ivor Maxse (Coldstream Guards)

(1st Division).* The 2nd Bn. Grenadier Guards, the 2nd and 3rd Bns. Coldstream Guards and the 1st Bn. Irish Guards, constituted the 4th (Guards) Bde. (2nd Division) under the command of Brig.-General R. Scott-Kerr (Grenadier Guards).† Two other battalions of Guards—the 1st Bn. Grenadier Guards and the 2nd Bn. Scots Guards—formed part of the 20th Infantry Bde. (7th Division),‡ and landed at Zeebrugge on the 7th of October, 1914, under the command of Brig.-General H. G. Ruggles-Brise (Grenadier Guards).§

(1) THE 4TH (GUARDS) BRIGADE, AUGUST, 1914, TO AUGUST, 1915.

At midday on the 23rd of August, 1914, Sir John French's Army was holding the line Binche-Mons-Condé. The I Corps on the right, under the command of Sir Douglas Haig, was facing north-east between Peissant and Mons, and Sir Horace Smith-Dorrien's II Corps was facing north along the canal from Mons to Condé. The front of the I Corps was held by the 1st and 2nd Divisions, on the right and left respectively, each division having one brigade (3rd and 6th Infantry Bdes.) in the front line.

Early in the afternoon of the 23rd, the 4th (Guards)

* The brigade was subsequently commanded by Brig.-General C. FitzClarence, V.C., Irish Guards. When he was killed on the 11th of November, 1914, Brig.-General H. C. Lowther, Scots Guards, succeeded to the command. The other battalions in the 1st (Guards) Bde. were the 1st Bn. The Black Watch and the 2nd Bn. The Royal Munster Fusiliers.

† Brig.-General Scott-Kerr was severely wounded at Villers Cottérêts and was compelled to give up the command of the brigade. Lieut.-Colonel N. A. L. Corry succeeded him and commanded the brigade until the 5th of September when he handed over the command to Lieut.-Colonel G. Feilding, who retained it until the arrival from England on the 18th of September of Brig.-General the Earl of Cavan (Grenadier Guards).

‡ The other battalions in the 20th Infantry Bde. were the 2nd Bn. The Border Regiment and the 2nd Bn. The Gordon Highlanders. Early in 1915 the 6th Bn. The Gordon Highlanders (T.F.) was also posted to the brigade.

§ When Brig.-General Ruggles-Brise was wounded in the Ypres fighting, he was succeeded in the command of the brigade by Brig.-General F. J. Heyworth (Scots Guards).

Bde., which was in reserve, was pushed forward to extend the line held by the 6th Infantry Bde. to the left northwestward towards Mons, and later in the day, when the news reached Sir Douglas Haig that the 3rd Division on his left was being seriously attacked by the Germans, two of the Guards battalions were ordered to take over the defence of a portion of the front of the 3rd Division. The Guards, however, were hardly involved in the fighting on the 23rd of August, the enemy's attack being directed upon the front of the II Corps.*

In the retreat, which began the next day, the withdrawal of the II Corps was covered by the I Corps and it fell to the lot of the 4th (Guards) Bde. to form the infantry rear guard of the latter corps. The Guards were not much molested by the enemy on the 24th or 25th of August,† but, on the 26th, they were seriously engaged in the Affair of Landrecies. In the afternoon of that day they reached Landrecies and the brigade went into billets, the 3rd Bn. Coldstream Guards (Lieut.-Colonel G. Feilding) providing the outposts. About 7 p.m. the Germans, who contrived to make their way close up to the Coldstream piquets by answering the challenge in French, attacked with the bayonet and succeeded in the first moments of surprise in capturing a machine gun. But the Coldstream, effectively assisted by the machine-gun section of the 2nd Bn. Grenadier Guards, quickly regained control of the situation. The piquets were reinforced, and, although the fighting continued until midnight, the enemy made no progress and withdrew about 1 a.m. after a howitzer of the 60th Battery, R.F.A., had succeeded in silencing his guns. The 3rd Bn. Coldstream Guards bore the brunt of the attack.‡ It was this battalion's baptism of fire and it

* *See* " History of the Grear War : Military Operations : France and Belgium, 1914," compiled by Brig.-General J. E. Edmonds, vol. i. p. 73.

† On the 24th of August " Even the rear guard was not really troubled : the 4th (Guards) Brigade retired by successive echelons from Harveng and Bougnies to a position two miles back between Quévy le Petit and Genly, pursued by heavy but ineffectual bursts of shrapnel." *See* " History of the Great War," vol. i. p. 89.

‡ The battalion lost 5 officers and 124 other ranks casualties in the engagement.

INTRODUCTORY

gloriously maintained the tradition of the regiment.* The Grenadiers suffered comparatively few casualties.

The following day, the 27th of August, the retreat was resumed. For the remaining days of August the Guards were not called upon to do any fighting, but the hard and continuous marching in the dust and heat, and the short time available for rest and sleep, severely tested their powers of endurance. Nevertheless, excellent march discipline was maintained, and but comparatively few men fell out.†

Soissons was reached on the 30th of August and the next day the 4th (Guards) Bde. again received orders to cover the retirement of the 2nd Division whose troops had reached Villers Cottérêts. On the 1st of September the 2nd Bn. Grenadier Guards and the 3rd Bn. Coldstream Guards, which were posted in the open south of Soucy, after checking the enemy's advance, were skilfully withdrawn to a line of defence round Rond de la Reine in Villers Cottérêts Forest. The enemy then advanced with a force of all arms and, at about 10 a.m., attacked the second line of defence between Vivières and Puiseux, held by the 2nd Bn. Coldstream Guards and 1st Bn. Irish Guards under the command of Lieut.-Colonel the Honble. George Morris, commanding the latter battalion. After a short artillery engagement the Germans

---

* "The 4th (Guards) Brigade in Landrecies was heavily attacked by troops of the Ninth German Army Corps, who were coming through the forest on the north of the town. This brigade fought most gallantly and caused the enemy to suffer tremendous loss in issuing from the forest into the narrow streets of the town." *See* Sir John French's Despatch, 7th Sept., 1914. As a matter of fact the German troops who attacked the Guards on this occasion belonged to the 14th Infantry Bde. of the IV Corps. *See* "History of the Great War," vol. i. p. 127.

At one period in the engagement the enemy's incendiary bombs set fire to some stacks of straw in a farmyard and disclosed to the Germans the smallness of the force which was checking their advance. Lance-Corporal G. H. Wyatt, 3rd Bn. Coldstream Guards, dashed forward and succeeded in extinguishing the flames although at the time the Germans were only a few yards from the spot. For this, and a subsequent act of gallantry at Villers Cottérêts on the 1st of September, Lance-Corporal Wyatt was awarded the Victoria Cross.

† *See* "The Grenadier Guards in the Great War," by Lieut.-Colonel the Right Honble. Sir Frederick Ponsonby, vol. i. pp. 30, 31; "The Irish Guards in the Great War," by Rudyard Kipling, vol. i. pp. 7–10.

VILLERS COTTÉRÊTS

withdrew and Lieut.-Colonel Morris ordered the 2nd Bn. Coldstream Guards to retire to a position north of Villers Cottérêts. He was himself about to follow with his own battalion when he received a message from Brig.-General Scott-Kerr telling him to hold on to his positions as the divisional commander proposed to give the main body a longer rest in Villers Cottérêts than had been originally intended. It was too late to recall the Coldstream, but the Irish Guards remained in their positions and withstood a hostile attack which was delivered by the Germans in considerable strength about 10.45 a.m. About this time in the day, however, the enemy succeeded in making his way into the wood and attacked the line held by the 2nd Bn. Grenadier Guards on the right and the 3rd Bn. Coldstream Guards on the left. Owing to the density of the trees and undergrowth the companies of both these battalions were somewhat widely extended and the Germans penetrated through the intervals between them. Some fierce and confused fighting at close quarters ensued, but the two battalions held to their ground with great pertinacity and were still in their positions when at length the Irish Guards, who had again been heavily attacked, were forced back through the forest. By this time Lieut.-Colonel Morris and his second-in-command, Major H. Crichton, had both been killed and Brig.-General Scott-Kerr severely wounded; * but the fighting in the wood was so much involved and units so inextricably intermingled that any kind of general supervision would have been out of the question. Officers and men of all three battalions behaved with the utmost steadiness and determination, and succeeded in fighting their way back to Villers Cottérêts, which they reached about 2 p.m.†

* The command of the brigade temporarily passed to Lieut.-Colonel N. A. L. Corry, Major G. Jeffreys taking over the command of the 2nd Bn. Grenadier Guards. The command of the 1st Bn. Irish Guards devolved upon Major H. H. Stepney, until the arrival of Lieut.-Colonel Lord Ardee on the 18th of September. The death of Lieut.-Colonel Morris deprived the Irish Guards of an extremely able commanding officer in whom all ranks had the greatest confidence.

† See " History of the Great War," vol. i. pp. 241, 242. " At Villers Cottérêts the men of the 4th Brigade became very much mixed, and

They had checked the advance of a considerably superior force of the enemy and inflicted serious casualties upon him.

The 4th (Guards) Bde. had no more fighting during the retreat.

On the 6th of September the Allied Armies returned to the offensive and two days later the 4th (Guards) Bde., now commanded by Lieut.-Colonel Feilding,* formed the infantry of the advanced guard of the 2nd Division and helped to force the passage of the Petit Morin after some considerable opposition from the enemy.† The following day the Marne was crossed without any fighting. On the 13th of September an attempt was made by the 2nd Bn. Coldstream Guards to cross the Aisne by means of a temporary bridge at Chavonne after the enemy had been driven out of that village. The battalion succeeded in crossing the river, but then came under heavy artillery fire as it reached the ridge on the farther bank and had to be withdrawn again across the river, a guard being left at the bridge.

The following day the 2nd Division effected the passage of the Aisne at Pont Arcy, the 4th (Guards) Bde., the last of its brigades to cross the river, being directed on the Soupir spur which had already been occupied by the 6th Infantry Bde. The 2nd Bn. Grenadier Guards led the advance which was vigorously shelled by the enemy. The Grenadiers began to reach their allotted positions in the neighbourhood of La Cour de Soupir Farm at about 10.30 a.m. and were almost immediately attacked by the Germans advancing in dense masses across the open. They held their ground and the 3rd Bn. Coldstream Guards, coming up on

---

officers took command of the men who happened to be near them. The wood, too, was so thick that at fifty yards' distance parties were practically out of sight of each other." *See* " The Grenadier Guards in the Great War," vol. i. p. 34. In this action the Grenadiers lost altogether 4 officers and 160 other ranks ; the Coldstream 3 officers and 37 other ranks ; the Irish Guards 9 officers and 115 other ranks.

* Major T. G. Matheson temporarily took over the command of the 3rd Bn. Coldstream Guards. On the 17th of September Brig.-General the Earl of Cavan arrived from England and assumed the command of the brigade, Lieut.-Colonel Feilding returning to his battalion. About the same time, Lieut.-Colonel W. Smith took over the command of the 2nd Bn. Grenadier Guards.

† *See* " History of the Great War," vol. i. pp. 282, 283.

their right, was in time to check the enemy's advance which had made some progress on that flank. Heavy fighting continued throughout the remainder of the day, but the Guards were able to hold their own, and, when darkness set in, entrenched on a line north and north-west of La Cour de Soupir Farm.*

The stand of the Germans on the Aisne brought to an end the Allied advance on this part of the front and began the period of trench warfare which was to last for so many months.

For nearly three weeks the Guards remained in their positions in the neighbourhood of Soupir. At first they suffered severely from the enemy's artillery fire, but by degrees the trenches were improved and the casualties steadily decreased.

By the end of September it was abundantly clear to the Allied leaders that no farther progress could be made on the Aisne front, and, at the beginning of October, Sir John French, with the approval of General Joffre, transferred his troops to Flanders.†

The I Corps was the last of the three British corps to move north and the 4th (Guards) Bde. did not reach Hazebrouck until the middle of October.

The 19th of October, 1914, is the official date of the opening of the first battle of Ypres which continued without intermission until the 22nd of November.‡ On the 20th of October the 2nd Division moved forward from Boeschepe.§

The 4th (Guards) Bde. formed the infantry of the advanced guard and its leading battalions, the 2nd and 3rd Coldstream Guards, got in touch with troops of the 7th Division in the vicinity of Zonnebeke where they dug themselves in for the night. The other two battalions of the brigade billetted that night at St. Jean. The following day the whole

---

* The casualties in the brigade during the day's fighting amounted to about 500.

† *See* " History of the Great War," vol. i. p. 406.

‡ *See* " Report of the Battles Nomenclature Committee as approved by the Army Council." [Cmd. 1138], 1921.

§ The division was ordered to march in the direction of Thourout, a town situated about ten miles east of Dixmude.

brigade moved forward towards Passchendaele and took up a defensive position a little to the east of the Zonnebeke-Langemarck road. The enemy was reported to be advancing in great strength through Houthulst Forest, and information was received that the progress of the troops on the right and left of the Guards had been brought to a standstill.

On the 22nd of October an attempt was made to continue the British advance. The 2nd Division moved forward to the attack with the 7th Division on its right and the 1st Division on its left. The 4th (Guards) Bde. was on the right of its divisional front. The 2nd and 3rd Bns. Coldstream Guards led the advance, but the fire of the enemy's artillery was very severe and little progress was made. At night the Guards were close to the Zonnebeke-Passchendaele road and the Grenadiers and Irish Guards were sent forward to fill the gaps in the line. The casualties in the brigade during the day's fighting had not been particularly heavy, but the Coldstream had lost 6 officers, including Lieut.-Colonel Feilding, who was slightly wounded,* and 80 other ranks.

The following day the positions held by the Guards were taken over by the French, and, as the brigade moved out of the line, the troops were able to get a tolerable night's rest. On the 25th of October the Guards were ordered to take the Reutel spur. The 1st Bn. Irish Guards led the attack, but its advance was fiercely opposed and was checked about 200 yards north of the village of Reutel. The 2nd Bn. Grenadier Guards, on the right, made even less progress. During the night the enemy made three counter-attacks, but was repulsed on each occasion. Further efforts were made to continue the advance the following day, but the German machine-gun and artillery superiority prevented any material progress being made. At dusk the 1st (Guards) Bde. (1st Division) took over the line of the 7th Division north of the Menin road and was thus on the immediate right of the 4th (Guards) Bde. Lord Cavan under the cover

* Major Matheson again took over the command of the 3rd Bn. Coldstream Guards. Lieut.-Colonel Feilding was able to return to his battalion on the 15th of November.

of darkness sent up the 2nd Bn. Coldstream Guards to link up the Irish Guards and Grenadiers in his front line. The 27th of October was a quiet day and the Guards seized the opportunity to improve their trenches. The Irish Guards were relieved by the 3rd Bn. Coldstream Guards.

The two Coldstream battalions, under the command of Lieut.-Colonel Pereira, who also had at times under his command units or portions of other units, held this line on the eastern edge of Polygon Wood facing Reutel and Becelaere until the night of the 15th–16th of November, when they were relieved by the French. They were not involved in any heavy fighting with the German infantry during this period, but they had no respite from the fire of the enemy's guns and his snipers were always busy. It was a long and trying ordeal for all ranks.*

On the 29th of October the Germans launched a heavy attack upon the point of junction between the 1st and 7th Divisions in the neighbourhood of the cross-roads south-east of Gheluvelt and for a time the British line was broken. The 2nd Bn. Grenadier Guards and the 1st Bn. Irish Guards were then in 2nd Divisional reserve and the latter battalion was sent forward to assist in restoring the situation northeast of Poezelhoek. The following day saw the 3rd Cavalry Bde. and the 7th Division pressed back towards Klein Zillebeke, and Lord Cavan, having under his command the 2nd Bn. Grenadier Guards, the 1st Bn. Irish Guards and the 2nd Bn. The Oxfordshire and Buckinghamshire Light Infantry, was ordered to move down to the right of the 7th Division. In the evening the Irish Guards and the Oxfordshire and Buckinghamshire Light Infantry dug in on the edge of the wood, which later on came to be known as Shrewsbury Forest. The Grenadiers were on the right supporting the cavalry. This

---

* Curiously enough the remnant of the 1st Bn. Coldstream Guards—about 120 strong, without officers or senior non-commissioned officers—also came under Lieut.-Colonel Pereira's command on the 5th of November. *See* p. 17.

From the 25th of October to the 17th of November the 2nd Bn. Coldstream Guards lost 7 officers and 216 men. On leaving Polygon Wood the two Coldstream battalions marched to Zillebeke, where they again came under the command of Lord Cavan.

line was heavily shelled by the enemy's artillery on the 31st of October, the Irish Guards being the principal sufferers. German attacks, too, farther to the left, uncovered the left flank of "Cavan's Force" for a time, but nevertheless the position was successfully maintained. The Grenadiers were relieved by the French at an early hour on the 1st of November, but the Irish Guards remained to suffer further losses from the enemy's continuous artillery bombardment.* Later in the same day, the Grenadiers were employed in a counter-attack which once more brought them up into the line on the left of the Irish Guards. This counter-attack restored the front which had been broken.

Heavy hostile shelling continued throughout the days which followed and the tired but indomitable troops were called upon to withstand repeated infantry attacks. The 6th of November was an especially trying one for the Irish Guards. The French troops on their right were forced to retire and the right company of the Irish Guards was overwhelmed. The following day Major Stepney, the officer commanding the battalion, was killed.† Two days later, on the night of the 9th, the Irish Guards were relieved and moved back into corps reserve, the survivors together with the reinforcements available only sufficing to form two companies each barely 150 strong.

The following day the Grenadiers were relieved after passing through what they themselves described as "the most gruelling day of the bombardment." ‡

Neither the Grenadiers nor the Irish Guards were deeply

---

* Casualties among the officers of the Irish Guards were very heavy on the 1st of November, Lord Ardee, the commanding officer, being among the wounded. Major Stepney assumed the command of the battalion.

† See "The Irish Guards in the Great War," vol. i. p. 42. Capt. N. Orr-Ewing commanded the battalion from this date until the night of the 9th of November when Major Webber took over the command from him. The battalion between the 31st of October and the 7th of November lost 16 officers and 597 other ranks.

‡ See "The Grenadier Guards in the Great War," vol. i. pp. 170, 171. "The 2nd Battalion Grenadiers made a wonderful stand to-day against enfilade fire of the worst description. They stuck it out simply magnificently." Extract from an account of the day's fighting by Lord Cavan.

involved in the battle of Nonne Boschen (Nuns' Wood) on the 11th of November, although the former had some casualties when moving up in support of the attack and spent a very unpleasant night and day under hostile artillery fire in the neighbourhood of the wood. In the evening of the 12th of November the two Guards battalions, together with the 2nd Bn. The Royal Munster Fusiliers and the 1st Bn. The Gloucestershire Regiment, were ordered to carry out a counter-attack under the command of Brig.-General FitzClarence. This counter-attack was never actually launched,* but the 1st Bn. Irish Guards, which led the advance from Nonne Boschen, came under a severe and accurate fire and had heavy casualties, with the result that at nightfall the battalion only mustered 4 officers and 160 men. Major Webber, commanding the Irish Guards,† was wounded and Brig.-General FitzClarence killed.‡

On the 15th of November the Grenadiers and Irish Guards, who had received a draft of men, rejoined " Cavan's Force " and went back into the trenches near Klein Zillebeke, the cavalry being on their right. On the 17th, the Germans made their last desperate effort to reach Ypres. Attack after attack was driven back with but comparatively slight losses to the Guards battalions. One company alone of the Grenadiers is reported to have fired over 24,000 rounds of ammunition and the enemy's losses were enormous.

On the 18th of November the 3rd Bn. Coldstream Guards took over the line held by the Grenadiers and Irish Guards and was in turn relieved by the French on the 20th of November. The 2nd Division was then withdrawn from the battle zone and the 4th (Guards) Bde. went back into billets at Meteren, together with the 1st Bn. The Hertfordshire

* See " The Grenadier Guards in the Great War," vol. i. pp. 175-177.

† Major the Honble. J. Trefusis, Scots Guards, succeeded him in the command on the 13th of December. Owing to the arrival of further drafts, the battalion mustered 15 officers and 700 men early in December.

‡ The death of Brig.-General FitzClarence, Irish Guards, was a serious loss to the Army. His great courage and brilliant leadership had already been amply proved on the 31st of October when his quick decision and initiative led to the recapture of Gheluvelt. See " 1914," by Field-Marshal Viscount French of Ypres, p. 254.

Regiment, which had joined it during the strenuous days at Ypres.*

In December the I Corps was ordered to relieve the Indian Corps, which was holding the area round Richebourg l'Avoué.† The 4th (Guards) Bde. reached Béthune on the 22nd of December, and the next day went into a very wet part of the line north-east of that town. The troops whilst in this area were subjected to the constant sniping and trench-mortar fire of the enemy, but their main source of trouble was due to the boggy nature of the ground which rendered the construction and maintenance of a trench system during the winter months an almost superhuman task. At the end of January, 1915, a move was made to the Cuinchy sector of the front, south of the La Bassée Canal. Early in the morning of the 1st of February, the day after the 4th (Guards) Bde. took over this new line, the 2nd Bn. Coldstream Guards was attacked by German bombers and lost some of its trenches. An immediate counter-attack in which the Irish Guards assisted, met with little success; but a second one, following a heavy artillery preparation, resulted in the re-capture of the lost ground as well as of some of the enemy's trenches.‡ A further attack on the brick stacks, which still remained in German hands, was carried out by the Irish Guards and the 3rd Bn. Coldstream Guards, on the 6th of February, and ended in their capture.

* In a letter to Colonel Sir Henry Streatfeild, Lord Cavan wrote as follows of the doings of the 4th (Guards) Bde. in the first battle of Ypres: "No words can ever describe what the devotion of the men and officers has been under the trials of dirt, squalor, cold, sleeplessness, and perpetual strain of the last three weeks. . . . We came into this theatre 3,700 strong, and we shall go back about 2,000, but nothing finer to my mind has ever been done by human men."

† The line actually occupied by the Indian Corps ran from beyond the canal south of Givenchy to the cross-roads just south of Neuve Chapelle. At this date the Indians were heavily engaged with the Germans and their line had been broken. The 1st Division, however, had succeeded in restoring the situation before the arrival of the 4th (Guards) Bde. *See* p. 18.

‡ The casualties on this fighting were rather heavy. The Coldstream lost 2 officers and 72 other ranks; the Irish Guards 5 officers and 32 other ranks; 32 prisoners and 2 machine guns were taken. Lance-Corporal O'Leary, Irish Guards, was awarded the Victoria Cross for his conspicuous bravery in this engagement.

BATTLE OF FESTUBERT

For the remainder of the winter and early spring the Guards remained in this part of the line, and by dint of hard and persistent work succeeded in converting an ill-constructed and ill-designed series of trenches into an organized defensive system.*

On the 15th of May began the battle of Festubert, in which the 2nd Division was engaged. The 4th (Guards) Bde. was in reserve for the first part of the attack. But, on the 17th, the 2nd Bn. Grenadier Guards and the 1st Bn. Irish Guards were pushed in in rear of the left flank of the 7th Division, and at night went forward to link up that division with the right flank of the 2nd Division. The general attack was resumed the following day. Both Grenadiers and Irish Guards came under a galling fire before the hour fixed for the advance, and, when at length the time came to move forward, they were met by so fierce a machine-gun fire that little progress was possible. The losses were very heavy, the Irish Guards in particular suffering terribly in their efforts to storm Cour d'Avoué Farm.†

After Festubert the 4th (Guards) Bde., before it left the 2nd Division to join the Guards Division, occupied various sectors on the front of the First Army—Vermelles, Auchy, Cambrin and Givenchy. Throughout these weeks the brigade did magnificent work in the line, in despite of the

---

* The 4th (Guards) Bde. was not called upon to take a leading part in the battle of Neuve Chapelle (10th–13th of March). Three of its battalions—the 2nd Bn. Grenadier Guards, the 2nd Bn. Coldstream Guards and the 1st Bn. Irish Guards—were in divisional reserve on the first day of the battle when the 6th Infantry Bde. attacked. The remaining two battalions—the 3rd Bn. Coldstream Guards and the 1st Bn. The Hertfordshire Regiment—were in corps reserve. The attack was to have been continued on the 11th of March, but it was found advisable to cancel the orders, and consequently instead of attempting to carry on the advance the Guards battalions went in to hold the line reached by the 6th Infantry Bde.

† See "The Irish Guards in the Great War," vol. i. pp. 85–89. The Irish Guards lost 18 officers and 461 other ranks; the Grenadiers 6 officers (including their commanding officer, Lieut.-Colonel W. Smith, who was mortally wounded), and 102 other ranks, killed, wounded or missing. The command of the battalion devolved upon Major G. Jeffreys. Early in May Lieut.-Colonel Pereira was appointed to command an infantry brigade, Major J. Steele succeeding him in the command of the 2nd Bn. Coldstream Guards.

persistent operations of the enemy's miners and bombers, and the constant activity of his trench mortars and artillery. The troops earned the unstinted admiration of their divisional commander and also of Sir Douglas Haig;* and, when the time came for them to leave the 2nd Division, the warmth of the send-off accorded to them marked the admiration and affection with which they were regarded by their comrades during a year of strenuous war. †

(2) THE 1ST (GUARDS) BRIGADE, AUGUST, 1914, TO AUGUST, 1915.

As already stated, the 1st Bn. Coldstream Guards and the 1st Bn. Scots Guards, together with the 1st Bn. The Black

---

* On the 18th of August, the day before the 4th (Guards) Bde. left the 2nd Division, Major-General Horne, commanding the division, sent the following message to the brigade : " The 4th (Guards) Bde. leaves the Second Division to-morrow. The G.O.C. speaks not only for himself, but for every officer, non-commissioned officer and man of the Division when he expresses sorrow that certain changes in organization have rendered necessary the severance of ties of comradeship commenced in peace and cemented by war. For the past year, by gallantry, devotion to duty, and sacrifice in battles and in the trenches the Brigade has maintained the high traditions of His Majesty's Guards and equally by thorough performance of duties, strict discipline, and the exhibition of many soldier-like qualities, has set an example of smartness which has tended to raise the standard and elevate the moral of all with whom it has been associated." On the 20th of August, Sir Douglas Haig, the First Army commander, sent the following message to the brigade : " The 4th (Guards) Bde. leaves my command to-day after over a year of active service in the field. During that time the Brigade has taken part in military operations of the most diverse kind and under varied conditions of country and weather, and throughout all ranks have displayed the greatest fortitude, tenacity and resolution."

† Various changes had taken place in the commands of the 4th (Guards) Bde. before it left the 2nd Division to become the 1st Guards Bde. in the Guards Division. At the end of June Lord Cavan was appointed G.O.C. the 50th (Northumbrian) Division, and Lieut.-Colonel G. Feilding succeeded him in the command of the 4th (Guards) Bde. Major Matheson, who then took over the command of the 3rd Bn. Coldstream Guards, soon afterwards obtained the command of an infantry brigade, and was succeeded by Major J. V. Campbell. In August Lieut.-Colonel the Honble. J. Trefusis also was appointed to command an infantry brigade and was succeeded in the command of the 1st Bn. Irish Guards by Major G. H. C. Madden.

Watch and the 2nd Bn. The Royal Munster Fusiliers, under the command of Brig.-General Maxse, formed the 1st (Guards) Bde. of the 1st Division in the British Expeditionary Force. Although this brigade shared in the hardships of the retreat from Mons, its battalions, which formed the rear guard of the division on the 27th of August, were not seriously engaged with the exception of the 2nd Bn. The Royal Munster Fusiliers, which was cut off and overwhelmed at Etreux.*

When the Allied Armies turned and advanced on the 6th of September, the 1st Bn. Coldstream Guards (Lieut.-Colonel J. Ponsonby) formed the infantry of the advanced guard of the 1st Division. The Petit Morin and the Marne were crossed without either of the two Guards battalions coming into action, and it was not until the 14th of September, the day after the passage of the Aisne had been effected, that they were really seriously engaged. That day the 1st Bn. Coldstream Guards was in the van of the 1st (Guards) Bde., and, after struggling up the wooded Vendresse valley, took up a position along the Chemin des Dames, where it suffered heavy losses from the enemy's artillery fire. Lieut.-Colonel Ponsonby eventually collected the equivalent of about a company of his men and continued the advance, penetrating about a mile within the enemy's line and occupying a very forward position beyond the village of Cerny. Then followed some confused fighting in the fog which was very thick. For a time the Guards were able to hold their own, but in the afternoon a heavy counter-attack, in which eighteen German battalions took part, was launched against the front held by the 1st Division. The Coldstream, Scots Guards and Cameron Highlanders made a gallant resistance and attacked in their turn, but the enemy's pressure was too great, and they were eventually obliged to relinquish their forward positions.†

* The heroic stand of the Munster Fusiliers was of the utmost service to the retreating force and arrested the enemy's pursuit for fully six hours. *See* " History of the Great War," vol. i. pp. 211, 212. The Munsters were replaced in the brigade by the 1st Bn. The Cameron Highlanders.

† *See* " History of the Great War," vol. i. pp. 342–346. The day's fighting cost the 1st Bn. Coldstream Guards 11 officers and 350 other ranks, Lieut.-Colonel Ponsonby being among the wounded. The casualties of the 1st Bn. Scots Guards amounted to 6 officers, including

From this day onwards the Coldstream and Scots Guards, although like all the other battalions in the Aisne area they suffered severely from the enemy's artillery fire, were not seriously engaged again with the German infantry until they appeared in the battle zone at Ypres late in October.

The 1st Division went into action on the 21st of that month on the left of the British line. Advancing in a north-easterly direction towards Koekuit with Bixschoote on its left, the 1st (Guards) Bde. made some progress, but repeated attacks by the German infantry, supported by intense artillery fire on the 22nd and 23rd of October, checked the advance and brought the battle of Langemarck to an end.* The brigade was relieved by the French in this area on the 25th of October, and the next evening took over the left portion of the front of the 7th Division north of the Menin road, where it found the 4th (Guards) Bde. on its left. Between the 26th and 29th of October the Coldstream and Scots Guards were allowed no rest by the enemy's artillery, the fire of which was as effective as it was persistent. The casualties were heavy, and the Coldstream became so much reduced in strength that it was found necessary to put in one company of the Black Watch at the Gheluvelt cross-roads on their right, and another company of the same battalion between them and the Scots Guards on their left. Even so, the line was much too thinly held.

Early in the morning of the 29th of October the Germans attacked in great strength along and on each side of the Menin road, and broke through the British line at the Gheluvelt cross-roads. They thus took the company of the Black Watch and two companies of the 1st Bn. Coldstream Guards in flank, and, after a fierce struggle, practically annihilated them. The remainder of the Coldstream swung back their right and managed to hold on to their position, but, later on in the day, the persistent attacks of the enemy

Lieut.-Colonel Lowther, and 114 other ranks. Major the Honble. L. d'H. Hamilton took over the command of the 1st Bn. Coldstream Guards, and Lieut.-Colonel the Honble. W. Hore-Ruthven succeeded Lieut.-Colonel Lowther in the command of the Scots Guards.

* The 1st Bn. Coldstream Guards had 200 casualties in the battle of Langemarck, the 1st Bn. Scots Guards about 50.

GERMAN ADVANCE DOWN MENIN ROAD

brought fresh disaster upon the defence. The Coldstream and the other company of the Black Watch were rolled up from the right. The Scots Guards a little farther to the north, with their right flank often in the air, were then in grave danger of sharing a similar fate. Two companies were overwhelmed and their positions captured by the Germans, but the remainder of the battalion fought with splendid determination and prevented any more progress being made by the enemy. The line was readjusted as soon as darkness set in.*

After this day's desperate engagement the 1st Bn. Coldstream Guards was given a few days for rest and reorganization, and the arrival of new drafts enabled it again to get into some sort of fighting trim. But the 1st Bn. Scots Guards remained in the line—and was actually in the front trenches without any kind of break from the 26th of October to the 13th of November.

The 2nd of November, by which date the Coldstream were once again in their forward position, was a day of very strenuous fighting, for the enemy again succeeded in breaking his way through the British line, and the Guards were called upon to face a succession of furious attacks, sometimes being surrounded on three sides. They held their ground manfully, but at the end of the day the Coldstream had lost all their officers and were reduced to 120 men. The battalion was then attached, as already related, to the other Coldstream battalions in the 4th (Guards) Bde.† The Scots Guards, however, remained with their own brigade and took part in repelling the German assaults on the 8th and 11th of November. On the first of these days their right flank was driven in and most gallantly restored; on the 11th, a day marked by a more than usually intense hostile artillery bombardment, they assisted in driving back the Prussian

* The casualties of the 1st Bn. Scots Guards during the day amounted to 8 officers and 336 other ranks. When darkness fell, there only remained 80 men of the 1st Coldstream Guards. They came under the command of the quartermaster, the only officer left to the battalion. Major the Honble. L. d'H. Hamilton, the commanding officer, was killed. Lieut.-Colonel J. Ponsonby returned to the battalion towards the end of November.

† *See* note, p. 9.

Guard with heavy losses. The day following this engagement the 1st (Guards) Bde. was sent back into reserve at Hooge.*

On the 21st of November the I Corps was relieved by the French on the Ypres front, and its troops spent a few weeks in billets behind the line. The 1st (Guards) Bde. was at Béthune on the 20th of December in time to take part in the sharp engagement known as the Defence of Givenchy. The troops of the Indian Corps had been heavily attacked on this part of the line, and the situation was by no means satisfactory.† In the evening on the 21st of December, therefore, the 1st (Guards) Bde. was ordered to take over the line of the Indian Corps, and, the following day, after some hard fighting, its troops succeeded in re-establishing the front at Givenchy. The 1st Bn. Coldstream Guards distinguished itself in the vigorous counter-attacks by which this important tactical position was regained and finally secured.‡

After several tours of duty in the trenches at Givenchy and Cuinchy, marked by no unusual incident, the Coldstream and Scots Guards, who were holding part of the Brickstacks salient at Cuinchy were attacked by the Germans on the 25th of January, 1915. After exploding some mines under the trenches occupied by the two front companies of the Coldstream and Scots Guards, the enemy made a vigorous assault upon the British position, and succeeded in gaining possession of the front line trench. His farther progress was checked, but a counter-attack failed to regain the lost trench.§

Trench warfare continued to be the lot of the 1st (Guards) Bde. throughout the remainder of the winter and spring. The two Guards battalions were not employed when the 1st Division took part in the disastrous failure at Rue du Bois on the 9th of May. They held the divisional line before the

---

* The 1st Bn. Scots Guards had lost 21 officers and 686 other ranks since going into action on the 21st of October.

† See " 1914," pp. 127, 128.

‡ When withdrawn from the line on the 22nd of December, it was found that the battalion's casualties amounted to 5 officers and nearly 200 other ranks.

§ Only 45 men were left in the two companies of Scots Guards which were attacked.

attack and were relieved by the other brigades which carried out the first assault. When that failed, the 1st (Guards) Bde. replaced the 2nd Infantry Bde. on the right of the line, but the 1st Bn. Coldstream Guards and the 1st Bn. Scots Guards were held in reserve, and at night the 1st Division was relieved by the 2nd Division.*

For the remainder of the summer, until they left the 1st Division to join the Guards Division, the Coldstream and Scots Guards were employed in the trenches south of the La Bassée Canal.

(3) THE 20TH INFANTRY BRIGADE, AUGUST, 1914, TO AUGUST, 1915.

It will be remembered that the 1st Bn. Grenadier Guards and the 2nd Bn. Scots Guards formed part of the 20th Infantry Bde. of the 7th Division. At the beginning of October, 1914, this division was embarked for Zeebrugge to operate in the defence of Antwerp, but, as events were to prove, it could do little more than help to cover the retreat of the Belgian Army, after which it took its place in the British line for the defence of Ypres.

After landing in Belgium on the 7th of October, the 7th Division moved to Ostend, and the following day covered the disembarcation of the 3rd Cavalry Division, which, with the 7th Division, formed the IV Corps. The 20th and the 22nd Infantry Bdes. were then sent by rail to Ghent.

The march which followed through Thielt—where the three brigades of the 7th Division were reunited—and Roulers to Ypres was a wearisome operation carried out over roads congested with traffic, but there was no hostile pressure to disturb the troops, although all the necessary precautions were taken. Ypres was reached on the 14th of October and here the outposts of the Grenadiers had their first brush with the Germans. By this time the Allies were

---

* The casualties on the 9th–10th of May were chiefly from shell fire. In the Scots Guards they amounted to 56, in the Coldstream to 20. In June Lieut.-Colonel S. H. Godman succeeded Lieut.-Colonel the Honble. W. Hore-Ruthven in the command of the 1st Bn. Scots Guards, the latter having been appointed G.S.O.1, 47th (London) Division.

about to take the offensive in this area and the 7th Division moved forward again between Hollebeke and Zandvoorde on the 16th of October, the 20th Infantry Bde., on the right, being in touch with the cavalry. The Grenadiers reached Zandvoorde about 11 a.m. and occupied outpost positions with the Scots Guards on their left. In the evening the latter were in Kruiseecke. The advance continued on the two following days towards the line Menin—Wervicq—Comines which, it was known, the enemy was holding.

On the 19th of October the 7th Division was ordered to attack, but this order was cancelled and the IV Corps again retired, the 1st Bn. Grenadier Guards occupying a position at Kruiseecke which formed an awkward salient. The next day hostile attacks began to develop, and, on the 21st of October—the day on which the I Corps reached the approximate line Bixschoote—Zonnebeke on the left of the 7th Division—a general action began. The troops of the 7th Division had little difficulty in driving back the enemy's attacks on their part of the front, although their line was thinly held, and it was found necessary to put in two companies of the Scots Guards on the right to reinforce the Grenadiers.

On the 23rd of October the trenches held by the 21st Infantry Bde. farther to the north, were heavily attacked, and two platoons of the 1st Bn. Grenadier Guards were sent to assist in their defence. The two reserve companies of this battalion were eventually used to reinforce the 2nd Bn. The Border Regiment, and a company of the 2nd Bn. Scots Guards went to the help of the 2nd Bn. The Wiltshire Regiment (21st Infantry Bde.). The following day the enemy burst his way through the thin British line and entered Polygon Wood, where confused fighting went on throughout the day. A company of the 1st Bn. Grenadier Guards, led by Major Colby, carried out a successful counter-attack, but had heavy losses.*

On the 25th of October came the fierce German assault

---

* The company lost 2 officers, including Major Colby, killed and 1 wounded, and suffered 100 casualties in the other ranks. *See* " The Grenadier Guards in the Great War," vol. i. pp. 115, 116.

DEFENCE OF KRUISEECKE SALIENT

on the Kruiseecke salient. The Scots Guards were driven out of some trenches on the left of their line, but the reserve companies of the battalion made a brilliant counter-attack, recapturing the lost ground and taking over 200 prisoners, among whom were 7 officers.

After several German attacks had been repulsed during the night, the enemy's artillery concentrated its fire on the salient in the early hours of the 26th of October.*

So violent was the shelling that it was almost impossible for the Guards to cling to their battered trenches, and at last, after the German infantry had succeeded in breaking its way through the line farther to the south, disaster befell the two companies of Scots Guards on the right. They were overwhelmed by the enemy and Lieut.-Colonel Bolton, the commanding officer, and the other survivors of the gallant defence were taken prisoners. Only one company of the Grenadiers appears to have been in this part of the line during the day. It retired fighting, but two platoons which did not get the order to withdraw shared the fate of the Scots Guards.† Eventually, Brig.-General Ruggles-Brise, commanding the 20th Infantry Bde., succeeded in withdrawing his troops to a new line between Zandvoorde and Gheluvelt, and the Guards battalions went back into reserve.‡

The 7th Division was now transferred to the I Corps, and, as has already been related, the 1st (Guards) Bde. took over the portion of the line, which ran through the cross-roads south-east of Gheluvelt, on the 26th of October.

Two days later, on the 28th, the 20th Infantry Bde. relieved the 22nd Infantry Bde. south of the Menin road, the

---

* "A terrific shelling of our trenches began early in the morning, and reached such a pitch that the men counted as many as sixty shells a minute on each small trench. The whole of the enemy's artillery fire was concentrated on Kruiseecke. Gallantly our men held on, in spite of the fact that again and again the shells blew in the trenches and buried half a dozen men at a time, all of whom had to be dug out with shovels. Some of them had as much as three feet of earth on top of them, and many were suffocated before they could be rescued." See "The Grenadier Guards in the Great War," vol. i. p. 118.

† See "The Grenadier Guards in the Great War," vol. i. pp. 121–123.

‡ The casualties of the 2nd Bn. Scots Guards amounted to 17 officers and 380 other ranks killed, wounded or missing.

1st Bn. Grenadier Guards going in on the left of the line with the 2nd Bn. The Gordon Highlanders on its right. The 2nd Bn. Scots Guards and the 2nd Bn. The Border Regiment, which were in support, were sent back before daybreak on the 29th of October in order to escape the enemy's artillery bombardment which it was certain would begin as soon as it was light. The Grenadiers, therefore, were unsupported when the enemy launched a very heavy infantry attack under cover of a fierce rifle and machine-gun fire. Almost surrounded, the Grenadiers fought magnificently, and even counter-attacked with the help of the Gordons. But they were too hopelessly outnumbered to be able to hold their line and were forced back to a position just east of the village of Gheluvelt. Here they managed to hold their ground until reinforcements arrived. The battalion was acknowledged to have saved a very critical situation.*

The 2nd Bn. Scots Guards came forward to participate in a counter-attack which was launched south of Gheluvelt, and succeeded in recovering some of the lost ground. But unfortunately the battalion went too far, and, in its withdrawal to conform with the general line, was fired upon by mistake and suffered serious losses.

During the night of the 29th–30th of October the remnants of the two Guards battalions were sent back to Hooge. The Grenadiers, under the command of Captain G. Rasch, could only muster 250 men; the Scots Guards, commanded by Captain G. Paynter, 200 men.

On the 31st of October the 21st and 22nd Infantry Bdes. were reported to have been shelled out of their trenches. The 2nd Bn. Scots Guards and the 2nd Bn. The Border Regiment were at the time holding a line in rear of the 21st Infantry Bde.† On receipt of this information Brig.-

---

* The battalion lost its commanding officer, Lieut.-Colonel M. Earle, wounded, and 19 other officers became casualties.

† "On the 31st, the day that Sir John French described as the most critical in the whole battle of Ypres, the remnant of the Seventh Division was holding a line from the Ypres-Menin road in front of the cross-roads at Veldhoek, to a point 500 yards north of Zandvoorde. At 1 a.m. it was decided to push up the Scots Guards and Border Regt., and entrench them close behind the left of the 21st Brigade." *See* "The Grenadier Guards in the Great War," vol. i. p. 132.

BATTLE OF NEUVE CHAPELLE

General Ruggles-Brise himself led forward the Grenadiers in order to prolong the line of the 20th Infantry Bde.

The situation for a time was critical in the extreme, but the front held firm, and by the evening the repeated attacks of the enemy had all been beaten back. At nightfall the two Guards battalions were withdrawn, but they were in the line again on the 1st of November. Four days later they were relieved by troops of the 3rd Division, when they left the battle zone and moved to billets at Meteren and Locre.*

In the middle of November the 7th Division again went into the line, the 20th Infantry Bde., now commanded by Brig.-General F. J. Heyworth,† taking over the trenches opposite Fromelles.

The 2nd Bn. Scots Guards was engaged in a local operation on the 18th of December when it was successful in capturing its objectives, but was forced to relinquish them in consequence of the failure of the rest of the attack.‡

Trench warfare continued for the Guards until the battle of Neuve Chapelle (10th–13th March, 1915), in which the 7th Division was engaged. On the 10th of March the Indian Corps and the 8th Division attacked successfully on both sides of the village of Neuve Chapelle. The following day the 1st Bn. Grenadier Guards was sent forward to link up the 21st Infantry Bde. with the right of the 8th Division in the trenches captured from the enemy near Moulin de Piétre. After this movement had been carried out under heavy fire, the Grenadiers and Gordon Highlanders endeavoured to advance, but could make little progress owing to the intensity of the German enfilade machine-gun fire.

The attack was resumed on the 12th of March. A successful advance was made by the 2nd Bn. Scots Guards and the 2nd Bn. The Border Regiment, the two battalions

---

* During this final period in the line at Ypres the 2nd Bn. Scots Guards lost 4 more officers and 136 other ranks. The 1st Bn. Grenadier Guards left the battle with a strength of one weak company commanded by Captain G. Rasch. Lieut.-Colonel L. R. Fisher-Rowe took over the command of the battalion at the end of November.

† *See* note on p. 2.

‡ The casualties on this occasion were heavy. The battalion lost 6 officers and 50 per cent. of the rank and file engaged.

gaining possession of some of the enemy's front line defences and capturing about 400 prisoners. The 1st Bn. Grenadier Guards, whose bombers earlier in the day had done good work in repelling the enemy's attacks on the left flank of the 21st Infantry Bde., then advanced on the right of the Scots Guards and consolidated the new positions.

The intention was to proceed with the operations the following day, but the various units were so much intermixed that it was found impossible to reorganize the brigade before daylight. The Scots Guards had been withdrawn after the previous day's fighting, but the Grenadiers and the other battalions of the brigade were not relieved until the evening of the 13th of March. They spent the day in the line and suffered very severely from the heavy fire of the enemy's guns.*

After its experience at Neuve Chapelle the 20th Infantry Bde. occupied trenches in the Fauquissart sector of the line, and had a comparatively quiet time until the middle of May, when it was called upon to take part in the battle of Festubert.

Following the night attack of the 2nd Division at Rue du Bois on the 15th–16th of May, the 7th Division, further on the right, attacked next morning. The 20th Infantry Bde. had two battalions in line, the 2nd Bn. Scots Guards being on the right, and the 2nd Bn. The Border Regt. on the left. The former penetrated far into the enemy's defensive system—too far, as it proved, for the two leading companies were eventually cut off owing to the failure of the rest of the attacking force.† The Grenadiers were

---

* See " The Grenadier Guards in the Great War," vol. i. pp. 242, 243. In the battle of Neuve Chapelle the 1st Bn. Grenadier Guards lost 14 officers (including its commanding officer, Lieut.-Colonel Fisher-Rowe, who was killed) and 328 other ranks. Two bombers of the Grenadiers—Lance-Corporal W. D. Fuller and Private T. Barber—were awarded the Victoria Cross for their gallantry during the fighting on the 12th of March. The 2nd Bn. Scots Guards lost 6 officers and 189 other ranks. Major G. Paynter, who commanded the battalion, was among the wounded. Major A. B. Cator succeeded him in the command and Lieut.-Colonel C. E. Corkran succeeded Lieut.-Colonel Fisher-Rowe in the command of the 1st Bn. Grenadier Guards.

† Later, when the British cleared this area, the bodies of a number of Scots Guardsmen were found lying in a circle with German dead all round them. They had evidently fought to the bitter end.

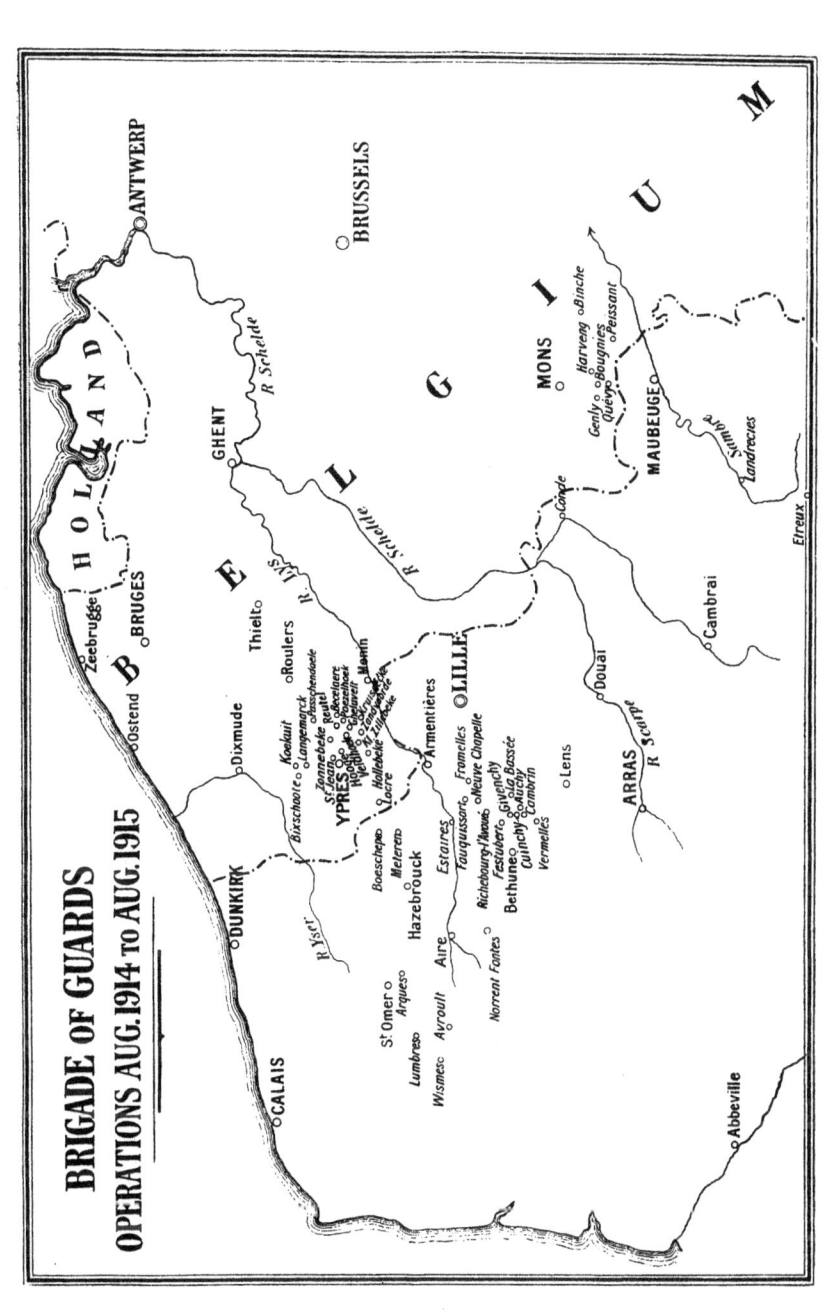

Vol. I., page 24.

then sent forward to prolong the line of the Scots Guards to the left, and the captured positions were successfully held. On the 17th of May the 4th (Guards) Bde. came through the Scots Guards and Grenadiers to continue the attack, and, for a time, the 1st and 2nd Bns. Grenadier Guards found themselves side by side. In the evening, on the 17th, the 20th Infantry Bde. was relieved,* and moved out of the battle zone. It remained in rest billets for the remainder of the month and then took over the line in front of Festubert and Givenchy.

The 1st Bn. Grenadier Guards was involved, to some extent, in the engagement which is known as the Second Action of Givenchy, on the 15th–16th of June.† The battalion was sent up to fill the gap between the 51st Division and the 21st Infantry Bde. But the attack of the troops on each of their flanks failed, and there was little chance for the Grenadiers to do more than cling to their ground.‡ For the remainder of their time with the 7th Division the two Guards battalions experienced the usual routine of trench warfare.

On the 3rd of August orders were received for them to join the Guards Division, which was then about to be formed, and, the next day, after an inspection by Major-General Hubert Gough, the divisional commander, the Grenadiers left the 7th Division. The remaining battalions of their brigade lined the street as they marched away, the pipers of the 2nd Bn. The Gordon Highlanders playing them out of the divisional area. The Scots Guards, who left the division a few days later, were also given a splendid, if less formal, send-off.

* The losses of the 2nd Bn. Scots Guards at Festubert amounted to 10 officers and about 400 other ranks ; those of the 1st Bn. Grenadier Guards to 4 officers and 113 other ranks.

† *See* "Report of the Battles Nomenclature Committee as approved by the Army Council." [Cmd. 1138], 1921.

‡ The losses of the battalion in this engagement amounted to 3 officers and 63 other ranks. In July Lieut.-Colonel Corkran was appointed to command an infantry brigade and was succeeded in the command of the 1st Bn. Grenadier Guards by Major G. Trotter.

II. THE FORMATION AND CONCENTRATION OF THE GUARDS DIVISION.

(1) THE FORMATION OF THE DIVISION DUE TO LORD KITCHENER.

The Guards Division was formed in August, 1915.

The idea of its creation appears to have been due solely to Lord Kitchener, who, after first obtaining His Majesty's permission to carry out his project, proceeded to form the division without taking into his confidence either the War Cabinet or the Commander-in-Chief in France.*

On the 16th of July he instructed Major-General Sir Francis Lloyd, who at that time was G.O.C., London District, to get ready the 3rd and 4th Bns. Grenadier Guards, the 2nd Bn. Irish Guards and the 1st Bn. Welsh Guards for service abroad, and to form a Pioneer Battalion, a Cyclist Company and a divisional Cavalry Squadron. These various units were to be sent to France with as little delay as possible in

---

* The following letter appears to have been the first intimation which Sir John French received with regard to the formation of the Guards Division :—

War Office,
Whitehall, S.W.
13th July, 1915.

MY DEAR FRENCH,—

The King has approved of the formation of a Guards Division to be commanded by the Earl of Cavan. To do this I propose to send you four battalions of Guards and four battalions of the Army Troops of the 1st and 2nd Army. You have the 19th Brigade still outside your Divisional formations, which might replace the Guards Brigade of the 2nd Division—while two battalions of the four I am sending you would replace the Guards in the 1st and 7th Divisions respectively. I will send you the artillery and divisional troops to complete the Division. Perhaps you may wish to mix them up with earlier formations in other Divisions so as to give the Guards a certain number of older units with those I can send.

If you will let me know that you like this idea I will go on with it and arrange about getting men ready.

Yours very truly,
(Sgd.) KITCHENER.

The Guards Division would have no number as in other Armies.

order to complete with the Guards battalions already in that country a Guards Division.*

There are unfortunately no documents in existence to explain the reasons which prompted Lord Kitchener's policy. It seems tolerably clear, however, that his intention was that a Guards Division should form a permanent part of the British Army and should not merely be called into being for the duration of the war. He was a great admirer of the Brigade of Guards and had a profound belief in its methods of discipline and training. It is only reasonable to suppose, therefore, that in forming the Guards Division Lord Kitchener was firmly convinced that he was carrying out a policy which would be to the advantage of the Army as a whole. The loyalty, the discipline, the devotion to duty and the proved efficiency of the Guards would be an example to the units of the other arms of the Service forming part of the division, and the very high standard of military excellence thus obtained could not fail to have a beneficial effect upon the troops of the New Armies.

There were, however, at the time many who viewed with considerable misgiving the creation of a Guards Division. Some military authorities considered that it was a mistake to concentrate so many fine battalions in a single division, and pointed out not unreasonably that the influence of their training and discipline would be more widely felt if the Guards battalions were distributed throughout the Army. Guardsmen themselves were divided in opinion, and the fear was expressed that it might not be possible to maintain the high standard of efficiency of the Brigade of Guards if its numbers had to be largely increased in order to keep a division up to strength.† This fear proved groundless. Both in the field and also behind the line the troops of the Guards Division from their first appearance on the battle-field of Loos in 1915 to the close of the war in 1918 amply maintained the great traditions of the Brigade of Guards, deservedly earning the

* Upon the receipt of these orders Sir Francis Lloyd at once made the necessary arrangements with the assistance of the Lieut.-Colonels commanding the regiments of Guards and the Household Cavalry.

† *See* "The Grenadier Guards in the Great War," vol. i. p. 283.

confidence and admiration of all with whom they came in contact. But Lord Kitchener's plan to make the division an integral part of the Army has not been acted upon. It has always been the practice of British Governments at the end of great wars to scrap the Army, and the practice at the end of the World War was no exception to the rule. The mighty force, which had raised the prestige of the British Empire throughout the world, was hurriedly, almost indecently, broken up, and the Guards Division among many others ceased to exist.

(2) APPOINTMENTS TO THE COMMANDS AND STAFF.

The honour of becoming the first commander of the Guards Division fell to Major-General the Earl of Cavan, whose successful record whilst in command of the 4th (Guards) Bde., and subsequently as G.O.C. the 50th (Northumbrian) Division, amply justified his selection for the appointment.

The divisional staff, with the exception of Major N. Davidson, R.A., who was appointed G.S.O.2, were all Guardsmen,* and of these Lieut.-Colonel the Honble. W. Hore-Ruthven, Scots Guards, G.S.O.1, and Lieut.-Colonel W. Darell, Coldstream Guards, A.A. and Q.M.G., were both Staff College graduates with considerable staff experience gained in the war. By His Majesty's wish H.R.H. the Prince of Wales was attached to the divisional staff and was employed on its administrative side.

Brig.-Generals Feilding, Lowther and Heyworth, who were commanding the 4th and 1st (Guards) and the 20th Infantry Bdes., at the time when the Guards Division was formed were appointed to command respectively the 1st, 2nd and 3rd Guards Bdes. in the new division. On the 20th of August, however, Brig.-General Lowther was selected by Sir John French to be his Military Secretary, and Lieut.-Colonel J. Ponsonby, who had been in command of the 1st Bn. Coldstream Guards since it landed in France, was then given the command of the 2nd Guards Bde.

* *See* Appendix II.

DIVISIONAL R.A. AND R.E.

Of the four artillery brigades allotted to the division* three came from the 16th Division, and one, the Howitzer Brigade, from the 11th Division. The brigade commanders and some of the officers had had experience in the war, and the batteries had received some shooting practice at Larkhill. But, although the material was excellent, the *personnel* as a whole had had but little training. The question of the command of the divisional Artillery, therefore, much exercised the mind of the Chief of the General Staff, who considered that it was essential that the C.R.A. should be a young and vigorous officer well versed in the artillery methods of the war.† Eventually Brig.-General A. E. Wardrop was selected for the post. He assumed the command of the divisional Artillery on the 13th of September, replacing Brig.-General C. E. Goulburn, who had been responsible for its earlier training and under whose command it came to France.

Lieut.-Colonel J. E. Vanrenen was the first C.R.E. of the division, but his health broke down very soon after the Guards went into the Loos area and he was succeeded in the command of the divisional R.E. by Lieut.-Colonel A. Brough, commanding the 55th Field Company, R.E.‡

(3) Concentration and Training of the Division West of St. Omer.

The concentration of the new division was carried out in and round the village of Lumbres which lies some miles to the west of St. Omer. Divisional headquarters was established in the château at Lumbres early in August, and the incoming troops of the division were comfortably billetted in the neighbouring villages.

---

* See Appendix I.
† The divisional commander fully agreed with General Robertson: " I look on it as vitally important to the future success of the division to have the very best artillery advisers. The infantry is so good that nothing but the closest and best artillery support will be good enough." *See* notes by Major-General the Earl of Cavan, W.D., Guards Division.
‡ This Field Company had been affiliated with the 20th Infantry Bde., and had followed the two Guards battalions of that brigade when they joined the Guards Division.

The weather during August and the early days of September was fine and warm, and the troops who came back from the line, as well as those fresh from England, appreciated to the full the beautiful countryside. There was a wonderful peace on the great undulating downs with their wooded slopes, and in the spacious meadows lying along the deep valleys through which the rivers Aa and the Bléquin wind their way to their junction at Lumbres and thence as a united stream flow eastward towards St. Omer. Amid such surroundings officers and men could enjoy the present, forgetful of the past and heedless of what the future might have in store for them.

The 4th (Guards) Bde., which now became the 1st Guards Bde., after taking its leave of the 2nd Division on the 19th of August, moved back to St. Omer, where it marched past the Commander-in-Chief in the town square, and then went into billets in the villages of Houlle and Moulle north of Lumbres.* The brigade retained the four battalions which had been with it throughout the war—the 2nd Bn. Grenadier Guards, the 2nd and 3rd Bns. Coldstream Guards and the 1st Bn. Irish Guards.†

The 2nd Guards Bde. was composed of the 1st Bn. Coldstream Guards ‡ and the 1st Bn. Scots Guards from the 1st Division, and the 3rd Bn. Grenadier Guards and the 2nd Bn. Irish Guards from England.

The 3rd Bn. Grenadier Guards was the only regular Guards battalion which had remained at home up to this period in the war.§ The formation of the Guards Division

---

* On the 24th of August the 1st Guards Bde. was moved to Thiembronne to make room for other troops arriving from England.

† A few days later Lieut.-Colonel J. Steele, commanding the 2nd Bn. Coldstream Guards, was appointed to command the 22nd Infantry Bde. and Major P. A. MacGregor succeeded him in the command of the 2nd Bn. Coldstream Guards.

‡ Major A. G. E. Egerton obtained the command of this battalion when Lieut.-Colonel J. Ponsonby was appointed to the command of the 2nd Guards Bde.

§ " Whether it was part of that mysterious thing called the British Constitution, or whether the idea of the keeping one regular battalion in London emanated from the brain of some timid member of the Cabinet, is not clear, but the 3rd Battalion remained at home after all the rest of the Regular army had gone. At first it was said that two

ARRIVAL OF UNITS FROM ENGLAND

made it necessary to send not only this battalion but also the 4th Bn. Grenadier Guards to France. The 3rd Battalion, under the command of Colonel N. A. L. Corry, reached Havre on the 27th of July, and the following day was moved by train into the Lumbres area, going into billets at Esquerdes.

The 2nd Bn. Irish Guards was formed officially on the 18th of July, 1915, and, as at that date there was a plentiful supply of men in reserve at Warley, there was no difficulty in dispatching the battalion to France in August.* It left Brentwood station on the 16th of that month, under the command of Lieut.-Colonel the Honble. L. J. P. Butler, and reached Lumbres three days later.

The 3rd Guards Bde., in addition to the 1st Bn. Grenadier Guards and the 2nd Bn. Scots Guards from the 7th Division, also included two new battalions from England—the 4th Bn. Grenadier Guards and the 1st Bn. Welsh Guards. The formation of the first of these battalions was authorized by Royal Warrant on the 15th of July, 1915, and the battalion, under the command of Lieut.-Colonel G. C. Hamilton, was ready to leave for the front a few weeks later. On its arrival in the Guards divisional area it was billetted at Blendecques.

The idea of raising a Welsh Regiment of Foot Guards appears to have originated with Lord Kitchener, and at once met with the hearty approval of His Majesty, who signed the Warrant for the creation of the regiment on the 26th of

---

regular battalions would have to remain behind in London, one for the King, the other for the Houses of Parliament, but His Majesty, having at once disposed of the idea that he needed the services of any regular battalion, Lord Kitchener decided to retain only one battalion, and that happened to be the 3rd Battalion Grenadier Guards." *See* "The Grenadier Guards in the Great War," vol. i. pp. 285, 286.

* " But . . . the 2nd Battalion was born in spirit as in substance, long ere the authorities bade it to be. The needs of the War commanded it; the abundance of the reserves then justified it. . . . Officers and men alike welcomed it, for it is less pleasing to be absorbed in drafts and driblets by an ever-hungry 1st Battalion in France, than to be set apart for the sacrifice as a veritable Battalion on its own responsibility, with its own traditions (they sprang up immediately) and its own jealous *esprit de corps*. A man may join for the sake of ' King and Country,' but he goes over the top for the honour of his own platoon, Company, and Battalion." *See* " The Irish Guards in the Great War," vol. ii. pp. 1, 2.

February, 1915. Three days later, on the 1st of March, St. David's Day, the 1st Bn. Welsh Guards mounted Guard at Buckingham Palace, Lieut.-Colonel W. Murray-Threipland, who had been given the command of the battalion, acting as Captain of the King's Guard.*

Many of the officers, warrant officers and senior non-commissioned officers, as well as a large proportion of the rank and file, of the new battalion, were transferred to the Welsh Guards from the other Guards regiments. With this nucleus at his disposal Lieut.-Colonel W. Murray-Threipland was soon able to form a very fine battalion in every way worthy to take its place beside the other battalions of the Guards Division. The Welsh Guards landed at Havre on the 18th of August. They reached St. Omer two days later and marched to billets in Arques.

The 4th Bn. Coldstream Guards, which was formed on the 17th of July, 1915, became the Pioneer Battalion of the Division.† It reached Lumbres from England under the command of Lieut.-Colonel R. C. Skeffington-Smyth on the 18th of August and went into billets at Elnes.

The Household Cavalry supplied the divisional squadron of cavalry and cyclist company.

All the units of the Guards Division were concentrated in the Lumbres area by about the 20th of August, and the

* "The order to raise the regiment was given by Lord Kitchener to Sir Francis Lloyd on February 6th. The actual conversation is so typical of both men that we give the note, made at the time by Sir Francis Lloyd :

Lord Kitchener (very abruptly) : " You have got to raise a Regiment of Welsh Guards."

Sir Francis Lloyd : " Sir, there are a great many difficulties in the way which I should like to point out first."

Lord Kitchener (very rudely) : " If you do not like to do it some one else will."

Sir Francis Lloyd : " Sir, when do you want them ? "

Lord Kitchener : " Immediately."

Sir Francis Lloyd : " Very well, sir ; they shall go on guard on St. David's Day."

See "History of the Welsh Guards," by C. H. Dudley Ward, pp. 3, 4, note.

† It was first described as the " Guards Pioneer Battalion," but this title was afterwards changed to the 4th Bn. Coldstream Guards (Pioneers), under the authority of W.O. Letter 20/Gen. No. 13935 (A.G. 1), 12.8.15.

TRAINING IN LUMBRES AREA

work of training for the coming British offensive at Loos in conjunction with French attacks farther south and in Champagne was already busily in progress.

On the 23rd of August an experimental embarcation of the 4th Bn. Grenadier Guards on barges on the canal at Aire was conducted in the presence of the divisional commander. On the 1st of September the first concentration of the infantry of the division took place when a tactical exercise was conducted in the neighbourhood of Wismes. The movements of all three brigades were carried out successfully, and, although some of the battalions were called upon to march for over seventeen miles, not a single man fell out during the day. About this date the 61st (Howitzer) and the 74th Bdes., R.F.A., were sent into the area of the First Army for a week's experience of actual service conditions, and, before the Guards left the Lumbres area, all the artillery of the division had been given a similar experience.

On the 15th of September Lieut.-General Haking, who had been appointed G.O.C. the new XI Corps to which the Guards Division was posted, was present at a field day of the 1st Guards Bde. After expressing his warm approval of the high standard of training of the troops, he addressed the officers of the three Guards brigades and explained to them how much depended upon the leadership of platoon commanders in modern warfare.*

On the two following days, the 16th and 17th of September, Lord Cavan reviewed the 2nd and 3rd Guards Bdes. He expressed his opinion that on each occasion the march past, the handling of arms and the general appearance of the troops were " at that high standard most proper for all Guardsmen under all and every condition." †

---

* " He advocated that platoon commanders should lead on and not worry about their flanks ; reserves would be behind them to fill up gaps, reinforce, clear up the situation and make good what had been won." *See* " History of the Welsh Guards," p. 22.

† " I was very particularly impressed with Brig.-General Ponsonby's word of command—with the marching of the left flank company of the 1st Bn. Scots Guards and the 4th Bn. Grenadier Guards—and with the exact timing of the motions of the ' Present ' and the ' Slope ' throughout both Brigades." *See* note by Major-General the Earl of Cavan, W.D., Guards Division.

On the 18th, the 2nd Guards Bde. carried out a field day in conjunction with the divisional Artillery, all the batteries of which had by this time returned to the Lumbres area.

The period of rest and training was now almost at an end; the moment for the Guards to take their place in the battle zone was fast approaching. On the 19th of September an order was received from the XI Corps for the division to move forward into an area due south of Aire by two night marches on the nights of the 22nd–23rd and 23rd–24th of September,* and, on the 21st, Lord Cavan issued his orders in accordance with these instructions.† This day the wind was in the east, and the sound of the British guns beginning the preliminary bombardment west of Loos could be distinctly heard while the 3rd Guards Bde. was carrying out a field exercise in conjunction with the 76th Bde., R.F.A., and while Field-Marshal Lord Kitchener, Colonel of the Irish Guards, inspected the 1st Battalion of his regiment in a field near Avroult.‡

On the 23rd of September divisional headquarters was moved from Lumbres to Norrent Fontes, and, during the night of the 23rd–24th, the whole of the division moved into the area south of Aire.§

On the 24th, Lieut.-General Haking held a conference at Lillers, at which he fully explained to the senior officers of the divisions under his command (1) the scope of the operations upon which the First Army in conjunction with the Tenth French Army was to embark the following day, and (2) the intended rôle of the XI Corps. In the afternoon of the same day Lord Cavan issued the following circular memorandum to the Guards Division:—

"On the eve of the biggest battle in the World's History the

---

* *See* XI Corps Order, No. 1.

† *See* Guards Division Order, No. 1, W.D., Guards Division, App. 2. The Guards were to move in rear of the 21st and 24th Divisions—the two other divisions of the XI Corps—and in front of the Cavalry Corps.

‡ After inspecting the battalion, Lord Kitchener thanked the officers and other ranks for their fine services in the war, and told them they would shortly be given another opportunity of repeating them. Lieut.-Colonel G. Madden was in command of the parade.

§ Divisional railhead was moved to Lillers on the 24th of September.

LORD CAVAN'S MESSAGE

General Officer commanding Guards Division wishes his troops God-speed. He has nothing to add to the stirring words spoken by the corps commander this morning, but he wishes to impress upon everybody two things—First, that the fate of future generations of Englishmen hangs on this battle—Second, that great things are expected of the Guards Division. He knows that as a Guardsman of over thirty years' service he need say no more."

CHAPTER II

THE BATTLE OF LOOS.

(1) Reasons for the Allied Offensive in the Autumn of 1915.

HAD the decision as to the autumn offensive of 1915 been left solely to the judgment of the Allied commanders on the Western Front, it is more than probable that it would not have taken place. Sir John French, the British Commander-in-Chief, in particular, after his experiences at Neuve Chapelle and Festubert earlier in the year, realized that he still had neither sufficient troops nor munitions for a prolonged series of attacks upon the enemy's strongly organized defensive positions, and was, therefore, at first opposed to a resumption of the offensive.

The natural anxiety, however, of the French Government and people to regain possession of the extensive coal mining district in the neighbourhood of Lens, combined with the urgent necessity of creating a diversion in the West to relieve the enemy's pressure in the Eastern theatre of operations,* were two powerful considerations which gravely affected the situation. It was felt that an Allied attack in France might oblige the Germans to withdraw some of their divisions from the Eastern Front, and so assist the Russians, whilst it was obvious that, if the enemy could be forced to withdraw from Lens and the country round it, the economic position in France, which at that time was somewhat precarious, would be greatly relieved.

These considerations ultimately prevailed, and it was decided to carry out a combined French and British attack

---

* Warsaw had fallen on the 5th of August.

towards the end of September. The scheme of operations entailed an advance towards Valenciennes by the First Army acting in conjunction with the Tenth French Army advancing north and south of Lens, while the main French attack was to be delivered in Champagne and directed upon Maubeuge—the intention being that the two forces should join hands in the area lying between Valenciennes and Maubeuge, and thus cut off such of the enemy's troops as might still be in the salient formed by Rheims—Noyon—Arras.

(2) TASK OF THE FIRST ARMY IN THE ALLIED OFFENSIVE.

The task assigned to the First Army, under the command of Sir Douglas Haig, in the Allied operations was to advance between the La Bassée Canal and Lens towards a line Henin-Liétard—Carvin, thus driving the Germans across the Haute-Deule Canal and protecting the left flank of the Tenth French Army which was to operate south of Lens.

For the execution of this task south of the La Bassée Canal, the First Army commander had only two corps (I and IV) and the 3rd Cavalry Division; the XI Corps and the Cavalry Corps (less one division) being held in General Reserve to be utilized should occasion arise.

The IV Corps, which was holding the southern portion of the British line, was ordered to capture the enemy's trenches between the Double Crassier, two great slag heaps lying side by side about a mile south-west of Loos, inclusive, and the Vermelles—Hulluch road, exclusive, after which the corps was to push forward with its left on the Hulluch—Vendin-le-Vieil road, and to seize the crossing of the Haute-Deule Canal at Pont-à-Vendin and the Lens—Carvin road south of Annay.

To the I Corps, which was holding the northern sector of the front of attack, was entrusted the task of storming the enemy's trenches between the Vermelles—Hulluch road, inclusive, and the La Bassée Canal; after which, the corps commander was instructed to advance with his right on the Hulluch—Vendin-le-Vieil road and to operate so as to seize the crossings of the Haute-Deule Canal from Pont-à-Vendin to Bauvin.

The 3rd Cavalry Division (less one brigade) was kept in Army reserve, in the Bois des Dames, south-west of Béthune, with orders to be in readiness to push forward to Carvin as soon as an advance was practicable.

It will be noticed that the town of Lens did not itself form an objective either for the British or for the French, the scheme of operations contemplating an encirclement of the town by the Allied Armies which would lead either to the hasty retreat of the enemy's garrison or to its surrender. The fact, however, that a hostile enclave might be left on the right of the British line of communications in the event of an advance necessitated the formation of a defensive flank in the south along the slopes of the ridge which extends between Grenay and the northern suburbs of Lens.

(3) Nature of the Country on the British Front.

The country over which the projected operations of the First Army were to take place is partly an agricultural, partly a mining district—the mining district being for the most part on the German side of the line.

Between the La Bassée Canal and Vermelles on the British side of the line, and also between La Bassée and Hulluch and as far east as the Haute-Deule Canal on the German side, stretches a great undulating plain of cultivated land, almost destitute of woods except for the orchards round some of the agricultural villages, such as Hulluch. The whole of this plain is thickly dotted with mining villages and their pitheads and slag heaps are the conspicuous landmarks of the district.

From Vermelles southward the country west of the British trenches, the soil of which is poor and chalky, rises gradually to a point just beyond Fosse No. 7 on the Vermelles—Lens road, whence it slopes down for about 1,000 yards. This road, which was to serve the British Army as its main line of communication in the first stages of its advance, runs in a south-easterly direction from Fosse No. 7 practically in a straight line to Lens.

The mining village of Loos, which at the time of the battle lay about 900 yards in rear of the German front line trenches, is situated about 1,000 yards east of the Vermelles— Lens road in a valley encircled on its southern and south-eastern sides by a spur of hilly ground that stretches from Grenay eastward as far as the mining village of Cité St. Auguste, its most noticeable features being the huge Double Crassier just east of Grenay and Hill 70, about 3,000 yards north of Lens. Practically the whole of this spur, which is covered with mining works and villages, lay within the enemy's lines, and the Germans thus commanded all the approaches to Loos,* from which village excellent observation could also be obtained from the two great pylons—which came to be known to the British troops as the "Tower Bridge." †

East of Loos the main Lens—La Bassée road runs almost due north across the top of Hill 70, a bare chalk down destitute of any kind of cover, and thence down its northern slopes past Puits No. 14 bis, Bois Hugo and the Chalk Pit— places which for ever will be associated with the Guards Division—to Hulluch and Cité St. Élie. East of this road, except for the eastern slopes of Hill 70 on which is situated the mining village of St. Auguste, the area of operations, which was bounded on two sides by the Haute-Deule Canal, is similar in its features to that north-east of Hulluch, which has already been described—although this district is slightly more wooded and contains fewer mining villages.

From a tactical point of view the general configuration of the country in which the operations were to take place, together with the artificial obstacles to an advance caused by the coal-mining industry, immensely favoured the

* The lower slope of this spur of hills—from the Double Crassier and thence in a north-easterly direction towards Loos—was to form the defensive flank of the British attack to which allusion was made on p. 38.

† This erection was of steel with double metal turrets connected by an overhead girder. It formed part of the machinery of the mining pits outside Loos.

defenders. The attacking troops had perforce to move forward throughout the whole battle either up or down great stretches of open country in which practically no cover was available, or to make their way through the intricate mazes of mining works, slag heaps and villages.

(4) GERMAN DEFENSIVE ORGANIZATION.

With every natural and artificial advantage of the ground in their favour, the Germans had not neglected to strengthen their position by means of a strong and elaborate system of trenches, the siting of which had been skilfully and carefully planned, and in the construction of which no labour had been spared.

South of the La Bassée Canal the enemy's front line extended in a southerly direction for a distance of about 8,000 yards to a point about 2,000 yards east of Grenay. From the northern boundary of this line—a point about 1,500 yards north-west of Auchy-lez-La Bassée—the German trenches ran almost due south to a point a little north-west of the spot where the railway line from Vermelles to La Bassée crosses the zone of trenches. In this sector the distance between the British and German lines nowhere exceeded 300 yards, and in many places the intervening space was considerably less.

South of the Vermelles—La Bassée railway the German line swung south-eastward, forming a great half circle and following the upward slope of the ground until it reached the point where the Vermelles—Loos and the Le Rutoire—Loos roads almost meet. In this part of the zone of operations the distance between the opposing trench lines was greater than farther north, a tract of open country, varying from 400 to 500 yards, separating the two armies.

South of the Vermelles—Loos road, the enemy's front line ran almost due south across the main Vermelles—Lens road, and thence just west of the Double Crassier along the spur of hills east of Grenay towards Souchez. In this sector the average distance between the British and German trenches was between 300 and 400 yards, except at the Double Crassier where the two lines were only a few yards apart.

The whole of the enemy's front line system was strongly wired and consisted of well dug fire trenches, communicating with a strong support line, throughout the whole length of which the Germans had constructed deep dug-outs and shell-proof machine-gun emplacements. In addition, almost every point in the line of especial tactical importance was defended by means of redoubts from which an enfilade fire could be brought to bear upon the attacking troops. In the northern sector of the enemy's defensive system the most important of these strongholds was the Hohenzollern Redoubt constructed on the slope south of Auchy-lez-La Bassée. It formed a salient in the enemy's line, jutting out for about 500 yards towards the British trenches, and was connected with his main line by two communication trenches—known as "South Face" and "North Face"—while two other trenches, "Big Willie" and "Little Willie," protected its flanks. Together with Fosse No. 8, and a great slag heap called the "Dump," from which the Germans commanded practically all the country lying between Vermelles and this portion of their line, the Hohenzollern Redoubt effectively guarded the approaches to Haisnes and Cité St. Élie.

The Germans' second line of defence was perhaps even a more formidable obstacle than their first line. It consisted of an organized and continuous trench system, extending from the La Bassée Canal about 1,000 yards east of Auchy-lez-La Bassée all the way to Lens. This line of trenches ran across the low-lying ground immediately south of the canal, thence along the rising ground through Haisnes, Cité St. Élie, Hulluch and Cité St. Auguste, at which last-mentioned place the line bore westward, crossing the Lens—La Bassée road along the southern slopes of Hill 70 on the outskirts of Cité St. Laurent.

In rear of this second line system of trenches there was no definitely organized defensive system, but, even if the British troops had succeeded in capturing the German second line, the difficulties in the way of their farther advance would have been considerable, especially in the low-lying water-logged country which extends from Douvrin—Wingles—Vendin-le-Vieil—Annay to the banks of the Haute-Deule Canal. In this district it would have been well nigh impossible in the wet weather of September, 1915, to conduct the advance except along the roads, so that even weak German rear guards might well have put up a formidable resistance and delayed the progress of the British troops until the enemy had been able to organize the defences of the Haute-Deule Canal. For a complete success, therefore, it was essential that the defeat of the Germans should be swift and catastrophic, and that the attacking troops, after overrunning their organized defensive system, should be able to maintain a continuous and relentless pressure upon them until they had been driven across the canal.

(5) Preparations for the Battle and the Results of the First Day's Fighting.

Although, in comparison with the battles that were to come, Loos was a small affair, it will always be remembered as the first of the greater offensive operations in which the British Army took part. The number of troops employed in the battle, the weight of artillery engaged, and the preparations made for it, exceeded anything that had hitherto been attempted by the British General Staff. New roads and tracks had to be made, miles of trenches had to be dug and telephonic communications to be laid. If, therefore, the organization was not always perfect, or the arrangements made for the reception and accommodation of the troops were not in every respect satisfactory, it should be borne in mind that the staff was confronted with a bigger proposition than it had ever before been called upon to face, while the difficulties entailed by the concentration of so many troops in a comparatively small area were intensified by the inexperience of many of the new divisions and the bad weather conditions which prevailed during the early days of the offensive.

The decision was made to utilize gas in the attack at Loos, and high hopes were entertained as to the value of this new weapon which was being employed by the British for the first time. It was hoped that it would demoralize the enemy and so do much to lighten the task of the infantry—more especially in its assault on the German second line trenches, the wire in front of which was in most places out of range of the British artillery. It was thought, indeed, that the employment of gas might be some compensation for the lack of artillery, for, although the guns and howitzers brought into the field for the operations at Loos greatly exceeded any previous concentration of British artillery during the war, it was yet realized that they were by no means sufficient for the work before them, especially in view of the fact that the supply of shells, especially H.E., was limited.*

In the preliminary artillery bombardment, which began on the 21st of September and was continued for four days, the task of cutting passages through the enemy's wire was entrusted to the field artillery, firing mainly with shrapnel, while the fire of the heavy guns and howitzers was directed against his rear defences and communications. In many places the wire was successfully cut, but this was not invariably the case, as, in more than one instance, the attacking troops reached the German front line trenches only to find themselves faced by an unbroken wire entanglement.†

The infantry attack was launched along the whole British line at 6.30 a.m. on the 25th of September, and from the first met with varying success.

On the extreme right of the IV Corps front, the 47th (London) Division carried out most of the task assigned to it, and, by its hold on the Double Crassier and the German trenches which lay between it and Loos, succeeded in securing the southern defensive flank. On the left of the 47th Division, the 15th (Scottish) Division drove the enemy

* One thousand guns of all calibres were employed in the battle, 400 north of the La Bassée Canal, 600 south of it. But although the concentration of guns was considerable, it should be remembered that the frontage to be covered by the British artillery was about five times greater than that at Neuve Chapelle.

† The German dug-outs were so deep and well-constructed that they suffered comparatively little damage during the 70 hours' bombardment. The Germans have always maintained, and probably with truth, that wherever the battery emplacements and dug-outs were well built, the material damage done by the British artillery was slight.

out of Loos and then pushed forward east of the village, overrunning Puits No. 14 bis and Hill 70. So great, indeed, was the impetus of this attack and so slight the German resistance that some of the troops of this division actually reached the outskirts of Cité St. Auguste. But unfortunately the majority of the attacking force which had been detailed for the capture of this village lost direction upon emerging from Loos and became involved in the attack on Cité St. Laurent. There was, therefore, no weight behind the attack on Cité St. Auguste, and, when later in the day the German defence stiffened,* the small force which had been checked by uncut wire outside the village was caught in a trap and either killed or compelled to surrender. Meanwhile, the troops who had occupied the redoubt on Hill 70 after making their way down the reverse slope as far as Cité St. Laurent (which was incorrectly described in the first reports of the engagement as Cité St. Auguste), were met by a vigorous German counter-attack at about 1.15 p.m. and forced back on to the north-western side of the hill.

On the left of the 15th Division, the advance of the 1st Division was also only partially successful. The attack was carried out by the 2nd and 1st Brigades, which succeeded, after severe fighting, in reaching by nightfall the line of the Lens—La Bassée road.

On the north of the Vermelles—Hulluch road the 22nd Brigade of the 7th Division forced its way to a position south of the Quarries facing Cité St. Élie, while the 20th Brigade of the same division succeeded in seizing the Quarries.

On the left of the 7th Division two battalions of the 26th Brigade of the 9th (Scottish) Division captured Fosse No. 8, while the two remaining battalions of the same brigade reached the enemy's second line defences opposite Haisnes. Farther north, however, the 28th Brigade of this division was unable to make any progress and was driven back into the original British line.

* The enemy brought up fresh troops who were in army reserve behind Lens. These reinforcements enabled him to hold his second line and to regain some of the lost ground.

RESULTS OF FIRST DAY'S FIGHTING

The 2nd Division, between the Vermelles—La Bassée railway and the canal, attacked through the gas, and, having failed to reach the German front line, returned to its own line.

On the evening of the 25th of September, consequently, as a result of the first day's fighting, the new British front extended approximately from about half-way across the Double Crassier in the south across the Vermelles—Lens road to the southern outskirts of Loos and thence along the western slopes of Hill 70. North of Hill 70 it followed the eastern side of the Lens—La Bassée road as far as Puits No. 14 bis, thence bending eastward through Bois Hugo, it ran along the western side of the subsidiary road which leads from Lens northward towards Hulluch, turning west again in the direction of the Lens—La Bassée road about 1,000 yards south-west of the last named village. From this point the line was believed at the time to follow the Lens—La Bassée road as far north as its junction with the Vermelles—Hulluch road, and there is no doubt that until quite late in the evening of the 25th of September British troops were holding a few more or less isolated posts along this road. It was then decided, in view of the chalky nature of the ground, that it was too late to set about the task of digging trenches, and, consequently, the order was given to withdraw the posts and to establish the line in the German trenches which ran from due west of Hulluch in a south-westerly direction towards the Loos—Haisnes road.

This change of position was to have an unfortunate bearing upon the next day's fighting—indeed, upon the whole subsequent course of the battle—for the Higher Command does not appear to have become aware of the withdrawal until some considerable time after it took place, and consequently ordered the two reserve divisions (the 21st and 24th Divisions of the XI Corps) to deliver an attack under the impression that they would start from a line nearly 1,000 yards farther east than was actually the case.*

* As a matter of fact, the troops of the 21st Division were in their right position when the time came for the attack to be delivered, but those of the 24th Division, owing to this withdrawal of the 1st Division, were not in their appointed place.

Northward from the western edge of Hulluch the new British front was more clearly defined. It ran westward from the junction of the Lens—La Bassée and Vermelles—Hulluch roads round the Quarries, thence northward round the eastern side of Fosse No. 8 and the Corons de Pékin and de Maron, and thence westward across the old German trenches north of the Hohenzollern Redoubt to the original British line between the Béthune—La Bassée road and the canal.

On the whole, the results of the day's fighting had been satisfactory, even if they had not come up to the expectations which had been indulged in by some of the more optimistic commanders. The Germans in many places had been pushed out of exceedingly strong positions and the divisions of the New Army had proved their fighting worth. At the same time, the losses had been very heavy, while the vigour and determination of the enemy's counter-attacks had made it clear that his troops were still full of fight. It was already abundantly evident that only by the maintenance of the most vigorous offensive would it be possible to break through the remaining German defences. That, in the opinion of the British Commander-in-Chief, it was still possible to reach the objectives which had been fixed upon before the offensive began, appears to be proved by the fact that he did not counter-order his decision to throw his reserves into the battle—a decision which he had made in the early hours of the day after he had received the news that the attack was making such good progress. At 9.30 a.m. he had placed the XI Corps, less the Guards Division, under the direct command of Sir Douglas Haig, and had himself issued orders for the acceleration of the advance of the Guards whom, however, he still retained in General reserve.

(6) CONCENTRATION OF THE XI CORPS IN THE ZONE OF OPERATIONS—FAILURE OF THE ATTACK ON THE 26TH OF SEPTEMBER.

Unfortunately, as matters turned out, the troops of the XI Corps were not near enough to the scene of action on the 25th of September, and the reserve divisions, consequently, were called upon to carry out long and exacting marches just before they were sent into action.*

On the 24th of September the 21st and 24th Divisions, which were then in the Ferfay and Nœux-les-Mines areas respectively, had received orders from the XI Corps commander to continue their march that night with the result that, in the early hours of the 25th, the head of the former division lay just west of Nœux-les-Mines and the tail half a mile south of Labuissière, while the head of the 24th Division was at Beuvry and its tail a little north-west of Béthune. It had originally been intended that the Guards Division, which, on the 24th of September, it will be remembered, was in billets in the area south of Aire, should also move forward on the night of the 24th–25th, and bivouac in the area round Ferfay vacated by the 21st Division. This movement, however, had been postponed in view of the congestion of traffic on the roads.

On the morning of the 25th of September, when, as has been already explained, Sir John French placed the 21st and 24th Divisions under the direct command of Sir Douglas Haig, these two divisions were still in column of route—the former in the neighbourhood of Mazingarbe, about a mile and a half south-west of Vermelles; the latter on the roads between Béthune and Nœux-les-Mines and Béthune and Vermelles.

The troops of the two divisions had had a most trying night march; the heavy rain, which began to fall on the evening of the 24th of September, and which continued all night, adding to their discomfort and difficulties.

* There can be little doubt that Sir John French made a mistake in keeping the XI Corps in General reserve. In view of the small scope of the operations, it was clear that the reserve troops could only be employed on the front of the First Army, and, had they been placed from the first at the disposal of Sir Douglas Haig, better arrangements could have been made for their concentration in the battle area. Even then it is more than doubtful whether success would have attended the attack of the 21st and 24th Divisions owing to the failure of the artillery to cut the enemy's wire, but, at any rate, a less severe trial would have been imposed upon inexperienced staffs and troops who were totally ignorant of active service conditions.

The Guards Division began to move forward from the area south of Aire at 6 a.m. on the 25th, and divisional headquarters was opened at Ferfay two hours later.

At 9.30 a.m. Lord Cavan, who had gone forward to advanced XI Corps headquarters at Nœux-les-Mines, received verbal instructions for his division to continue its advance in the afternoon. At 11.30 a.m., therefore, the necessary orders were issued, and the division, whose concentration in the Ferfay area was only completed at 10.30 a.m., moved forward again at 2 p.m. with instructions to occupy the area just vacated by the 21st Division—viz. the head of the division at Nœux-les-Mines, the tail at Labuissière.

This march, throughout the course of which rain fell almost incessantly, proved a terribly trying ordeal even for seasoned troops. The actual distance which had to be traversed varied from between fifteen and a half to seventeen and a half miles, but it was not so much the length of the march—although it should be remembered that the infantry had already been marching for about four hours in the morning—as the continuous stoppages on the roads which proved so tiring for the troops. There was no kind of traffic control, and units and transport of the 21st and 24th Divisions, and transport of the 47th Division, blocked the entire line of route, while, to add to the general congestion, the tail of the column was cut off by the Cavalry Corps, orders having been received that the cavalry was to be allowed to pass through the infantry.

Owing to these incessant delays, the rear troops did not reach their destinations until after midnight, the majority of the units having been on the road for between seven and eight hours. Notwithstanding their trying ordeal, the men behaved with their customary cheerfulness and determination, only a very small number falling out, and, on reaching the end of their journey, they were rewarded as they found that billets had been provided for them—the 1st Guards Bde. group at Nœux-les-Mines; the 2nd Guards Bde. group at Houchin; and the 3rd Guards Bde. group at Hallicourt. The troops were thus enabled to sleep under cover and to dry their clothes, with the result that, on the following morning, when the divisional commander visited the various units, he found his men fit and cheery and apparently none the worse for their long march.

The operations of the First Army on the 26th of September were wholly unsuccessful. The attacks delivered by the 1st Division on Hulluch and by the 21st and 24th Divisions on the enemy's positions between that village and Hill 70 ended in complete failure, nor was the attempt made by the 15th Division to regain possession of the redoubt on Hill 70 attended with any more success.

At nightfall, consequently, on the 26th, the southern part of the British line, as a result of a severe day's fighting, remained much the same as it had been on the previous evening. The redoubt on Hill 70 was still in the possession of the Germans, whose defensive positions from that point ran northward just west of the Lens—La Bassée road to the western outskirts of Hulluch.

(7) THE GUARDS DIVISION TAKES OVER THE LINE FROM THE 21ST AND 24TH DIVISIONS.

The time had now come for the Guards to take their share in the great offensive, but the rôle which they were called upon to play was entirely different from that for which they had been originally cast. The hour for the resumption of open warfare had not yet arrived and the Guards Division, instead of being pushed through the attacking divisions to lead the victorious advance to the Haute-Deule Canal, had to be employed to recapture important tactical points from which the enemy had succeeded in ejecting the British troops, and to consolidate in the face of violent German counter-attacks the new British line which had been gained at the cost of so much heroism and so many casualties.

As soon as Sir John French heard of the failure of the operations on the 26th of September, he placed the Guards Division at the disposal of Sir Douglas Haig, and it came once again under the direct command of the XI Corps.

At 11.45 a.m. on the 26th, an order was issued by Lieut-General Haking, in accordance with instructions sent from

G.H.Q., for the Guards Division to march at 1 p.m. to a position of readiness in, and in rear of, the old British first line trenches between the Le Rutoire—Loos and Vermelles—Hulluch roads.

The three Guards brigades accordingly began to move forward at that hour from the billets in which they had spent the night of the 25th. The divisional Artillery, including the D.A.C., the movements of which from this time onwards throughout the battle were controlled by the XI Corps through the C.R.A., Guards Division,* was ordered to move into the billets vacated by the infantry, and the divisional Train was sent forward to Nœux-les-Mines. The Field Companies, R.E., accompanied their respective infantry brigades, while the Field Ambulances and the 4th Bn. Coldstream Guards (Pioneers), which remained under the direct orders of the divisional commander, followed the 3rd Guards Bde. The mounted troops did not advance with the division, and the remainder of the first line transport which did not accompany the battalions was parked in the billeting area relinquished by the infantry. Advanced divisional headquarters was established in a small house in the main street of Sailly-Labourse, while the Administrative Staff remained for the time being in Nœux-les-Mines, subsequently moving to Labourse.

At 2.10 p.m., on receipt of further instructions from the XI Corps issued after the full effects of the failure of the morning's attack had become known, a revised order was sent out to the 1st and 2nd Guards Bdes. bidding them to continue their advance to the old German front line trenches immediately in front of the sectors already allotted to them, and there during the night to strengthen their position to the utmost of their power. To assist the infantry in this task, a company of the 4th Bn. Coldstream Guards (Pioneers) was attached to each brigade.

The 1st Guards Bde. reached its appointed line in the course of the afternoon and its headquarters was established in a cellar at Le Rutoir Farm. At 9.45 p.m. Lord Cavan visited Brig.-General Feilding and told him that the 1st

---

* *See* W.D., Guards Division, September, 1915.

and 2nd Guards Bdes. were to relieve the 21st and 24th Divisions, the relief to begin at 1 a.m. on the 27th of September. In accordance with these instructions, Brig.-General Feilding ordered the 2nd and 3rd Bns. Coldstream Guards to take over the front line from the point where it bent back west of the Lens—La Bassée road, about 800 yards south-west of Hulluch, to a point about 600 yards south-east of "Lone Tree." He also gave orders that patrols were to be pushed out under cover of the early morning mist with instructions to dig themselves in, so as to establish posts in advance of the main line of defence. Commanding officers were strictly warned not to commit themselves to any offensive movement and to seize every opportunity of consolidating the line, getting into touch on their left with the 1st Division and on their right with the 2nd Guards Bde.

By 6 a.m. this relief had been successfully accomplished by the 3rd Bn. Coldstream Guards on the left and the 2nd Bn. Coldstream Guards on the right, and two advanced posts had also been established.

The 2nd Guards Bde. moved forward at the same time as the 1st Guards Bde., and, by about 3 a.m., the 1st Bn. Scots Guards, on the right, and the 2nd Bn. Irish Guards, on the left, had taken over the stretch of front line which ran from "Fort Glatz," on the north-western outskirts of Loos, northward along the western side of the Lens—La Bassée road, the Irish Guards being in touch with the 1st Guards Bde. and the Scots Guards with the dismounted troops of the 6th Cavalry Bde., who were then holding the line immediately north-east of Loos. The 3rd Bn. Grenadier Guards and the 1st Bn. Coldstream Guards, the two remaining battalions of the brigade, also advanced during the night and occupied the first and second line trenches in the old German defensive system north of Loos. By 6 a.m., when the 2nd Guards Bde. headquarters was shifted from Le Rutoire Farm to Loos, the position occupied by the brigade had already been much improved and the machine-gun defence as carefully organized as was possible in the darkness.

It is not easy to exaggerate the difficulties of this relief and the arduous and prolonged work which it entailed for officers and men. The distance which had to be traversed by each brigade was considerable, the ground was slippery and inches deep with mud; the trenches were for the most part crumbling ruins and filled with dead bodies and every kind of equipment, while the progress of the incoming battalions was still further impeded by stragglers belonging to the outgoing divisions who had to be collected and sent back to Vermelles. The confusion was at times almost indescribable, and it is doubtful whether the higher authorities had any idea of the immense difficulties which had to be overcome by the troops on their way into the line. Luckily, although there was some shelling during the night, there were few casualties, and by the time day broke the Guards had succeeded in making themselves as safe and comfortable as was humanly possible. Their night's work had been a fine feat of efficiency and endurance.

At 1.50 p.m. on the 27th of September, in accordance with verbal instructions given to him by Lieut.-General Haking, Lord Cavan issued an order* for the Guards Division to attack the Chalk Pit and Puits No. 14 bis on the Lens—La Bassée road and Hill 70.

In order to consolidate the new British line, the ejection of the enemy from these positions was deemed to be of the utmost importance. From the redoubt on Hill 70 the Germans not only commanded Loos with machine-gun fire, but also could enfilade the British trenches which ran northward from that village, while the Chalk Pit and Puits No. 14 bis afforded him excellent *points d'appui* for the purposes of counter-attack. Whether or not it was a wise policy, however, at this stage of the battle and when there were so few available reserves, to attempt the capture of these extremely strong positions with so comparatively little artillery preparation is open to doubt. It is tolerably clear, at any rate, that had Sir Douglas Haig known a little earlier of the loss of Fosse No. 8 and " the Dump," † he

* *See* Guards Division Operation Order, Appendix IV.
† On the night of the 25th-26th of September the 73rd Infantry Bde. relieved the 26th Infantry Bde. at Fosse No. 8, and held the

would have counter-ordered altogether this attack by the Guards Division: as it was, he instructed Lieut.-General Haking that the Guards were on no account to advance beyond the line the Chalk Pit—Puits No. 14 bis—Hill 70.

Lord Cavan's plan of action was to seize his objectives—the Chalk Pit and Puits No. 14 bis opposite his centre and Hill 70 on his right—then to consolidate the ground gained, and link it up with the line which he already held on his left. If this work were successfully carried out, the defensive position held by the Guards Division would be greatly strengthened, and, if it were decided to undertake further offensive operations, the line would be much better adapted for the launching of a fresh attack.* He decided, therefore,

---

position until 8.30 a.m. on the 27th when the line was broken at Corons alley. A strong German attack then developed and at 2.30 p.m. the whole of Fosse No. 8 had fallen into the enemy's hands (*see* I Corps narrative). Sir Douglas Haig, who received this information shortly after Lord Cavan had sent out his orders for the Guards' attack, immediately instructed Major-General R. H. Butler, who was at the time at I Corps headquarters, to find out from the XI Corps commander whether there was time to stop this attack, or at any rate to postpone it, as he did not wish to use up a fresh division having nothing behind it except the 28th Division, which would now be required to reinforce the I Corps in front of Fosse No. 8. Lieut.-General Haking, who appears only to have received Major-General Butler's message at 3 p.m., replied that the Guards were already advancing to the attack, and that, owing to the difficulties of communication, he feared that it would be impossible for him to get orders to Lord Cavan in time to countermand the attack. For a record of this conversation *see* W.D., First Army, September, 1915.

* It was the original intention of the XI Corps commander, in the event of the capture of the Chalk Pit and Puits No. 14 bis, to push forward the 1st Guards Bde. and to secure the line of the Lens—La Bassée road. *See* Lieut.-General Haking's telegram to Sir Douglas Haig, dispatched at 8.30 a.m. on the 27th of September. Early in the morning of the 28th, however, Brig.-General Feilding, who was somewhat sceptical as to the feasibility of such an advance, with his commanding officers, made a personal reconnaissance of the enemy's positions round Hulluch, and reported that the German defences were too strong for the operation to be successful. He stated that the enemy was so placed that he could enfilade any trench that could be dug forward as a starting point for the advance, while the German wire was so strong and thick that he doubted whether it could be broken by artillery fire. In view of this report, and also of the failure of the 2nd Guards Bde. to take Puits No. 14 bis, Lieut.-General Haking's proposed advance did not take place.

to leave the 1st Guards Bde. in the position which it already occupied, in order to form a defensive flank on the left of the line, and to carry out his attack with the 2nd and 3rd Guards Bdes., the latter of which was still in the neighbourhood of Vermelles. His orders to Brig.-General Feilding were to protect the left of the 2nd Guards Bde. with covering fire as soon as the attack began, and then, after the Chalk Pit had been captured, to gain touch with the 2nd Guards Bde. and to consolidate a new line a little in advance of that which his troops were occupying.

Brig.-General Feilding carried out these instructions very effectively, and, in addition to providing the covering fire, made arrangements for the discharge of a cloud of smoke at 4 p.m., which had the effect of drawing the enemy's fire and of concealing the attack of the Irish Guards on the Chalk Pit from the view of the German gunners in the Hulluch area.*

The arrangements made for the artillery bombardment before the attack and for the artillery support during the operation, were as good as were possible in the circumstances, the time available being so short and the positions of the enemy's machine guns so difficult to locate. To assist the 2nd Guards Bde., Puits No. 14 bis was bombarded by the heavy artillery from 12 noon to 3 p.m., the fire of certain guns being concentrated on the houses at the western edge of Bois Hugo, and, at 3.40 p.m., for five minutes before the infantry attack was launched a hurricane bombardment by every available gun was directed on all the objectives. A brigade, R.F.A., of the 21st Division was allotted to the 2nd Guards Bde., and its commander was attached to Brig.-General Ponsonby with orders to be ready at any moment to switch off his target on to any other which the brigadier might select. The 76th and 95th Brigades, R.F.A., were allotted in a similar way to the 3rd Guards Bde., and their commanders were instructed to carry out the orders of Brig.-General Heyworth.†

---

* *See* pp. 55–56.
† At 6.15 a.m. on the 27th of September Brig.-General Wardrop, C.R.A., Guards Division, was placed in command of the 21st and 24th

ATTACK ON THE CHALK PIT

(8) ATTACK BY THE 2ND GUARDS BRIGADE ON THE CHALK PIT AND PUITS No. 14 BIS.

On the receipt of Lord Cavan's order for the attack, Brig.-General Ponsonby assembled his commanding officers, and, after he had made as thorough an inspection as was possible of the ground over which the troops were to advance,* issued his orders. The 2nd Bn. Irish Guards was to attack the Chalk Pit at 4 p.m., and to establish itself on the northeast side of Chalk Pit Wood. It was to be supported by the 1st Bn. Coldstream Guards, which was to hold the northern end of the Chalk Pit. When the Chalk Pit had been effectually secured, the 1st Bn. Scots Guards was to advance echelonned to the right rear of the Irish Guards and to attack Puits No. 14 bis, moving round the south side of Chalk Pit Wood. To cover this attack, the Irish Guards were to bring a heavy fire to bear on the Puits and, to assist in this task, four machine guns were detailed to accompany them. The 3rd Bn. Grenadier Guards was to remain in support, ready, if necessity arose, to go to the assistance of the Scots Guards.

In conformity with these orders two companies (Nos. 3 and 2) of the 2nd Bn. Irish Guards moved forward down the western slope of the valley at 4 p.m., and, meeting with little opposition, reached the western edge of Chalk Pit Wood and the Chalk Pit with few casualties. The successful

---

divisional Artillery in support of the Guards Division. The task assigned to the artillery at the disposal of the XI Corps was " to keep down all fire on or near the Lens—La Bassée road—Hill 70—to west of Hulluch." Ten 18-pdr. bdes. and six howitzer bdes. were employed for this purpose, the majority of which only fired for a little over an hour. Each field battery had four guns, and each howitzer battery only four howitzers.

* " From where I issued my orders to battalion commanders one could plainly see on the other side of the valley the Chalk Pit and the two ruined red houses. A small narrow wood runs south from the Pit, and farther south stands the Puits, a prominent looking building with a high chimney. Close to the Puits and nearer to the wood stands a small red house known as 'the Keep.' To the right is Hill 70, which is practically on the sky-line as one looks at it from Loos." See Brig.-General Ponsonby's account of the operations of the 2nd Guards Bde., W.D., Guards Division, App. 7c.

advance of the battalion was undoubtedly assisted by the cloud of smoke discharged by the 1st Guards Bde. from the trenches south-west of Hulluch, the smoke effectually screening the movements of the Irish Guards from the enemy's artillery observers, and the machine-gun and rifle fire which accompanied it drawing his fire.*

As soon as the Irish Guards were in possession of Chalk Pit Wood and the Chalk Pit, No. 1 Company was sent to the southern end of the wood to reinforce No. 3 Company and to assist the 1st Bn. Scots Guards, which was already advancing to the assault of Puits No. 14 bis, while two platoons of No. 4 Company were sent forward to strengthen the defence of the Chalk Pit.

Meanwhile the Scots Guards, the Left Flank Company and " C " Company leading, in extended order, had doubled down the slope from the British trenches and almost immediately had come under heavy shrapnel fire from the enemy's guns concealed in rear of Bois Hugo. They succeeded, however, in reaching the Loos—Hulluch road without much difficulty.

But as soon as they began to ascend the slope on the eastern side of the road, where they were joined by the two companies of Irish Guards from Chalk Pit Wood, they were met by a withering machine-gun fire from Bois Hugo, " the Keep " and the Puits. Notwithstanding the destructive nature of this fire, however, and a certain amount of confusion caused by the leading companies of the Scots Guards becoming mixed up with the Irish Guards, an assault on " the Keep " and the Puits was quickly organized.† This attack was delivered with vigour and determination, but the enemy's positions were of exceptional strength and his

---

* *See* Report of the officer commanding the 8th Bn. of the Berkshire Regiment, W.D., Guards Division, App. 7E. The smoke was actually discharged from the trenches occupied by this Battalion on the I Corps front.

† In this attack the Scots and Irish Guards were unexpectedly reinforced on the right by a detachment of the 4th Bn. Grenadier Guards, under Captain Morrison, belonging to the 3rd Guards Bde. This party had lost touch with the remainder of its battalion after entering Loos preparatory to the attack on Hill 70 (*see* p. 60), and, having received no orders in reply to various messages, Captain Morrison decided to join in the operations of the 2nd Guards Bde.

machine-gun fire was so effective and deadly that, by the time the assaulting troops had reached the Puits, their numbers were so much reduced that success was no longer possible.* A small party only, most gallantly led by Captain J. H. Cuthbert, Scots Guards, succeeded in entering the Puits where it held on for some time, engaged in fierce hand-to-hand fighting with the Germans.

Meanwhile, on the left of the attack, the leading companies of the 1st Bn. Coldstream Guards had come up in support of the Irish Guards, who had been compelled owing to the intensity of the enemy's machine-gun fire, to fall back to the western side of Chalk Pit Wood. They were now re-formed, and, advancing in conjunction with the Coldstream on their left, quickly re-established themselves on the eastern side of the wood, while the Coldstream pushed forward and regained possession of the eastern side of the Chalk Pit.

About the same time, two companies of the 3rd Bn. Grenadier Guards came up in support of the Scots Guards. They were met with very heavy machine-gun fire as they advanced up the slope south of Chalk Pit Wood and had heavy losses. One platoon, however, led by Lieutenant A. T. Ayres-Richie, managed to penetrate as far as the Puits, thus bringing a welcome reinforcement to Captain Cuthbert's hard-pressed detachment which was still holding out. But so deadly was the enfilade machine-gun fire in the area between the Chalk Pit and the Puits that it was sheer waste of life to send forward more men to Captain Cuthbert's assistance, with the result that, after a splendid attempt, the Puits had to be evacuated, and the Scots Guards and Grenadiers then dug themselves in for the night on a line running southward from Chalk Pit Wood towards Loos.

The position of the 2nd Guards Brigade, as the result of the day's fighting, was, therefore, as follows: the Chalk Pit had been captured and was held by the 1st Bn. Coldstream Guards, which was in touch with the 2nd Battalion

* No fewer than 11 officers, including the commanding officer, Lieut.-Colonel S. H. Godman, who was severely wounded, became casualties in this attack.

of the same regiment (1st Guards Bde.) on its left; the 2nd Bn. Irish Guards was in possession of Chalk Pit Wood; and two companies of the 1st Bn. Scots Guards and one company of the 3rd Bn. Grenadier Guards held a line of trenches along the lower slopes of the rising ground on which Puits No. 14 bis is situated.

The losses suffered by the brigade, especially in officers, had been very severe, but all ranks had behaved with splendid gallantry and steadiness in most trying circumstances, and, although they failed to keep possession of the Puits, they were able to consolidate their position on the ground they had won, in despite of the intensity of the enemy's artillery and machine-gun fire.

(9) ATTACK BY THE 3RD GUARDS BRIGADE ON HILL 70.

In his orders for the attack on the 27th of September Lord Cavan made the operation to be carried out by the 3rd Guards Bde. against Hill 70 contingent upon the success of the 2nd Guards Bde. in its assault on the Chalk Pit and Puits No. 14 bis. The reason which influenced him is obvious —with the Puits still in the enemy's hands, the task of capturing the redoubt on Hill 70 would be infinitely more difficult as an enfilade fire could be brought to bear from this position upon nearly all the ground which would have to be crossed by troops attacking Hill 70 from Loos. During the course of a battle, however, owing to the difficulties of communication and the general confusion, it is seldom possible to carry out orders to the letter, and, as events turned out, the 3rd Guards Bde. made its attack on Hill 70 notwithstanding the fact that the 2nd Guards Bde. had failed in its attempt to capture the Puits.

On the morning of the 27th of September Lord Cavan visited Brig.-General Heyworth in Vermelles and explained fully to him the operation which he wished his brigade to carry out. The latter then made clear the situation to his commanding officers, and, after issuing his orders for the attack, went forward with his brigade-major and Lieut.-

Colonel G. Hamilton, commanding the 4th Bn. Grenadier Guards, to reconnoitre the ground.

The four battalions of the brigade, marching in the following order, viz. : 4th Bn. Grenadier Guards, 1st Bn. Welsh Guards, 2nd Bn. Scots Guards, 1st Bn. Grenadier Guards—began their advance from the Vermelles area about 2.30 p.m. Commanding officers had been warned that as soon as the troops appeared over the sky-line beyond Fosse No. 7 they would probably come under the enemy's artillery fire. Before reaching the top of the hill, consequently, the commanding officer of the leading battalion deployed into artillery formation and the other battalions conformed. In this formation the brigade moved down the long stretch of sloping ground into Loos—a distance of about a mile. From the moment the leading troops appeared over the crest of the hill, and for the remainder of the advance, the brigade came under a heavy shrapnel and H.E. fire. All four battalions displayed magnificent coolness and discipline. The men moved steadily forward as if on parade. There was no sign of confusion, each platoon in succession keeping distance and intervals, and advancing quietly and in excellent order.*

The commanding officers of the various battalions, too, handled their men with skill and judgment, and, by promptly availing themselves of the cover afforded by the old German communication trenches on the lower slopes of the hill north and north-west of Loos, succeeded in reducing the number of casualties and in maintaining the cohesion of their troops.

Unluckily, however, just as the 4th Bn. Grenadier Guards was debouching from one of these communication trenches and entering Loos, it encountered a violent discharge of gas-shells. This caused some delay and confusion as the men had to put on their gas-masks, while their commanding

* " . . . the men on reaching the ridge were met by a tornado of shrapnel fire. Nevertheless, the Brigade . . . advanced with the steadiness of men on parade, and men of other battalions, who could see the manœuvre from their own trenches, have spoken again and again of that wonderful advance as being one of the most glorious and impressive sights of the war, and of how they were thrilled to see those large silhouettes pressing silently and inexorably forward against the sky-line." *See* " The Guards at Loos," the *Times*, 8th of November, 1915.

officer, who was on his way from Brig.-General Heyworth's headquarters to rejoin his battalion as it entered the town, was himself gassed and compelled to leave the scene of action. The command of the battalion thus unexpectedly devolved upon Major the Honble. Myles Ponsonby.

It was during this temporary confusion that about two and a half companies of the 4th Bn. Grenadier Guards, under the command of Captain Morrison, the leading company commander, got detached from the remainder of the battalion, and, losing their way in the network of narrow streets, worked round to the northern edge of the village instead of advancing straight through it. As soon as he realized that he had made a mistake in direction, Captain Morrison sent off several messengers to brigade headquarters for instructions, but, as he received no replies to these messages and found himself in touch with the 2nd Guards Bde., he thought it best to join in the attack of the Scots Guards on Puits No. 14 bis and then to endeavour to rejoin his own battalion for the attack on Hill 70 as soon as the Puits had been taken.

The failure of the attack on the Puits, however, made this intention impossible as Captain Morrison's detachment was called upon to guard temporarily the right flank of the 2nd Guards Bde. along the Loos—Bénifontaine road and was in consequence unable to return to its own battalion until a late hour in the evening.

As soon as he was informed of the reduction in strength of the 4th Bn. Grenadier Guards caused by the loss of Captain Morrison's detachment, Brig.-General Heyworth, finding that not more than 200 men of his battalion were left to Major Ponsonby, decided to launch his attack on Hill 70 with the 1st Bn. Welsh Guards supported by the remaining men of the 4th Bn. Grenadier Guards. At this time, having himself seen the 2nd Guards Bde. enter Puits No. 14 bis, the brigadier was under the impression that there was no reason for him to delay his own attack.* He left his headquarters, therefore,

* " I should have stated that my instructions were that I was not to attack if the 2nd Guards Bde. attack failed, but, having myself seen the attack of the 2nd Guards Brigade enter Puits No. 14 bis, I concluded the attack was successful and went to organize my own attack. I was not aware till later that the attacking troops had

ARRANGEMENTS FOR THE ATTACK

in order to find Lieut.-Colonel Murray-Threipland, commanding the 1st Bn. Welsh Guards, and personally to give him his instructions. He was lucky enough to find that officer without much delay and ordered him to bring up his battalion, which was still in a communication trench outside the village, and to carry out the assault on Hill 70 forthwith.

Lieut.-Colonel Murray-Threipland lost no time in his preparations for the attack. He ordered Major Ponsonby with his Grenadiers and two machine guns to direct the operation on the left, with No. 3 Company of the Welsh Guards in support, and the Prince of Wales's Company of the Welsh Guards, with a frontage of two platoons, and supported by No. 2 Company of the same regiment, to prolong the line on the right. He also instructed Captain Rhys Williams to go forward with two machine guns to some trenches on the right of the attack occupied by the 10th Hussars and the Blues, and to work along them with the object of driving out the Germans who were in the neighbouring trenches. He kept No. 4 Company of the Welsh Guards and two machine guns in battalion reserve.

The attack was launched at 5.30 p.m. and shortly afterwards Lieut.-Colonel Murray-Threipland heard from his liaison officer at brigade headquarters that the brigadier, who had by this time learned that the attack of the 2nd Guards Bde. had ended in partial failure, had sent orders cancelling the attack on Hill 70. It was then of course too late to act upon this information, as the troops were already in action.* The leading companies of Grenadiers and Welsh Guards had little difficulty in scaling Hill 70; there

---

subsequently to retire." *See* Brig.-General Heyworth's "Account of the Capture of Hill 70 by 3rd Guards Brigade," W.D., Guards Division, App. 7D. As a matter of fact, the brigadier was actually carrying out Lord Cavan's wishes by attacking Hill 70, because, as soon as the latter knew that the Chalk Pit had been captured, but that the Puits was still held by the enemy, he sent an order to the 3rd Guards Bde. to press the attack on Hill 70. This order, which was sent off at 5.20 p.m., did not reach Brig.-General Heyworth until much later.

* *See* Lieut.-Colonel Murray-Threipland's letter to Lord Harlech, W.D., Guards Division. As a matter of fact this order had not actually left brigade headquarters when the news that the attack had started reached Brig.-General Heyworth, and it was accordingly cancelled.

was at first comparatively little machine-gun or rifle fire while the enemy was concentrating his guns on Loos and on the last two battalions of the 3rd Guards Bde. which were still moving down the slope into the village. As soon, however, as the attacking troops reached the crest of Hill 70, they encountered a furious machine-gun fire directed upon them from the redoubt which was held in strength by the Germans, and also from Puits No. 14 bis. Both the Grenadiers and the Welsh Guards suffered severely during this stage of the advance, but, notwithstanding their losses, the troops succeeded in reaching to within about 25 yards of the enemy's position.* Explicit orders had been given to all commanding officers by the brigadier that on no account were they to go beyond the crest of Hill 70. The Welsh Guards, therefore, remained just below the top of the hill, but, owing to the fact that Lieut.-Colonel Hamilton had become a casualty so early in the day, it would appear that this order had not been communicated to Major Ponsonby,† and the Grenadiers accordingly pressed on towards the redoubt. To this unfortunate circumstance must be attributed the greater part of the casualties suffered by the 4th Bn. Grenadier Guards in this action.‡

It was not until some time after darkness had set in that any information as to the progress of the fight reached battalion headquarters. A message at last reached Lieut.-Colonel Murray-Threipland from Captain Bulkeley, commanding No. 2 Company Welsh Guards, stating that he had got on to the hill, but that he could make no farther progress without reinforcement as his casualties had been heavy. He added that his men were in tolerable safety under the

* See "The Grenadier Guards in the Great War, 1914–1918," vol. i. p. 313.

† Major Ponsonby, who had led his men with conspicuous gallantry and determination, was mortally wounded at this period in the attack. His adjutant, Captain T. F. J. N. Thorne, remained with him for the remainder of the evening, but was himself killed whilst endeavouring to rescue some of the wounded men during the night.

‡ It should also be noted, as a further explanation for the continued advance of the Grenadiers, that on the maps with which the troops had been supplied the redoubt was shown as being on the northern slope of Hill 70, whereas it actually was situated on the reverse slope.

shelter of a bank, but that any one who attempted to advance immediately came under machine-gun fire. About the same time this message was received, news reached battalion headquarters from Captain Rhys Williams, who reported that he was doing good work and could usefully employ two more machine guns.

It appeared to Lieut.-Colonel Murray-Threipland from Captain Bulkeley's report, which was corroborated verbally by Lieut. Rupert Lewis, who arrived shortly afterwards at battalion headquarters, that No. 2 Company had reached the point which had been fixed upon as its objective. He accordingly sent orders to Captain Bulkeley to consolidate the position which he had gained, and sent his two remaining machine guns to Captain Rhys Williams. He also ordered Captain Palmer to take No. 4 Company (Welsh Guards) to fill up a gap between the right of No. 2 Company and the trenches held by the 10th Hussars, and to consolidate.

Soon after he had given these orders, Lieut.-Colonel Murray-Threipland sent word back to Brig.-General Heyworth that his troops had captured their objectives on Hill 70, but that the attacking force was somewhat scattered and that he considered it advisable that the 2nd Bn. Scots Guards should relieve the Welsh Guards and the Grenadiers, and consolidate a line on the ground that had been gained. In response to this message, Lieut.-Colonel Cator, commanding the 2nd Bn. Scots Guards, arrived with two companies of his own battalion and the remnants of Captain Morrison's detachment of the 4th Bn. Grenadier Guards, which had by this time rejoined the 3rd Guards Bde. Up to this period in the evening Lieut.-Colonel Murray-Threipland had received no news of any kind from the Grenadiers or the Prince of Wales's Company (Welsh Guards), but he appears to have been confident that they had reached and were holding their objective. He now went round the forward positions with Lieut.-Colonel Cator and Major Brough, R.E.,* and it was soon clear to all three officers that no organized digging-in was possible on the

* Major Brough was still in command of the 55th Field Company, R.E., at this time. He succeeded Lieut.-Colonel Vanrenen as C.R.E. of the Guards Division on the 30th of September.

line then held, the enemy's machine-gun fire being far too fierce and the positions occupied by the troops too much exposed. Lieut.-Colonel Cator immediately returned to brigade headquarters and recommended that a line should be dug on the near slope of the hill in continuation of the trenches held by the cavalry on the right. This necessitated a withdrawal of about 100 yards behind the crest of Hill 70—the farthest point reached in the attack—whilst it also rendered the task of recovering the wounded a matter of great difficulty. In the circumstances, however, Brig.-General Heyworth had no alternative but to agree to the proposed withdrawal and his decision was approved by the divisional commander.*

The work of digging and wiring the new line was admirably carried out by the 2nd Bn. Scots Guards during the night, and by an early hour the following morning the new positions were safely consolidated. Connexion had been established with the cavalry on the right; whilst on the left, where Lieut.-Colonel Cator had not been able to get in touch with the 2nd Guards Bde., the line had been drawn back about 500 yards south-west of Puits No. 14 bis, forming a strong point from which the gap between the two brigades could be covered by machine-gun fire, should occasion arise.

As soon as he had been relieved by Lieut.-Colonel Cator, Lieut.-Colonel Murray-Threipland set to work to collect the various units of the attacking force on Hill 70, and to rescue the wounded, many of whom lay between the new line and the crest of the hill. This latter task was one of much danger and difficulty as the Germans kept up an intense machine-gun fire throughout the night. So splendid, however, was still the moral of the unwounded men of the two battalions, which had carried out the attack, that it was only when their commanding officer was able to give the order personally to them that they could be induced to leave the hill.†

* " The O.C. 2nd Bn. Scots Guards made a wise decision on Hill 70 to dig in just on reverse side of crest and not at farthest point gained, although this entailed a sacrifice of some of our wounded in between, and some officers' bodies." *See* note by Major-General the Earl of Cavan, W.D., Guards Division.

† " I found it very difficult to get our men back, unless I personally

Eventually, Nos. 2, 3 and 4 Companies, Welsh Guards, and a few men belonging to the Prince of Wales's Company of the same regiment and to the 4th Bn. Grenadier Guards were successfully withdrawn. But it was found impossible to rescue many of the wounded who lay along the crest of the hill as no one could reach them and live owing to the intensity of the enemy's fire.*

As a result of the operation a firm line of defence was consolidated along the slopes of Hill 70 which added considerably to the security of the British position at Loos. Both Grenadiers and Welsh Guards had displayed a magnificent courage in the attack and a dogged tenacity in holding on to the ground which they had won. Of the latter Lieut.-Colonel Murray-Threipland was justified in saying when describing his battalion's baptism of fire on Hill 70, that the men had borne themselves "up to the best Brigade of Guards standard."

But in this attack, as in the case of that of the 2nd Guards Brigade, the losses were very severe, especially in officers, and the enemy still held the redoubt on Hill 70.

(10) THE SECOND ATTACK OF THE 2ND GUARDS BRIGADE ON PUITS NO. 14 BIS.

Lord Cavan, who had spent the day in his battle headquarters at Le Rutoire Farm, visited the headquarters of the 2nd and 3rd Guards Bdes. in the evening of the 27th of September in order to make himself fully acquainted with the details of the day's fighting and to discuss future plans with his brigadiers. He decided that no good purpose would be

---

got at them, even then they all wanted to go forward and not back."
See Lieut.-Colonel Murray-Threipland's letter to Lord Harlech, W.D., Guards Division, September, 1915.

* A small party of men belonging to the 4th Bn. Grenadier Guards together with a machine-gun section of the same battalion, under the command of Lieut. M. G. Williams, which had accompanied the attack, remained on Hill 70 until late on the 28th of September. This party, with the assistance of some men belonging to one of the Field Companies, R.E., managed to dig itself in and put out some wire. Some of the wounded men on the hill succeeded in making their way to this party and were brought back on its withdrawal.

served by attempting a fresh attack upon the redoubt on Hill 70, but he gave orders that every effort must be made to strengthen the defences of the new line on the hill. With regard to a further offensive operation on the 2nd Guards Bde. front for the capture of Puits No. 14 bis, the decision was not left to the Guards divisional commander, as the order for the renewal of the attack upon that position emanated from First Army headquarters.*

In consequence of this decision of the Higher Command, Lord Cavan, at 12 noon on the 28th of September, issued an order to Brig.-General Ponsonby instructing him to attack the Puits at 3.45 p.m. that day. The infantry attack was to be preceded by a bombardment by the heavy artillery of the Puits and some ruined houses a little south-east of it and by a hurricane bombardment of the same area by the divisional Artillery for five minutes before the assault was actually launched.† The attack was to be delivered from the southern edge of Chalk Pit Wood.

As soon as he received this order, Brig.-General Ponsonby sent a message to Lord Cavan stating that in his opinion the attack had little chance of success. But this message never reached the division, and, although the brigadier was anxious to postpone the operation, at any rate until it could be carried out under cover of darkness, he considered that as

---

* The intention presumably of the Higher Command was to complete the task which had originally been set the Guards Division and to secure the line of the Lens—La Bassée road; but it is difficult to understand why it was thought that an attack on a position of exceptional strength should be more successful as a single isolated operation on the 28th of September than it had proved to be when part of a larger operation on the 27th. The failure of the Scots Guards to capture the Puits had been solely due to the enemy's fierce machine-gun fire from concealed positions on three sides, and there was no apparent reason to suppose that the British artillery would be any more able to locate and to destroy these positions by means of a short bombardment on the 28th than had been the case the previous day.

† Lord Cavan states in his notes on the battle of Loos that his " plan was faulty in the light of knowledge gained since of the enemy's position, in that our artillery preparation was too much centred on what we believed to be the strong points, whereas they were about 100 to 200 yards farther east." *See* W.D., Guards Division, September, 1915. *Cf.* Operation Order No. 2 by Brig.-General A. E. Wardrop, R.A., *ib.* App. 8A.

SECOND ATTACK ON PUITS NO. 14 BIS

he could not get into communication with the divisional commander he had no alternative but to carry out his instructions. He entrusted the attack to the 1st Bn. Coldstream Guards, which was occupying the Chalk Pit, and ordered Lieut.-Colonel A. G. Egerton, after securing the enemy's position, to establish himself on the railway line immediately south of the Puits. All the available machine guns were to cover the attacking troops, concentrating their fire on Bois Hugo, while the 2nd Bn. Irish Guards on the right of the line was to cooperate with rifle fire directed on the enemy's trenches in front of that wood.

The Coldstream Guards carried out the assault with their customary dash and determination. Despite the most galling fire of machine guns from three sides, but mainly from Bois Hugo, the leading companies pushed forward and some of the men, led by Lieut. C. J. M. Riley and 2nd Lieut. O. G. Style, actually reached the Puits. The enemy's machine-gun fire, however, which by this time had been augmented by an artillery bombardment, became so terrific, and the losses were so severe,* that Brig.-General Ponsonby decided that success was out of the question and ordered the battalion to discontinue the attack. The withdrawal was admirably conducted and the enemy attempted no counter-attack either then or during the night, so that it was possible to collect the wounded and to strengthen the line on the 2nd Guards Bde. front.

(11) EXTENSION NORTHWARD OF THE LINE HELD BY THE GUARDS DIVISION AND RELIEF OF THE DIVISION.

The following day, the 29th of September, although the Germans actually made no counter-attack, they shelled the Chalk Pit and Chalk Pit Wood very heavily.† Loos and its

---

* 9 officers and 250 other ranks were either killed or wounded in this abortive attack. Of the party which reached the Puits only Lieut. Riley, wounded, and two men got back. *See* W.D., 1st Bn. Coldstream Guards.

† Lieut.-Colonel Egerton, commanding the 1st Bn. Coldstream Guards, and his adjutant, Lieut. the Honble. M. D. Browne, were

vicinity were also severely bombarded during the day, but, as a result of good dispositions by the various commanding officers, and of the hard work in the construction and renovation of trenches done by the men, the losses were comparatively light.

On the 30th of September detailed instructions from the XI Corps were received at divisional headquarters with regard to work in connexion with the construction of a starting line for a fresh offensive operation which was then in contemplation.* The scheme of this proposed attack which, it was hoped, would take place on the 3rd of October in conjunction with the French, who had just taken over Loos, was as follows : the I Corps was to carry out an attack under cover of gas south of the La Bassée Canal, its objectives being the line of the Vermelles— La Bassée railway and Fosse No. 8; the XI Corps was to attack the enemy's trenches along the Lens— La Bassée road south and south-west of Hulluch, and also, in cooperation with a French attack on Hill 70 on the right, to endeavour to gain a more advanced defensive position designed to connect the Chalk Pit on the left with the north-eastern edge of the wood which extends east of the Lens—La Bassée road south of Bois Hugo ; the IV Corps was to be in reserve.

In order to carry out the preparations necessary for these operations, which involved the digging of several new fire trenches and numerous communication trenches, the 1st Guards Bde. had to take over part of the line occupied by the 3rd Infantry Bde. (1st Division) opposite Hulluch and

---

killed by the same shell just outside the battalion's headquarters in the Chalk Pit. Captain E. B. G. Gregge-Hopwood took over the command of the battalion temporarily until Lieut.-Colonel the Honble. G. V. Baring was brought in from the 4th Bn. Coldstream Guards (Pioneers) as commanding officer. Of Lieut.-Colonel Egerton, Brig.-General Ponsonby wrote: "The Coldstream Guards have lost a most valuable commanding officer in whom all ranks had the greatest confidence."

* This order was given verbally on the telephone to Major Davidson, G.S.O.2, Guards Division, by Lieut.-General Haking and confirmed by a written order from the corps received later in the day. *See* W.D., Guards Division, App. 12 and 12A.

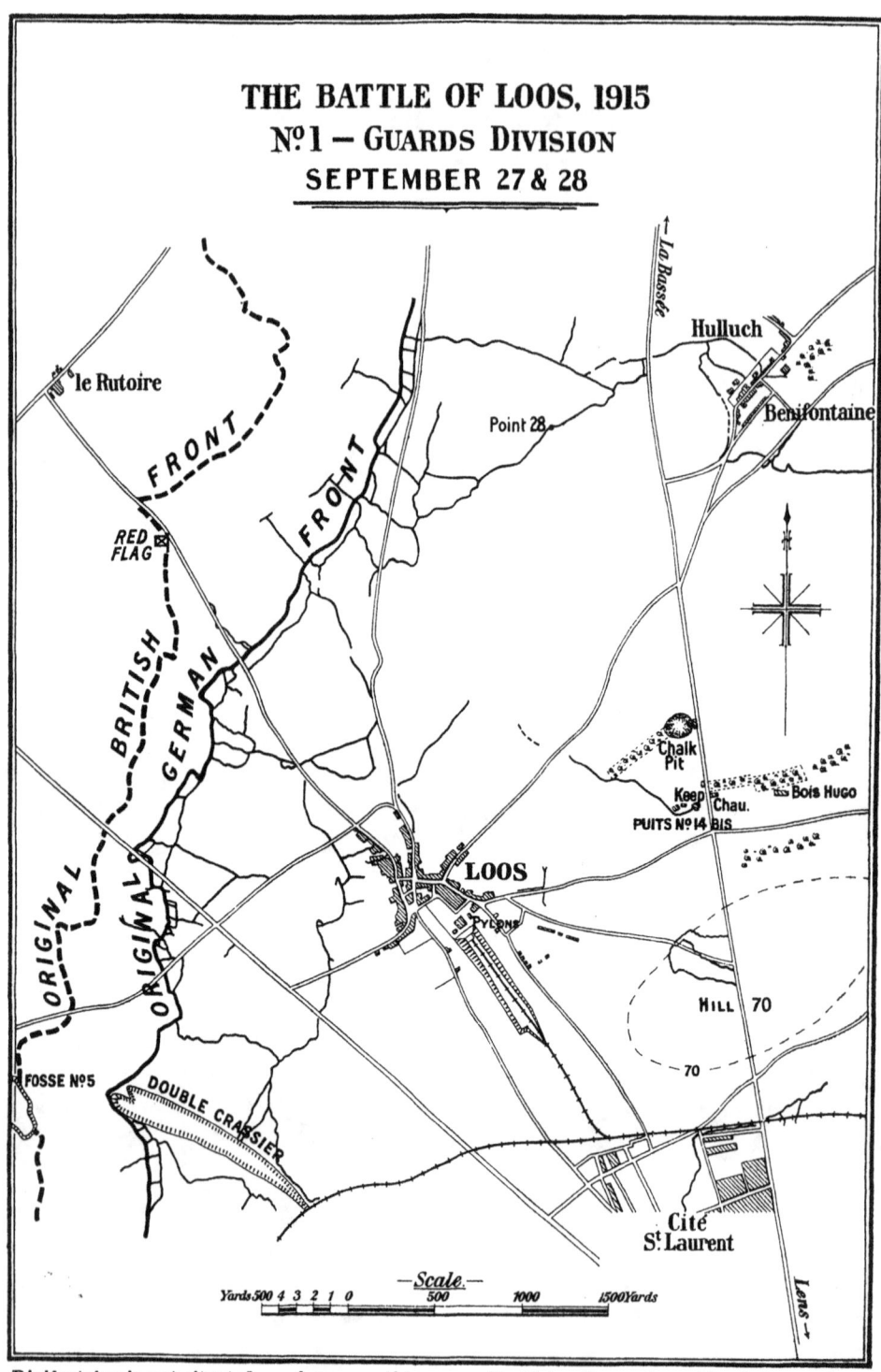

Bénifontaine is not situated as shown on this map. It adjoins the *eastern* side of the northern portion of Hulluch. (*See* Report on Loos country, G.S., 1st Div., Sept., 1915.) All the maps used appear to have been wrong in this regard.

Vol. I., page 68.

RELIEF OF THE GUARDS

the 2nd Guards Bde. to extend its left so as to keep in touch with the 1st Guards Bde.

The two brigades carried out these movements as soon as it was dark on the night of the 30th, and their working parties laboured unceasingly until 4 a.m. the next day. By this hour the 1st Guards Bde., with the assistance of the 4th Coldstream Guards (Pioneers), had constructed a new fire trench running parallel to the Lens—La Bassée road southward towards the eastern edge of the Chalk Pit, with which the 2nd Guards Bde., digging northward from Chalk Pit Wood, had linked up. It was a magnificent night's work of which officers and men were justly proud.

Meanwhile, the relief of the Guards Division had already begun. The 3rd Guards Bde. was relieved by the 142nd Infantry Bde. (47th Division) on the night of the 29th–30th of September,* and, although Loos was being heavily shelled at the time of the relief, the brigade escaped without a single casualty. It moved into billets in the neighbourhood of Labourse.

The relief of the 1st and 2nd Guards Bdes. by troops of the 12th Division was effected between midnight on the 30th of September and 4 a.m. on the 1st of October, the 1st Guards Bde. going into billets in the Mazingarbe area, the 2nd Guards Bde. near Verquigneul. Notwithstanding the bad weather and the terrible condition of the ground, both reliefs were carried out successfully, and, although there was a good deal of hostile artillery fire, with few casualties.

All ranks in the two brigades were worn out by their arduous exertions, and, after such a strenuous period in the line, even the squalid and overcrowded billets, which were all that were available in the area, represented comparative comfort to the men. The administrative branches of the divisional and brigade staffs had done their best to make things as comfortable as possible, and the troops found hot food and big fires awaiting their arrival.

* This brigade was to hold the line until the arrival of the troops of the French IX Corps, who, it had been arranged, were to take over the Loos sector.

CHAPTER III

THE BATTLE OF LOOS—*continued*.

ACTIONS OF THE HOHENZOLLERN REDOUBT.

(1) THE GUARDS TAKE OVER THE LINE OPPOSITE THE QUARRIES, 4TH OF OCTOBER—ALTERATION OF THEIR FRONT OWING TO THE LOSS OF THE HOHENZOLLERN REDOUBT.

ON the night of the 3rd–4th of October the Guards Division was again called upon to go into the line. The XI Corps had by this time been reconstituted, the 12th and 46th Divisions replacing the 21st and 24th Divisions, which had been withdrawn out of the battle area for the purposes of reorganization and refitment. The contemplated attack, too, in conjunction with the French, which it had been proposed to make on the 3rd of October and the preparations for which had occupied the Guards Division during its last night in the trenches,* had been definitely abandoned on the 1st of October owing to the inability of the French to be ready in time.†

So unsatisfactory, however, did Sir Douglas Haig consider the British line to be in front of Fosse No. 8 and southward to the Vermelles—Hulluch road that he determined to carry out this attack with his own troops in a somewhat modified form. He decided to make no further effort for the time being to capture the redoubt on Hill 70, but to attempt to drive the Germans out of Fosse No. 8 and the Quarries just

---

* The objects of this operation, it will be remembered, were the recapture of Fosse No. 8 and the formation of a more advanced defensive line between Hill 70 and the Chalk Pit.

† *See* XI Corps Op. Ord., R.H. 5. 79.

west of Puits No. 13 and to establish a defensive flank east of those places. He entrusted to the I Corps the task of recapturing Fosse No. 8, and to the XI Corps that of capturing the Quarries and pushing forward the line to the Lens—La Bassée road northward from the Chalk Pit to the salient opposite Hulluch.

Orders to this effect were issued from First Army headquarters on the 1st of October, and, later in the course of the same day, Lord Cavan received an order from the XI Corps instructing him to prepare a plan by the following day for the capture of the Quarries,* and to relieve the 2nd Division on the night of the 3rd–4th of October on the front extending southward from a point about 600 yards south of the Dump.

At 12.15 noon the following day the preliminary instructions for the relief were issued. The 1st Guards Bde. was ordered to relieve the 6th Infantry Bde. on the left with its right flank just south of the Quarries and the 3rd Guards Bde. to relieve the 5th Infantry Bde. and hold the line on the right. The 2nd Guards Bde. was to be in reserve at Vermelles, and the 4th Bn. Coldstream Guards (Pioneers) was to remain with divisional headquarters until further orders.

Shortly before midnight the same day, after consultation with the 2nd Division, detailed orders to the above effect, as well as for the movements of the other units of the Guards Division affected by the relief, were issued from divisional headquarters which, it was stated, would be opened at Noyelles-lez-Vermelles Château on the completion of the relief.† The relief was an exceedingly difficult one to carry out owing to the extremely bad condition of the communication trenches ‡ and the activity of the Germans on

---

* An order was sent at the same time from the XI Corps to the G.O.C. the 12th Division, to prepare a plan for the capture of the sector of the Lens—La Bassée road opposite his front.

† *See* Guards Division, G.R. 385. W.D., Guards Division, App. 13B.

‡ "The trenches were in poor condition after days of continuous fighting. The parapets of the fire trenches had been freely undercut to try and afford protection against shell fire. The communication trenches were badly damaged and battalion and brigade headquarters were not very safe. The German trench mortars were very attentive

the front of the 2nd Division—so aggressive, indeed, were they reported to be that it was felt that they might seize the opportunity of making an attack during the progress of the relief. Lord Cavan, therefore, early in the afternoon of the 3rd of October, sent special instructions to Brig.-General Feilding warning him to take every possible precaution against an attack as his troops were approaching the enemy's trenches south of the Quarries and to attempt no offensive operation until he was firmly established in the line. He also instructed both Brigadiers to have parties of bombers in readiness during the progress of the relief and emphasized the paramount importance of the troops settling to work on the construction of good communication trenches with the least possible delay.

The urgent necessity for precaution was proved about 6 p.m. when the 2nd Division reported heavy shelling of the British positions just north of the Vermelles—Hulluch road. As soon as this message was received at divisional headquarters, the 3rd Guards Bde., whose battalions were still in the neighbourhood of Sailly-Labourse, was ordered to stand fast until further orders. An hour later, on the receipt of a message from the 2nd Division that the situation was well in hand, an order was sent out for the relief to proceed, and it was completed shortly after 3 a.m. on the 4th of October; the relief of the 6th Infantry Bde. by the 1st Guards Bde. having been successfully effected a few hours earlier.

During the small hours of the morning, however, an attack by the enemy a little farther north succeeded in driving the troops of the 28th Division out of the Hohenzollern Redoubt—an incident which materially changed the situation on this part of the front. The loss of this important system of trenches rendered insecure the left flank of the line now held by the Guards Division and so made the proposed offensive operation against the Quarries extremely hazardous. Sir Douglas Haig, therefore, decided to abandon for the time being any further thought of an attack and to concentrate

---

and accurate. Lastly, our drainage led towards the enemy which was a great drawback after the persistent rain." Extract from note supplied by Lieut.-Colonel Brough, C.R.E., Guards Division.

A SIDE-SLIP IN THE LINE

the activities of his troops upon the work of strengthening the front of which they were actually in possession. This decision necessitated a readjustment of the line, whilst it was also necessary to relieve the 28th Division.

Accordingly, the XI Corps handed over to the IV Corps the frontage which it was holding from Loos on the French left to a point about 2,000 yards north of the eastern edge of that village, and in its turn took over from the I Corps the frontage from the left of the line held by the Guards Division to the Vermelles—Auchy-lez-la-Bassée road which runs north of Fosse No. 8. Of this frontage the southern sector was allotted to the 12th Division and the northern sector, from just south of the Quarries to the Vermelles—Auchy-lez-la-Bassée road, to the Guards Division. It was arranged that the front held by the 12th Division should be covered by the artillery of the Guards Division, the 12th Division and the 7th Division (less one brigade R.F.A.), and that held by the Guards Division by the artillery of the 28th Division and one brigade of the artillery of the 7th Division.

The order of the XI Corps commander, containing these instructions, reached Lord Cavan at 9 a.m. on the 4th of October, shortly after divisional headquarters had been opened at Noyelles-lez-Vermelles, and, at 6 a.m. the following morning the preliminary orders for the proposed side-slip in the line were issued to the Guards brigades. The 3rd Guards Bde. was warned that it would be relieved that night by the 37th Infantry Bde. (12th Division) and would then take over the billets occupied by the 2nd Guards Bde.; the 2nd Guards Bde. that it would relieve the 83rd Infantry Bde. (28th Division), which was then holding a frontage of about 1,500 yards with its left on the Vermelles—Auchy-lez-la-Bassée road; and the 1st Guards Bde. that it would extend its left so as to join the right of the 2nd Guards Bde. The 4th Bn. Coldstream Guards (Pioneers) was ordered to billet in Vermelles under arrangements to be made by the 3rd Guards Bde.*

Meanwhile, during the night of the 4th–5th of October,

* See G.R. 437, W.D., Guards Division, App. 21.

in spite of heavy shelling by the enemy, the 3rd Guards Bde. had succeeded in strengthening materially its position, and the 1st Guards Bde., although somewhat impeded by the activity of the enemy's bombers, had also done much to improve and to consolidate the trenches in its sector of the line.

By 4.15 a.m. on the 6th of October the various reliefs, to which reference has just been made, had been successfully carried out, and at 10 a.m. divisional headquarters was opened at the Château des Pres at Sailly-Labourse.

An order was now received from the XI Corps that gas cylinders were to be installed along the frontage held by the Guards in preparation for an attack which was to be carried out at a subsequent date by the 46th Division, and a conference was held at divisional headquarters at which the necessary arrangements were discussed by Lord Cavan, the C.R.E. and representatives from the brigades in the line. Detailed instructions with regard to the preparation of the positions for the cylinders, the construction of " jumping off " trenches for the proposed attack, and the manner in which the cylinders were to be conveyed to the front line trenches so as to avoid, as far as possible, any undue congestion of traffic in the various communication trenches were issued later in the day.*

The paucity of the routes to and from the front on this part of the line, and the strenuous and incessant work which was required to keep them open owing to the enemy's accurate artillery and trench-mortar fire was a source of constant anxiety to the divisional and brigade staffs. It was only by the strict observance of traffic regulations and the maintenance of a rigid trench discipline that it was possible to keep these routes clear for the supply of food and ammunition to the troops in the line. The installation of gas cylinders thus added immensely to the difficulties of the situation. All the necessary preparations, however, for the placing in position of 120 cylinders on the front of each brigade had been made by the evening of the 7th of October and full instructions for the carrying out of the work of their

* See W.D., Guards Division, App. 27A.

installation in the line, on the night of the 8th–9th, were issued from divisional headquarters at 11 p.m. on the night of the 7th.

(2) GERMAN ATTACK ON THE 2ND GUARDS BDE. ON THE 8TH OF OCTOBER.

The night of the 7th–8th of October passed comparatively quietly, but, shortly after noon the following day, a report from the XI Corps reached divisional headquarters, stating that the enemy had cut passages through his wire near Hill 70, whilst, about the same time, the German artillery began a brisk bombardment of Vermelles as well as of the railway line north-east of it and the front line trenches held by the Guards Division. It was now tolerably clear that the enemy was contemplating an offensive operation, but on which particular sector or sectors of the British line the attack would be delivered was still uncertain. This question, however, was not left long in doubt. At 4.30 p.m. a message was received at divisional headquarters from the 2nd Guards Bde. to the effect that the enemy was attacking " Big Willie " and that Brig.-General Ponsonby had already requested the 3rd Guards Bde. to have a battalion in readiness to reinforce the line should such assistance become necessary.* About half an hour after the receipt of this message, the 1st Guards Bde. reported that the bombardment on its front had become very severe all along the line; that the front and support trenches had been considerably damaged; and that touch with its left battalion was only being maintained by orderlies. A message was also received from the 4th Bn. Coldstream Guards (Pioneers) that the battalion had been shelled out of its billets at Noyelles-lez-Vermelles.

As it was now certain that an attack, possibly on a big scale, was already in progress, Lord Cavan sent out an order cancelling his previous instructions for the installation of gas cylinders in the line that night, and made arrangements with the 12th Division for the reinforcement of the Guards Division by the 35th Infantry Bde. should the necessity arise.

* The 3rd Guards Bde. reported later that the 2nd Bn. Scots Guards had been detailed for this purpose.

The German infantry attack on the front held by the 2nd Guards Bde. began about 4 p.m. The brunt of it was directed against the narrow salient in the line just south of "Big Willie" where the track leading from Le Rutoire to the Loos—Haisnes road crosses the trenches, and its object was to drive the British out of these trenches and thus to straighten the enemy's line just south of "Big Willie." *
The attack was carried out by battalions belonging to three different regiments † and was pressed with extreme determination, the German bombers advancing down the trench that led from the southern face of the Hohenzollern Redoubt and also attacking along the communication trench that ran east and south of the British position. They thus attacked from three sides the two companies of the 3rd Bn. Grenadier Guards which formed the garrison of this part of the line and succeeded in driving them back out of their trench. Most of the Grenadiers' bombers were put out of action as their supply of bombs was quickly exhausted, with the result that the situation on this part of the front became precarious in the extreme.

It was then that Sergeant Brooks, 3rd Bn. Coldstream Guards, on his own initiative, organized a bombing party from his battalion on the right and began attacking the Germans, moving forward along the lost trenches. This prompt and gallant action was the turning point of the engagement. Sergeant Brooks and his party, followed by No. 1 Company of the 3rd Bn. Grenadier Guards and two companies of the 1st Bn. Scots Guards, which had been sent forward by Brig.-General Ponsonby to reinforce the Grenadiers as soon as he heard of the German attack, bombed the enemy out of the trenches, and, when the German bombers attempted to cross the open ground to the south of the Dump, they were decimated by machine-gun fire. The guns of the 3rd Brigade, R.F.A., were also brought to bear with great effect on the communication trenches leading to the Hohenzollern Redoubt. During this vigorous British counter-

---

* *See* information obtained from prisoners captured by the 1st Guards Bde. on the 8th of October. W.D., Guards Division, App. 39.
† The 97th the 55th and the 77th Infantry Regiments.

attack a constant supply of bombs and additional bombers was supplied by the 1st Bn. Irish Guards, the 1st Bn. Scots Guards and the 2nd Bn. Irish Guards, with the result that the Germans were driven back after suffering heavy casualties. By 7 p.m. the lost portion of the line had been recaptured and was held by the attacking force until Colonel Corry, commanding the 3rd Bn. Grenadier Guards, was able to consolidate his position by blocking the northern end of the trench and forming a defensive front running in a north-easterly direction from the Le-Rutoire—Haisnes track.

Meanwhile, the front held by the 2nd Bn. Coldstream Guards, on the right of the line occupied by the 1st Guards Bde., had also been attacked by German bombers after an artillery and trench-mortar bombardment lasting for nearly four hours. The enemy, however, failed in his attempt to effect a lodgment in the trench in front of the Quarries which he attacked, and, after a series of unsuccessful bombing encounters with the Coldstream which lasted until darkness set in, withdrew. The artillery support given to the 1st Guards Bde. throughout the day was most efficient and was of great assistance to the infantry. The manner, too, in which the Signal Service contrived to keep up the communications between the two brigades, throughout the whole course of this engagement, was admirable and earned a special word of praise from Brig.-General Ponsonby.

The successful result of the afternoon's fighting, after the initial failure of the defence on the front of the 2nd Guards Bde. was due primarily, if not entirely, to the splendid courage and initiative of Sergeant Brooks * and of a few men belonging to the 3rd Bn. Coldstream Guards; and secondly, to the excellent cooperation between all three brigades.

The action proved that in modern warfare—and particularly in intricate trench to trench fighting—everything may ultimately depend upon the bravery and resource of the individual soldier. But the efforts of the bombers led by Sergeant Brooks might have been unavailing, had not a

* Sergeant Brooks was awarded the Victoria Cross for his conduct in this engagement. *See* Appendix III.

continuous supply of bombs been forthcoming and their distribution been carefully organized.* The ease and comparative celerity with which this work was accomplished were due to the good discipline which prevailed and to the close liaison existing between the brigades and battalions. In this respect the Guards Division always had a great advantage over other divisions. It started with a feeling of corporate unity and with a common training which less fortunate divisions only obtained after months of war. Its commanders were all Guardsmen, as were also the staff officers of the division † and the brigades—most of whom had lived and served throughout the greater part of their military careers with the various Guards regiments and who thus shared with the regimental officers and men the feeling of confidence and pride which is bound up with the traditions of the Brigade of Guards. From the first, therefore, the division was a happy family in which the team work was excellent—for the other arms of the Service included in the formation were soon inspired by the same divisional *esprit de corps*, vying with each other in their efforts to maintain and to increase the high reputation of the division.

The gallant behaviour of all ranks on the 8th of October earned the unstinted praise of the XI Corps commander and also of the Commander-in-Chief himself ; ‡ but the incidents

* From the beginning of the attack valuable assistance was given to the Grenadiers by the 1st Bn. Irish Guards on their left. "The Grenadiers, most of their bombers killed, borrowed No. 1 Company's bombers, who ' did good work,' while No. 1 Company itself formed a flank to defend the left of the Brigade in case the Germans broke through, as for a time seemed possible." *See* "The Irish Guards in the Great War," vol. i. p. 119.

† Except for Major N. Davidson, R.A., who was the original G.S.O.2 of the Division and Lieut.-Colonel R. S. McClintock, R.E., who was G.S.O.1 for a short time in 1917–1918, all the staff officers of the Guards Division throughout the campaign were Guardsmen, although the connexion of some of them with " the Brigade " was only due to the war.

‡ " I have once more to express to you, and the troops under your command, my deep appreciation of their splendid conduct yesterday in the severe repulse inflicted upon the enemy's violent attack all along your line south of the La Bassée Canal. Please communicate this to the troops." *See* telegram from Field-Marshal Sir J. French to Lieut.-General Haking, 9th of October, 1915, W.D., Guards Division, App. 46.

of the fighting, especially the manner in which the German bombers had been able to rush the trenches occupied by the 3rd Bn. Grenadier Guards, showed Lord Cavan that certain lessons with regard to trench warfare at close quarters had still to be learned—at any rate, by the battalions which had only recently arrived from England. He seized the opportunity, therefore, of drawing up a memorandum on bomb-fighting in which he laid down the main principles to be observed in the conduct of this kind of warfare. This memorandum was circulated to the division on the 9th of October and was subsequently considerably amplified and expanded.* Lord Cavan also wrote a letter to the XI Corps, which was forwarded to Sir Douglas Haig.

In this letter Lord Cavan drew attention to that which he considered to be the main lesson of the recent engagement, namely, the necessity of keeping open at all costs as many avenues of approach as possible to the front line trenches during a bombing attack in order to ensure a continuous supply of bombs reaching the fighting troops. He also suggested that a carefully-worded memorandum should be supplied to the battalion commanders of the New Army, pointing out that in close trench fighting it might often be advisable to make slight tactical rearrangements of the line in order to protect an exposed flank, even if such changes of position might necessitate a local withdrawal.†

(3) DECISION TO CONTINUE THE BRITISH ADVANCE—RÔLE ASSIGNED TO THE GUARDS—GERMAN ATTACK ON THE 1ST GUARDS BRIGADE REPULSED—RELIEF OF THE GUARDS DIVISION COMPLETED, 13TH OF OCTOBER— FAILURE OF THE ATTACK OF THE 46TH DIVISION—THE GUARDS ORDERED TO RETURN TO THE LINE.

The German attack on the 8th of October, as has already been narrated, led to the temporary cancellation of the order for the installation of gas cylinders on the Guards divisional front, but, in spite of the exertions of the previous

* *See* W.D., Guards Division, App. 47.
† *See* W.D., Guards Division, App. 48.

day's fighting and the dilapidated state of the trenches after the bombardment, this work was successfully begun the following day when 240 cylinders were placed in position on the front held by the 2nd Guards Bde.*

On the 10th of October orders from the XI Corps were received at divisional headquarters stating that the Guards would be relieved, on the night of the 10th–11th, by the 12th and 46th Divisions and explaining the objects and scope of the forthcoming operation to be carried out by the First Army.† The intention of Sir Douglas Haig was to endeavour to continue his advance towards the line Henin-Liétard—Pont à Vendin. As the first stage in this forward movement, the IV Corps was ordered to gain the line of the Lens—La Bassée road on the 13th of October, and the I, Indian and III Corps were to support the attack with fire and smoke, while the XI Corps was to establish a strong defensive flank on the north—an operation which entailed the capture of Fosse No. 8 and of the Quarries.

In order to carry out the task assigned to him, Lieut.-General Haking ordered the 12th Division to attack the Quarries, and, after consolidating the ground won and gaining touch with the IV Corps on its right and the 46th Division on its left, to send forward strong patrols towards Cité St. Élie in order to ascertain whether that place was still held by the enemy. He ordered the 46th Division to capture Fosse No. 8 and the Dump, and then to consolidate a line north and north-east of the Corons de Maron, gaining touch with the 12th Division and the I Corps on its right and left respectively.

The Guards were ordered to arrange for the protection of both these attacks by means of a discharge of gas and smoke.

Full instructions for the guidance of the *personnel* of the Guards Division who were to be left in the line on the relief of the division in order to carry out the smoke and gas arrangements were issued from divisional headquarters on

---

* By 6 a.m. on the 11th of October 840 gas cylinders had been installed on the front of the Guards Division.

† *See* XI Corps Op. Ords. Nos. 7 and 8.

the 10th of October, and, on the following day, the orders for the relief of the Guards by the 12th and 46th Divisions were dispatched to the brigades. On relief, the 1st Guards Bde. was to move to Verquin, the 2nd Guards Bde. to Prieure St. Pry, Vaudricourt and Drouvin, the 3rd Guards Bde. to Sailly-Labourse, and the 4th Bn. Coldstream Guards (Pioneers) to Fouquières. According to corps instructions, the infantry and R.E. of the division were to remain in corps reserve, whilst one brigade (3rd Guards Bde.) and one Field Company, R.E., were to be in readiness to move at one hour's notice from 2 p.m. on the 13th of October, the remainder of the division at two hours' notice.*

Before the relief was timed to take place, however, the Guards brigades in the line were called upon to resist another German attack, the enemy's bombers making a determined effort on the afternoon of the 12th of October to recapture certain sapheads on the left of the 1st Guards Bde. front, from which they had been ejected by the 2nd Bn. Grenadier Guards during the night of the 10th, whilst, at the same time, a heavy and effective trench-mortar bombardment was directed on the trenches behind this part of the line. The fight, which was a fierce one, lasted for four hours, and it was not until 8 p.m. that the enemy was finally forced to retire, having failed to gain any ground and suffered heavy casualties. This engagement, however, naturally delayed the progress of the relief which was not completed until 6 a.m. on the 13th of October.

The British offensive operation on the afternoon of that day was not successful. The attack of the 46th Division—

---

* On the 11th of October a German shell fell close to the entrance of the headquarters dug-out of the 1st Bn. Irish Guards. It mortally wounded the Rev. Father Gwynne, the battalion chaplain, and also wounded Lieut.-Colonel Madden, the commanding officer, and Lord Desmond FitzGerald, the adjutant. Father Gwynne died the next day. He was "a man unusually beloved" and his death was universally mourned. Lieut.-Colonel Madden, who had been a keen and untiring commanding officer, died a few weeks later. As Lord Desmond FitzGerald was incapacitated by his wound, Major the Honble. H. R. Alexander, from the 2nd Battalion, took over the command of the 1st Battalion until the 31st of October when Lieut.-Colonel R. C. A. McCalmont assumed the command.

the failure of which immediately affected the Guards Division —was carried out by the 137th and 138th Infantry Bdes. Although the enemy's positions were subjected to a discharge of gas and a bombardment by the heavy artillery, his machine-gun fire was so fierce and well-sustained that the 137th Infantry Bde. on the right failed to reach " Big Willie," and after heavy losses was compelled to fall back as far as the old German front line. On the left, the 138th Infantry Bde., after storming the Hohenzollern Redoubt, succeeded in reaching Fosse trench, but was then driven back again to the west face of the Redoubt where some of its units held on with fine tenacity, in the face of violent German counter-attacks, until they were relieved the following day.

On the 13th of October, however, the situation was at times critical and it was feared that the enemy might succeed in regaining his old line. By order of the XI Corps, therefore, two battalions of the 3rd Guards Bde.—the 1st Bn. Grenadier Guards and the 1st Bn. Welsh Guards—moved out of billets in the course of the afternoon in order to reinforce the 139th Infantry Bde., the reserve brigade of the 46th Division. Later, in the evening of the same day, in view of the heavy casualties which had been suffered by the two attacking brigades of the 46th Division, it became evident that it would be necessary to withdraw them speedily from the line, and, consequently, Brig.-General Heyworth, at Sailly-Labourse, was warned to be in readiness to take over the front of the 46th Division with the 3rd Guards Bde. the following day.

In the early hours of the morning of the 14th of October, the decision to relieve the two brigades of the 46th Division having been made by Lieut.-General Haking, Lord Cavan ordered the 3rd Guards Bde. to carry out the relief on the night of the 14th–15th. At 4 p.m., the same day, he received Lieut.-General Haking's order for the Guards Division again to go into the line, relieving the 46th Division on the nights of the 14th–15th and 15th–16th of October.

TERRIBLE CONDITION OF TRENCHES 83

(4) Relief of the 46th Division successfully carried out on the 15th–16th of October—Attack by the 2nd and 3rd Guards Bdes. on the Hohenzollern Redoubt and Dump trench.

Even after the unfortunate prelude to the new offensive on the 14th of October, it still remained the intention of Sir Douglas Haig to continue the attack, and the task set the Guards, on their return to the line, was to capture and hold Dump and Fosse trenches, and then to form a defensive flank facing north to cover a farther advance on Fosse No. 8.

Although the actual distance to be covered in this attack was not considerable, the task before the troops of the Guards Division was an extremely formidable one. The enemy's artillery and trench mortars, on the 14th, had completely demolished the remnants of a trench system which had until then been in existence in the forward portion of the line, and had also rendered most of the communication trenches almost impassable, in addition to which, they were in many places blocked with dead bodies and littered with every imaginable kind of *débris*.* The enemy's defensive organization, too, had been proved to be particularly strong and his troops were naturally elated by their successful repulse of the attack of the 46th Division.

In view of the above considerations, therefore, it was decided, after a conference at divisional headquarters on the 14th of October, at which Lieut.-General Haking was present, not to attempt to carry out the whole operation

* " The state of the trenches was terrible, unburied bodies lying everywhere, and the parapets and communication trenches blown in on all sides. The trenches allotted to the battalion were knocked about and we found dead bodies, equipment and *débris* of all kinds mixed up together. Salvage parties worked all day. Just as much damage was done to the communication trenches as to the front line trenches." *See* W.D., 1st Bn. Coldstream Guards, October, 1915. So bad was the condition of the ground that Brig.-General Heyworth, after a personal reconnaissance of the line on the 14th of October, informed Lord Cavan that it was out of the question to carry out an offensive on a large scale before the 17th. Lord Cavan concurred with this opinion and reported accordingly to the XI Corps.

allotted to the division by means of a single attack. The following preliminary objectives, which were to be secured by a series of bombing attacks supported by artillery and trench-mortar fire, were assigned, therefore, to the attacking brigades : *—to the 3rd Guards Bde. on the right, the junction of Slag Alley trench and Dump trench, and the triangle formed by the South Face of the Hohenzollern Redoubt and the southern section of Dump trench; to the 2nd Guards Bde., on the left, the chord of the Hohenzollern Redoubt and the northern part of " Little Willie."

During the course of the relief German infantry, who displayed much courage and initiative, carried out three distinct bombing attacks on the west front of the Hohenzollern Redoubt. All these attacks were driven back by the bombs and rifle fire of the incoming Guards battalions, but they naturally added to the manifold difficulties of the situation. The incessant fire of the enemy's guns, which was directed with great accuracy on the British communication trenches, also gravely impeded the progress of the work that was being set in hand for the contemplated offensive. The night of the 15th–16th of October was thus a very trying one for all ranks in the two brigades. Despite every difficulty, however, the attack was launched punctually at the appointed hour, 5 a.m. on the 17th of October. It was supported by a carefully arranged artillery and trench-mortar bombardment, and was pressed with the utmost gallantry by the 1st Bn. Grenadier Guards and 2nd Bn. Scots Guards, supported by the 4th Bn. Grenadier Guards, on the front of the 3rd Guards Bde., and by the 1st Bn. Coldstream Guards, supported by the 3rd Bn. Grenadier Guards, on the front of the 2nd Guards Bde. But it was soon clear to both brigadiers that, in view of the intense severity of the enemy's enfilade machine-gun fire and the terrible condition of the ground, it was not humanly possible for their

---

* These two brigades took over the line during the course of the 15th–16th of October, the 1st Guards Bde. remaining in divisional reserve at Vermelles and Sailly-Labourse. One battalion of this last-mentioned brigade was ordered to hold itself in readiness to move forward at thirty minutes' notice from 5 a.m. on the 17th of October. *See* W.D., Guards Division, 16th of October, 1915.

troops to reach the objectives. At 8 a.m., therefore, as soon as this information had been communicated to him, Lord Cavan authorized them to break off the attack and to consolidate such ground as had been gained. Very little progress had actually been made by either brigade and the casualties had been heavy,* but, nevertheless, the ground that had been secured was of some tactical value as it facilitated the construction of blocks in the trenches leading west from Dump trench and made easier the work of sapping forward towards the west front of the Hohenzollern Redoubt, which by this time had been reduced to a heap of earth and broken sandbags.

(5) WORK OF THE GUARDS IN THE LINE—BOMBING ATTACK BY THE 2ND BN. IRISH GUARDS ON THE WEST FRONT OF THE HOHENZOLLERN REDOUBT—RELIEF OF THE GUARDS DIVISION 26TH-27TH OF OCTOBER.

The small results achieved by the fighting on the 17th of October seem finally to have convinced Sir Douglas Haig that it was useless to attempt the recapture of Fosse No. 8 and the network of defences round the Dump until the Germans had been systematically driven out of their outlying trenches. Although, therefore, the taking of Fosse No. 8 still remained the principal objective on this part of the front, the tactical method of achieving this purpose was changed.† It was hoped that by means of periodic artillery

* Four officers were killed and 7 wounded in the course of this attack, and 400 other ranks were either killed or wounded. Some idea of the severity of the fighting may be obtained from the fact that the two Guards brigades between them made use of 15,000 bombs, while both brigadiers agreed that they had experienced no more heavy shell fire during the war than between dawn and midday on the 17th. The fire of the bulk of the enemy's guns was of course concentrated on the front held by the Guards Division.

† The advisability of adopting a policy of " biting off " the enemy's defences trench by trench by means of constant bombing attacks and persistent sapping was advocated by Lieut.-General Haking in a report written for Sir Douglas Haig on the 14th of October :—" I am of opinion," wrote the XI Corps Commander, " that before any further attack is made against Fosse 8 we must establish our line along Dump trench and Fosse trench. I think this can best be done by organizing

bombardments of the enemy's trenches and communications round the Fosse and the Dump, his machine guns and trench mortars would be destroyed and his defensive positions in the vicinity of these places rendered untenable, thus making it comparatively easy for the British troops to gain ground by means of persistent bombing attacks and sapping operations.*

The Guards, in consequence of this decision, were not called upon, during the remainder of their period of duty in this part of the line, to make another general attack, their task being to consolidate and to reorganize the divisional sector in order to make it as straight and convenient as possible for the 12th Division, which was to relieve them and to carry on the operations for the recapture of Fosse No. 8.

The task of " biting off " portions of the enemy's defences in the vicinity of the Hohenzollern Redoubt was no light one, and the days and nights between the 17th and 26th of October, when the Guards were relieved by the 12th Division, were strenuous ones for the troops in the line.

On the evening of the 19th of October the 1st Guards Bde. relieved the 3rd Guards Bde., and, on the 21st, the 2nd Guards Bde. took over a portion of the line from the 5th Infantry Bde. (2nd Division) on its left.† But, previous to this change of position, on the night of the 20th–21st, the 2nd Bn. Irish Guards had made a fine attempt to storm the trenches held by the Germans behind the west front of the

---

bombing attacks, covered by artillery fire carefully concentrated on certain definite points, and made along Dump trench from the south-east, along South Face and North Face from the south-west, and along ' Little Willie ' from the south. An attack of this nature is somewhat slow, but it should be sure, and, with Dump trench and Fosse trench in our hands, with a good barrage on Mad Point and Mad Alley, we can arrange a far better assaulting line against Fosse 8 than we have at present."

* *See* First Army No. G.S. 194/10 (a), 20th of October, 1915.

† This readjustment of the line was made necessary as a result of a fresh decision as to the conduct of future operations against Fosse No. 8. The task of recapturing the Fosse was now assigned to the XI Corps and for this reason that Corps took over from the I Corps on its left the line as far as a point a little north of the Vermelles—La Bassée railway, whilst it relinquished to the IV Corps on its right the part of the sector it was holding south of the Quarries.

Hohenzollern Redoubt. Two parties of bombers, converging from the north and south, were employed in this attack which was covered by the guns of the divisional Artillery directed on "Little Willie," North Face and South Face, and by the rifle fire of the 2nd Bn. Coldstream Guards on the right flank. The northern party, after twice being driven back, succeeded in its third attempt in seizing the enemy's barricade about twenty-five yards from its starting point and there established itself. The southern party, which at first met with less resistance, made a little more progress, but was eventually attacked by the enemy's bombers on three sides and forced to consolidate.

After this attack, during the remaining days of their sojourn in the line, the Guards attempted no further offensive movement, but worked with splendid energy to improve the positions which they held, and, notwithstanding the enemy's incessant bombing attacks and persistent artillery and trench-mortar fire, they had strengthened the line considerably and immensely improved the communications by the night of the 26th–27th of October, when their two brigades were relieved by the 35th and 37th Infantry Bdes. (12th Division).

The Guards had now played their part in the operations at Loos and were withdrawn from the battle area.

(6) SOME CONSIDERATIONS ON THE LOOS OPERATIONS—
SHARE IN THEM OF THE GUARDS DIVISION.

This is not the place in which to attempt any detailed examination of the strategy of the Allied commanders which led to the offensive in the autumn of 1915 of which the operations round Loos formed part. Nor is it necessary to examine in too critical a spirit the tactical conduct of the battle of Loos itself. In the light of subsequent knowledge it is clear that the chief importance of this battle in British military history will be due to the fact that it was the experience gained in it which settled the tactics of the British Higher Command in the first battle of the Somme in 1916, and, indeed, to the end of the period of trench warfare.

The barren strategical results obtained by the gallant efforts of the British Army at Loos, at the cost of so many casualties, proved that in modern warfare, unless an attacking army has an overwhelming superiority in men and guns, a "break-through" on a front wide enough to have any decisive effect is not possible against a stubborn and well-armed enemy in strong defensive positions. Success at one point in the line is neutralized by failure at other points, and provided that the defence is organized in sufficient depth, the impetus of the attack as the advance proceeds is almost bound to come to a standstill owing to the difficulty of the keeping up of communications, the physical exhaustion of the troops and the want of adequate artillery support. But in September, 1915, these facts had not been made clear.*

Loos was the real baptism of fire of the New Army which had been raised by Lord Kitchener; it proved the courage and fighting qualities of the citizen troops who had responded to his call; but it also proved that their training was incomplete, that they still lacked the disciplined experience and the confidence in themselves and in their leaders without which complete success in the hard school of war is impossible. The new divisions were called upon to attack positions of amazing strength held by first-class fighting men, and in their first impetuous rush they achieved wonders. On the 25th of September there is no doubt that the enemy was much shaken, and had Sir Douglas Haig been in a position to seize his opportunity and to push forward at once, it is conceivable that he might have been able to reach the Haute-Deule Canal. But the strength and recuperative powers of the Germans were underrated, while the further mistake was made of sending into the battle at its most critical moment troops who had never before been in action and who, in addition, were worn out with long marching and insufficient

* Whilst it was recognized that both the previous offensive operations during the year—Neuve Chapelle and Festubert—had failed to achieve any decisive results, their failure was attributed not so much to the intrinsic difficulties of the tasks set the infantry as to the inadequacy of the available artillery owing to the lack of munitions, and to the comparatively small scale upon which the operations were conducted.

THE SPIRIT OF THE DIVISION

food. After the failure of the attack on the 26th of September any chance there might have been of gaining a strategical success was over. By the time the Guards appeared on the scene of action the enemy had recovered his moral and resumed the offensive. The British Commander-in-Chief had neither the men nor the guns to make it possible for him to carry out his original scheme, and, consequently, the remainder of the operations in the Loos area really resolved themselves into a series of hard fought local engagements carried out for the purpose of improving the tactical position on the British front, and for keeping employed as many German troops as possible in order to assist the French operations in Champagne.

In these engagements the Guards behaved with the courage and pertinacity which were expected of them. If no large measure of success crowned their efforts, they yet gave a striking example of the physical and moral endurance which can only be achieved by good discipline, long training and *esprit de corps*. In the fighting on Hill 70, at the Chalk Pit and Puits No. 14 bis, and again round the Hohenzollern Redoubt, the Guards not only maintained, but even increased, the prestige which their previous record in the war had already given to them.*

And during the four weeks spent either in the shattered trenches in the Loos area or in the crowded billetting district behind the line, the various units of the division, under the tireless personal supervision of its commander and his staff, were welded together into a first-class fighting machine.

* During the Loos operations many of the remaining regimental officers who had come out with the original Expeditionary Force were killed, but the new officers in the Guards regiments had proved their worth. After the battle of Loos, even old-fashioned Guardsmen became convinced that officers of the Special Reserve could safely be employed as company commanders, and from this time onwards the battalions of the Guards Division were officered to a large extent by officers of the Special Reserve with very short training behind them. There was a general idea in the Army that the Guards Division did not encourage the new officer—at any rate until a much later date. But this was not the case. The breadth of view with which, as a general rule, the old officers after Loos welcomed and pushed forward the new ones was very noticeable, and did much to promote the happiness and family pride of the division.

The divisional Artillery, under the command of Brig.-General Wardrop, after its baptism of fire, made rapid strides in efficiency, and the close liaison, which was set up from the beginning between the infantry leaders in the line and the gunners responsible for the protection of their troops,* helped to bring about a mutual understanding between the two arms without which any kind of effective cooperation between them is impossible. The divisional R.E., too, did yeoman service both in and behind the line. The construction and maintenance of the defences and communication trenches in a modern battle are tasks which test the courage and endurance of the most seasoned troops, but on the battle-field of Loos the inevitable difficulties of the situation were greatly increased as a result of the almost incessant wet weather, and owing to the open nature of the country. No cross-country tracks were available, and the supply of duck-boards at this period in the war was limited. In addition, therefore, to the other tasks which fell to their lot in the battle, the Field Companies, R.E., were called upon to improvise means for draining the water out of the trenches—a task of no little difficulty which necessitated much pumping and the digging of numerous water channels and new trenches.†

* *See* "Extracts from instructions issued by the C.R.A., Guards Division, to his Artillery Brigade Commanders." W.D., Guards Division, App. 87.

† The principal difficulty which confronted the C.R.E. when the Guards first went into the line opposite the Hohenzollern Redoubt was the supplying of R.E. stores quickly to the troops in the forward area. The "battle dumps" were unsuitably situated for the purpose, and the demands for materials of all kinds, especially of timber for the artillery, were very great and urgent. A new R.E. dump was opened, therefore, at Vermelles and hastily stocked with the stores which were most imperatively required. The institution of this dump somewhat eased the situation, but even Vermelles was a considerable distance from the front. The task of carrying up R.E. stores to the fighting troops was a severe strain upon the R.E. and the 4th Bn. Coldstream Guards (Pioneers) which was placed at the disposal of the C.R.E. throughout most of this period of the battle. It is interesting to note that for some days after the Guards took over the line opposite the Hohenzollern Redoubt stores were actually conveyed in carts during the hours of darkness to within 400 yards of the front line trenches on the southern portion of the divisional front. The practice was then discovered by the Germans and had to be discontinued.

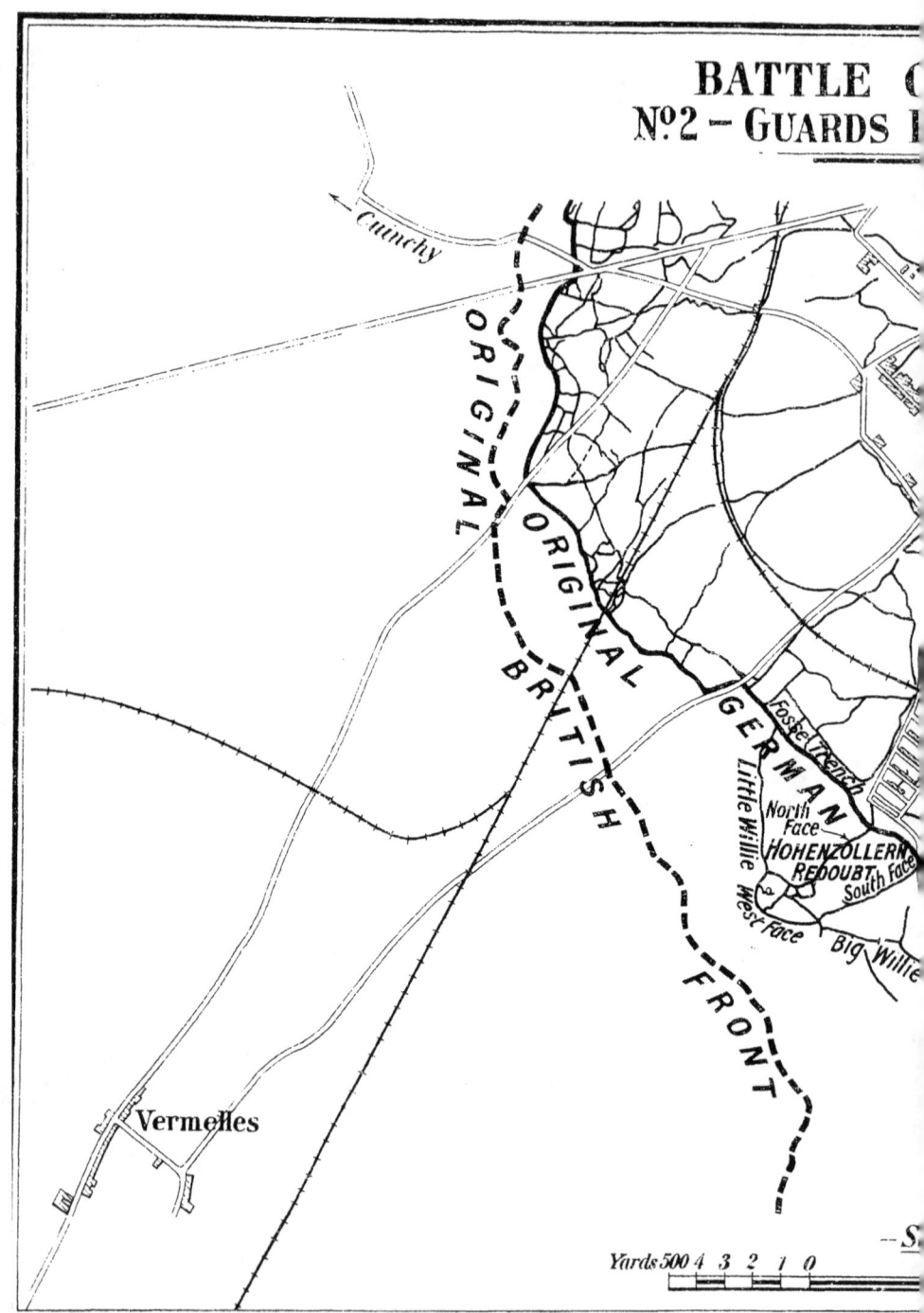

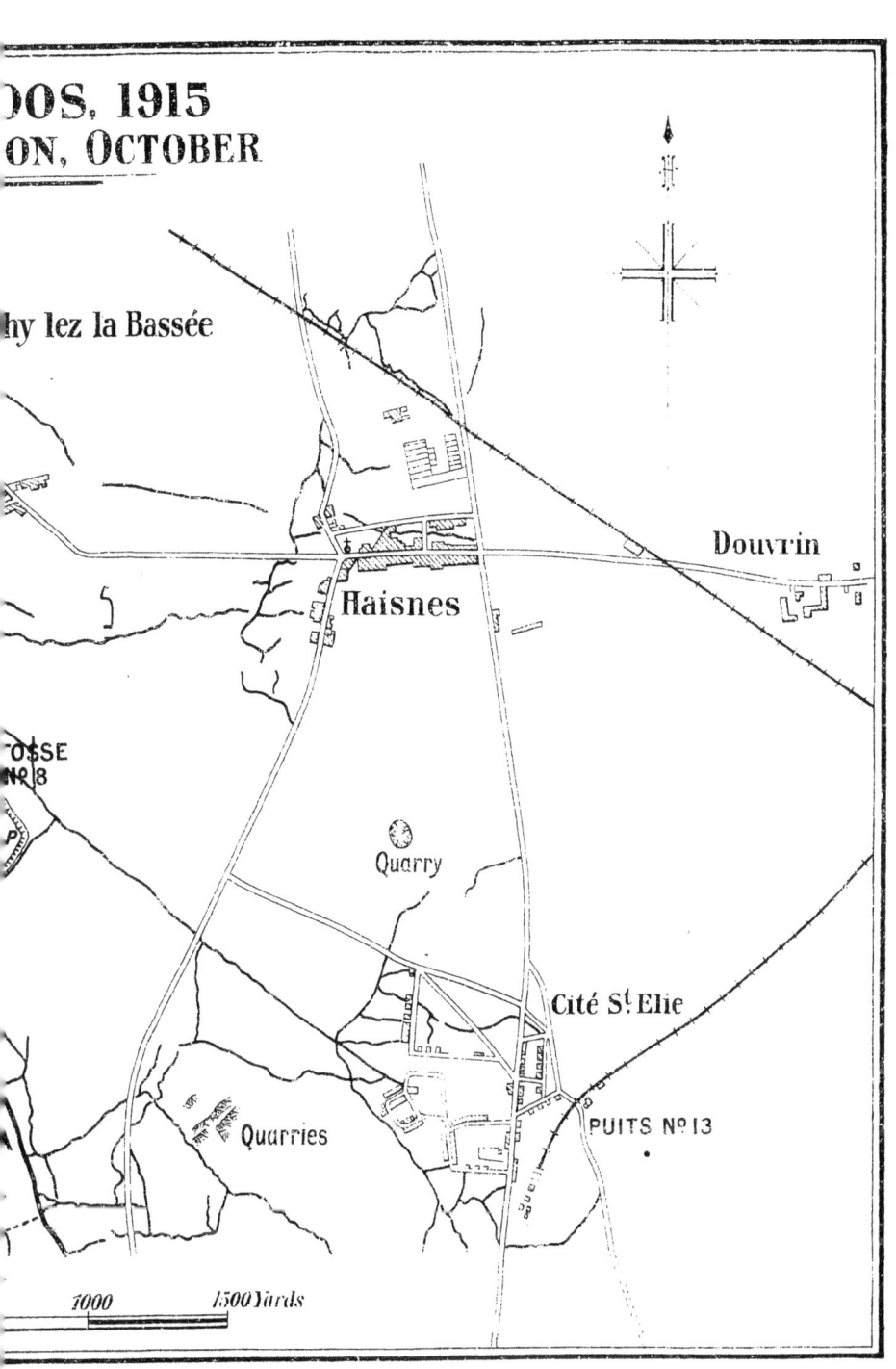

CHAPTER IV

THE WINTER OF 1915-1916.

(1) IN REST BILLETS IN THE BÉTHUNE AREA.

ON leaving the battle zone the Guards Division was withdrawn to the billetting area west and south-west of Béthune, divisional heaquarters being opened on the 27th of October at Gosnay (Les Charmeux), a village about half way between Béthune and Bruay.*

In despite of the days and nights of strenuous exertion through which they had passed and the heavy casualties which they had suffered, all the battalions of the Guards Division were in excellent health and spirits, and, on coming out of the line, set to work without a moment's delay to restore their normal routine and discipline. It was a real disappointment to the division when the inspection by His Majesty the King, which had been arranged to take place on the 28th of October in a great field of stubble between Lillers and Allouagne, had to be abandoned owing to the unfortunate accident which befell His Majesty. All ranks had been looking forward to this ceremony—conscious of the historic significance of the presence of the King among his Guardsmen, and anxious to display their enthusiastic devotion and loyalty to the Sovereign who personified the unity, the courage and the patriotism of the Empire.

During the remainder of their stay in rest billets, the Guards spent their time in steady drill and in field exercises,

---

* The divisional Artillery remained in the line after the infantry had been withdrawn and came under the command of the G.O.C. the 12th Division. It did not rejoin its own division until just before the Guards moved into their new line.

every opportunity being given to commanding officers to train their new drafts and to reorganize their battalions after the wear and tear of battle.

(2) Relief of the Indian Corps by the XI Corps on the Front East and South-East of Laventie.

The decision to relieve the Indian troops from further service in France before the winter set in necessitated a readjustment of the line on the front held by the First Army, and the XI Corps was selected by Sir Douglas Haig to take over the sector north of the La Bassée Canal then occupied by the Indian Corps. In order to cause as little dislocation as possible on the front south of the canal where active operations for the recapture of Fosse No. 8 were still contemplated, the XI Corps was reconstituted; the 12th Division, which, it will be remembered, had relieved the Guards Division opposite the Hohenzollern Redoubt was transferred to the I Corps, while the 19th Division, which was then in the line in the vicinity of Festubert, was incorporated in the XI Corps.

When Lieut.-General Haking's Corps moved north, therefore, it consisted of the Guards, the 19th and the 46th Divisions.*

(3) The New Line Occupied by the XI Corps.

The front which was now taken over by the XI Corps extended from La Quinque Rue—a point about 1,000 yards south of Richebourg L'Avoué—northward to Picantin—a village about two miles east of Laventie. The whole of this defensive system was situated in low-lying country, the greater part of which was subject to inundation in the winter months; and at no point along the line, which ran in a north-north-easterly direction just east of the Rue du Bois

* Various details were transferred to the XI Corps by the Indian Corps when it left the line. Of these No. 13 Trench Mortar Battery, consisting of twelve 4-pdr. mortars converted from 95 mm., and "L" Stokes Mortar Battery, both from the Lahore Division, were allotted to the Guards Division.

and the Rue Tilleloy, was the distance between the British and German trenches more than a few hundred yards apart —in many places, indeed, it was considerably less. The whole of the British positions were also overlooked from the Aubers ridge, along the slopes of which lay the enemy's main defensive system. As was usually the case on the Western Front, all the natural advantages of the ground both for attack and defence had been secured by the Germans.

The northern portion of the Corps sector was allotted to the Guards Division, from a point about 1,000 yards south-east of Neuve Chapelle where the La Bassée—Estaires road crosses the Rue du Bois, to a point north of Fauquissart, a ruined hamlet on the Rue Tilleloy. About ten days after the division took over the line, its front was extended northward to a point in the neighbourhood of Picantin, about 2,500 yards north-east of Fauquissart. It was destined to remain in continuous occupation of this line until the beginning of February, 1916.

(4) Move of the Guards Division into its New Area.

Orders respecting the move of the Guards Division into the new area reached divisional headquarters at Les Charmeux on the 3rd and 4th of November, and on the former day the G.S.O.1 and D.A.A. & Q.M.G. visited the Lahore Division, which the Guards Division was to relieve, and made all the necessary arrangements for the taking over of the line. On the 8th, the 2nd Guards Bde. and the divisional Cavalry moved to the neighbourhood of La Gorgue, and the divisional Artillery, which had by this time rejoined the division, and the Field Companies, R.E., to the area north-west of Merville. The following day the 3rd Guards Bde. marched to Merville, and, on the 10th of November, divisional headquarters was opened at La Gorgue and that of the 1st Guards Bde. at Merville. Four days later the relief was completed and the Guards Division took over the line. The 2nd Guards Bde., with its headquarters at Pont du Hem, relieved the 137th Infantry Bde. and part of the 60th Infantry Bde.

on the front between Rue du Bois and a point just north of Mauquissart, while the 3rd Guards Bde., with its headquarters at " Cockshy House," * Rue de Paradis, relieved the 59th Infantry Bde. and the remainder of the 60th Infantry Bde. northward as far as Fauquissart. The 1st Guards Bde. was in divisional reserve. Its headquarters was at La Gorgue and two of its battalions were billetted in the La Gorgue area, the two others being respectively north-west and north-east of Merville.†

(5) Bad Condition of the Trenches in the New Line—
Drainage Difficulties.

The front line defences in the new sector occupied by the Guards Division, owing to the marshy ground in which they were situated, consisted of breastworks and not trenches. These breastworks had been much neglected during the summer months and, although of great thickness at their base, were by no means bullet-proof at the top. In many places along the line the parapets were tumbling to pieces and the revetments were in a state of complete dilapidation throughout the entire area. It was at once realized that unless immediate steps were taken to improve the defences the bad weather of the winter would bring about a total collapse of the front line.‡ The conditions in rear were

* A rather pretentious three-storeyed red-brick villa which formed a conspicuous landmark for the enemy's gunners—hence its nickname.
 † When the Guards Division extended its line to the north on the night of the 24th–25th of November, relieving the 20th Division on part of its front, the divisional front was definitely divided into two brigade sectors. The headquarters of the brigade in the southern sector was established at " Cockshy House," Rue de Paradis, and that of the brigade in the northern sector in Laventie. The brigade in reserve was thenceforward billetted in Merville.
 ‡ Detailed instructions with regard to the method of holding the line, and the sequence in which the work of repairing and improving the defences and communications was to be carried out, were issued from divisional headquarters on the 13th of November. The respective tasks to be undertaken by the infantry, the R.E. and the other units in the division were also carefully allotted. *See* W.D., Guards Division, App. 182. In order to ensure continuity in the work, it was arranged that a scheme showing the work in hand should be drawn up by the

WORK IN THE LINE

if anything worse. The communication trenches, which were of especial importance in a region where there was so little cover and in which the enemy had such excellent observation, were already full of water, and the detached posts and defended localities, which formed the rear defences along the Rue du Bacquerot and farther west, had been much neglected and were crumbling to pieces.

The work of repairing the front line breastworks was taken in hand as soon as the division went into the trenches. An attempt was also made to construct simultaneously a new support line, but this proved too big an undertaking and had to be discontinued, the task of the restoration and drainage of the front line and the strong points in rear absorbing for the time being all the available labour of the division.*

The restoration of the communication trenches was carried out mainly by the 4th Bn. Coldstream Guards (Pioneers) assisted by a Tunnelling Company, and by dint of most strenuous work by day and night these routes to the front line were soon much improved.† The main difficulty, however, which confronted Lord Cavan and his C.R.E., was not so much the actual reconstruction of the defences and the communications as the drainage of the whole trench system. The flow of water from the Aubers ridge was caught and distributed by the Rivière des Laies, an artificial channel which ran just behind the German front line. The whole area between this watercourse and the river Lys had been furnished with a network of open drains and channels

C.R.E., in consultation with the General Staff, and should be given to each Brigadier on going into the line. It was left to the Brigadier to apportion the work among his battalions, but he was required to supply the division with a careful record of the work done when his brigade's tour of duty came to an end.

* Some idea of the amount of work done during the first few weeks of the occupation of this sector of the line by the Guards Division may be gathered from the fact that for quite a considerable period of time an average of 40,000 sandbags were laid in position every day.

† At a conference held at divisional headquarters on the 18th of November it was decided that battalions in the front line should be responsible for the upkeep of the communication trenches as far back and including Rue Tilleloy, and that the Pioneers under the directions of the C.R.E. should take charge of them westward from Rue Tilleloy.

designed for the purpose of controlled irrigation during the winter months.

The engineering problem that presented itself to the staff of the Guards Division was to discover which of these numerous water-ways which connected the Rivière des Laies and the river Lys would prove effective for carrying away the water from the front line.

It soon became apparent that three main streams would have to be utilized for the drainage of the central portion of the divisional trench system. The Cyclist Company was at once set to work to clear out these ditches, working forward from the river Lys to the front line, while the R.E. were employed to clear out all the local drains and water-ways round and immediately behind the front line. Much of this latter work, owing to the want of cover and the close proximity of the enemy, could only be done, in the daytime, by one or two men working together at the same time. It was, consequently, a long and tedious task.

The drainage on the extreme right of the divisional sector caused even more difficulty, and it was not until a series of investigations had been carried out that the actual course of the flow of water towards the river Lys was discovered and satisfactorily dealt with. On the left of the line most of the water ran into a large pond, which had to be drained almost completely by means of a new channel dug by the division. The labour required for all this drainage work was so great that a Land Drainage Company was allotted to the division, and it did excellent work in the location and the clearance of the blocks in the drainage system throughout the area.

The result of all this clearance work was that after the first winter storms the pumping station, which was being installed on the river Lys opposite Estaires, was flooded out, while the front line remained tolerably dry. This was satisfactory so far as it went, but, as much of the country east of Laventie was still under water owing to the natural gradient of the ground being not steep enough to carry off the surface water sufficiently quickly, leave was obtained to move forward a big pump into this area. As soon as this pump was in working order, conditions behind this part of the line became much more satisfactory.*

Throughout the winter months the energies of the R.E. and Tunnelling Company had to be largely diverted to mining operations owing to the enemy's mining activity on various parts of the line. There were three separate systems of mining on the divisional front, mainly of a defensive nature.

As a complete defensive system, the sector never fulfilled all the necessary requirements, but, by the time the Guards Division left it, it was at any rate habitable even in wet weather, and its defences and communication trenches were well revetted and in a sound state of repair—so secure and solid, indeed, was the line that at least one division, which subsequently occupied it, expressed the wish to remain in it for the duration of the war.

(6) Method of holding the Line on the XI Corps Front.

In view of the kind of country in which the XI Corps now found itself, no attack on a large scale by the enemy was to be anticipated during the winter months. The Germans were installed in comparative comfort on the Aubers ridge and there was no reason to suppose that, even if they had any inclination to indulge in more fighting after their recent experiences, they would be foolish enough to exchange the high ground for the wet and muddy plain held by the British. At the same time, the opposing lines were so close together that some offensive action by the enemy was always possible and the problem, therefore, which had to be solved by the General Staff was how best to organize a sound defensive system with the employment of the smallest possible number of men in the forward zone.

---

* In forwarding the " Winter Line Report " to the XI Corps on the 22nd of December, 1915, is added the following note :—" I think the drainage efforts of the C.R.E., in addition to his other work, have been wonderfully successful "—a word of appreciation which was thoroughly deserved. *See* W.D., Guards Division, App. 269.

After the lessons of the previous winter there was no inclination among the higher authorities to maintain larger garrisons in the front line trenches than was absolutely necessary—especially in an area such as that which extended southward from Laventie to the La Bassée Canal. It was decided, therefore, that each corps in the First Army should only employ two divisions in the front line and that its remaining division should be in Army reserve, in order that its troops could be comfortably billetted and its commander given an opportunity of training his officers and men.

In accordance with this scheme, the front of the XI Corps was divided between the Guards Division and the 46th Division, while the 19th Division was withdrawn into Army reserve. Lieut.-General Haking's original intention was that each division in the line should in turn go into Army reserve. Lord Cavan, however, after consultation with his own brigadiers and also with the G.O.C.'s of the two other divisions in the corps, put forward a proposal that the Guards should remain permanently in the line which they occupied—so long, that is to say, as the XI Corps remained in this particular sector—and that the two other divisions should relieve each other according to the original scheme. His reasons for making this proposal were that he would always be able to have a brigade in reserve in good billets behind the line for six out of eighteen days, and that he could also arrange that no battalion should be actually in the line for more than forty-eight hours. As the Guards Division had already undergone a month's field training in the Lumbres area, and as all the divisional and brigade schools and courses of instruction could be maintained in full working order while the division was in the line, Lord Cavan urged that the advantages to be gained from his proposal were considerable. Each division in the corps would get to know its own sector and an all important continuity in the work on the defensive system would be secured, while, from the point of view of offensive action, the scheme had everything to commend it. The troops in the line would become acquainted with the enemy's positions and his methods of trench warfare, and an effective

ADMINISTRATIVE ARRANGEMENTS

system of cooperation and mutual understanding could be established between the artillery and the infantry.*

Lieut.-General Haking raised no objection to a trial being given to Lord Cavan's scheme, and it was accordingly adopted. It proved so entirely satisfactory in practice that it remained in force throughout the winter. Each Guards brigade spent six days in every eighteen days in divisional reserve, and during a brigade's period of duty in the line only two of its battalions were kept in the front trenches, the remaining two battalions being in reserve in an area some little distance behind the line where it was possible to provide them with tolerably comfortable billets in various ruined farms and cottages.†

(7) Arrangements for the Comfort and Well-being of the Troops during the Winter Months.

As soon as the work and location of the division for the coming months had been more or less definitely settled, Lord Cavan, with the assistance of his staff, set to work to make his arrangements for the winter months. The health and general well-being of the troops were the two main considerations which occupied his attention. The experience which he had gained during the previous winter whilst in command of the 4th (Guards) Bde. had shown him that

---

* *See* W.D., Guards Division, App. 144.

† In reply to a return called for by the XI Corps on the 1st of December, 1915, as to the number of men employed in the line by each Guards Brigade, the following statement was sent:—

(a) Number of men per yard who are actually in the trenches .. Right Bde. 0·33. Left Bde. 0·57
(b) Number of men per yard in immediate support of (a) .. ,, ,, 0·1. ,, ,, 0·11
(c) Strength of battalion reserve .. ,, ,, Nil. ,, ,, Nil.
(d) Strength of brigade reserve .. ,, ,, 2 Coys. ,, ,, 2¼ Coys.

Note:—Garrisons of posts in front line system are included in (b). Garrisons of posts in the Croix Barbée system (the defended localities north of Richebourg St. Vaast and along, and in rear of, the Fleurbaix road) which are all found by these brigades are not included in (d).

See W.D., Guards Division, App. 197.

the men's health could be maintained, in far worse conditions than were likely to prevail in that of 1915–1916, provided that stringent precautions were adopted and a rigid discipline enforced.

Soon after the Guards took over their new sector of the front, therefore, regulations were laid down by their Commander for the preservation of health, and the duties and responsibilities of the various branches of the staff and of the Brigadiers were carefully enumerated. The " Q " Staff of the division was made responsible to the divisional Commander for the maintenance of an adequate supply of grease and lubricants and of fuel; for the provision of drying rooms for the brigade in divisional reserve; for winter clothing and gum boots. It was left to the Brigadiers to see that the discipline of grease parades was duly enforced; to insist upon the men wearing their gum boots and keeping their puttees loose in the trenches; to arrange for drying rooms for their reserve battalions; and to attend to the carrying out in detail of the general instructions of the division with regard to the comfort, cleanliness and well-being of their troops both in the line and in billets.*

The A.D.M.S., Colonel G. S. McLoughlin, was instructed to assist the Brigadiers by giving lectures to the men in the care of their feet and in the best methods of keeping themselves warm. This officer was also made responsible for the exercise of a close supervision in all matters affecting cleanliness and sanitation in the Divisional area.

The billets available west of Laventie—in La Gorgue and Merville—were both good and plentiful. All the units of the division, therefore, which were not actually in the line, were lodged in tolerable comfort. But even in Laventie itself and in other villages in the forward area, the billetting accommodation was better than was usually to be found in the neighbourhood of the front trenches, so that the reserve

---

* On two matters, however, definite instructions were laid down by the divisional commander. No battalion was to be kept in the line for more than forty-eight hours and no man was to be permitted to stand in water up to the knee.

battalions of the brigades in the line had little of which to complain.

The division had the use of some good baths which had been installed by the Indian Corps in a brewery at La Gorgue. These were placed under the charge of the officer commanding the 45th Sanitary Company, Lieutenant Pearson, and were gradually enlarged and improved. Baths were also fitted up in a building at Pont du Hem for the use of the two reserve battalions of the brigade occupying the southern sector of the front. A soldiers' club, with reading and recreation rooms, was opened at La Gorgue and proved a great boon to the troops during the winter. The first serious attempt, too, was made at this time to supply some kind of organized entertainment for the division. This work was entrusted by the " Q " Staff to the joint management of the Senior Chaplain of the division, the Rev. R. J. Fleming,* and the officer commanding the divisional Supply Column, Major Sir W. E. T. Avery, Bart.† A cinema was purchased out of divisional funds and a small hall at La Gorgue was then converted into a theatre where the latest films from England were regularly "released." In the charge of energetic chaplains the cinema was also taken round the divisional area for the entertainment of troops in their billets.

Throughout the months spent in this low-lying sector of the British front where—in spite of the most vigorous and persistent drainage operations—much of the country was usually under water, the moral of the Guards Division was excellent, and its health record a good one, the percentage of sickness being remarkably low.

(8) THE DIVISIONAL DEFENCE SCHEME.

The defences of the Guards Division in the area between the front line and La Gorgue were organized in three zones :—
(a) the front system, which consisted of the front line

---

* This officer was succeeded as Senior Chaplain by the Rev. Pat McCormick on the 23rd of December, 1915.

† The officer commanding the Employment Company subsequently performed these duties.

trenches and breastworks and a series of strong points close in rear of them along the Rue Tilleloy; * (*b*) the Croix Barbée system, formed by a chain of supporting posts, the majority of which were constructed along the Rue du Bacquerot although a few were farther westward; and (*c*) the Le Drumez system, which included various works and defended localities covering La Gorgue and Estaires and also certain bridgeheads on the rivers Lys and Lawe.†

The front system, which was "to be defended at all costs," ‡ was garrisoned in each brigade area by two battalions, the left front battalion of the brigade in the southern portion of the line being also called upon to furnish a garrison for " Winchester " post, one of the principal strong points in the Croix Barbée system.§ In this last-named system, each brigade in the line was responsible for the upkeep and improvement of the posts in its own area and was also required to find garrisons for them from its reserve battalions. The actual number of men needed for these garrisons was left to the discretion of the brigadiers, but Lord Cavan insisted that a garrison should be definitely allotted to each post and that it should be drawn from a battalion billetted as near to it as possible.‖

---

* The original intention when the Guards Division came into the line was to reconstruct the support line in the front system which had fallen into disrepair and to make a new reserve line in the same area. Owing, however, to the difficulties caused by the drainage work and the shortage of labour, the latter scheme had to be abandoned altogether, and, although the reconstruction of the support line was persevered with, its completion was not accomplished by the division.

† See W.D., Guards Division, App. 184.

‡ See XI Corps R.H.S. 399, W.D., Guards Division, App. 155.

§ Part of one of the doors from this building, which was decorated in the taste of the period by officers of various battalions, is preserved in the Officers' Guard Room at St. James's Palace.

‖ The Brig.-General, commanding the 1st Guards Brigade, pointed out, that, if he had to find garrisons for the posts in the Croix Barbée system, his brigade reserve would be so much reduced that it would be of no practical value in an emergency. Lord Cavan, while recognizing this fact, refused to alter his policy, pointing out that it was based on two principles of defence which experience in the war had proved to be sound—namely, that a counter-attack to be successful must be delivered either immediately after the line had been broken, or postponed until it could be organized with artillery support on a larger scale than was possible with a brigade reserve. His objects, he

DIVISIONAL DEFENCE SCHEME

The works and defended localities in the Le Drumez system were not permanently occupied, but caretakers were kept in them. The responsibility for the garrisoning of these strong points, should occasion arise, were entrusted, west of the Estaires—La Bassée road, to the brigade in divisional reserve, and, east of that road, to the 4th Bn. Coldstream Guards (Pioneers).

The rôle of the divisional reserve in the defensive organization was to carry out a strong counter-attack supported by the guns of all the available artillery. If, however, the enemy succeeded in penetrating so far and in such strength that there was little prospect of such a counter-attack being successful in the forward area, all the reserve battalions were to garrison the posts in the Le Drumez system and the bridgeheads and to hold the line until the arrival of the division in corps reserve.

In the event of a serious attack by the Germans in strength, the Guards divisional Artillery was ordered to remain in its usual positions for as long a time as possible in order to be able to support any counter-attack by the divisional reserve. But the C.R.A. was instructed to reconnoitre routes, and to have in readiness new positions for his batteries in rear suitably sited for the defence of the Le Drumez system, in case the Croix Barbée system fell into the enemy's hands. A plan for liaison artillery barrages was also drawn up in conjunction with the divisions on either flank, by which mutual support was ensured in the event of an attack on any of the divisional fronts.

Throughout the three months during which the Guards Division held this portion of the XI Corps sector of the line, the enemy made no real attempt to attack the division —his offensive efforts, indeed, were mainly confined to

explained, were to prevent abortive counter-attacks, and to make certain that the posts in the Croix Barbée system were securely held so that a good starting off line might be available, if necessity should arise, for a big counter-attack to be delivered by the divisional reserve. He also stated that, in his opinion, twenty or thirty men, issuing from the post or posts nearest to the point in the line to which the enemy might have penetrated, would be able to render very effective assistance in an emergency in view of the broken condition of the ground which lay between the Rue Tilleloy and the front line defences.

intermittent artillery bombardments and mining enterprises. The prompt and effective retaliation by the divisional Artillery, which invariably followed any hostile bombardment, was usually sufficient to check these displays. The policy laid down by Lord Cavan with regard to such artillery retaliation was that it should be " marked," that is to say, that batteries should not waste ammunition by firing a few rounds every few minutes during the day, but should reserve their fire until the enemy did something to which it was worth while replying, and then fire at their utmost speed for a definite period of time.*

The German mining operations opposite the Guards divisional front caused a certain amount of anxiety on various occasions during the winter, especially during the month of December when the enemy's miners contrived to slip past the protective galleries in the area just north of Mauquissart, getting to within close proximity of the British front line breastworks. As soon as the danger was reported, the garrison in this part of the line was withdrawn, and warnings were issued along the front as to the precautions to be taken in any area in which hostile mining operations were suspected. Instructions were also given to the troops to occupy without delay the near edge of any crater which might be formed by the explosion of a German mine. As the liaison between the tunnelling companies in the line and the brigades at this time did not appear to be very effective, an order was given by the division to the officers in command of the tunnelling companies to report daily to the Brigadier, on whose part of the line their men were working, full particulars as to the work done during the previous twenty-four hours and the work proposed to be carried out.†

The vital necessity of good communications as a factor in the strength of the defensive organization was fully realized and stringent precautions were insisted upon by the division in the matter of the laying and the maintenance of telephone lines throughout the whole of the divisional

* *See* the divisional order with regard to " Artillery Retaliation." W.D., Guards Division, App. 194.
  † *See* W.D., Guards Division, Apps. 219, 221 and 223.

area. Infantry brigade signalling officers were made responsible for all the lines in their areas. The lines between battalions and companies in the forward system were laid whenever possible by the brigades, and, in cases where this could not be arranged, it was still the duty of the brigade signalling section to patrol the lines as soon as possible after they had been laid in order to test them. All such lines were maintained by the battalions and it was a divisional order that they should be patrolled each day. The lines from batteries to their forward observing officers were laid by the artillery, but it was again the duty of the infantry brigade signalling officer to inspect them and all other artillery lines, and to report at once to the various battery commanders if any of their lines required attention.*

It was during the winter months of 1915–1916, too, that the immense importance of accurate intelligence to the successful conduct of the defence in trench warfare first began really to be understood and appreciated. The maintenance of a close observation of the enemy's movements in, and in rear of, his front line trenches; the careful location of his guns, trench mortars and machine guns; a day to day report as to the state of his wire and the condition of his defences; the identification of his units in the line; were all items of information, the collection of which was of the utmost importance not only to the divisional staff for the defence of the line, but also to the higher authorities.

In the Guards Division, as in most other divisions of the British Army, all such intelligence was sent daily to divisional headquarters by the brigades in the line and also by the gunners. It was then carefully tabulated by the General Staff and circulated to the troops by means of daily summaries. In this way detailed information, describing the habits of the enemy and his defensive organization and methods, was always available to the brigadiers, whilst it also formed a permanent record for the use of the corps and any division which might subsequently take over the line.†

* *See* W.D., Guards Division, App. 245.
† As the war continued and the methods of obtaining intelligence

106   THE WINTER OF 1915–1916

(9) Winter Operations—Raids and Reconnaissance.

Although, as has already been stated, there was no possibility of carrying out any large offensive operation during the winter, Lieut.-General Haking, on first taking over the new line, expressed his wish that everything should be done to harass the enemy during the coming months.* He also informed divisions that the corps might be called upon by the First Army to carry out attacks on small localities in cooperation with similar attacks made by neighbouring corps, and also to endeavour to gain ground which might facilitate the capture of the Aubers ridge, " as a preparation for the great offensive in the spring."

As a matter of fact the XI Corps was not called upon to participate in any organized attack for purposes such as those outlined by Lieut.-General Haking in his memorandum on " the Winter Campaign, 1915–1916." The contemplated

were improved and multiplied, there was a general tendency among the fighting troops to underestimate the value of intelligence summaries. This was no doubt due to the natural inclination of the man on the spot to view the war entirely from his own particular standpoint, and also perhaps to the elaborate manner in which some army and corps staffs insisted upon these records being maintained by the lower formations without sufficiently explaining to them the necessity for so much extra work. There can be no doubt, however, that in trench warfare, as in any other kind of warfare, there is only one road to success either in attack or defence—and that is, to keep in touch with the enemy. This can only be done if an accurate and never-ceasing watch is kept upon him by the troops who are actually facing him, and the knowledge so obtained is placed promptly at the disposal of the General Staff.

* " The corps has been distinguished since its formation for the constant offensive action it has been called upon to carry out, and a fine offensive spirit is apparent in all units. It is of vital importance for the vigorous prosecution of the campaign that every effort should be made from the highest to the lowest to foster and increase this spirit throughout the winter months which lie before us. By constantly harassing the enemy, compelling him to keep his reserves on the move, gaining a small success in one place and then in another, we can greatly improve the moral of our own troops and wear out and depress the enemy . . . the offensive spirit of the troops must be carefully encouraged throughout the winter months and the natural desire of the troops to have a quiet time in the trenches must be discouraged in every possible way." *See* XI Corps Memorandum on the Winter Campaign, 1915–1916, W.D., Guards Division, App. 118.

"step by step" capture—and presumably retention—of tactical localities on the lower slopes of the Aubers ridge in midwinter was happily not embarked upon. Nor were the corps commander's warnings against the hibernating habit required by the Guards Division. Its regimental officers and men, like other troops in the line, were sometimes apt to consider that the higher authorities exaggerated the moral value of an aggressive policy in trench warfare, and to resent being continually called upon to carry out raids and reconnaissances for apparently no other purpose than to satisfy the insatiable curiosity of the Intelligence branch of the General Staff. But, nevertheless, they possessed the true spirit of the offensive—due in their case to a proud confidence in themselves borne of good discipline and training, and the fighting tradition of "the Brigade." They were never satisfied until they had established a moral ascendancy over the Germans in any part of the line in which they happened to find themselves. And nowhere was this ascendancy more fully established and maintained than on the front between Neuve Chapelle and Picantin in the winter of 1915–1916. The narrow strip of No Man's Land, which divided the two defensive systems, was constantly patrolled and denied to the enemy, while several daring and successful raids were made into his trenches.* The offensive policy of the division, which was adhered to during its sojourn on this part of the front, was laid down by Lord Cavan in a memorandum issued on the 19th of November.† After pointing out that the conditions with regard to the number of troops and amount of munitions available were infinitely

* In January, 1916, the work of the divisional raiding patrols was so conspicuously successful that Sir Henry Rawlinson, who was then in command of the First Army, wrote the following letter of congratulation to Major-General Feilding through the XI Corps :—" I observe that during the past four weeks raiding expeditions into the enemy's trenches have been undertaken on six different occasions by the Guards Division. This shows that a commendable spirit of enterprise exists, and that the success which has been attained is the result of carefully laid plans well and boldly executed. It is evident that the division has established a moral ascendancy over the enemy which is of the highest value, and I desire to compliment them on their good work."

† See W.D., Guards Division, App. 148.

more favourable to the British Army than during the preceding winter, the divisional commander directed (1) that lanes from 50 to 100 yards wide were to be cut by the artillery through the wire at various points in the enemy's wire, and kept permanently open;* and (2) that raids were to be carried out from time to time during the hours of darkness on one or other of these selected points. The raiders, whose assault was to be preceded by a short and intensive artillery bombardment or discharge of gas, and whose strength was not to exceed two companies, were instructed to rush the enemy's front line trenches and to kill or capture the defenders, to demolish machine guns and trench mortars, and to blow up and damage the defences and dug-outs to the best of their ability; but they were to return to their own line with the least possible delay.

Lord Cavan was confident that, by the adoption of these tactics, it would always be possible to surprise the Germans as they would never be certain by which lane through their wire the raiding parties might make their appearance; that the casualties would be comparatively slight as experience had proved that losses were suffered not so much in the actual assault as when captured positions were held; that aggressive action of this kind would keep up the moral of the troops and be a good antidote to the inevitable slackness resulting from life in the trenches; and, finally, that if the enemy were continually harassed the spirit of his troops would deteriorate, and he would thus be compelled to augment the garrison of his front line system and to utilize for the purpose his best-trained men instead of Landwehr troops.

In accordance with the foregoing policy, periodic artillery bombardments for the purpose of cutting lanes in the enemy's wire, or for the destruction of particular strong points in his trench system, were undertaken by the divisional Artillery. As an example of the kind of work accomplished by these bombardments, the results of a " shoot " which

* The estimated amount of ammunition required for the original wire-cutting was 500 rounds for each locality chosen, and 40 rounds a day for the keeping open of the gap.

took place on the 24th of November are worth recording. In the course of a little over an hour one 18-pdr. battery, D/76, and two howitzer batteries, A/61 and B/61, firing H.E. shell,* damaged a German blockhouse and battered down the breastworks of a strong point opposite Mauquissart on a width of 60 yards, cutting a stretch 40 yards wide in the enemy's wire. The gap thus made was then sprayed with machine-gun fire throughout the night, whilst, in order effectually to prevent the enemy from repairing the damage already done by the artillery, occasional rounds of shrapnel were also fired upon the same area at stated intervals. In addition to these preliminary bombardments and the constant task of retaliation the divisional Artillery was continually called upon to take its share, in conjunction with the machine gunners, in covering the small raiding operations which were carried out by the infantry." †

In the first half of the month of December, and again in the early days of January, 1916, this form of enterprise became quite popular on the front of the Guards Division, each battalion in turn carrying out some inroad into the enemy's trenches. The almost uniform success of these attacks earned for the division the congratulations of the

---

* This was one of the first occasions on which H.E. shell was used by the 18-pdr. batteries. It will be remembered that H.E. shell was not issued to the field batteries when the B.E.F. was first dispatched to France. Brig.-General Wardrop, C.R.A., Guards Division, in his report on the work of his batteries on the 24th of November, stated that he was unable to say how much of the damage done to the German defences was due to the 18-pdr. guns and 4·5 howitzers respectively—in view of the failure of some of the 4·5 ammunition; however, he was inclined to agree with the officer commanding the 18-pdr. battery that his guns did most of the work. He considered that the 18-pdr. H.E. was very satisfactory and this opinion was confirmed by an officer of the divisional staff who was an observer of the bombardment. *See* W.D., Guards Division, Apps. 170, 171.

† Lord Cavan was delighted with the rapid improvement made by the divisional Artillery. In a message to the division, on the 15th of December, congratulating the fighting units on the successes which had been achieved during the preceding fortnight, he made especial allusion to the cooperation of the artillery in the various infantry attacks as having been " well-timed and thoroughly accurate, thus giving confidence to the raiding parties and safely covering their withdrawal."

Higher Command, and led to the immediate award of some thoroughly well-deserved decorations.* It is unfortunately impossible in the space available in this book to do more than to make a passing allusion to one of these little operations—a raid which Sir Douglas Haig himself described as " a well-planned and well-executed operation, reflecting the highest credit on all concerned, from Lieut.-Colonel Lord H. Seymour, commanding the 4th Bn. Grenadier Guards, downwards.† Every detail of this raid was most carefully thought out beforehand, and the actual attack was preceded by a daring personal reconnaissance along the enemy's line conducted by Captain Sir Robert Filmer, the leader of the raiding party, accompanied by Sergeant Higgins and three men belonging to No. 3 Company, 4th Bn. Grenadier Guards. The enemy was taken completely by surprise and suffered a good many casualties. Considerable material damage was also done to his trenches in which the raiders remained for twenty minutes while the artillery placed an effective barrage for the protection of their flanks. The attackers' casualties on this occasion were only one officer and four men wounded, all of whom were brought back to the British line.

* Some months later, the 31st of May, Lieut.-General Haking wrote as follows to Lord Cavan :—" I see in the Commander-in-Chief's Despatches that four battalions of the Guards Division [the 2nd Bn. Grenadier Guards, the 1st Bn. Coldstream Guards, the 2nd Bn. Irish Guards and the 1st Bn. Welsh Guards] have been included, and I shall be very glad if you will permit me to send them congratulations with thanks. I also wish to express to you how much I appreciate your successful efforts to initiate these raids in the corps when you were commanding the Guards Division. The raids carried out by your battalions were a great incentive to other divisions in the corps, and we learned a great deal from them ; in fact it is chiefly owing to the example set by the Guards Division that the XI Corps has earned sixteen ' mentions.' "

† For a more detailed account of this raid, see " The Grenadier Guards in the Great War, 1914–1918," vol. i. pp. 347–349. For the preliminary arrangements made by Lord Henry Seymour and his remarks on the carrying out of the enterprise, see W.D., Guards Division, App. 236.

SCHOOLS FOR SPECIALISTS

(10) WINTER TRAINING-SCHOOLS AND COURSES OF INSTRUCTION.

Early in November, 1915, the First Army commander issued an important memorandum outlining the training which he wished to be carried out in the Army during the winter months.* In this document a general scheme of individual and combined training was laid down for the guidance of divisional commanders to whom was wisely assigned the task of training their own troops. Much of the scheme was of course only applicable to divisions in Army reserve and consequently did not directly affect the Guards Division, which remained constantly in the line. But the training of specialists—such as machine gunners, bombers and trench-mortar *personnel*—the necessity of which was emphasized in Sir Douglas Haig's memorandum, was carried on by the Guards Division without cessation throughout the winter. As many officers as it was permissible to send always attended the various special courses of instruction and conferences, organized by the First Army and G.H.Q. In the Guards Division a divisional Bombing School had been established before the division left the Loos sector, with Major B. Baden-Powell, Scots Guards, as commandant. This School was kept in being in the new sector of the line under the more high-sounding title of the School of Explosives, and throughout the winter courses of instruction were given by Major Baden-Powell and his staff in the use of trench mortars,† in the methods of bomb-fighting, and in the employment of Very lights, rockets and other explosive apparatus.

A divisional Signalling Class was also formed in which were given courses of instruction in the care and use of telephones, laying, operating, and maintaining of lines,

* *See* First Army, No. 431 (G), "Instructions for Training." W. D., Guards Division, App. 125.

† During the winter of 1915–1916 three 4-pdr. batteries of 4 mortars were allotted to divisions in the line. The *personnel* of one of these batteries had to be found by each division. The *personnel* of the Guards Division battery was drawn from the 1st Guards Bde. and trained in the divisional School of Explosives.

and the use of visual equipment. Each of these courses was attended by thirty men, six from each Guards brigade and twelve from the artillery, and their duration, like those in the School of Explosives, depended upon the progress made by the students. They usually lasted for about three weeks.

Signalling courses of a more elementary character were also conducted by the brigade signalling officers.

The general training and instruction in their duties of regimental officers and non-commissioned officers, whilst in the trenches and also whilst in divisional reserve, were left to their natural instructors—their commanding officers and company commanders respectively, under the supervision of the brigadiers. In order, however, that there might always be a supply of trained machine gunners it was laid down by the division that a large number of men—at least 50 per cent. in excess of the recognized establishment—should be kept with each brigade machine-gun company.

In addition to these various forms of training, lectures on subjects dealing with the organization and administration of the Army were given to the troops of the brigade in divisional reserve by the divisional commander himself and by other officers of the division, while the services of outside lecturers were always eagerly welcomed.*

Besides receiving instruction it also fell to the lot of the Guards to impart it, for towards the middle of December six battalions of the 38th (Welsh) Division were sent in turn to be trained by the Guards Division for a period of eight days in the trenches. Other units of the 38th Division—the Pioneers, R.E., and Field Ambulances—were also attached for the same purpose to similar units in the Guards Division.

* Probably the most generally popular lecture was that given by Captain H. Hesketh-Prichard in December on "The Art of Sniping." Captain Prichard's expert advice on the care and use of telescopic sights, and his general information on the subject of sniping, greatly interested the men, and gave an impetus to the sniping activities of the division.

(11) PROMOTION OF LORD CAVAN : BRIG.-GENERAL FEILDING APPOINTED G.O.C., GUARDS DIVISION—OTHER CHANGES IN THE COMMANDS.

On the 22nd of December, Lord Cavan was selected to command the XIV Corps which was then in process of formation. His early promotion had been anticipated for some time, but its actual announcement caused a feeling akin to consternation throughout the Guards Division, so universal was the respect for him as a man and so implicit the confidence in him as a commander. For Lord Cavan himself the task of saying good-bye to his division was a sad one, but the parting was made much easier for him than would otherwise have been the case owing to the news which reached him on the 27th of December, that the Guards Division was to join the XIV Corps.

On the 3rd of January, 1916, Brig.-General G. Feilding was appointed to succeed Lord Cavan in the command of the Guards Division, with the temporary rank of Major-General. His fine record in the war clearly marked him out for the succession. He had come to France in command of the 3rd Bn. Coldstream Guards. He had handled his battalion with great skill and boldness during the retreat from Mons, on the Aisne, and throughout the strenuous fighting round Ypres in the autumn of 1914. He had succeeded Lord Cavan in the command of the 4th (Guards) Bde. in the summer of 1915, and he had at once proved himself to be an efficient and resourceful brigadier. His personal courage, his fearless and independent character, his acknowledged military capacity and judgment, his tried experience in the war, amply justified his promotion.

The command of the 1st Guards Bde., made vacant by the promotion of Major-General Feilding, was given to Brig.-General C. E. Pereira * who reported for duty on the 9th of January. Ten days later Lieut.-Colonel G. D. Jeffreys gave up the command of the 2nd Bn. Grenadier Guards on being appointed to command the 58th Infantry Bde., and, much to his own regret and that of his battalion, left

* At the time in command of an infantry brigade.

the Guards Division.* About this date, also, Colonel N. A. L. Corry, who had been in command of the 3rd Bn. Grenadier Guards since its arrival in France the previous July, was obliged to return to England owing to the state of his health. He was succeeded in the command of the battalion by Lieut.-Colonel B. N. Sergison-Brooke. On the 13th of February yet another change took place among the commanding officers of the Guards, when Lieut.-Colonel A. B. E. Cator was appointed to command the 37th Infantry Bde., Major R. S. Tempest succeeding him in the command of the 2nd Bn. Scots Guards. On the 28th of February Brig.-General Wardrop left the division on his promotion to command the artillery of the XIV Corps and was succeeded as C.R.A. by Brig.-General W. Evans.

(12) THE DIVISION LEAVES THE XI CORPS AND JOINS THE XIV CORPS.

Throughout the month of January and the early days of February the ordinary routine of trench life continued. Except for the activity of the patrols, to which allusion has already been made, there were no particular incidents which call for comment. The enemy showed no kind of inclination to attack the Guards, and the latter were mainly occupied in the unremitting labour required to keep their defences standing and their communications open in the wet weather which was prevalent all through the month.

In the second week of February the 35th Division was posted to the XI Corps, and, a few days later, definite orders were received for the Guards Division to join the XIV Corps.†

* The command of the 2nd Bn. Grenadier Guards devolved upon Major A. St. L. Glyn until the 1st of February, when Major C. Champion de Crespigny assumed the command.

† The units of the XIV Corps were being concentrated in and near Doullens in the area of the Third Army, where it was at first thought that the Guards would go on leaving the Laventie sector of the front. But just before the division left the line the XIV Corps commander received orders to move into the area of the Second Army, leaving his two divisions—the 36th and 55th Divisions—with the Third Army and assuming the command of the 6th, 14th and 20th Divisions in the Ypres salient. The Guards, therefore, moved north from La Gorgue and Merville, and, upon their arrival in Flanders, replaced the 14th Division in the XIV Corps.

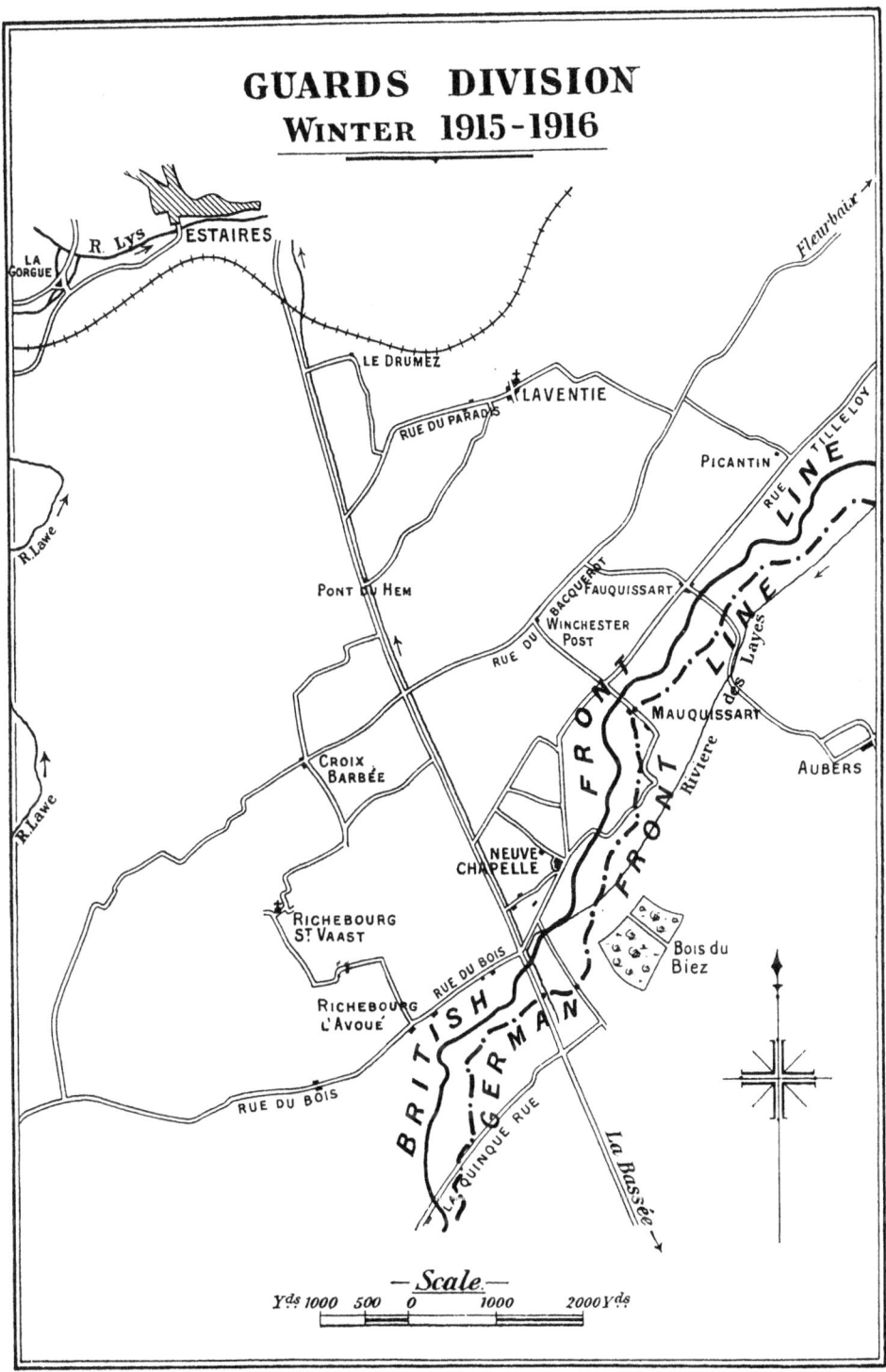

MOVE TO SECOND ARMY AREA

The relief of the division began on the 14th of February and was completed by the evening of the 16th.* The following day divisional headquarters was opened at Hazebrouck, and, by the 19th, the whole of the troops of the Guards Division, after some trying marching on the slippery and snow-covered roads, had arrived in the area of the Second Army, where they came under the command of General Sir Herbert Plumer.

* On the 17th of February Lieut.-General Haking sent the following message to Major-General Feilding :—" The military situation does not permit of my seeing your division on its departure from the corps, in order to say good-bye to you all, and thank all ranks for the fine services they have performed during the time the division has been in the corps. I am compelled, therefore, to write what I should have liked to speak.

" Ever since the division was formed and posted to this corps, it has proved itself to possess the finest possible military spirit. Lord Cavan, and since his departure, General Feilding, ably assisted by Lieut.-Colonel the Honble. W. P. Hore-Ruthven, G.S.O.1, Lieut.-Colonel Darell, A.A. & Q.M.G., and a most efficient staff, have carried out several offensive operations with distinguished success, including the attacks during the fighting round Loos, the consolidation of a difficult and unmade line about the Hohenzollern Redoubt, and the raids into the hostile trenches along the Rue Tilleloy front. The careful planning of these operations by the divisional commander and his General and Administrative Staff, the accurate reconnaissance and detailed organization of each by the brigade commanders, Brigadier-Generals Heyworth, Ponsonby and Pereira, and also General Feilding until he succeeded Lord Cavan in command of the division, together with their staffs, has been a model of good fighting. The infantry operations have been ably seconded by the artillery of the division under Brigadier-General Wardrop and his brigade commanders, who have spared no pains, both in the construction of forward observing posts and the training and organization of good observing officers, to secure the success of the infantry. The Royal Engineers, also, under Lieut.-Colonel Brough and his Field Company commanders, have been indefatigable in their work on the defences, the water drainage in rear of our line, and in assisting the artillery in the construction of some of the best observing posts in any part of the British line. The battalion commanders, officers and non-commissioned officers and men, who have been called upon to bear the brunt of all this fighting, have shown throughout an offensive spirit, which, in my opinion, surpasses any standard reached by the Guards or any other infantry in past campaigns, and which will be the admiration of future generations of soldiers. The fine discipline and soldierly bearing of all ranks is also a matter for you all to be proud of ; you have been an example to other divisions with whom you have been associated, and that example has produced the best results, and has raised the fighting value and efficiency of the whole corps."

CHAPTER V

IN THE YPRES SALIENT, MARCH–JULY, 1916.

(1) THE GUARDS JOIN THE XIV CORPS IN THE SECOND ARMY AREA—IN CORPS RESERVE ROUND CASSEL AND AT CALAIS—RELIEF OF THE 6TH DIVISION IN THE YPRES SALIENT, 16TH–20TH OF MARCH.

WHEN the Guards arrived in Flanders the troops of the XIV Corps were holding the left of the British front—the northern portion of the Ypres salient from the Bellewaarde stream, north west of Hooge, on the right to the junction with the French Army just south of the village of Boesinghe on the left. The 6th Division was on the right of the line and the 20th Division on the left, the boundary between the two divisions running just north of Wieltje Farm. The 14th Division, which the Guards Division was to replace in the corps, had just come back from the line into corps reserve. For some weeks, consequently, the Guards were not called upon to go into the trenches, and the opportunity was taken of sending each brigade in turn into camp at Calais, where, in addition to the benefit of a change of air, there were greater facilities for the training and the recreation of the troops than existed in the closely cultivated agricultural district round Cassel.* Thus between the time of their

---

* While the division was in corps reserve there were four serious bombing accidents which resulted in 8 officers and 25 other ranks being either killed or wounded. These accidents were caused by the premature explosion of the Mills bombs used. On the 16th of March Major-General Feilding wrote a letter to the XIV Corps, pointing out that these bombs were timed to burst in three instead of five seconds. He considered this an insufficient margin of safety and urged that there should be a return to the old five seconds fuze in order that confidence in the bomb might be restored. *See* W.D., Guards Division, App. 541.

arrival in the area of the Second Army and their taking over the front on the 16th of March the three brigades were located either in immediate corps reserve in and round Poperinghe, or in the Wormhoudt—Herzeele area north of Cassel, or at Calais. Divisional headquarters was moved on the 22nd of February from Hazebrouck to Esquelbecq Château near Wormhoudt and the divisional Artillery was billetted round Zeggers Cappel. The weather at this time was very wet and cold and a good deal of snow fell, so that much training in the open was not possible.* At Calais the conditions of life under canvas were, as may be imagined, somewhat trying, but, nevertheless, the bracing sea air and the change of scene and surroundings proved an excellent tonic for the troops for whom their officers arranged plenty of football, athletic sports and other amusements.† But this pleasant period of relaxation could not last for ever, and, on the 14th of March, orders came for the Guards to relieve the 6th Division in the line.

The relief began two days later and was completed in the evening of the 20th of March,‡ the 3rd Guards Bde., on the

---

* Major-General Feilding seized the opportunity of visiting the various battalions and explaining to officers and men the importance of making the line which they were to occupy north of Hooge strong and defensible. He warned them of the difficulties against which they would have to contend in the salient where they would be continuously under the enemy's observation, and outlined the method of defence. *See* " The Grenadier Guards in the Great War," vol. ii. p. 3.

About this time the Major-General instituted a system of giving signed parchments to non-commissioned officers and men in recognition of his appreciation of their good work. This practice was adopted in some other divisions as well as the Guards Division, and enabled the G.O.C. to show his appreciation of services in cases in which it was not always possible for him to obtain any other form of recognition.

† The greatest sporting event at Calais was undoubtedly the " Great Calais First Spring Meeting," organized by the 2nd Guards Bde. It was held on the sands " in some doubt as to whether the tide would not wipe out the steeplechase course " and was an unqualified success. *See* Appendix XIII. " Every soul in the Brigade who owned a horse, and several who had procured one, turned out and rode, including Father Knapp (Chaplain, 2nd Bn. Irish Guards), aged fifty-eight. There were five races, and a roaring multitude who wanted to bet on anything in or out of sight." *See* " The Irish Guards in the Great War," vol. ii. p. 67.

‡ Major-General Feilding assumed the command of the sector at

right, and 1st Guards Bde., on the left, taking over a front of about 3,700 yards from the Bellewaarde stream just north of the Menin road to a point a little to the north of Wieltje Farm, while the 2nd Guards Bde. remained in divisional reserve in and round Poperinghe.* Each brigade in the line had two battalions in the front system and two in reserve, the forward battalions being relieved in the line every four days.† For the greater part of the period passed by the Guards in the salient each brigade spent two weeks in one sector, two weeks out of the line, and two weeks in the other sector.‡

(2) Work in the Line—Restoration and reconstruction of the Trench System—Activity of the German Artillery.

The sector of the line on which the Guards Division now found itself was incomparably the most unpleasant part

10 p.m. on the 18th of March. By the 20th, the artillery relief had also been completed. *See* W.D., Guards Division, March, 1916.

The artillery was organized in two groups in battery positions round the northern outskirts of Ypres. B/74, which had been in action with the artillery of the 20th Division, did not go into the line until later in the month. *See* W.D., C.R.A., Guards Division, March, 1916.

* While the Guards occupied this sector of the line the headquarters of the division, of the C.R.A. and of the brigade in reserve were at Poperinghe; that of the brigade on the right in the ramparts of Ypres, and that of the brigade on the left in dug-outs along the canal bank. The 4th Bn. Coldstream Guards (Pioneers) was located in a camp just east of Poperinghe; the Field Companies, R.E., on the canal bank and the divisional Cavalry and Cyclists south and north-east of Poperinghe respectively.

† When it first went into this sector the 1st Guards Bde. tried the plan of relieving the battalion in the line every two days, but, as only one of the forward battalions was ever relieved on the same night, this meant a nightly relief on the brigade front. The system of relief described above was that adopted by the 3rd Guards Bde. when it went into the line and eventually became the practice throughout the division.

‡ A few days before the Guards went into the line, on the 7th of March, Lieut.-Colonel the Honble. W. P. Hore-Ruthven left the division upon his appointment as B.G.G.S., VIII Corps, and was succeeded as G.S.O.1, by Lieut.-Colonel C. P. Heywood, Coldstream Guards. Ten days later Lieut.-Colonel G. F. Trotter was appointed to the command of the 27th Infantry Bde. and Major A. St. L. Glyn obtained the command of the 1st Bn. Grenadier Guards.

of the whole British front. The holding of the Ypres salient at any time in the year was a task which made greater demands upon the stamina and moral of the defending troops than did that of any other portion of the front. But in the cold and wet weather of the early spring of 1916 the conditions of life in this dismal and water-logged area, overlooked on three sides by the enemy's artillery, were even more deplorable than usual.

It was invariably the custom in the British Armies in France, and no doubt the custom prevailed in every other theatre of war, for any division when taking over a new line to describe the state of the trenches as lamentably neglected by the outgoing troops; but in the Ypres sector in wet weather such a description was almost inevitable, for, however much work might have been expended upon the trenches, a few days' rain or a hostile bombardment generally reduced them to crumbling heaps of dismantled sandbags and mud.

The state of things found by the Guards when they relieved the 6th Division was no exception to the rule. The whole trench system was in a state of dilapidation and ruin. Part of the reserve line in front of the White Château * was untenable in daytime and the communication trenches, which were of great length in this sector, were so badly damaged by the enemy's artillery fire that it was impossible to use them—men had either to get out of them and walk across the open in full view of the enemy or to struggle along them up to their waists in water. The front line trenches were also far from satisfactory as the parapets were very low, at any rate for the Guards, and by no means bullet-proof.†

Throughout the course of the war there was usually a rumour current of an impending German attack upon Ypres

---

* In reply to an inquiry by the corps Major-General Feilding reported that the White Château was a shell-trap and could not be occupied. He arranged to cover it by some trenches in the neighbourhood, and hoped to construct a small work to the west of it. *See* W.D., Guards Division, App. 552.

† *See* Notes on the line to be taken over, W.D., Guards Division, App. 517.

and in this respect the spring of 1916 was no exception to the rule. Every effort was made, therefore, to strengthen the defences in the immediate neighbourhood of the town, and the R.E. of the Guards Division were at first almost wholly engaged in the construction of a series of machine-gun positions in ruined buildings in the ramparts, between the town and the village of St. Jean and along the canal bank. They also dug some new trenches for local defence in rear of the White Château. While the Field Companies, R.E., were thus employed, the 4th Bn. Coldstream Guards (Pioneers) set to work upon the restoration of the communication trenches and soon succeeded in securing cover from view, although it was some time before it was possible to place much reliance in the protection afforded by these approaches to the front line against the enemy's rifle and machine-gun fire.

Meanwhile, the infantry of the two brigades in the line worked hard upon the strengthening and the draining of the forward system, and, in a comparatively short space of time, there was a marked improvement in the defences. But these first weeks in the salient were a severe strain upon all ranks. There was no attempt at infantry action by the enemy, but his artillery was seldom silent—it rarely was in this sector of the line—and the fierce, concentrated area bombardments, which at this time were fired by the Germans, took a heavy toll of casualties and destroyed the trenches almost as fast as they were repaired.*

As the fire of the divisional Artillery had no appreciable effect in keeping down that of the enemy's batteries, a special bombardment of the German lines was carried out by the corps heavy artillery in conjunction with the field guns on the

* " These various activities did not pass unnoticed and the enemy subjected our whole trench system to a thorough good bombardment, doing an immense amount of damage. I think West Lane communication trench alone received 52 direct hits and the damage all round was on much the same scale. It took us the rest of our time in this sector to get repairs effected." Extract from note supplied by Lieut.-Colonel Brough, C.R.E., Guards Division.

During March the losses in the division, mainly caused by shell fire, amounted to 10 officers and 323 other ranks. *See* **General Staff Summary, Guards Division.**

4th and 5th of April. This " shoot " was much hindered by bad visibility; but, nevertheless, an immense amount of damage was done to the hostile trench system, and its effect was beneficial, as, although the enemy's artillery fire continued to be persistent and annoying, his gunners did not again carry out any concentrated bombardments on particular areas while the Guards remained in this sector of the line.

As soon as the work necessitated by the scheme for the immediate defence of Ypres had been completed, the Field Companies, R.E., were sent into the forward area to assist the infantry. Their main task was to strengthen and develop the machine-gun defence in the event of a hostile attack breaking through the front line system, and their time was largely occupied in the building of concrete and steel emplacements for machine guns, linked up with belts of wire and sited so as to bring flanking fire to bear upon the various avenues of approach to Ypres. Their work was rendered particularly arduous owing to the drainage difficulties.*

In addition to the devising and the carrying out of these various defences, a vast amount of work was thrown on the C.R.E. and his men in the reconstruction of the shelters and dug-outs along the canal bank, the majority of which when the Guards went into the line had no pretensions to being shell-proof, and in increasing the accommodation in the ramparts and cellars of Ypres. A new brigade headquarters was made in the ramparts and a new artillery brigade headquarters was built just north of the town. The cellars in the ruined houses east of the moat were cleared of *débris* and fitted with bunks for the troops.†

* " Our great difficulty in this sector was that the ground, having been repeatedly and heavily shelled, had become water-logged during the winter, and it was very difficult to keep one's drainage cuts open in the greasy, yellow clay." Extract from note supplied by Lieut.-Colonel Brough, C.R.E., Guards Division.

† " Corps and army workshops for R.E. material were organized at this time, but a great deal of manufacturing work still fell on the Field Companies in the line, which, apart from making up R.E. stores for the front line, had to provide a good deal of hutting. This meant having a number of small scattered shops, and it proved a perfect curse getting raw material to them and manufactured stuff away. We

(3) HOSTILE RAID ON THE 19TH OF APRIL—DEATH OF BRIG.-
GENERAL HEYWORTH—THE GUARDS RELIEVED BY THE
20TH DIVISION—THE 2ND GUARDS BRIGADE SENT TO
RELIEVE THE CANADIANS OPPOSITE HOOGE—THE GUARDS
DIVISION TAKES OVER THE LEFT SECTOR OF THE FRONT
OF THE XIV CORPS, 16TH–19TH OF JUNE—WORK IN
THE LINE.

In the evening of the 19th of April the enemy's infantry made a raid north of Wieltje and some of the raiders succeeded in penetrating the front held by the 2nd Bn. Scots Guards in that village. They made their way into the line at a point where a trench, which had been heavily shelled, had been evacuated. But they were promptly bombed out again and the lost ground regained.*

During the month of May there was an increase in mining activities, but in other respects there was little incident on the Guards front. Ammunition had now to be used with great economy in view of the coming operations on the Somme, and, consequently, the work of the divisional Artillery was strictly limited to such retaliatory fire as was

had only the one road from Poperinghe to Ypres upon which to send up large quantities of stores to the front line. The transport difficulties were great enough even when the enemy was not shelling our communications. I think that we often had as many as 50 D.A.C. wagons out on a night carting up stores to Ypres. The railway line was of little use to us as the track was too badly damaged at and beyond Ypres." Extract from note supplied by Lieut.-Colonel Brough, C.R.E., Guards Division.

* This affair cost the Scots Guards 49 casualties and the 4th Bn. Grenadier Guards on their right 27. *See* W.D., Guards Division, App. 624.

The total casualties in the division during April amounted to nearly 400 all ranks. At the end of the month the O.C. Guards Division Base Depôt sent in a return showing the number of reinforcements sent to the front during the period 25th of August, 1915, to the 26th of April, 1916. The following figures are of interest :—

Grenadier Guards	..	69 officers,	2587	other ranks.
Coldstream Guards	..	45 ,,	2078	,, ,,
Scots Guards ..	..	46 ,,	1714	,, ,,
Irish Guards	..	35 ,,	1532	,, ,,
Welsh Guards	..	5 ,,	434	,, ,,

deemed necessary. On the 9th of May Brig.-General Heyworth was unfortunately killed by a German sniper as he was going round the line, and in him the 3rd Guards Bde. lost a most gallant commander who was universally popular and deservedly respected. He was succeeded in the command of the brigade by Brig.-General C. E. Corkran.

On the 21st of May the Guards were relieved in the line by the 20th Division,* and moved back to the Wormhoudt area, divisional headquarters being established in Esquelbecq Château.†

The division had been enjoying its well-earned rest for about a fortnight when the news arrived that the Canadians had been driven out of Hooge,‡ and orders were soon afterwards received from the XIV Corps for one of the Guards brigades to move forward in order to take over part of the front held by the Canadians.

* The divisional Artillery was relieved by that of the 20th Division on the 20th of May and went back to the Zeggers Cappel area. It received a message of congratulation from Major-General Feilding for the work done on battery positions and O.P.'s. *See* W.D., C.R.A., Guards Division, May, 1916, and App. 34.

Lieut.-Colonel G. R. V. Kinsman left the division owing to ill-health early in the month and was succeeded in the command of the 76th Bde., R.F.A., by Lieut.-Colonel F. C. Bryant.

Lieut.-Colonel C. B. Watkins replaced Lieut.-Colonel H. Fawcus in the command of the D.A.C. about the same time for a similar reason. The D.A.C. sustained its first casualties in action in May, losing 3 men and 46 animals. *See* W.D., D.A.C., Guards Division, May, 1916.

Lieut.-Colonel Ravenhill relinquished the command of the 74th Bde., R.F.A., early in June and was succeeded by Lieut.-Colonel J. B. Riddell.

† Just before the Guards left the line the B.G.G.S., XIV Corps sent the following note to Major-General Feilding :—" The corps commander wishes me to express to you and all ranks of the Guards Division his sincere thanks for the work done during the last two months, both in and behind the line. The cost has been heavy, but the defence has been sure, and a very great improvement effected in the line."

‡ On the 2nd of June the Germans, after a very intense artillery bombardment, which completely obliterated the trenches, broke through the Canadian line from the northern edge of Sanctuary Wood to Mount Sorrel. They penetrated as far as Maple Copse, and, although they were driven out of it again, they succeeded in establishing themselves for a time on Observatory ridge. Obstinate fighting continued for some days and the enemy captured Hooge on the 6th. On the 13th a Canadian counter-attack regained much of the lost ground, but Hooge still remained in German hands.

The 2nd Guards Bde., to which the 76th Field Company, R.E., was attached, was at once dispatched in lorries to Vlamertinghe and went into the line opposite Hooge on the 15th–16th of June. The conditions in the trenches were terrible and the enemy's artillery fire was very severe;* but the Guards were not called upon to resist any infantry attack, and, on the night of the 21st–22nd, the brigade was relieved by the Canadians and rejoined the division.

The 1st and 3rd Guards Bdes. remained behind the line in G.H.Q. Reserve until the nights of the 16th–17th and 18th–19th of June when they relieved the 6th Division in the left sector of the XIV Corps front, the 3rd Guards Bde. going in on the right and the 1st Guards Bde. on the left of the line. Divisional headquarters was then moved from Esquelbecq to the convent of St. Sixte, north of Poperinghe.†

The trenches in the new sector, which extended from north of Wieltje Farm to Boesinghe, were in poor condition, but, as the ground was now beginning to dry out, it was possible

---

* "We've been having stirring times these last months. We were rushed up in motor-buses in the middle of our rest as an emergency measure to relieve the Canadians after their counter-attack at Hooge. We took over what was in effect a battle-field and untidy one at that. Mined trenches, confluent craters, bodies and bits of bodies, woods turned into a wilderness of stubby blackened stumps and a stink of death and corruption which was supernaturally beastly. The Canadians fought extremely well and are brave and enterprising, but they are deficient in system and routine. No troops can be first-rate unless they are punished for small faults and get their meals with regularity. The Canadians are frequently famished and never rebuked, whereas the Brigade of Guards are gorged and d——d the whole time." Extract from a letter of Lieutenant Raymond Asquith. *See* "The Autobiography of Margot Asquith," vol. ii. pp. 240, 241.

† The divisional Artillery relieved the 6th Divisional Artillery on the 18th of June, the battery positions being outside Ypres on the Wieltje road, and farther north behind the canal. The D.A.C. formed a big forward ammunition dump containing 40,000 rounds, 32,000 for the 18-pdrs. and 8,000 for the howitzers. *See* W.D's., C.R.A., and D.A.C., Guards Division, June, 1916.

In the middle of May an important reorganization of the divisional Artillery had taken place. The 61st Bde., R.F.A., had parted with all its howitzer batteries, one battery going to each of the 74th, 75th and 76th Bdes., R.F.A. Henceforward the 61st Bde. consisted of three 18-pdr. batteries, and the other three brigades each had three 18-pdr. batteries and one howitzer battery. *See* W.D., 61st Bde., R.F.A., May, 1916.

to get a little cover by digging down and draining; and so, by dint of hard work, the support line was soon made habitable and the communication trenches much improved.* The bridges across the Yser Canal were at first a source of great trouble as they were frequently shelled and the northernmost of them, which was only protected by a canvas screen, was continually subjected to the enemy's rifle and machine-gun fire. The R.E. put up a series of trench grid bridges on piles, the grids being placed just below water level so that they might escape detection by aeroplane observers. The R.E. were also kept continuously employed in assisting the infantry with the drainage and the reconstruction of the front line trench system.† The line now occupied by the division was a long one, and it was no easy matter to keep up its defences and its communications; but during their sojourn in this area the Guards certainly effected considerable improvements, and when they left it a man's safety in the front area, as one writer has expressed it, no longer depended upon his ability " to imitate a Russian dancer." ‡

* " The enemy had at least one deadly and big trench mortar opposite the point where our trenches turned north-west from the canal bank, and he not infrequently put up ' Brock's benefit,' which obliterated all vestige of our trenches within its range. We tried digging fresh trenches here, but we really held a line behind this point." Extract from note supplied by Lieut.-Colonel Brough, C.R.E., Guards Division.

† The damage done by shell fire to the natural system of drainage in this area which ran down to the canal necessitated an immense amount of labour. Much of this could only be done by daylight and of course only scattered groups of men could be employed. Nevertheless, a new front line trench about 300 yards long was dug to straighten up the point of junction with the division on the right.

‡ " We had one great asset in this sector. A really good central divisional R.E. workshop to which the railway delivered material. Moreover, by arrangement with the local Railway Construction Company, we were able to send up four broad gauge truck loads of material nightly to just west of Ypres. Here we harnessed horse teams to the railway wagons (the country being dead flat) and pulled them up to our dumps just close behind the canal bank in our sector. This arrangement worked very well, the empty railway trucks being dragged back and delivered at Ypres before dawn. The enemy, strange to say, acquiesced in our proceedings." Extract from note supplied by Lieut.-Colonel Brough, C.R.E., Guards Division.

IN THE YPRES SALIENT

(4) RESUMPTION OF AN AGGRESSIVE POLICY ON THE FRONT OF THE SECOND ARMY—RAIDS BY THE GUARDS—DEPARTURE OF THE DIVISION TO THE SOMME AREA, 27TH OF JULY.

A more offensive policy was now inaugurated all along the front of the Second Army " with the object of assisting the offensive in other areas and also to assist any future offensive in this area." *

In conformity with this policy, on the 24th of June, the left group of guns covering the Guards' front carried out a bombardment of the German line, cutting three gaps in the enemy's wire and making four breaches in his parapet. These gaps were somewhat difficult to keep under observation owing to the long grass, but they appeared to be well cut and were kept open by systematic shooting.† On the night of the 25th–26th of June the 1st Bn. Grenadier Guards carried out a raid and advanced the line of the 3rd Guards Bde. about 200 yards on a frontage of 300 yards, digging a forward trench north-west of Forward Cottage.

The enemy showed no inclination to fight at this time and appeared to be mainly occupied in the strengthening of his defences. But even in this comparative calm the salient exacted its heavy toll of casualties.‡

On the night of the 1st–2nd of July a company of the 1st Bn. Welsh Guards, under the command of Captain H. Dene carried out a very successful attack in the right sector of the line. A hostile post at Morteldje Estaminet, which stood at the cross-roads where Admiral's road running north-west from Wieltje met Boundary road running north from Ypres, was captured and two prisoners were taken. This enterprise was supported by the concentrated fire of

---

* *See* Guards Division Op. Ord. No. 44, and General Staff Summary, Guards Division.

† Another bombardment of the same character was carried out on the 27th of June by both artillery groups. The breaches made in the enemy's line were kept under machine-gun and Lewis-gun fire.

‡ The losses in the division during the week 21st–28th of June amounted to 8 officers and 253 other ranks.

THE RAID AT MORTELDJE ESTAMINET 127

the 4·5 howitzers, and two bombing posts were successfully established at the ruins of the estaminet. The following day the German artillery and *minenwerfer*-fire rendered these posts untenable and they had to be withdrawn; but a Lewis gun was placed so as to cover the ruins with its fire, and deny them to the enemy. The Welsh Guards, who displayed great courage and determination in this affair, then set to work to sap forward in order to reestablish the posts and were still engaged upon this task when they were relieved in the line by the 2nd Bn. Scots Guards.*

The following night the 2nd Bn. Irish Guards † raided the south-western face of the German salient at Krupp Farm on the Pilckem road. The raiders, who consisted of 40 Guardsmen and a small detachment of R.E., advanced as soon as the British artillery barrage had lifted from the enemy's trenches. They took 2 prisoners and carried out some demolition work, remaining for about ten minutes in the captured position in spite of an intense hostile barrage. Lieutenant Pym, who was in command of the raiding party, never returned, and the casualties in the raid and subsequent artillery bombardment were unfortunately somewhat numerous.‡

On the night of the 3rd–4th of July the 1st Bn. Grenadier Guards, in cooperation with troops of the 20th Division on their right, succeeded in digging a new forward trench which advanced the line about 250 yards between Wieltje and Cross Roads Farm, but an attempt by the 4th Battalion of the same regiment to raid the locality known as Canadian dug-outs near the cross-roads-north west of Wieltje a few

---

* See "History of the Welsh Guards," pp. 88–89. The Welsh Guards lost 4 officers and 76 other ranks. But most of these casualties were incurred after the capture of the objective.

"We got the place with one casualty and while consolidating the Bosch guns were turned on the men who continued digging all through the night under intense shrapnel fire." Extract from a letter written by Lieut.-Colonel Murray-Threipland.

† The 2nd Guards Bde. had relieved the 1st Guards Bde. before the end of June.

‡ See W.D., 2nd Guards Bde., July, 1916. *Cf.* "The Irish Guards in the Great War," vol. ii. pp. 88–92. The Irish Guards had 52 casualties as a result of this affair.

days later ended in failure, the enemy being found very much on the alert and ready for the raiders.*

Throughout the remainder of July—until the 25th of the month when the relief of the Guards Division began—except for some patrol encounters, there was little incident on the divisional front.

The Allied operations on the Somme were now in full progress, and, although no sane man was personally anxious to take part in the offensive, there was yet a feeling throughout the division that the proper place for the Guards was in the battle zone. The call duly came, the XIV Corps received orders to relieve the VIII Corps in the Somme area, and, at 4 p.m., on the 27th of July, Major-General Feilding handed over the command of the Boesinghe sector to the G.O.C. the 4th Division. Three days later the Guards Division was billetted in the area Bouquemaison—Lucheux—Halloy, with divisional headquarters at Doullens.†

(5) Arrival of the Guards in the Area of the Reserve Army—The Division goes into the Line opposite Beaumont Hamel.

When the Guards reached the battle area, the troops of the XIV Corps were already holding the front of the Reserve Army (General Hubert Gough) from the river Ancre to the Puisieux—Hébuterne road, the 6th Division being in occupation of the right, the 25th Division of the centre, and the 20th Division of the left of the line. The Guards Division thus found itself for the time being in corps reserve. The troops were in the Bus-les-Artois—Vauchelles-les-Authie area and divisional headquarters at Bus-les-Artois.‡

* *See* W.D., Guards Division, Report, July, 1916.
† *See* W.D., Guards Division, July, 1916, also App. 947. The casualties in the division from the 28th of June to the date when it left the salient amounted to 800 all ranks.
‡ *See* W.D., Guards Division, August, 1916, and App. 960. The divisional Artillery, whose relief by the 4th Divisional Artillery in the salient was completed a few days later than that of the infantry, moved on the 1st of August to the Thievres—Authie—St. Leger-les-Authie area, relieved the centre and left groups of the 38th divi-

Three hundred men from the infantry of the division, however, were at once called for by the corps to assist the 252nd Tunnelling Company, while two battalions—the 3rd Bn. Coldstream Guards and the 2nd Bn. Irish Guards—were also attached for work with the 20th and 25th Divisions respectively from the 4th of August onwards.*

On the 8th of August, as soon as orders had been received for the Guards to move into the line, Major-General Feilding held a conference at which the work that would have to be done in the trenches was fully discussed. In view, too, of a contemplated offensive " at some future date " in conjunction with the 6th Division on the right, the Major-General impressed upon officers the importance of reconnaissance as soon as they went into the line.

On the 9th of August, the day on which the Guards began to relieve a brigade of the 6th Division and the whole of the 25th Division, His Majesty the King, accompanied by H.R.H. the Prince of Wales and the Commander-in-Chief, called upon the divisional commander and visited all three Guards brigades. The following day divisional headquarters was transferred to Bertrancourt and the relief was completed on the 11th.

The Guards, with all three brigades in the line, the 1st, 2nd, and 3rd from right to left, now held the centre of the XIV Corps front—that portion of the sector of the Reserve Army which faced the German positions from west of Beaumont Hamel to a point opposite Serre. They remained in this area until the 15th of August when certain changes in the distribution of the 1st and 2nd Guards Bdes. were rendered necessary as a preliminary to the movement southward of the XIV Corps.† This change of location brought

---

sional Artillery, and were covering the 20th Division in the line on the 8th of August. The battery positions were at Courcelles, east and south-east of Colincamps, midway between Colincamps and Hébuterne, and between Sailly-au-Bois and Hébuterne. The D.A.C. formed at Coigneux a large forward dump containing 400 rounds per 18-pdr. and 300 per howitzer. This dump was stocked in two days. *See* W.D's., C.R.A., and D.A.C., Guards Division, August, 1916.

* Both battalions rejoined the division on the 7th of August.

† *See* p. 139.

the Guards Division temporarily under the orders of the V Corps.

Except for the activity of the British artillery and of the enemy's *minenwerfer* there was little incident during the short period spent by the division on the Ancre front. Patrolling was carried out with great energy, and the troops worked hard in the improvement of their line—one piece of work done by the 1st Bn. Scots Guards earning a special word of praise from the V Corps Commander.*

(6) The Social Life of the Division—The " Daily Dump "—Work of the Chaplains.

During the months spent by the Guards in the area of the Second Army the life of the division out of the line was not an altogether unpleasant one. In fine weather conditions in the camps near Poperinghe were by no means bad and Poperinghe itself at that period in the war was not much shelled by the enemy and had its attractions for the troops. There was plenty of ground available for football and cricket and athletic sports. The rivalry between battalions and brigades was keen and many a hard fought game took place. There was a great interchange of hospitality, too, and the good feeling and friendship which already existed between officers and men of the various units in the division became greater and closer.

It was during the summer of 1916 while the Guards were in the salient that the famous " Daily Dump," the " Punch " of the 2nd Guards Bde., made its first appearance. It was initiated by Brig.-General J. Ponsonby and for a long time kept in existence by him and his brigade staff.† For fifty consecutive nights it was regularly issued with the orders.

---

* The battalion sapped out for about 180 yards to " 16 Poplars " on the Hébuterne—Puisieux road and established two posts. *See* W.D's., Guards Division, App. 1047, and 2nd Guards Bde., App. 41.

† *See* " Henry Dundas, Scots Guards, a Memoir," in which occur many allusions to and quotations from this journal. The 1st Guards Bde. also produced a journal with the title of " The Canal Chronicle," but it appears to have had rather a brief career.

Then for a short time it only appeared weekly. But subsequently it was revived as a " daily " and was continued as such for another fifty numbers, until on the 20th of June, 1917, its editors confessed that the unpleasant conditions of life at Elverdinghe before the opening of the third Ypres offensive forced them to admit that Minerva must yield to Mars.* Many journals and news sheets were circulated among the formations and units of the British Army in France, but few, if any, can have equalled " The Dump " in length of existence, and it is certain that not one surpassed it in real humour or in literary excellence.

The effort to give some kind of amusement to the troops which had been so successfully begun at La Gorgue was considerably developed in the Ypres area, and became an important feature in the life of the Guards Division. At Poperinghe there was a large hall near the railway station which had been converted into a theatre by the 6th Division and was capable of accommodating an audience of 1,000 persons. This building was taken over by the divisional staff. A cinema was installed in it and a canteen fitted up. An entertainment, lasting from 2.30 to 6.30 p.m., was given daily while the troops were in the salient and the hall was invariably crowded. It was an enormous boon to all ranks when they came out of the mud and squalor of the trenches to be able to go to a place in which they could

* " The ' Dump ' has sunk once more to rest
The century is past.
Obeying Destiny's behest,
We make this sheet our last.
 *   *   *   *
Behind—in dalliance divine
With words we mocked at Fate.
Here, in the very foremost line,
We find the strain too great.

The calm of letters is displaced
By War's unruly jars
Beaten at last—though not disgraced,
Minerva yields to Mars.
Pens can't compete with H.E. shell—
And so, dear public, fare you well."

See " The Daily Dump," No. 100, vol. 2.

find rest and refreshment, listen to good music and witness a show which was both instructive and amusing.* An officer, usually one of the divisional chaplains, was always in charge at the hall in case it had to be cleared owing to a sudden bombardment by the enemy's artillery—a by no means unusual interruption for theatre goers at Poperinghe.

The chaplains naturally did their utmost to assist in the social life of the division, and one of them, the Rev. Sydney Jones, under the direction of the " Q " Staff, attended most efficiently to the material wants of the men. He always contrived to keep the divisional canteen well supplied with every kind of food and tobacco, even at times when other divisions were running short of such things. His business acumen was also great, and the large profits which resulted from his management of the canteen were distributed among the units of the division for the provision of athletic requisites and prizes.

The Guards were fortunate in their chaplains of all denominations. They worked together with the utmost cordiality and friendliness. Both in the field and behind the line they carried out their multifarious duties with energy and devotion.† When the division was engaged in an

---

* In addition to the cinema entertainment, the bands of the various Guards regiments, which came out in turn to France, gave many excellent concerts. Colonel Mackenzie Rogan of the Coldstream Guards band added to the success of these concerts by bringing with him a giant gramophone with a trumpet attachment which enabled songs by Melba, Caruso, Clara Butt and others to be heard all over the Hall.

The Guards never had a divisional Concert Party. But this omission was made good by the 3rd Bn. Coldstream Guards which in 1916, with the approval and encouragement of its commanding officer, Lieut.-Colonel R. B. Crawford, formed an admirable theatrical company known as the " Lilywhites." The players in this troupe, who were all officers, warrant officers, non-commissioned officers and men of the battalion, unlike the members of most other such parties in the B.E.F., were not struck off the strength. They performed their ordinary military duties and gave their spare time to the task of entertaining their comrades. The " Lilywhites " continued in existence until the Guards returned to England.

† " At the beginning of the war many commanding officers thought that the chief duty of a padre was to bury the dead, but they soon came to realize their value when they found that they were men as well as chaplains. At first the chaplains in the Guards Division used to live with the Field Ambulances, but they soon came to live with the

offensive operation two of the Church of England chaplains were always sent to the main dressing station to help with the wounded as they came in and one to the advanced dressing station. The remaining chaplains were with the attacking or supporting battalions. They followed the infantry as soon as possible after the assault had been delivered and helped the stretcher-bearer parties to find and succour the wounded and dying.* In other ways, too, the chaplains were often useful while the troops were in the front line. They could carry messages and act as guides, and there is more than one case on record in which a chaplain proved himself of value in an emergency.

There can be no doubt of the wonderful influence which their priests had upon the Roman Catholics : it is only necessary to read Mr. Kipling's story of the Irish Guards to appreciate what men like Fathers Gwynne and Knapp did for their respective battalions.† It is naturally less easy to estimate the spiritual influence exercised by the chaplains of the Church of England and the Non-Conformist ministers.

---

battalions and used to go up with them to the line and be with them wherever they were. . . . It was sometimes difficult to persuade a commanding officer to take a chaplain into his battalion, but, so long as the chaplain was of the right stuff, a commanding officer when he had once got him was only too anxious not to lose him." Extract from a note supplied by one of the divisional chaplains.

* The following note addressed by Major-General Feilding to the Rev. Pat McCormick, Senior Chaplain of the division, after the fighting on the Somme in 1916, gives some idea of the work done by the chaplains on the field of battle :—" I am very glad to have your reports on the work of the chaplains during the fighting that took place on September 15th–25th. From all sources I have heard the same story that the chaplains were doing everything that was possible in comforting the dying and helping the wounded. They themselves were exposing themselves continuously to the hottest shell fire helping to find and collect the wounded. And what I think is perhaps grander, they were doing it not to get for themselves merit or honour, but because it was their duty. I am told on all sides that Rogers, Hubbard, Llewellyn, Jones and Crawley were especially splendid. I feel sure from all I heard that Head was also amongst those who were most conspicuous. I cannot thank the chaplains too much for all tha they did."

† Both these priests were killed. The only chaplain of the Church of England who was killed with the Guards Division was the Rev. E. Gibbs.

But there is no doubt that the earnestness, unselfishness and sincerity of most of the padres had a great effect upon both officers and men. If ministers of religion sometimes failed to seize their opportunity in the war, this was certainly not the case in the Guards Division.*

* Mr. Stephen Graham in his book " A Private in the Guards " speaks somewhat disparagingly of the divisional chaplains. He formed an impression, presumably as a result of his experiences with the Guards that " in the war Chaplains' work had failed." But it should be remembered that this writer's experience at the front was of short duration and somewhat limited in scope. Had he himself been an eyewitness of the work actually done by many of the padres—at Loos, on the Somme, at Ypres, at Cambrai—had he seen with his own eyes their calm courage and unswerving devotion to duty in the most trying conditions, he would, in common fairness to very gallant gentlemen, have told a different tale. And had he been present at any Service held before an attack, he would scarcely have ventured to suggest that they had failed in their principal duty as ministers of religion.

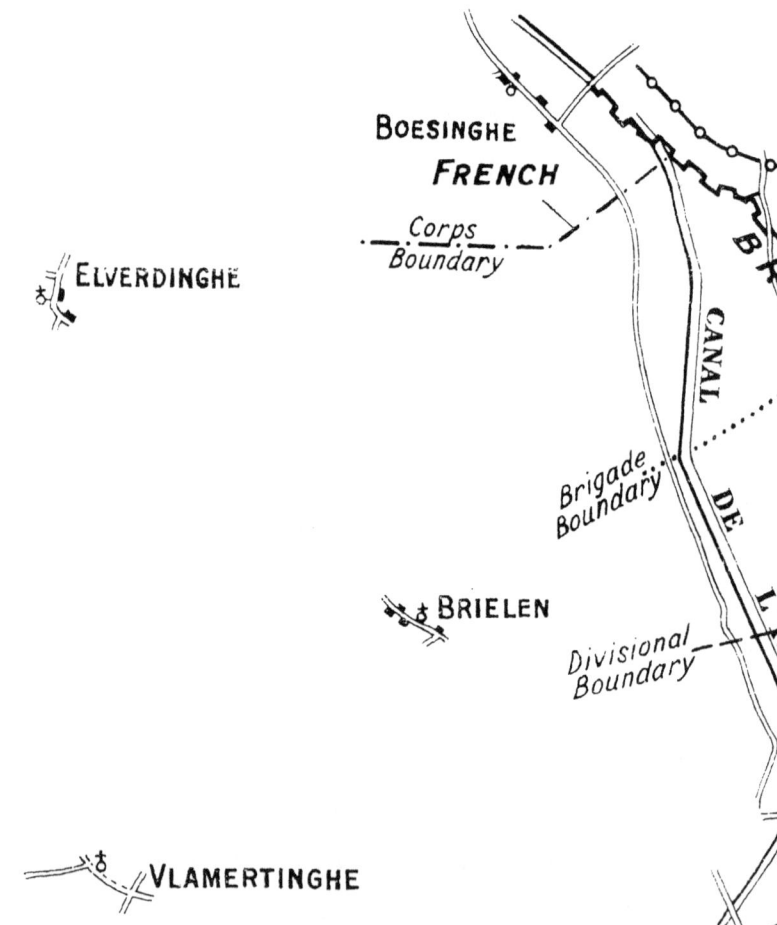

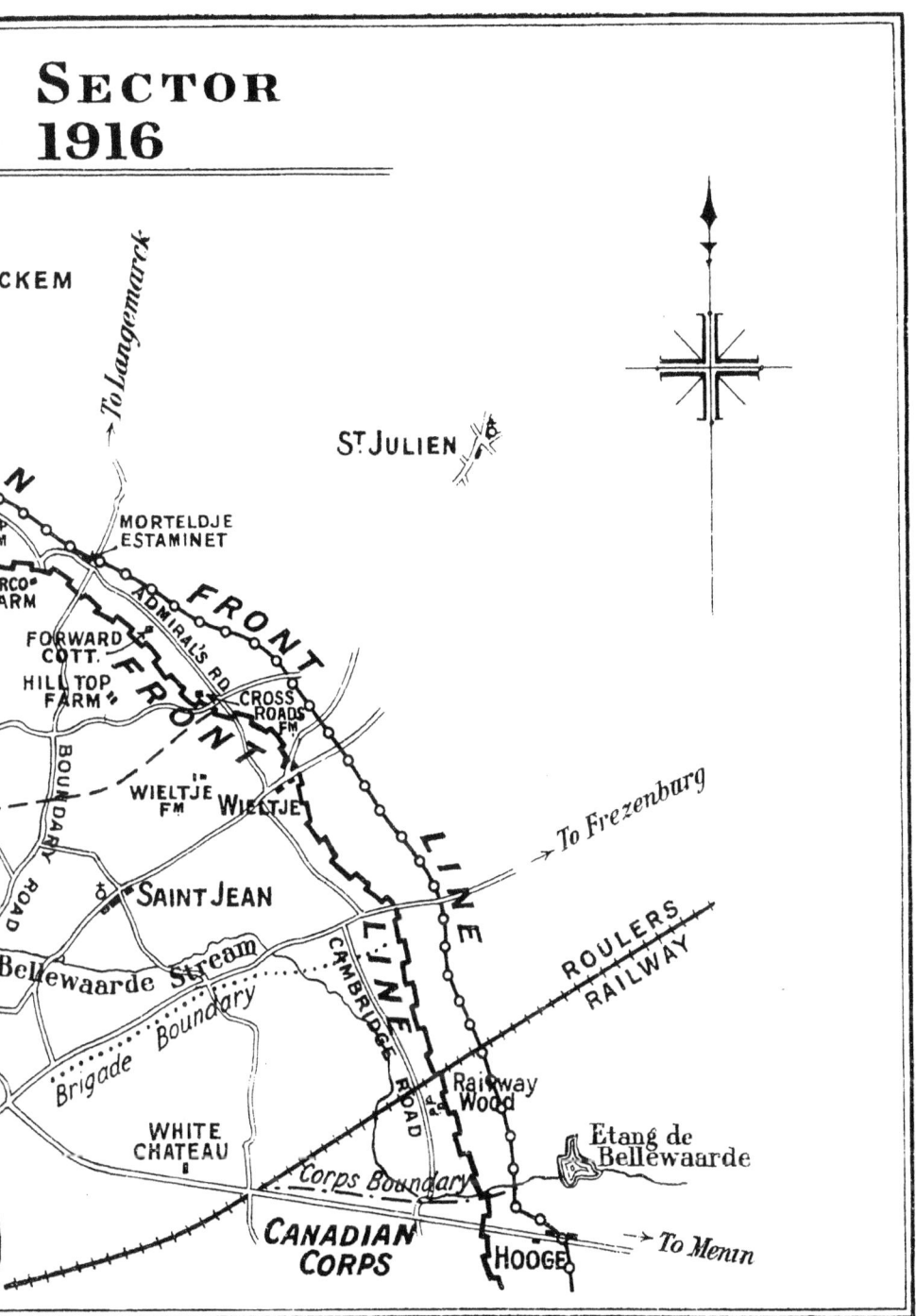

CHAPTER VI

THE OPERATIONS ON THE SOMME—THE BATTLES OF FLERS-COURCELETTE AND MORVAL, SEPTEMBER, 1916.

(1) OBJECTS OF THE ALLIES IN THE BATTLE OF THE SOMME —SCOPE OF THE OPERATIONS—NATURE OF THE TERRAIN.

THE battles of the Somme, 1st of July—18th of November, 1916, were fought with three main objects in view :—(1) to relieve the pressure upon Verdun where the French Army was being " bled white " ; (2) to assist the Allied Armies in the other theatres of war by preventing any further transference of German troops from the Western Front ; * and (3) to wear down the strength of the enemy's forces in France and Belgium.

The original scheme of operations for the summer of 1916, drawn up and agreed upon by General Joffre and Sir Douglas Haig, had been designed upon a far more ambitious scale than the offensive which actually took place.† The German attack upon Verdun in February, 1916, completely upset the Allied programme, the drain made upon the resources of the French Army in its magnificent defence of that town being so great that it was incapable of taking the share assigned to it in the summer offensive. The battle, therefore, which had been intended as " a supreme French stroke for a decision," had to be transformed into " a British battle of

---

* The Austrian offensive in the Trentino during the month of May led the Russians to embark upon an offensive in Galicia early in June. It was urgently necessary, therefore, for the Allies in France, more especially in view of the political situation in Russia, to do all that they could to pin down the Germans in the Western theatre of operations.

† See " Sir Douglas Haig's Despatches," p. 20.

attrition " and gave the British Army for the first time the dominant rôle in the Allied operations in the principal theatre of war." *

The German defensive positions in the area in which the Allied advance was to take place had been carefully chosen and sited.† They lay along the succession of undulating ridges and spurs which form the watershed between the Somme and the rivers of south-western Belgium. Incessant labour throughout the winter of 1915 and the spring of 1916 had covered the whole of the countryside lying north and south of Albert on the German side of the line—from north of the Ancre to south of the Somme—with an intricate series of deeply dug trenches which stretched eastward as far as Bapaume and Péronne.‡

Between these organized trench systems § every village and every point of tactical vantage, every wood and every pit or quarry, had been put into a state of defence, so that no line of approach towards the enemy's positions was not effectively covered, and usually enfiladed, by artillery and

* See " Sir Douglas Haig's Command," vol. i. p. 86.

† The first of these organized systems of defence opposite the British front extended from the village of Curlu on the right bank of the Somme northward for about 3,000 yards to a point a little to the east of Maricourt Wood, thence west and north for another 7,000 yards to the Ancre. North of this latter river the German line jutted westward at Beaumont Hamel and then ran northward again to Hébuterne and Gommecourt.

‡ " During nearly two years' preparation he (the enemy) had spared no pains to render these defences impregnable. The first and second systems each consisted of several lines of deep trenches, well provided with bomb-proof shelters and with numerous communication trenches connecting them. The front of the trenches in each system was protected by wire entanglements, many of them in two belts forty yards broad, built of iron stakes interlaced with barbed wire, often almost as thick as a man's finger." See " Sir Douglas Haig's Despatches," p. 22.

§ The enemy's second main line of defence was at a distance, varying from 3,000 to 5,000 yards according to the nature of the country, in rear of the front line system. It lay along the southern crest of the ridge, which formed the highest portion of the watershed from north of Péronne through Combles, Longueval, Bazentin-le-Grand, Pozières, east of Thiepval and thence northward through Grandcourt to the high ground east of Gommecourt. In rear of this line there were at least three other lines either constructed or in course of construction when the battle began.

machine-gun fire. The enemy's defences, therefore, against which the British and French troops were now called upon to advance formed, to quote the words of Sir Douglas Haig, "not merely a series of successive lines, but one composite system of enormous depth and strength." *

(2) OPENING OF THE ALLIED ATTACK ON THE 1ST OF JULY—
PROGRESS OF THE ADVANCE TO THE MIDDLE OF SEPTEMBER.

The initial assault in the battle of the Somme was launched on the 1st of July. The Fourth Army (General Sir Henry Rawlinson) attacked on a front of about 10 miles extending from Maricourt in the south, round the German salient just south of Fricourt, northward to the river Ancre a little to the west of St. Pierre Divion and north of the Ancre as far as Serre, in cooperation with the French under the command of General Foch operating on a front of about 8 miles on both sides of the river Somme. A subsidiary British attack by the Third Army (General Sir E. H. Allenby) was also made the same day on a front of about 5 miles on both sides of the German salient at Gommecourt.†

The results of the first day's operations were such as to

* *See* "Sir Douglas Haig's Despatches," p. 23. "The numerous woods and villages in and between these systems of defence had been turned into veritable fortresses. The deep cellars usually to be found in the villages, and the numerous pits and quarries common to a chalk country, were used to provide cover for machine guns and trench mortars. The existing cellars were supplemented by elaborate dug-outs, sometimes in two storeys, and these were connected up by passages as much as thirty feet below the surface of the ground. The salients in the enemy's line, from which he could bring enfilade fire across his front, were made into self-contained forts, and often protected by mine fields; while strong redoubts and concrete machine-gun emplacements had been constructed in positions from which he could sweep his own trenches should these be taken. The ground lent itself to good artillery observation on the enemy's part, and he had skilfully arranged for cross fire by his guns." *Ib.* p. 22.

† In the attack on the 1st of July Sir Douglas Haig had 13 divisions in the front line, and 6 divisions in close reserve, 2 of which came into action that day. The French employed 5 divisions. In the original scheme of operations it had been intended to use 39 French divisions on a front of 30 miles. This gives some idea of the change which the German attack upon Verdun made in the Allied plans.

determine the British Commander-in-Chief to press forward his attack between the Franco-British junction and " a point half way between La Boisselle and Contalmaison, and to limit the offensive on our left to a slow and methodical advance." *

For the next fortnight the British troops slowly forged their way forward through the enemy's defensive positions in spite of a stubborn resistance on the part of the Germans, and, by the end of the first phase of the battle on the 17th of July, they had succeeded in establishing their line from a point just west of Hardecourt-aux-Bois, where touch was maintained with the French, northward along the eastern edge of Trônes Wood to Longueval; whence the front bent westward past Bazentin-le-Grand to the northern corner of Bazentin-le-Petit round Bazentin-le-Petit Wood past the southern face of Pozières to a point a little to the north of Ovillers la Boisselle.†

In the second phase of the battle, which extended from the latter part of July to the end of the second week in September, the main struggle raged for the possession of the high ground lying between Delville Wood and the Somme, whilst a vigorous pressure had also to be maintained on the remainder of the front in order to strengthen the British positions on the Ancre and to secure the hold which had already been gained on the main ridge west of Delville Wood. By dint of the most determined fighting the British and French troops pushed back the enemy, who obstinately contested every inch of the ground, with the result that by the 12th of September, the British line ran from about 2,000 yards south-west of Combles along the eastern edge of Leuze Wood, round the eastern sides of Ginchy and Delville Wood, and thence westward skirting High Wood and north of Pozières. On the right the French had also made con-

---

* *See* " Sir Douglas Haig's Despatches," p. 26. In order to enable Sir Henry Rawlinson " to concentrate his attention on the portion of the front where the attack was to be pushed home," the British Commander-in-Chief now placed the conduct of the operations between La Boisselle and Serre under the command of General Hubert Gough to whom he gave the two northern corps of the Fourth Army.

† *See* " Sir Douglas Haig's Despatches," pp. 31, 32.

siderable progress, having reached a line running approximately from Cléry-sur-Somme northward to le Forest and a point just south of Combles.*

(3) THE XIV CORPS TRANSFERRED TO THE FOURTH ARMY—SITUATION ON THE FOURTH ARMY FRONT—PREPARATIONS FOR THE ATTACK ON THE MORVAL—LESBŒUFS—GUEUDECOURT LINE BY THE GUARDS DIVISION.

About the middle of August the XIV Corps was moved to the Fourth Army area south of the Ancre in order to replace the XIII Corps on the battle front between Longueval and Combles. Lord Cavan † established his headquarters at Etinghem near Bray-sur-Somme on the 16th of August and the southern movement of his divisions began soon afterwards, the 20th Division being the first to leave the northern area.

The movement of the Guards Division to the area of the Fourth Army began on the 19th of August. On that day the 3rd Guards Bde. moved to Bus-les-Artois. The following day the 1st Guards Bde. moved into Bois de Warnimont, while the 3rd Guards Bde. reached Vauchelles and Sarton. On the 21st, the 2nd Guards Bde. moved to Bus-les-Artois, where Major-General Feilding established his headquarters.

During the next few days the Guards continued their journey southward, the troops moving partly by road and partly by rail according to a pre-arranged time-table which worked without a hitch of any description. On the 25th of August the division rejoined the XIV Corps.‡ On that day divisional headquarters was opened at Treux; the 1st Guards Bde. was at Méaulte; the 2nd at Morlancourt; and the 3rd at Vignacourt.§

* *See* " Sir Douglas Haig's Despatches," p. 39.

† Lord Cavan was obliged about this time to go into hospital for a few weeks. During his absence the XIV Corps was commanded by Lieut.-General Morland, G.O.C. the X Corps.

‡ The divisional Artillery rejoined the division on the 1st of September and was billetted in Sailly-le-Sec and Vaux.

§ After relieving the XIII Corps the XIV Corps was composed of the following divisions:—the Guards, 5th, 6th, 16th, 20th and 56th. The last-named division joined the corps on the 1st of

The Guards reached their new destination, therefore, at the time when the troops of the Fourth Army were still endeavouring to break their way through the enemy's defences at Guillemont and in its vicinity. The capture of this village and of Falfemont Farm south-east of it was achieved by the XIV Corps in the course of operations which extended from the 3rd to the 5th of September—operations in which the Guards were not called upon to take part.*

For the ten days following its arrival in the Treux area the division remained in corps reserve and the opportunity was utilized to give the troops as much training as was possible for the hard work in store for them. Every phase in an attack upon the enemy's prepared positions was rehearsed by the various battalions in conditions which were made as realistic as circumstances would allow. Every detail of the equipment and arms to be carried by the fighting troops was carefully studied and decided upon.† The actual training of their battalions was of course left entirely to the commanding officers, but Major-General Feilding and his brigadiers were generally present at these attack practices and exercised a close supervision over all the work done. In this way a uniformity of tactical doctrine was established throughout the division which was to prove of great value in the confused fighting in which the Guards were so soon to be engaged.‡

In view of the difficulties which he anticipated with regard to the maintenance of communications in the forward area, Major-General Feilding instituted special signalling courses

September. The 6th Division did not reach the area of the XIV Corps until the 7th of that month.

* The capture of these strongly fortified positions, together with Leuze Wood and the south-eastern portion of Delville Wood, broke down a barrier which had delayed the British advance for seven weeks.

† A special parade for this purpose was held on the 3rd of September, a detachment from each Guards brigade carrying out an attack practice. Different " fighting orders " were worn by the leading and rear waves. W.D., Guards Division, September, 1916, App. 1063.

‡ A conference, attended by the staffs of the Guards brigades, C.R.E., etc., was held at divisional headquarters on the 28th of August, when the probable task of the division was outlined and the methods of carrying it out were discussed and settled. *See* W.D., 2nd Guards Bde., App. (unnumbered).

in each Guards brigade. All forms of visual signalling were assiduously practised and eight additional runners were trained in each battalion.* The divisional Signal Company was also instructed to carry forward a single trunk system to the most advanced point possible rather than to endeavour to set up and maintain independent lines to the various units engaged in the battle.† The Major-General came to this decision because he felt that one main line on which the whole of the energies of the divisional Signal Company could be concentrated, would be easier to keep in working order, and consequently more reliable, than numerous lines the satisfactory maintenance of which, in conditions such as existed on the Somme, was beyond the powers of the signallers available.‡ On the 3rd of September § a conference was held at divisional headquarters at which Major-General Feilding indicated to his brigadiers and commanding officers the

---

* Twenty-seven men from each brigade were also instructed in the handling of pigeons. *See* W.D., Guards Division, September, 1916.

† All lines worked well during the attack on the 15th of September, although the necessary equipment was hard to procure. The bad state of the roads made the use of despatch riders in the forward area impossible. Cavalry messengers were, therefore, used. The contact aeroplanes and pigeons both did satisfactory service. *See* W.D., Guards Divisional Signal Company, September, 1916.

‡ Only one casualty occurred in the division during this period of training. Second-Lieutenant C. de L. Leach, 1st Bn. Scots Guards, was mortally wounded whilst examining bombs at Morlancourt and was awarded the Albert Medal in Gold as a posthumous recognition of his conspicuous gallantry. The following are the terms of the award :—
" In France on September 3rd, 1916, Second-Lieutenant Leach was detonating bombs in buildings in which two non-commissioned officers were also at work when the fuze of one of the bombs ignited. Shouting a warning he made for the door, carrying the bomb pressed close to his body, but on reaching the door he found a party of men assembling for church parade, so that he could not throw the bomb away without exposing them to grave danger. He continued, therefore, to press the bomb to his body till it exploded and mortally wounded him. Second-Lieutenant Leach might easily have saved his life by throwing the bomb away, or dropping it on the ground, and seeking shelter, but either course would have endangered the lives of those in or around the building. He sacrificed his own life to save the lives of others." *See* also W.D., 1st Bn. Scots Guards, September, 1916.

This is the first instance of an officer of the Brigade of Guards being awarded this much prized decoration.

§ *See* W.D., Guards Division, September, 1916, App. 1069.

intentions of the XIV Corps commander in the next advance of the Fourth Army which was provisionally fixed for the 15th of September. The general idea was that, so soon as the line Leuze Wood—Ginchy had been definitely secured, the Guards and the 6th and 56th Divisions should attack the enemy's positions between Ginchy and Flers, in order to gain possession of the line Morval—Lesbœufs—Gueudecourt, in conjunction with a French advance on the right.*

Two Guards brigades were to be employed in the initial attack with the third in divisional reserve. The advance would have to take place on a narrow front of probably not more than 1,000 yards. The exact tactical formations to be adopted in the coming offensive were discussed at some length at this conference as in view of the narrowness of the front and the open nature of the country it was clear that the troops would be terribly exposed to the enemy's artillery fire. Major-General Feilding eventually decided, with the general approval of those present, that the attacking brigades should advance with a maximum number of men in the front ranks and in as little depth as possible in the hope that they would thus escape the German artillery barrage which was certain to be laid down as soon as the assault had been launched. The brigade in reserve was to move forward as closely as possible on the heels of the leading brigades and its commander was told to seize the most favourable opportunity for passing through the barrage and to keep his troops in hand as long as he could.

* "The general plan of the combined Allied attack which was opened on the 15th September was to pivot on the high ground south of the Ancre and north of the Albert—Bapaume road, while the Fourth Army devoted its whole effort to the rearmost of the enemy's original systems of defence between Morval and Le Sars. Should our success in this direction warrant it, I made arrangements to enable me to extend the left of the attack to embrace the villages of Martinpuich and Courcelette. As soon as our advance on this front had reached the Morval line, the time would have arrived to bring forward my left across the Thiepval Ridge. Meanwhile on my right our Allies arranged to continue the line of advance, in close cooperation with me, from the Somme to the slopes above Combles; but directing their main effort northwards against the villages of Rancourt and Frégicourt, so as to complete the isolation of Combles and open the way for their attack upon Sailly-Saillisel." *See* "Sir Douglas Haig's Despatches," p. 41.

(4) THE 3RD GUARDS BRIGADE RELIEVES THE 47TH AND 48TH INFANTRY BDES. IN THE LINE AT GINCHY, 9TH–10TH OF SEPTEMBER—GERMAN COUNTER-ATTACKS IN THE NEIGHBOURHOOD OF GINCHY—ATTEMPT TO CAPTURE THE " QUADRILATERAL "—INTER-BRIGADE RELIEF ON THE GUARDS DIVISIONAL FRONT.

On the 8th of September Brig.-General Corkran, 3rd Guards Bde., established his headquarters at Carnoy, the road between which village and Wedge Wood his troops were engaged in repairing. The following day, in the evening about 7 o'clock, he received orders to relieve the 47th and 48th Infantry Bdes. which had suffered severely during the day in an attack upon Ginchy and the " Quadrilateral," a strongly fortified defensive work on the Ginchy—Morval road.*

The 3rd Guards Bde. with the 3rd Guards Bde. Machine-Gun Company † accordingly moved forward from Carnoy at 8 p.m., the 4th Bn. Grenadier Guards being ordered to relieve the 47th Infantry Bde., and the 1st Bn. Welsh Guards, the 48th Infantry Bde.‡ The 1st Bn. Grenadier Guards moved to Bernafay Wood in support of the two leading

* In order to facilitate the arrangements for the intended attack upon the Gueudecourt—Lesbœufs—Morval line, it was considered advisable first to gain possession of Ginchy. With this object in view, therefore, an attack was launched in the afternoon of the 9th of September by the 16th Division which had relieved the 20th Division in the line on the 4th of September. The 48th Infantry Bde. carried Ginchy by assault and advanced through the village to some trenches on its north-eastern outskirts. The 47th Infantry Bde. was not equally successful, for, after losing many men, it found its advance checked in front of the " Quadrilateral." On the right of the 47th Infantry Bde. the 167th Infantry Bde. (56th Division) succeeded in forcing its way into Bouleaux Wood, but then could make no farther progress owing to the fact that its left flank was uncovered as a result of the failure of the 47th Infantry Bde. to reach its objective.

† For a summary of the work of the machine-gun companies in the operations on the Somme, see p. 177.

‡ On coming into the line these two battalions were under the orders of the 16th Division. Major-General Feilding took over the command of the sector at 10 a.m., 10th of September, when his headquarters was opened at Minden Post. See W.D., Guards Division, September, 1916.

battalions, while the 2nd Bn. Scots Guards remained in the Carnoy area in brigade reserve.

The 4th Bn. Grenadier Guards had no little difficulty in finding the positions occupied by the units of the 47th Infantry Bde., which lay a little to the south-east of Ginchy south of the "Quadrilateral," and it was not until 5 a.m. on the 10th of September that the relief was completed.* The situation on this part of the front at that period in the day was decidedly obscure, and it was some time before Lord Henry Seymour could get into touch with his various companies. The trenches in which the Grenadiers found themselves were broken and disconnected, and were filled with the dead and wounded of the 47th Infantry Bde. Throughout the day every effort was made to improve the line, but the troops were exposed to the persistent fire of the enemy's artillery and suffered a good many casualties.

On the left the Welsh Guards on the outskirts of Ginchy were in an even more uncomfortable position. The relief of the 48th Infantry Bde. was completed about 3.30 a.m.; but Lieut.-Colonel Murray-Threipland then found that he was not in touch with the Grenadiers on his right and for a time his battalion was in a precarious position, as the Germans made a vigorous counter-attack almost immediately after it took over the line and drove back the Prince of Wales's Company which was trying to gain touch with the 4th Bn. Grenadier Guards. The situation was a dangerous one until, in response to a request by Lieut.-Colonel Murray-Threipland for reinforcements, Brig.-General Corkran sent forward a company of the 1st Bn. Grenadier Guards, under the command of Captain E. N. Vaughan, to the assistance of the Welsh Guards. The Grenadiers held the right flank while the Welsh Guards reorganized, and subsequently some of the lost ground was regained and the line re-established north of Ginchy.†

* See "The Grenadier Guards in the Great War," vol. ii. pp. 128, 129.

† See "History of the Welsh Guards," pp. 114–119. In this engagement at Ginchy the 1st Bn. Welsh Guards lost 10 officers and 195 other ranks, killed, wounded or missing. See W.D., 1st Bn. Welsh Guards, September, 1917.

DISPOSITIONS FOR THE ATTACK

During the night of the 11th, the Welsh Guards were relieved and withdrew to Bernafay Wood. The front which they had occupied was then divided into two sectors—one being held by the 1st Bn. Grenadier Guards, the other by the 2nd Bn. Scots Guards. On the right of this brigade front the troops of the 6th Division relieved the 4th Bn. Grenadier Guards which was withdrawn to Happy Valley Camp near Fricourt. The line of the Guards Division was then held by the 3rd Guards Bde. with the 1st Bn. Grenadier Guards and the 2nd Bn. Scots Guards from right to left.

In the early hours of the morning of the 12th, a gallant attempt was made by a company of the 1st Bn. Grenadier Guards, under the command of Captain A. C. Graham,* to bomb its way across the gap in the line south-east of Ginchy and to attack the southern end of the "Quadrilateral." This attempt, and also a subsequent one carried out later in the morning in conjunction with troops of the 56th Division moving forward from Bouleaux Wood, ended in failure owing to the intensity of the enemy's machine-gun fire.†

During the night of the 12th–13th of September the 3rd Guards Bde. was relieved in the line by the 1st Guards Bde. and the 2nd Guards Bde., and moved back to Happy Valley Camp where it remained until the 14th when it advanced to Trônes Wood in support of the forthcoming attack by the two other brigades.

(5) THE 1ST AND 2ND GUARDS BDES. IN THE LINE—PREPARATIONS AND DISPOSITIONS FOR THE ATTACK OF THE 15TH OF SEPTEMBER.

The front of the Guards Division was now held by the two brigades which were to carry out the attack on the Gueudecourt—Lesbœufs—Morval line. The 2nd Guards Bde., with its headquarters in Dummy trench west of Trônes Wood, held the right, and the 1st Guards Bde., with its headquarters in Bernafay Wood, the left of the line.

* Captain Graham was killed by a shell in the afternoon. *See* W.D., 1st Bn. Grenadier Guards, September, 1916.

† *See* "The Grenadier Guards in the Great War," vol. ii. pp. 113, 114.

The 15th of September was fixed as the date of the attack. The XIV Corps, as already arranged, was to advance with three divisions in the line—the 56th Division on the right, the 6th Division in the centre, and the Guards on the left.*

Four objectives were assigned to the Guards Division.† The first of these—the " green line "—lay about 1,000 yards to the north and north-east of Ginchy, and ran in a south-easterly direction from a point just south-east of the Ginchy—Gueudecourt road to a point beyond the German defensive work known as the " Triangle." The second objective—the " brown line "—the capture of which was to be effected by the left attacking brigade while the brigade on the right held firm, ran almost due north from the " green line " for about 500 yards and then swung westward towards the Ginchy—Gueudecourt road. The " blue line "—the third objective—which was from 800 to 1,000 yards east of the " brown line," ran from a point on the Flers—Lesbœufs road about 800 yards north-west of Lesbœufs in a southerly direction in front of that village. The fourth objective—the " red line "—lay just east of Lesbœufs.

The boundary line between the Guards Division and the 14th Division (XV Corps) on its left ran from the junction of the Ginchy—Flers and the Ginchy—Gueudecourt roads, a little to the north of Ginchy, along the latter road for about 800 yards, and thence in a north-easterly direction towards Lesbœufs. On the right flank the boundary line between the Guards and the 6th Division was about 500 yards south of the Ginchy—Lesbœufs road. Each Guards brigade had to move forward on a front approximately of about 500 yards. The attack was to be preceded by an artillery bombardment which was to begin on the 12th of September and to be carried on daily from 6 a.m. to 6 p.m. until zero hour on the 15th.‡ Half the available artillery was to be employed in firing a creeping barrage to cover the advance

* *See* Map facing p. 164.
† The 5th Division was to be kept in XIV Corps reserve and the 20th Division in General Reserve.
‡ Night firing was to continue from the 12th to the 14th inclusive. *See* W.D., C.R.A., Guards Division, September, 1916.

of the infantry,* and the other half was to put down a stationary barrage which was to be lifted back as soon as the creeping barrage got level with it. The creeping barrage was to open 100 yards in front of the starting off line of the infantry and was to be carried forward at the rate of 50 yards a minute until it reached a line 200 yards in front of the first objective when it was to be made stationary.†

Nine tanks were detailed to cooperate with the Guards, the day marking the first appearance of this new engine of warfare on the field of battle.‡ Very careful instructions were laid down for their employment.

The attacking troops were instructed on no account to wait for them as it was not expected that they would exceed the pace of 15 yards a minute over heavily shelled ground.

The Cavalry Corps was to be disposed in depth by 10 a.m. on the 15th of September, with its head at Carnoy, ready so soon as the infantry had reached its final objectives, to move forward and seize the high ground Rocquigny—Villers-au-Flos—Riencourt-les-Bapaume—Bapaume.§

On the 13th of September the troops of the two attacking Guards brigades were disposed as follows:—in the right sector of the divisional front held by the 2nd Guards Bde. Brig.-General Ponsonby had the 2nd Bn. Irish Guards ‖ in the front line, with the 1st Bn. Scots Guards in support. The 3rd Bn. Grenadier Guards and the 1st Bn. Coldstream

---

* *See* Guards Divisional Artillery Operation Order, No. 49.

† Gaps of 100 yards in width were to be left in the creeping barrage to allow of the forward movement of the tanks to the first and second objectives. The advance to the third and subsequent objectives was to be led by the tanks preceded by a barrage. The infantry was to follow without any covering barrage. *See* "Instructions for employment of tanks" to accompany Guards Division Order, No. 75, Appendix IV.

‡ The number of tanks was subsequently increased to ten. *See* Supplementary Instructions attached to Guards Division Order No. 75.

§ *See* Guards Division Order No. 76, Appendix IV.

‖ Major Rocke took over the command of the battalion on the 11th of September when Lieut.-Colonel Reid was placed on the sick list owing to trench fever. *See* W.D., 2nd Bn. Irish Guards, September, 1916.

Guards remained in brigade reserve.* In the left sector, held by the 1st Guards Bde., Brig.-General Pereira had the 2nd Bn. Grenadier Guards in the front line with the 1st Bn. Irish Guards in support in Trônes Wood. The 2nd and 3rd Bns. Coldstream Guards, which were to carry out the attack on the 15th, remained at Carnoy.

(6) EVENTS OF THE 13TH AND 14TH OF SEPTEMBER—ASSEMBLY OF THE GUARDS BATTALIONS FOR THE ATTACK.

In the morning of the 13th of September Major-General Feilding held a conference at divisional headquarters at which he gave his final instructions to his brigadiers and commanding officers. He emphasized the great importance before the main attack was launched of driving the Germans out of any trenches they might be occupying on the north-eastern outskirts of Ginchy, pointing out that any opposition from this quarter at the outset of the day's fighting on the 15th of September might hamper the whole operation and would assuredly lead to many additional casualties.†

The two particular places just north-east of Ginchy—the possession of which by the enemy appeared to the Major-General to be of most consequence—had been cleared of Germans before the 2nd Bn. Irish Guards and the 2nd Bn. Grenadier Guards took over the line; but, in order to gain more ground for the launching of the attack on the right of the Guards, it was thought advisable to take possession of a

* These two battalions were to carry out the attack on the 15th of September.
† So much convinced was the Major-General of the necessity of clearing up the situation on the immediate front of each of the Guards brigades before the attack began that in the afternoon of the 13th he wrote to the two brigadiers instructing them to seize and consolidate any trenches in close proximity to their lines which might be held by the enemy. He also laid stress upon the importance of settling the forming up places of battalions that night so that nothing might be left to chance. "This is perhaps the greatest battle that has ever been fought. The Guards Division has been specially selected for the operation—the eyes of the whole of England will be watching us and I have absolute confidence that we shall live up to our reputation; but we must start without initial difficulties." *See* W.D., Guards Division, App. 1119.

THE ORCHARD CLEARED OF GERMANS

trench east of Ginchy which actually formed part of the "Quadrilateral." The G.O.C., the 6th Division, organized an artillery bombardment of this trench, and a company of the 2nd Bn. Irish Guards was then ordered to cooperate with troops of the 71st Infantry Bde. in an attack upon it on the night of the 13th of September. This attack appears to have been hurriedly and inadequately organized, and it ended in failure. The wire-cutting by the artillery had been ineffective and the company of Irish Guards was mown down by rifle and machine-gun fire, only thirty survivors returning to the British line.* The attack of the 71st Infantry Bde. was equally unsuccessful.†

During the night of the 13th–14th of September the 2nd Bn. Grenadier Guards advancing along the Ginchy—Flers road drove the enemy out of the orchard about 400 yards north of Ginchy. Here the Grenadiers dug themselves in as they were unable to make any more progress.‡

The 14th of September passed uneventfully.§ Divisional headquarters was moved forward to Bernafay Wood and the brigadiers and commanding officers were busily employed in making their final arrangements for the attack the following day. It was laid down ‖ that the assaulting battalions should advance in four successive waves with a frontage of four platoons, the men being in single file in columns of half companies, and the platoons 500 yards apart. Two machine guns were to accompany each of the leading battalions and

---

* See W.D.; 2nd Bn. Irish Guards, September, 1916.

† See "The Irish Guards in the Great War," vol. ii. pp. 98, 99. "I attribute the failure of the attack to the feebleness of the barrage which preceded it. The trench which No. 2 Company had to attack was full of the enemy, who shot at their ease over the parapet supported by machine guns. The men behaved with great gallantry, and only stopped when ordered to do so." Extract from the report of Major C. A. Rocke, commanding 2nd Bn. Irish Guards.

‡ This small advance cost the battalion 100 casualties. See W.D., 2nd Bn. Grenadier Guards, Narrative, 13th of September, 1916.

§ The 2nd Bn. Grenadier Guards record that their trenches were bombarded all day and much knocked about before they handed over to the assaulting battalions. See Narrative in the battalion War Diary. On the right the 2nd Bn. Irish Guards records a quiet day. See W.D., 2nd Bn. Irish Guards, September, 1916.

‖ See W.D., 2nd Guards Bde. O.O. No. 129/G, shows formations.

four were to move forward with each supporting battalion. Three more machine guns were to follow in rear with a Stokes mortar on each flank.

During the night of the 14th–15th of September the troops of the Guards Division went into their respective positions of assembly.* The night was a cold one and the men suffered a good deal from the exposure, but there were singularly few casualties from the enemy's artillery and machine-gun fire. This immunity was largely due to the skill with which the various commanding officers avoided as much as possible the areas which were usually bombarded by the enemy's gunners. The almost invariable uniformity of the Germans' artillery programme during the war was often exceedingly helpful to their opponents.

On the right, on the front of the 2nd Guards Bde., the 3rd Bn. Grenadier Guards and the 1st Bn. Coldstream Guards took over the line from the 1st Bn. Scots Guards and the 2nd Bn. Irish Guards. The trenches now occupied by the Grenadiers ran about 300 yards east of Ginchy, those of the Coldstream on their left being astride the Ginchy—Lesbœufs road. The Scots Guards remained in rear of the Grenadiers and the Irish Guards in rear of the Coldstream. The front of the 6th Division, on the right of the 2nd Guards Bde., ran in a south-easterly direction along the Ginchy—Combles road about 300 yards behind the right flank of the 1st Bn. Scots Guards.

On the front of the 1st Guards Bde. the 2nd and 3rd Bns. Coldstream Guards, on the right and left of the line respectively, relieved the 2nd Bn. Grenadier Guards and the 1st Bn. Irish Guards.† The starting off position of the 2nd Bn. Coldstream Guards was in the orchard recently captured by the 2nd Bn. Grenadier Guards, while that of its sister battalion was a little farther to the left facing in a north-westerly

---

* The divisional front was about 1,200 yards in length. There was no front trench system to accommodate this assembly of troops, and the various positions were indicated by means of tapes and sign posts provided by the R.E. *See* p. 181.

† The line of the 1st Guards Bde. was held by the 2nd Bn. Grenadier Guards with the 1st Bn. Irish Guards in support until the two Coldstream battalions came in.

direction towards Flers. The 2nd Bn. Grenadier Guards remained in rear of the 2nd Bn. Coldstream Guards and the 1st Bn. Irish Guards in rear of the 3rd Bn. Coldstream Guards. On the left of the 1st Guards Bde. the troops of the 14th Division (XV Corps) held the eastern outskirts of Delville Wood, but between the two British forces the Germans were still in occupation of some trenches out of which the 14th Division had been unable to eject them.

The 3rd Guards Bde., which, it will be remembered, was in divisional reserve, moved forward into Trônes Wood and Guillemont during the night.

The line from which the Guards Division was called upon to launch its attack was one of considerable tactical difficulty. The semi-circular and cramped position in which the two attacking brigades were placed rendered their advance singularly dependent upon the ability of the 6th and 14th Divisions to clear their flanks. It was obvious before the battle began that if the troops of these divisions were unable to make their way forward, the Guards would be exposed to short range fire from the " Quadrilateral " on the right and from the German trenches lying between Ginchy and Delville Wood on the left.

(7) THE ATTACK BY THE 1ST AND 2ND GUARDS BRIGADES ON THE 15TH OF SEPTEMBER.

Throughout the night of the 14th–15th of September the British heavy artillery maintained a continuous bombardment of the enemy's positions opposite the front of the Fourth Army. At 6.20 a.m., zero hour, on the 15th, the creeping barrage came down and the two Guards brigades moved forward to the attack. For the first time in the history of the regiment three battalions of Coldstream Guards attacked in line together, advancing, as one eye-witness described the scene, " as steadily as though they were walking down the Mall." *

From the first moment of the attack the troops were

* *See* " The War Story of Dillwyn Parrish Starr," p. 88.

called upon to fight their way across the broken and featureless country which lay between them and their objective. The enemy's riflemen and machine gunners, posted in slits of wrecked trenches and shell-holes, held on to their ground with the utmost gallantry and tenacity. The inability of the troops of the 6th Division on the right to make any progress north of the Ginchy—Combles road * also added materially to the difficulties of the 2nd Guards Bde., its leading battalions in addition to having to face the fire of the enemy in front being fiercely enfiladed by machine-gun fire from the " Quadrilateral." † In order, if possible, to check this enfilade fire, Lieut.-Colonel Sergison-Brooke, commanding the 3rd Bn. Grenadier Guards ‡ on the right of the brigade front, threw out a defensive flank § on the right, while the remainder of his battalion pressed on to the first objective. Meanwhile, the 1st Bn. Coldstream Guards, on the left, in the impetus of its advance had come under the British creeping barrage. In the confusion caused by this mishap it lost its bearings amid the smoke, and moved forward in a northerly, instead of in a north-easterly, direction. This swinging to the left by the 1st Bn. Coldstream Guards unfortunately resulted in a similar movement on

---

* The failure of the 6th Division to advance " was due to inadequate artillery preparation which arose from lack of time for reconnaissance, difficulties of weather and ground, and an artillery which had taken over the front on the previous day." *See* W.D., 6th Division, September, 1916.

† " About 300 yards from the jumping off line we came on a practically continuous line of badly knocked about trenches held by about half a battalion of Germans. They shot at us till we got to within about 20 yards or less, and then tried to bolt, but as far as I could see most of them were shot or caught by our barrage into which they ran back." Note supplied by Colonel Sergison-Brooke.

‡ Most of the casualties of the 3rd Bn. Grenadier Guards occurred on the right flank. These included Lieut.-Colonel B. N. S. Brooke (wounded), and most of the officers. *See* W.D., 3rd Bn. Grenadier Guards, September, 1916.

§ Later in the day, after the capture of the " green line," it was found possible to get a machine gun into a position from which its fire could be brought to bear on the " Quadrilateral." This had the effect of checking the enemy's enfilade fire from this direction and the Grenadiers who had formed the defensive flank rejoined their battalion on the " green line."

2ND GUARDS BDE. REACHES FIRST OBJECTIVE

the part of the two other battalions of the same regiment on the front of the 1st Guards Bde.,* and also of a portion of the 3rd Bn. Grenadier Guards on the right of the 2nd Guards Bde.,† thus making a gap in the line of attack just north of the Guinchy—Lesbœufs road. The loss of cohesion caused by the change of direction and by the intensity of the German machine-gun fire to a certain extent broke up the attack of the 2nd Guards Bde. and led to an intermingling of units, officers and men fighting their way forward in small groups without being able to pay much attention to what was happening on their flanks. But nothing daunted, and in spite of heavy losses,‡ the 3rd Bn. Grenadier Guards and the 1st Bn. Coldstream Guards, reinforced by men from both the supporting battalions, succeeded in reaching the line of their first objective. Efforts were then made to establish the new position—a line of broken trenches lying north-east of the Ginchy—Lesbœufs road. The Germans in the " Triangle "—a strong point just in front of the first

---

* " The check (caused by the 1st Bn. Coldstream Guards coming under the British creeping barrage) was momentary, but caused the whole Battalion to swing slightly to the left. This led the 2nd and 3rd Battalions Coldstream in the 1st Guards Brigade also to ease off slightly to the left, and, as often happens, the slight deviation was exaggerated as the advance continued, and soon all the Coldstream battalions were moving in a northerly instead of a north-easterly direction." *See* " The Grenadier Guards in the Great War." vol. ii. p. 100.

† " When the 1st Bn. Coldstream began to swing to the left a gap was made between the two front battalions of the 2nd Guards Brigade, which widened out as the advance progressed. Observing this, Captain Oliver Lyttelton pushed up 100 men of the 3rd Battalion Grenadiers to fill the intermediate space, but as the gap gradually extended, and the smoke and dust made it impossible for them to see where they were going, these hundred men were able to keep touch with the 1st Battalion Coldstream only, and became detached from the rest of the Battalion." *See ib.* p. 101.

‡ Lieut.-Colonel the Honble. Guy Baring, commanding the 1st Bn. Coldstream Guards, was killed. He had proved himself a capable commander and his death was deeply regretted by all ranks. The Coldstream went into action with 17 officers and 690 other ranks. They came out of the battle with 3 officers, one of whom was wounded, and 221 other ranks. The Grenadiers lost 17 officers either killed or wounded out of the 22 who went into action, and had 395 casualties in the other ranks. *See* W.D's., 1st Bn. Coldstream and 3rd Bn. Grenadier Guards, September, 1916.

objective—continued to hold out for some time longer, but, by about 11 a.m., their resistance had been overcome and the whole of the new position had been roughly consolidated.

Lieut.-Colonel Godman, commanding the 1st Bn. Scots Guards, came up about this time and assumed the command of the mixed force of Grenadiers, Coldstream, Scots Guards and Irish Guards, which had reached the first objective.*

The advance to the "green line" of the 1st Guards Bde. on the left of the divisional front must now be followed. Its two leading battalions—the 2nd and 3rd Bns. Coldstream Guards—were met by a withering machine-gun fire from hostile posts in the sunken road north of Ginchy and lost the majority of their officers and many of their rank and file before they had advanced 100 yards. For a few minutes the men hesitated, but Lieut.-Colonel J. Campbell, commanding the 2nd Battalion, rallied his troops magnificently.† A few notes from the hunting horn which he carried were sufficient to restore the confidence of the leading waves and the attack went forward in one headlong and irresistible rush. Followed by detachments of the 1st Bn. Irish Guards, the two Coldstream battalions swept over the ground to their first objective of which they were in possession at about 7.15 a.m. Large numbers of Germans were either killed or made prisoners, and several machine guns and trench mortars were captured.‡ The line actually reached was the "green line," but, owing to the loss of direction to which allusion has already been made,§ the leading battalions had reached it at a point more to the north than had been intended. They had, indeed, trespassed into the area assigned to the 14th Division. But, nevertheless, the 1st Guards Bde. on the left was in touch with the 2nd Guards Bde. on the right,

---

* *See* W.D., 2nd Bn. Irish Guards, September, 1916.

† "Very few troops would have attempted to go on against the tremendous fire, but the Coldstream, led by John Campbell, swung off their proper line, and went for the Boche like tigers, got into them with the bayonet, and killed every man of them." Extract from a letter of Major Aubrey Fletcher, Grenadier Guards.

‡ *See* p. 156.

§ *See* Report on Operations, 1st Guards Brigade.

the positions which the two Guards brigades had captured forming part of the enemy's defensive system running in a north-easterly direction from the northern edge of High Wood to the Longueval—Flers road south of the village of Flers and thence across the Ginchy—Lesbœufs road to the " Triangle."

The fact that the divisional line at this hour of the day was a more or less continuous one was largely due to the action of Lieut.-Colonel de Crespigny, commanding the 2nd Bn. Grenadier Guards. This battalion, it will be remembered, had been ordered to follow in rear of the 2nd Bn. Coldstream Guards.* After emerging from Ginchy, where his battalion had come under a heavy hostile artillery barrage, with his right, as ordered, on the Ginchy—Lesbœufs road, Lieut.-Colonel de Crespigny could see no sign of the Coldstream, but, knowing that his own men were in their right position, he decided to push forward and to carry out the instructions given to him.† He was still under the impression that the Coldstream had carried their appointed objective and were pushing on to the " brown line," and that the task, therefore, of his battalion was to occupy the captured position. But it soon became apparent that, far from having been driven out of the " green line " opposite the Grenadiers, the Germans were still in possession of an advanced trench in front of their main line of defence. Lieut.-Colonel de Crespigny's men were met with a hail of rifle and machine-gun bullets from this trench as well as from the flanks as soon as they began

---

* " The 2nd Battalion Grenadier Guards will move in rear of the 2nd and 3rd Battalions Coldstream Guards. When the latter advance to the assault of the second objective the 2nd Bn. Grenadier Guards will occupy the first objective until the 1st Battalion Irish Guards have passed through them ; they will then follow and support them in their attack on the fourth objective." *See* 1st Guards Bde. Order No. 78.

† " He sent a message to General Pereira and received the following reply : ' Your pigeon message timed 7.45 a.m. not quite clear. Irish Guards reported their headquarters in green line (first objective) and in touch with 41st Brigade on left at 8.45 a.m. You state no signs of Coldstream. Presume they are pushing on to next objective. Am sending bombs up.' " *See* " The Grenadier Guards in the Great War," vol. ii. p. 60.

to move forward.* They succeeded, however, in driving back the enemy, and the companies on the right then rushed the line of the first objective. Here they came in touch with the 3rd Battalion of their regiment and strengthened the right flank of the Guards Division † which, owing to the failure of the 6th Division to advance on the right, was in a dangerously exposed position. The companies on the left after a stiff fight gained possession of the section of the "green line" opposite to them. One company was then pushed out and at last succeeded in gaining touch with the Coldstream on its left, thus filling the gap in the divisional line.

To return now to the doings of the two Coldstream battalions.

After reaching the line of the first objective, Lieut.-Colonel Campbell was at first under the impression that his troops were on the line of the third objective,‡ so difficult was it in the torn and broken region in which he found himself to distinguish any guiding landmarks.§ But, after a conference held in a shell-hole with other commanding officers, he realized that he had only reached the first objective,‖ and he promptly decided to push forward

---

* "... they were in artillery formation instead of in line, marching forward under the impression that the two battalions of Coldstream were in front of them. To approach the trench with any prospect of success it was necessary to deploy into line, and in doing this they lost very heavily. Our creeping barrage had, so to speak, run away, and there was now no artillery support of any kind." See "The Grenadier Guards in the Great War," vol. ii. p. 61.

† A platoon of No. 1 Company with one machine gun is mentioned as having rendered great service here. See Narrative, 2nd Bn. Grenadier Guards.

‡ See 1st Guards Brigade, Report of Operations.

§ "Even had maps been issued to the officers a week, instead of a day or so, before the attack; even had those maps marked all known danger-points—such as the Ginchy—Flers sunk road; even had the kaleidoscopic instructions about the Brown and Yellow lines been more intelligible, or had the village of Ginchy been distinguishable from a map of the pitted moon—once the affair was launched there was little chance of seeing far or living long." See "The Irish Guards in the Great War," vol. i. p. 171.

‖ The Brigade Narrative says, "From 2.30 p.m. and throughout the remainder of the day Lieut.-Colonel Campbell and Lieut.-Colonel McCalmont both reported their position as being in our 3rd objective just N.W. of Lesbœufs."

to the next objective about 500 yards farther forward. Before doing so, however, he did all in his power to reorganize his mixed force, ordering men who belonged to battalions in the 2nd Guards Bde. to side-slip to the right and collecting the remnants of the 2nd and 3rd Bns. Coldstream Guards and 1st Bn. Irish Guards.

Then the advance was resumed, and the troops of the 1st Guards Bde., following the notes of their leader's hunting horn, with the same splendid courage and determination as had carried all before it in the first attack, speedily gained possession of their second objective—the "brown line." * Lieut.-Colonel Campbell at once pushed forward patrols towards the line of the third objective—the "blue line "— and sent back a message to Lieut.-Colonel McCalmont, 1st Bn. Irish Guards, asking him to bring up the remainder of his battalion to the support of the Coldstream.† This message reached Lieut.-Colonel McCalmont at about 11.15 a.m. He was at this time with the greater part of his battalion in the "green line." ‡ He at once led forward his men to the "brown line," where they set to work to improve the new positions, which consisted of a few shallow trenches with no traverses and afforded little protection against artillery fire.§ The enemy could now be observed

* At dusk the 1st Guards Bde. had 250–300 rifles—men belonging to each of its battalion—holding the second objective with its left on the Guinchy—Gueudecourt road in the XV Corps area. *See* 1st Guards Brigade Report on Operations.

† Lieut.-Colonel Campbell was awarded the Victoria Cross for his conspicuous gallantry and able leadership in this day's fighting. *See* Appendix III. "John Campbell was splendid; leading his men everywhere and fighting like a tiger." Extract from a letter of Major-General Feilding.

‡ Practically the whole of one company and part of another belonging to this battalion had become involved in the advance of the Coldstream, but the remainder had maintained the right direction, advancing in rear of the 2nd Bn. Grenadier Guards and reaching the "green line" about 200 yards north-west of the Ginchy—Lesbœufs road. *See* W.D., 1st Bn. Irish Guards, September, 1916.

§ It was deemed advisable as there was practically no field of fire from the new positions to consolidate a line of shell-holes about 300 yards in front of them. This line was held throughout the remainder of the day, but at nightfall the troops were withdrawn to the "brown line" upon the further consolidation of which every effort was then concentrated. *See* **Report of Operations, 1st Guards Brigade.**

retreating towards Bapaume, and the general impression among the officers who had reached this part of the line appears to have been that the enemy's resistance had been temporarily overcome and that a rapid continuation of the advance might result in the capture of Lesbœufs. In anticipation of a speedy resumption of the advance, therefore, a party of about 120 men was hurriedly organized on the front of the 2nd Guards Brigade, by Captain Sir Ian Colquhoun, 1st Bn. Scots Guards, and Captain O. Lyttelton, 3rd Bn. Grenadier Guards.* It pushed forward from the " green line " for a distance of about 800 yards. Here the leaders found a trench † where they decided to halt, as they realized that, although they might be able to seize Lesbœufs, the force at their disposal would be too small to hold the village. An urgent message was sent back asking for reinforcements and every effort was concentrated on converting the trench in which the party found itself into a defensive position. It was out of the question, however, for Brig.-General Ponsonby with the force which still remained at his disposal to contemplate a farther advance.‡ He applied, therefore, to the division for reinforcements. But by this time in the day it was clear to Major-General Feilding from information received from aeroplane observers that the Guards had not actually got so far as from previous reports he had been led to believe.§ He was also aware

* This party was subsequently joined by Major Rocke and some officers and men of the 2nd Bn. Irish Guards. *See* Captain Lyttelton's report to the 2nd Guards Brigade.

† This trench was just short of the third objective and was a little south of the Guinchy—Lesbœufs road (right brigade area). *See* W.D., 3rd Bn. Grenadier Guards, September, 1916. The left flank was refused until it met the road north-west of the first objective (" green line "). *See ib.*

‡ About midday after the capture and partial consolidation of " the green " and " brown lines " all ranks in the two Guards Bdes. were undoubtedly ready and anxious to continue the advance. But bayonets were lacking. All the battalions had been heavily engaged ; between them the two brigades had lost approximately three-quarters of their officers and two-thirds of their rank and file.

§ At 6 p.m. the XIV Corps commander telephoned that he was convinced that the division had no men in the " blue line " and that he was going to shell it. His information was received from contact aeroplanes. The misleading reports that the leading brigades had reached

FURTHER ADVANCE STAYED

that the want of success of the 6th and 14th Divisions rendered far from secure the situation on both his flanks and that the enemy was massing in Lesbœufs and Morval. In view of this knowledge, he decided that it would be unwise for him to commit the whole of his reserve, the 3rd Guards Bde., for which Brig.-General Ponsonby had asked, or to continue the advance to the third objective. He decided, however, to send forward the 4th Bn. Grenadier Guards to strengthen the right flank of the 2nd Guards Bde. and the 2nd Bn. Scots Guards to reinforce the 1st Guards Bde.* Meanwhile, the Germans, as soon as they realized that the British advance was not being pressed, had recovered from their first alarm, and began concentrating in small bodies. About 5 p.m. they came on in considerable strength and endeavoured first to envelop, then to rush the trench held by the advanced party which was now under the command of Major Rocke, 2nd Bn. Irish Guards. After a strenuous struggle, this gallant little band of Guardsmen succeeded in effecting its withdrawal to the main position, having suffered singularly few casualties,† considering the violent nature of the attack to which it had been subjected.

For the remainder of the evening and throughout the

---

the " blue line " were mostly received at divisional headquarters from F.O.O.'s. *See* W.D., Guards Division, September, 1916.

* The 3rd Guards Bde. had reached the area between Ginchy and Guillemont between 6 and 7 a.m. Here it remained until about 9.15 a.m. when its two leading battalions—the 4th Bn. Grenadier Guards on the right and the 2nd Bn. Scots Guards on the left—moved forward to the sunken road about 800 yards north-west of Ginchy, the two other battalions remaining south-west of that village. The two leading battalions remained in their position until they were sent to reinforce the attacking brigades. The Grenadiers, who had comparatively few casualties throughout the day, moved up to the assistance of the 2nd Guards Bde. at 5 p.m. The Scots Guards did not leave the sunken road until about 6 p.m. and suffered a good many casualties on their way to the " brown line." Two officers were killed and several others, including Lieut.-Colonel Tempest, the commanding officer, wounded. Major the Honble. R. Coke, who was sent for to take over the command of the battalion, was wounded on his way up to the front line, and consequently the command devolved temporarily on Lieut. W. A. Boyd. *See* W.D's., 3rd Guards Brigade and 2nd Bn. Scots Guards, September, 1916.

† About 60 per cent. of the party got back. *See* Captain Lyttelton's Report to the 2nd Guards Bde.

night of the 15th–16th of September, which was a wet and cold one, the tired troops holding the front of the 2nd Guards Bde. were called upon to resist numerous determined bombing attacks by the Germans.* But every attempt by the enemy to regain his lost positions was successfully defeated, and, on the 16th, when the 61st Infantry Bde. passed through, the Guards still held intact the line which they had gained at so heavy a cost.

On the front of the 1st Guards Bde. the night passed comparatively quietly.† On the 16th of September, however, the positions which the brigade continued to hold on the left of the divisional front were very severely bombarded throughout the day by the enemy's artillery,‡ and, by nightfall, when it was relieved by the troops of the 20th Division, all ranks were absolutely worn out—for five nights they had had practically no sleep.§ Human nature had reached the limit of its physical endurance. The attack by the Guards Division on the 15th of September will rank for all time as a splendid military achievement, and, if it failed to obtain a full measure of success, the failure was due to causes over which the attacking troops themselves had no control. There is little doubt that, had the divisions on the flanks of the Guards been able to carry out their share in the advance, the 1st and 2nd Guards Bdes. would have reached their final objectives.

The German defence was worthy of the highest praise

---

* " All that night the right flank of the 2nd Guards Brigade was being bombed, and Captain J. Hopley, who behaved with great gallantry, at one time had his men standing back to back and firing both ways." *See* " The Grenadier Guards in the Great War," vol. ii. p. 106.

† At 6.30 p.m. and 7.15 p.m. counter-attacks made from the right and right rear on the troops holding the 2nd objective (" brown line ") were repulsed. *See* Narrative of Operations, 1st Guards Bde.

‡ " The men were dumb—tired with mere work and suffering ; the few officers doubly tired out by that and the responsibility of keeping awake and thinking consecutively, even when their words of command clotted on their tongues through sheer weariness." *See* " The Irish Guards in the Great War," vol. i. p. 178.

§ " Casualties were comparatively light in spite of the fact that all lines were greatly overcrowded." *See* Narrative of Operations, 1st Guards Bde.

AN INFANTRY BATTLE

and it was only the splendid leadership of the regimental officers and the fine fighting qualities and admirable discipline of their men which enabled the Guards to break through the enemy's defences and to gain possession of their second objectives. It was an infantry battle throughout, for the tanks in this their first cooperation in the field with the troops of the Guards Division proved of little or no assistance to the infantry. They were late in crossing the parapet and so were unable to move forward in advance of the leading battalions.* The tank to which had been entrusted the important task of dislodging the Germans from their positions at the south-eastern corner of Delville Wood does not appear to have come into action. The remaining tanks wandered about in various directions and are reported to have done a certain amount of useful fighting on their own account either in the area of the Guards Division or in that of the 6th Division, but they certainly failed on this occasion to carry out their main task and were of no help to the infantry in the subduing of machine-gun fire.†

(8) THE ATTACK OF THE 3RD GUARDS BRIGADE ON THE 16TH OF SEPTEMBER—RELIEF OF THE GUARDS DIVISION.

The line actually reached by the two Guards brigades on the 15th of September ran from a point on the Ginchy—Lesbœufs road a little to the north of the "Triangle" in a north-westerly direction to a point approximately 300 yards from the Ginchy—Gueudecourt road about three-quarters

---

* At 3 a.m. on the 15th of September the officer in command of the tanks detailed to cooperate with the Guards reported to Major-General Feilding that seven of his machines were concentrated in their appointed rendezvous on the southern outskirts of Trônes Wood. *See* Major-General Feilding's Report to the XIV Corps, 19th of September, 1916. Apparently nine tanks were eventually allotted to the Guards Division, two of which had engine trouble before zero hour. *See* W.D., Guards Division, September, 1916.

† "To summarize the services rendered by the tanks—it must be admitted that they were of no assistance in the attack chiefly owing to the fact that they started too late to enable them to fulfil their proper task, and also owing to the fact that the moment they started they lost all sense of direction and wandered about aimlessly." *See* Report of Major-General G. P. Feilding, 19th of September, 1916.

of a mile north of Ginchy. It thus formed a slight salient on the front of the Fourth Army as the 6th Division on the right had failed to advance from its original line and the 14th Division on the left had only reached its first objective.

In the evening of the 15th Lord Cavan, as soon as he decided not to press the attack further that day, ordered the heavy artillery to bombard the line of the third objective; and, later, he ordered Major-General Feilding to make the necessary arrangements for the renewal of the infantry advance the following day. At 9.45 p.m. on the 15th, the Major-General issued his orders * accordingly.

On the right the assault was to be delivered by the 61st Infantry Bde., which was placed under the orders of Major-General Feilding, and, on the left, by the 3rd Guards Bde.

The first objective assigned to the attacking troops was the third objective of the previous day—the " blue line "—and the second, the fourth objective of the previous day—the " red line." The simultaneous attack by the troops of the 14th Division was to be directed upon Gueudecourt. The 3rd Guards Bde. was to advance approximately from the line held by the 1st Guards Bde. The attack was to be covered by the usual artillery barrages.†

* *See* Guards Division, Operation Order No. 78.

† Brig.-General Corkran was warned over the telephone at 7 p.m. on the 15th of September that his brigade would have to carry out this operation at 9.30 a.m. the following day. The written operation order reached him at 10.30 p.m. It contained all the arrangements for the attack, artillery barrages, etc. *See* W.D., 3rd Guards Bde., September, 1916.

There was never any question of the attacking troops relieving the troops already in the line as it is expressly stated in the operation order that the 1st and 2nd Guards Bdes. " will not be withdrawn to-night."

At midnight, on the 15th–16th, Brig.-General Corkran reported that the conditions under which he was being ordered to attack were extremely unfavourable, as the trenches in the front area were packed with other units and there were no alternative positions available for the assembly of the assaulting battalions. He went so far as to predict that the attack could not be successful. *See* W.D., Guards Division, September, 1916. This information was at once communicated to corps headquarters. In view of the fact that the Guards' attack formed part of an offensive along the front of the Fourth Army, the corps commander decided that it must take place as arranged.

ATTACK BY THE 3RD GUARDS BDE. 163

Brig.-General Corkran ordered the 1st Bn. Grenadier Guards and the 1st Bn. Welsh Guards, on the right and left respectively, to pass through the front held by the 1st Guards Bde. and to carry out the attack. The 4th Bn. Grenadier Guards, less two companies which had been attached the previous day to the 2nd Battalion of the same Regiment and were still with it, was instructed to follow in support of the leading battalions, while the 2nd Bn. Scots Guards was to remain in reserve, attached to the 1st Guards Bde.

The attack was fixed to begin at 9.25 a.m., but, owing to a variety of causes, neither of the leading battalions was in a position of readiness until about midday and the actual assault by the Guards was not launched until about 1 p.m.* By this time the 61st Infantry Bde. (20th Division) on the right had already reached its first objective and was consolidating its new positions.†

---

* The brigade orders for the attack did not reach the battalions of the 3rd Guards Bde. until after midnight on the 15th–16th of September. It was a pouring wet night and the condition of the ground east of Ginchy was very bad. The 1st Bn. Grenadier Guards lost its way while moving up to the front line :—" At 3 a.m. (on the 16th) the battalion moved up to be in readiness for the attack at 9.30 a.m., but our guides got lost, and, after three hours' wandering, the battalion returned to its old position when the order came at 9 a.m. to go up again so as to get in with the attack at 9.25 a.m. We arrived at a position just behind the starting point at 11.15 a.m." *See* W.D., 1st Bn. Grenadier Guards, September, 1916. The Welsh Guards had much the same experience as the Grenadiers. When he led his battalion forward, Lieut.-Colonel Murray-Threipland found the only available assembly positions occupied by the 4th Bn. Grenadier Guards and the 2nd Bn. Scots Guards. There was no time to dig new trenches and so he decided to withdraw the Welsh Guards to Ginchy. The War Diary of the 3rd Guards Bde. records that at 2.30 a.m. the Welsh Guards reported that there was great congestion in the area allotted to them for their assembly and that this information was passed on to divisional headquarters, presumably to confirm Brig.-General Corkran's previous message (*see* note on p. 162). At 8.30 a.m. a further report was received from the Welsh Guards stating that they could not reach the starting off line by 9.25 a.m. Orders were then issued to both the assaulting battalions to push forward to the attack as soon as possible. *See* W.D., 3rd Guards Bde., September, 1916.

† Reliable air reports stated that the 61st Infantry Bde. was on the line of its first objective at 1.5 p.m.—roughly from the divisional boundary on the right to the sunken road from Ginchy to Lesbœufs—

The troops of the 14th Division, on the left, had also begun their attack although they were making but slow progress. Any hope, therefore, which there might have been of taking the enemy by surprise was lost to the Guards, and, with the element of surprise eliminated, a small infantry attack over heavy country unsupported by artillery had little or no chance of success.* The casualties in the assaulting battalions were heavy from the moment the troops crossed the parapet, and, as on the previous day, the leading waves lost direction, moving towards the north instead of to the north-east.† This diversion became more pronounced as the advance proceeded owing partly to the failure of the 14th Division to clear the left flank of the 3rd Guards Bde., and partly to the quantity of standing crops in the area which made it difficult for the men to see where they were going. The 1st Bn. Grenadier Guards succeeded in advancing to the high ground west of Lesbœufs.‡ It there came under very heavy machine-gun fire, and, being unable to make any farther progress, was ordered to consolidate a position. On the left, the 1st Bn. Welsh Guards, after some stiff fighting, reached a line south of the Flers—Lesbœufs road,§ where it also was ordered to dig in.

The 4th Bn. Grenadier Guards was then sent up to strengthen the right flank of the 3rd Guards Bde. front, while the 3rd Bn. Coldstream Guards was employed to link up the line of the 1st Bn. Grenadier Guards with that of the Welsh Guards.

and that beyond the latter point the enemy was holding the trench in strength. *See* W.D., Guards Division, September, 1916.

* In the Diary of the 1st Bn. Grenadier Guards it is stated that the advance took place " without artillery or other support." The obvious inference is that the artillery barrage which had covered the attack of the 61st Infantry Bde. was not repeated when the Guards battalions went forward.

† " Casualties were heavy. . . . The advance had to be made in sectional rushes, and the assaulting troops got into standing crops, where they lost direction, and, mistaking Gueudecourt for Lesbœufs, swung round to the left." *See* " History of the Welsh Guards," p. 122.

‡ *See* W.D., 1st Bn. Grenadier Guards, September, 1916.

§ It was not until the next morning that the commanding officer found that his battalion was about 200 yards short of the first objective. *See* W.D., 1st Bn. Welsh Guards, September, 1916.

GUARDS DIVISION
Operations, Sept. 15, 1916

Assembly Trenches of 2nd & 1st Guards Brigades .... ———
1st Objective .... – – – – –
2nd   ,, ... –·—·—·—
3rd   ,, ... ••••••••••
4th   ,, ... xxxxxxxx
Trenches .... ∼∼∼∼∼
Germans on Left Flank before attack .... ♥♥♥♥♥♥♥

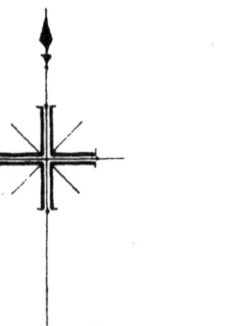

Scale
yds 1000   500   0   1000 Yds

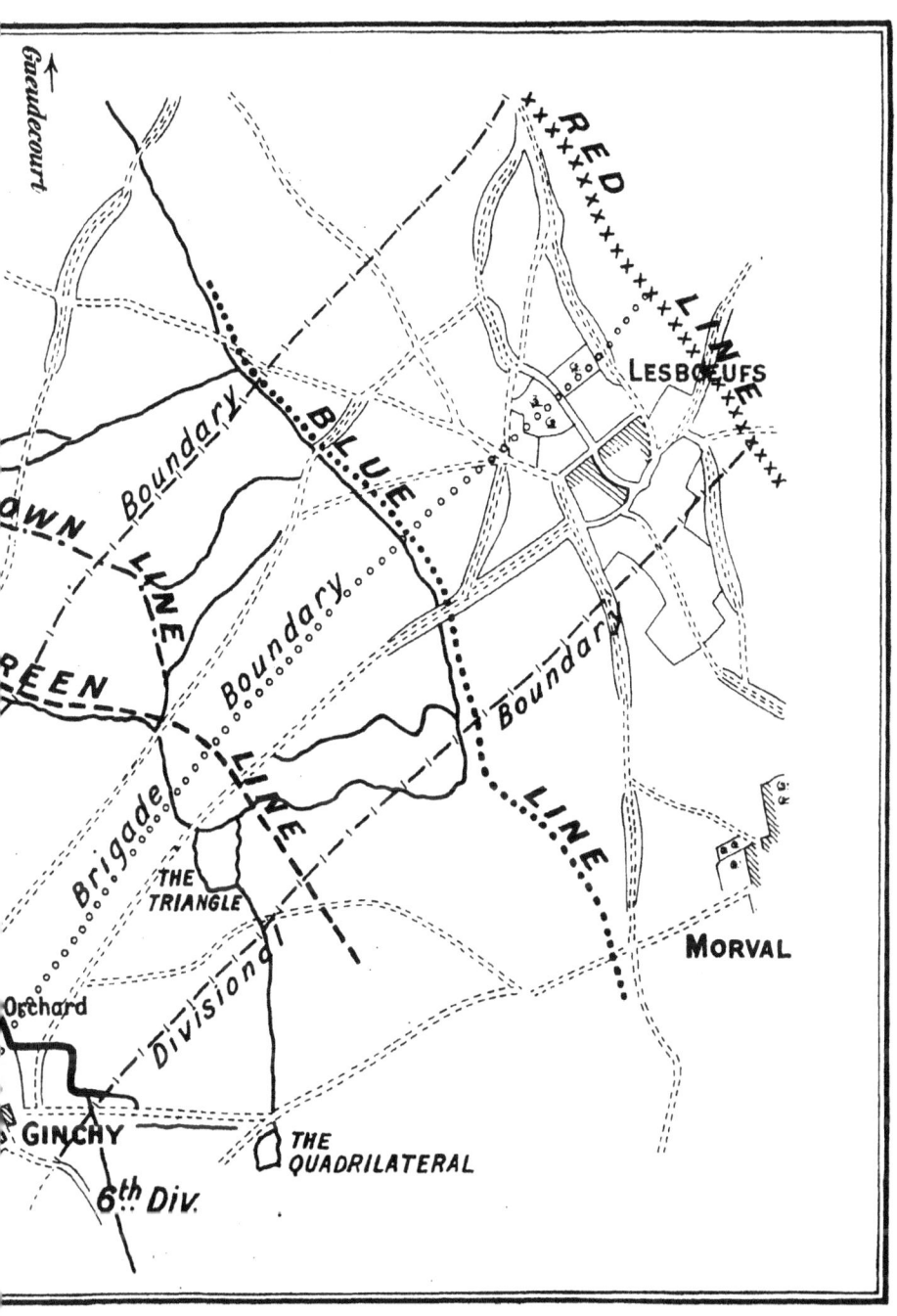

LOSSES OF THE GUARDS DIVISION

In view of the heavy casualties suffered by the Guards Division on the 15th and 16th of September Lord Cavan now decided to give the division a few days' rest out of the line. This relief was completed on the night of the 16th–17th of September,* the 1st Guards Bde. moving back to the neighbourhood of Fricourt, and the 2nd and 3rd Guards Bdes. to Carnoy.

(9) Return of the Guards to the Line—Preparations for the Renewal of the Offensive.

The Guards were only out of the line for three days—a very short period in which to refit and to reorganize the battalions after the heavy fighting in which they had been engaged. The casualties in all three brigades had been very severe, the losses in officers and non-commissioned officers being especially serious.† But in the matter of filling up their ranks after a battle the battalions of the Guards Division were always more fortunate than other units in the British Armies in France, for their drafts from England, which at this period in the war were plentiful, consisted of trained men imbued by their instructors with the methods, the tradition and the moral of the Brigade of Guards, fit and ready to take their places in the line. In the few days'

* The 20th Division came into the line, the command passing at 8 a.m. on the 17th of September. *See* W.D., Guards Division, September, 1916.

† Casualties in the Guards Division between the 10th and 17th of September, 1916 :—

	Killed.		Wounded.		Missing.		Total.	
	O.	O.R.	O.	O.R.	O.	O.R.	O.	O.R.
1st Guards Bde. ..	15	280	42	1082	2	423	59	1785
2nd Guards Bde. ..	25	153	26	796	10	757	61	1706
3rd Guards Bde. ..	13	163	26	849	—	141	39	1153
4th Bn. Coldstream Guards (Pioneers)	1	2	—	28	—	5	1	35
R.A.	—	4	3	19	—	—	3	23
R.E.	—	4	2	37	—	2	2	43
R.A.M.C.	—	6	6	40	1	1	7	47
Total ..	54	612	105	2851	13	1329	172	4792

See W.D. ("A" & "Q"), Guards Division.

respite which was allowed to them, therefore, the new drafts were absorbed into the various battalions and the three Guards brigades were once again made ready for their next trial of strength with the enemy.

On the 19th of September, Major-General Feilding held a conference at 2nd Guards Brigade headquarters,* at which future arrangements were discussed in the light of the lessons learnt during the recent fighting. The Major-General stated that the intention of the XIV Corps was to call upon the Guards Division to complete the work begun on the 15th of September. Its task would be to cooperate with the French and other British divisions in the capture of the line, Morval—Lesbœufs—Gueudecourt. It was clear that a strenuous resistance was to be expected from the enemy and that success could only be secured by means of the closest liaison between the artillery and the infantry.

The Major-General then drew attention to the vital necessity of subordinate commanders doing their utmost to maintain the direction of the attack, although he fully appreciated the immense difficulty of their task in the confusion inseparable from battle. With regard to the approaching advance, he explained that the capture of Lesbœufs would be entrusted to the Guards and warned the commanders of the 1st and 3rd Guards Bdes., who would be in charge of the attack, to make special arrangements for the effectual clearance of the dug-outs and cellars in the village.†

---

* See Notes on Conference, G.D. No. 2284/C. W.D., Guards Division, App. 1099.

† Subsequent to this conference, Major-General Feilding issued a short memorandum to his brigadiers urging them to have assembly trenches constructed, if possible, in order that their final dispositions for the attack might be carried out while the troops were in positions of comparative safety. He also laid it down that strong reserves should be posted in rear of the starting off positions in case the attacking troops should be driven back by a counter-attack from Lesbœufs, and gave instructions that all the battalions actually entrusted with the launching of the attack should be well forward before zero hour in view of the certain difficulty of bringing up reinforcing troops when once the battle had begun. See W.D., Guards Division, App. 1115.

THE GUARDS IN THE LINE AGAIN

Orders for the relief by the Guards of the 20th Division on the night of the 20th–21st of September reached divisional headquarters on the 19th.* The 1st Guards Bde. was then directed to relieve the 60th Infantry Bde. in the right sector of the line, and the 3rd Guards Bde. to relieve the 59th Infantry Bde. in the left sector. The 2nd Guards Bde. was ordered to remain in reserve.

At 7.30 a.m. on the 21st of September the completion of this relief was reported to Major-General Feilding and half an hour later divisional headquarters was opened at Minden Post.

The operation orders † for the coming attack were now issued to the Guards brigades. The Allied advance was to be directed on the whole line between the Somme and Martinpuich with the French on the right and the Fourth Army on the left, while the Reserve Army, under the command of General Gough, was to attack Thiepval and the Thiepval ridge the following day.

The objectives of the XIV Corps included Morval and Lesbœufs, the capture of Gueudecourt being entrusted to the XV Corps. The attack on the front of the XIV Corps was to be carried out by the 5th Division on the right, the 6th Division in the centre and the Guards Division on the left. The 56th Division was to form a defensive flank to the south of the 5th Division.‡ The 21st Division (XV Corps) was to operate on the left of the Guards.

---

* On the 18th of September, at 10.15 p.m., orders were issued for the relief of the 20th Division by the Guards on the night of the 19th–20th of September. This relief was postponed for 24 hours by an amended order issued early next day. *See* W.D., Guards Division, September, 1916.

† *See* Guards Division O.O. No. 82, issued at 12 noon on the 21st of September. On the 20th of September the day of attack had been altered—on account of bad weather—from the 22nd to the 23rd and on the 21st of September a further postponement was made until the 25th for the same reason. *See* W.D., Guards Division. On the night of the 21st–22nd of September the 1st Guards Bde. handed over the front south of the Ginchy—Lesbœufs road (exclusive) to troops of the 6th Division. This left each Guards brigade in the line with a frontage of about 500 yards. *See* W.D's., Guards Division and 1st Guards Bde.

‡ Since the 16th of September the situation on the front of the XIV Corps had been considerably improved as a result of a successful

The objectives given to the Guards Division were as follows : *—

The " green line "—a line running for about 1,500 yards in a northerly direction from a point about 500 yards west of Lesbœufs on the more southern of the two roads leading from Ginchy to Lesbœufs.

The " brown line "—a line running from the cross roads south of Lesbœufs along the western outskirts of the village.

The " blue line "—a line running just east of Lesbœufs from the Lesbœufs—le Transloy road northward along the Lesbœufs—Gueudecourt road.

The Guards attack, as already stated, was to be carried out by the 1st and 3rd Guards Bdes., and the task assigned to their commanders was to press through to the final objectives, maintaining a sufficient flow of troops throughout the day's fighting to ensure that the impetus of the advance was kept up to the final objective. The 75th Field Company, R.E., was attached to the 1st, and the 55th Field Company, R.E., to the 3rd Guards Bde.† Three tanks were allotted to cooperate with the division in the attack and were ordered to remain in divisional reserve.‡

All the available artillery was to be organized in two groups.§ The right group, consisting of the 24th, 74th and

attack, delivered on the 18th, by the 6th and 56th Divisions. The former had captured the " Quadrilateral " and the latter had reached a line Middle Copse—Bouleaux Wood. After the capture of the " Quadrilateral " the 6th Division had linked up with the 20th Division on the left and with the 56th Division at Middle Copse. A subsequent attempt by the 56th Division to clear up the northern portion of Bouleaux had been unsuccessful.

* *See* Map facing p. 186.

† The 4th Bn. Coldstream Guards (Pioneers) was kept in divisional reserve.

‡ The tanks were ordered to assemble at the south-west corner of Trônes Wood, and, as soon as the infantry attack had been launched, their commander was to take his machines to the north-east corner of Ginchy, and then to go to Brig.-General Pereira's headquarters and wait for his orders from Major-General Feilding. Instructions for tanks were issued with Guards divisional Order No. 82. But there is no mention in the divisional, brigade or battalion War Diaries of work being done by the tanks on the 25th of September.

§ *See* W.D., C.R.A., Guards Division, September, 1916. For a

75th Bdes., R.F.A., under the command of Lieut.-Colonel A. Bethell, was to cover the front of the 1st Guards Bde., while that of the 3rd Guards Bde. was to be covered by the left group consisting of the 61st, the 36th and 93rd Bdes., R.F.A., commanded by Lieut.-Colonel F. A. Buzzard. Both groups were to carry out a bombardment of the enemy's positions from 7 a.m. to 6 p.m. on the day before the attack. To cover the actual attack half of the artillery on the divisional front was to be employed in firing standing barrages, while the remainder was to supply the creeping barrages to cover the advance of the infantry to the various objectives. A standing barrage was to be placed on the " green line " at zero hour, and was subsequently to be transferred to the " brown " and " blue " lines according to an arranged time-table.* The creeping barrage was to be laid down 100 yards in front of the line occupied by the attacking troops at zero hour, and was then to be moved forward at the rate of 50 yards a minute until it reached a line 200 yards beyond the " green " line when it was to be made stationary. At zero + one hour, and at zero + two hours, respectively, the creeping barrage was to be resumed in the same manner as in the initial attack in order to cover the advance of the infantry to the second and third objectives.

(10) CAPTURE OF LESBŒUFS BY THE 1ST AND 3RD GUARDS BRIGADES, 25TH OF SEPTEMBER—THE GUARDS DIVISION WITHDRAWN FROM THE LINE FOR REST AND TRAINING.

By an early hour on the morning of the 25th of September the troops of the 1st and 3rd Guards Bdes. were all in their respective positions ready for the advance. The 2nd Bn. Grenadier Guards and the 1st Bn. Irish Guards, on the right

summary of the work of the artillery in the operations on the Somme, see p. 182.
 * The 14th Horse Artillery Bde. was ordered to form a standing barrage on certain points in the enemy's positions which were not allotted to the R.F.A. batteries. In all cases the standing barrage was to be lifted back when it was reached by the creeping barrage. See W.D., C.R.A., Guards Division Operation Order.

and left respectively, held the front of the 1st Guards Bde. extending from the Ginchy—Lesbœufs road to a point rather more than 500 yards to the north-west.*

The 2nd and 3rd Bns. Coldstream Guards, under the command of Lieut.-Colonel J. Campbell, were in support.

The 2nd Bn. Scots Guards was on the right, and the 4th Bn. Grenadier Guards on the left, of the sector of the line held by the 3rd Guards Bde., the right of the Scots Guards being in touch with the left of the 1st Guards Bde.†

The 1st Bn. Grenadier Guards was in support and the 1st Bn. Welsh Guards in reserve.‡

The weather on the 25th of September was fine and clear, and the state of the ground was more favourable for the attacking troops than it had been on the 15th or 16th. After a quiet morning the creeping barrage was put down punctually and effectively by the British gunners at 12.35 p.m., zero hour, and the Guards battalion, advancing in two waves with 75 yards distance between each wave, went forward to the attack.

Within about a minute after the troops had crossed the parapet the enemy's artillery put down a heavy counter-barrage on the front of the 1st Guards Bde. and upon the trenches in rear,§ but, although this bombardment considerably impeded the movements of the supporting companies, the leading waves of Grenadiers and Irish Guards had rushed forward so quickly that they escaped it. They were close up to the enemy's line when the British barrage was lifted. The Irish Guards captured their objective with little

* *See* Map facing p. 186.
† *See ibid.*
‡ In front of the Guards on the 25th of September the Germans had the 56th and 111th Infantry Divisions and two battalions of the 24th Reserve Infantry Division.
§ " Immediately after Nos. 1 and 2 Companies had advanced, a hostile barrage was put on our assembly trenches which very much hampered Nos. 3 and 4 Companies whose orders were to move into the front assembly trench under cover. There were a good many casualties. . . . Eventually these companies got so held up by the shelling that they advanced ' over the top ' to the first objective (' green line ') soon after 1 p.m." *See* Report by Lieut.-Colonel McCalmont, 1st Bn. Irish Guards.

difficulty, but the Grenadiers on the right were less fortunate. They found that the German wire in front of them was uncut. The officers promptly ordered their men to lie down in the standing crops in which the wire was concealed and to open a covering fire while they themselves went forward to cut a passage through the wire. This coolness and devotion to duty on the part of the officers and the steadiness of the men saved a critical situation—a path was cut through the enemy's entanglements, and, although most of their officers lost their lives in the carrying out of their task, the Grenadiers were enabled to sweep forward and capture their first objective at the point of the bayonet.*

Notwithstanding the delay caused by the uncut wire on the right, both the leading battalions of the 1st Guards Bde. were concentrated on the " green line " by about 1.20 p.m.† The Germans had fought bravely, but had proved no match in hand-to-hand fighting with the Guards, the bulk of the defenders of the " green " line having been either killed or captured.‡

Punctually, at 1.35 p.m., the advance to the second objective was begun under the protection of a creeping barrage and in ten minutes' time the " brown line " was in possession of the 1st Guards Bde. which was in touch with the 18th Infantry Bde. (6th Division) on the right and the 3rd Guards Bde. on the left. The opposition encountered in this second advance was slight, as was also that when the Guards went forward to the attack on the " blue line " at 2.35 p.m. The enemy for the time being had had sufficient fighting and surrendered freely, with the result that, shortly after 3.30 p.m., the two leading battalions of the 1st Guards

---

* " About 12.39 or 12.40 our first objective was gained with a certain amount of difficulty as our artillery fire had failed to cut a single strand of wire. While the companies were cutting it, the Germans picked off almost all our officers." *See* Report of Lieut.-Colonel C. De Crespigny, September, 1916. Captain A. Cunninghame, 2nd Lieutenant G. Arbuthnot and Lieut. the Honble. W. A. D. Parnell were killed, and Lieut. A. F. Irvine wounded whilst engaged in cutting the wire in front of the first objective.

† In the 1st Guards Bde. Report the time is given as 1.15 p.m.

‡ In the 1st Guards Bde. Report it is stated that 3 machine guns were captured.

Bde. had passed through Lesbœufs and were firmly established on the eastern outskirts of that village,* touch having been maintained with the troops on each flank throughout the advance. By this hour the 2nd and 3rd Bns. Coldstream Guards, which had followed closely in support of the Grenadiers and Irish Guards, had consolidated the " green " and " brown lines," and were completing the clearance of the village of Lesbœufs.

The course of events on the front of the 3rd Guards Bde. must now be followed. The two leading battalions—the 2nd Bn. Scots Guards on the right and the 4th Bn. Grenadier Guards on the left—moved forward at zero hour under cover of the creeping barrage. The Scots Guards reached and captured their first objective with but few casualties ; but the Grenadiers, soon after their advance began, came upon a German trench which had escaped the British artillery bombardment and was strongly held by the enemy.† But in despite of the fierce rifle and machine-gun fire of its defenders which caused many casualties in their ranks, the Grenadiers stormed this trench, killing about 150 of the enemy.‡ Quickly, reforming their ranks, they then pushed on to their first objective of which they were in possession at 1.35 p.m. It was now found that the left flank of the 3rd Guards Bde. was uncovered as the 64th Infantry Bde. (21st Division) had not succeeded in reaching Gird trench.§ A defensive flank, therefore, was hastily formed by the left

---

* *See* 1st Guards Bde. Report.

† " In perfect order, with not a man out of place, the line swept on until it came to the two intermediate lines, which the officers had been warned to expect somewhere in front of the first objective. These had only recently been discovered, and no one quite knew how strongly they were held." *See* " The Grenadier Guards in the Great War," vol. ii. p. 140.

‡ " The Battalion (4th Bn. Grenadier Guards) did what they were told to do, and I don't think they could have done better. I know there was not a single shirker in the lot. Our dead lay in front of the first German trench, but there were 100 to 150 German corpses there when I came up." Extract from a letter of Lord Henry Seymour to Sir Henry Streatfeild, 27th of September, 1916.

§ The advance of the 64th Infantry Bde. was checked by a line of uncut wire. *See* " Narrative of Operations of the 64th Infantry Bde. from 21st to 27th September, 1916."

ALL OBJECTIVES GAINED

flank company of the Grenadiers, while the remnants of the company on the right of the line, keeping touch with the Scots Guards, went forward to the second objective. This was gained without much difficulty.* At 2.35 p.m. after two companies of the 1st Bn. Welsh Guards † had been sent forward to strengthen the left flank, the 1st Bn. Grenadier Guards passed through the leading battalions, and, by about 3.30 p.m., was in possession of the third objective. The situation in the evening, therefore, on the front of the Guards Division as a result of the day's fighting, was as follows :—all the objectives had been taken ; Lesbœufs was cleared of Germans ; and the troops of the 1st and 3rd Guards Bdes. were busily engaged in consolidating their new positions, from the Lesbœufs—le Transloy road just north of the village of Lesbœufs to Windy trench. On the right the Guards were in touch with the 6th Division,‡ but on the left there was a considerable gap between the 3rd Guards Bde. and the troops of the 21st Division. This gap was held by a strong defensive flank.

It was mainly the uncertainty with regard to the safety of the left flank which decided Major-General Feilding and Lord Cavan not to make any attempt to carry forward the advance in the evening of the 25th of September.§ After the capture of Lesbœufs it was clear that the enemy's troops in the forward area were completely demoralized, and some of the Guards commanding officers, who witnessed the Germans hurrying away northward without their arms, had called anxiously for cavalry to complete the rout.‖

* This advance was led by Sergeant Pitt, as all the officers had become casualties. *See* " The Grenadier Guards in the Great War," vol. ii. p. 141.

† *See* W.D., 1st Bn. Welsh Guards, September, 1916.

‡ Still farther to the right the situation was equally satisfactory. Morval had fallen to the 5th Division and the French had captured Frégicourt, and, in conjunction with the 56th Division, were encircling Combles.

§ This decision was come to over the telephone at 7 p.m. The XIV Corps ordered an artillery barrage to be kept on all fronts during the night. *See* W.D., Guards Division, September, 1916.

‖ Brig.-General Corkran, 3rd Guards Bde., recommended the employment of cavalry. *See* W.D., 3rd Guards Bde., September, 1916.

Apparently a squadron of cavalry was brought up somewhere in

But it is doubtful whether even if sufficient cavalry had been in a position to advance immediately from Lesbœufs, men on horses would have been able to make much progress in the few hours of daylight still available, for, in view of the failure to capture Gueudecourt, the front of advance was certainly too narrow for effective cavalry manœuvre, while any local infantry advance would have been a risky undertaking.*

The situation on the Guards front remained unchanged during the night of the 25th–26th of September. The troops, in spite of their exertions and losses during the previous day's fighting, were in high spirits, and the enemy made no serious attempt at a counter attack. Early in the morning, on the 26th, any further anxiety as to the safety of the left flank was removed, as the 64th Infantry Bde., with the assistance of a tank, gained possession of Gird trench,† and, at about 4 p.m., the troops of the 21st Division captured Gueudecourt and linked up connexion with the 3rd Guards Bde. midway between that village and Lesbœufs.

After the capture of Gird trench in the morning the Guards again enjoyed the spectacle of parties of Germans hurrying away from their trenches between Gueudecourt and le Transloy, and on this occasion the British artillery was able to inflict serious casualties on the retreating enemy. But, although the moral of the German front line troops was affected in this particular area, it was soon made evident that there was no serious demoralization in rear. A squadron of cavalry, which attempted to feel its way forward in the

---

the neighbourhood of Gueudecourt in the afternoon, but could make no progress. *See* W.D., Fourth Army, September, 1916.

* "Our salient was very pronounced. Gueudecourt was not taken, and our left flank was absolutely in the air. . . . It has been a good show, and not so difficult as the one on the 15th, for this time we did not have to make a long advance exposed to enfilade fire from both flanks; but we have met fresh troops and beaten them soundly in an open fight." Extract from a letter of Major-General Feilding to Lieut.-General Sir Francis Lloyd, 26th of September, 1916.

† Between 300 and 400 of the enemy in the trench surrendered to the 64th Infantry Bde. about 9 a.m., the remainder being driven towards the refused flank of the 3rd Guards Bde. About 6 officers and 100 of the rank and file surrendered to the Guards.

morning towards Gueudecourt, was speedily forced to come back and patrols which the Guards themselves pushed out from Lesbœufs were also unable to make much progress. Whatever might have been the result had it been possible to renew the general attack with fresh infantry covered by artillery all along the Allied front after the capture of Gueudecourt and Combles,* it was clear that the enemy's machine gunners, who, by the afternoon of the 26th, had formed a chain of posts on the high ground east of Lesbœufs northward to le Transloy, were well able to check any local advance by small parties of calvary and infantry. The German artillery, too, which had fired comparatively little during the night of the 25th–26th and the early hours of the 26th of September, became much more active as the day wore on, and the whole energies of the Guards had to be directed to the strengthening and deepening of their new defensive positions.

During the night of the 26th of September the 2nd Guards Bde. relieved the two other brigades in the line, the relief being completed by 11.30 p.m.†

The 2nd Guards Bde. remained in the line until the night of the 30th of September, when in its turn it was relieved by the 167th Infantry Bde. (56th Division). By this date a new line of trenches had been dug at a distance varying from 200 to 250 yards east of Lesbœufs. This line extended along the whole front of the Guards Division except in the area immediately north of the Lesbœufs—le Transloy road, where there was a gap in it of about 200 yards.‡

---

* The news of the joint occupation of Combles by the French and the 56th Division reached Guards divisional headquarters at 10.5 a.m. on the 26th of September.

† The machine-gun companies of the outgoing brigades remained in the line until the 28th of September. The 2nd Bn. Irish Guards relieved the 2nd Bn. Grenadier and 1st Bn. Irish Guards on the front of the 1st Guards Bde., while the 1st Bn. Scots Guards relieved the 1st Bn. Grenadiers and the 2nd Bn. Scots Guards on that of the 3rd Guards Bde. The relief was completed at 2.15 a.m. on the 27th. *See* W.D., 2nd Guards Bde., O.O. No. 66.

‡ A reconnaissance was made on the 29th of September by a company of the 1st Bn. Coldstream Guards, the object of which was to fill this gap by the capture, if possible, of Rainy trench and the linking it up with a trench which another company of the same battalion

The casualties in the Guards Division during the battle of Morval * on the 25th of September were less severe than they had been on the 15th–16th of September, but they were sufficiently heavy to reduce the effective strength of the battalions to such an extent that the XIV Corps commander decided to give the division a period of rest behind the line.†

On the 2nd and 3rd of October, therefore, the Guards moved from the Carnoy—Fricourt areas to No. 4 Training Area south-west of Amiens.

In the two battles in the Operations on the Somme in which it took part the Guards Division enhanced its reputation and well deserved the tribute of praise which it received from Lord Cavan and Sir Henry Rawlinson.‡ On the 15th of September, in particular, the

---

was digging north of the Lesbœufs—le Transloy road. The enemy's machine-gun fire was so heavy, however, that the attack was not pressed, and the company was ordered to withdraw. *See* Report to Guards Division, W.D., 2nd Guards Bde., App. 80.

* *See* " Report of the Battles Nomenclature Committee as approved by the Army Council." [Cmd. 1138], 1921.

† Casualties in the Guards Division, 18th–30th of September—

Unit.	Killed. O.	Killed. O.R.	Wounded. O.	Wounded. O.R.	Missing. O.	Missing. O.R.	Total. O.	Total. O.R.
1st Guards Bde.	9	110	14	609	—	168	23	887
2nd Guards Bde.	1	27	4	117	—	2	5	146
3rd Guards Bde.	12	161	14	694	—	280	26	1135
4th Bn. Coldstream Gds. (Pioneers)	—	4	—	14	—	—	—	18
R.A.	—	8	2	40	—	2	2	50
R.E.	—	—	1	14	—	—	1	14
R.A.M.C.	—	4	2	26	—	—	2	30
Chaplains	—	—	1	—	—	—	1	—
Totals	22	314	38	1514	—	452	60	2280

The casualties in the fighting on the 25th of September accounted for more than 90 per cent. of the above figures. *See* W.D., Guards Division (" A " & " Q "), September, 1916.

‡ Sir Henry Rawlinson issued the following appreciative order on the 8th of October :—" It is only since the reports have come in that it has become clear that the gallantry and perseverance of the Guards Division in the battles of the 15th and 25th of September were paramount factors in the success of the Fourth Army on these days. On the 15th of September, especially, the vigorous attack of the Guards in circumstances of great difficulty, with both flanks exposed to the enfilade fire of the enemy, reflects the highest credit on all concerned,

infantry of the division was required to make an attack of exceptional difficulty, advancing from an awkward line with both flanks exposed to a heavy enfilade fire. It was entirely due " to the gallantry and perseverance " of the officers and other ranks of the Guards Division that the front of the XIV Corps was carried forward that day to a line which made the subsequent assault upon Morval and Lesbœufs " a feasible operation." On the 25th of September the task of the Guards was a less difficult one, but the capture of Lesbœufs was a thoroughly well-planned and admirably conducted feat of arms which reflected the greatest credit upon every unit in the division. The staff arrangements worked without a hitch; communications were well maintained; and the infantry, covered by an effective artillery barrage and magnificently led, routed the enemy and captured all its objectives.

(11) WORK OF THE GUARDS MACHINE-GUN COMPANIES DURING THE FIGHTING ON THE 15TH AND 25TH OF SEPTEMBER.

The part played by the machine gunners of the Guards Division in the fighting on the 15th and 25th of September was a prominent and gallant one, but unfortunately it is not an easy matter to give anything like a full account of their achievements on the 15th, because on that day the machine gunners were involved in the general confusion and many

and I desire to tender to every officer, N.C.O., and man my congratulations and best thanks for their exemplary valour on that occasion. Their success established the battle front of the XIV Corps well forward on the high ridge leading towards Morval and Lesbœufs, and made the assault of these villages on the 25th a feasible operation. On the 25th September the attack of the hostile trenches in front and north of Lesbœufs was conducted with equal gallantry and determination. In this attack the division gained all the objectives allotted to them, and I offer to all concerned my warmest thanks and gratitude for their fine performance." Fourth Army, No. 373 (G).

Lord Cavan, the XIV Corps commander, sent the following message to Major-General Feilding and the Guards Division :—" Hearty thanks and sincere congratulations to you all. A very fine achievement, splendidly executed." 25th of September, 1916.

of the gun sections were practically wiped out of existence. The 3rd Guards Bde. Machine-Gun Company relieved the 47th and 48th Machine-Gun Companies (20th Division) in the line at Ginchy and south-east of that village on the 9th of September.* The relief was a very difficult one, but the guns were in position to assist in the defence of the line against the German counter-attack on the 10th.† On the night of the 12th–13th of September the 1st and 2nd Guards Bdes. Machine-Gun Companies relieved the 3rd Guards Bde. Machine-Gun Company when the 1st and 2nd Guards Bdes. took over the line from the 3rd Guards Bde. In the attack on the 15th, the machine-gun sections moved forward with the infantry. It is difficult to follow the fortunes of the 2nd Company on the right as its commander and all its other officers became casualties, the majority of them, indeed, being either killed or wounded before the first objective was reached. There is no record of the fate of the guns which accompanied the 3rd Bn. Grenadier Guards in the assault. But, later in the day, two guns of the Coldstream section, one gun of the Scots Guards section and two guns of the Grenadiers' section were used to cover the defensive flank on the right of the 2nd Guards Bde. It is also clear that one of the reserve guns with the 1st Bn. Scots Guards, which was brought up on the left flank with the ninth wave of the attacking infantry, was of much assistance in repelling attempts at counter-attacks made by the enemy in this area. The gunners made use only of the light tripod and it proved both handy and effective. The Irish Guards section had three of its guns put out of action by hostile fire. Its remaining gun is reported to have been seen firing in the German " second line," but it is impossible to say where exactly it went as no more was heard of it. All its team became casualties.‡ The movements of the gun-sections of the 1st Company are equally difficult to trace with any certainty in the confusion which prevailed after

* See p. 143.
† See W.D., 3rd Guards Bde., Machine-Gun Company, September, 1916.
‡ See W.D., 2nd Guards Bde., Machine-Gun Company, September, 1916.

the first objective had been reached. No. 2 Section is reported to have had three guns damaged by shell fire and No. 4 Section sustained very heavy losses in *personnel* early in the advance. No. 3 Section was successful in getting all four of its guns as far as the first objective and eventually took up a position " just south of Flers." Of the three guns belonging to No. 1 Section two were sent to the defensive right flank of the division and the other was placed in position on the left of the 2nd Bn. Grenadier Guards to cover its junction with the Coldstream. No. 4 Section provided covering fire for the infantry in the advance to the third objective. One of its guns was put out of action by close-range artillery fire and all its *personnel* became casualties. But the remaining guns found some good targets, and their fire was very effective until they had to be withdrawn from the advanced positions which had been taken up.*

On the 16th of September the 2nd Guards Bde. Machine-Gun Company was able to bring up more of its guns into positions in the support line, but its last remaining officer was killed. When the 1st and 2nd Companies were relieved, on the 17th, by the 3rd Company, the 1st Company had lost 4 officers and about 90 other ranks, and the 2nd Company, 9 officers and 83 other ranks, killed, wounded or missing.† In the attack on the 25th of September the 1st Guards Bde. did not attach its machine gunners to its battalions for the advance. Brig.-General Pereira, in the light of the experience gained on the 15th, decided that it was impossible for the gun-sections to maintain the same rate of progress as the infantry. He ordered them, therefore, to advance at their own time and pace, although he indicated very precisely what he wished them to do. This arrangement answered satisfactorily. When the final objective had been gained by the infantry, No. 1 Section soon had four guns in position in front of Lesbœufs, and another four guns were in the line of the second objective west of that village. The reserve

* *See* W.D., 1st Guards Bde., Machine-Gun Company, September, 1916. The 3rd Guards Bde. Machine-Gun Company was in reserve with the 3rd Guards Bde. on the 15th of September.

† *See* W.D's., 1st and 2nd Guards Bdes. Machine-Gun Companies, September, 1916.

guns were brought up a little later, and one was used in the front line to replace a gun that had been lent to the 3rd Guards Bde. for the defence of the open flank on the left of the Division.* The 3rd Guards Machine-Gun Company was also successful in carrying forward eight of its guns with the infantry of the brigade, all of which were placed in positions on the line of the captured objectives.†

On the 26th of September the guns of both companies fired with considerable effects upon bodies of the enemy retreating across the open.

(12) Work of the Divisional R.E. and the 4th Bn. Coldstream Guards (Pioneers) during the course of the Operations on the Somme.

When the Guards Division moved to the Fourth Army area preparatory to taking part in the British offensive, the difficulty of getting together the requisite engineer stores for the coming operations was, as usual, the problem that had to be solved by the divisional R.E. All the dumps in the back area had already been denuded of most of the useful materials, and such available stores as had been taken forward were in bulk and not in " one-man loads." So great, too, was the congestion of traffic on the main line of communication that lorries, the supply of which was limited, could barely do one trip in the day from railhead to the main dump at Minden Post. But every obstacle in his way was successfully overcome by the C.R.E., and the necessary engineer stores had all been collected and were in readiness for the attack before the 15th of September.‡ A forward depôt had been established in Bernafay Wood and sufficient

---

* *See* Narrative 1st Guards Bde., also W.D., 1st Guards Bde. Machine-Gun Company, September, 1916.

† *See* W.D., 3rd Guards Bde. Machine-Gun Company, September, 1916.

‡ " After exerting much pressure I got 20 lorries for one day, so just succeeded in getting our dumps ship-shape for the 15th September attack." Extract from a note supplied by Lieut.-Colonel Brough, C.R.E., Guards Division.

WORK OF THE FIELD COMPANIES

R.E. stores for the purposes of the initial assault had been carried forward and dumped near the R.E. assembly trenches which were close to the headquarters of the 1st and 2nd Guards Bdes.

During the days before the attack the R.E. laid out and marked several routes for horse-transport leading to Bernafay Wood, and began the heavy task of clearing a track from the northern end of that wood through Trônes Wood to Ginchy; they were busily employed also in the construction of new, or in the improvement of old, battle headquarters for the division and the brigades.

On the night of the 14th-15th of September the various positions of assembly for the battalions of the two attacking brigades were laid out with tapes by the R.E.* assisted by the brigade staff officers. Before this, the C.R.E. had held a conference of R.E. commanders, and, in addition to giving them their orders for the attack, had explained to them fully the various duties they would be called upon to perform, impressing upon them the value of reconnaissance. On the 15th of September the 75th and 76th Field Companies were employed with the 1st and 2nd Guards Bdes. The 55th Field Company and the 4th Bn. Coldstream Guards (Pioneers) remained in reserve under the orders of the C.R.E.

As the attack developed one company of the 4th Bn. Coldstream Guards was sent forward from Bernafay Wood in order to try and clear a track up to and past Ginchy. This attempt ended in failure as the men came into view of the enemy's artillery, and the company was forced to withdraw after suffering some casualties. Later in the day, however, two other companies of the same battalion undertook the task and did some good work. The 76th Field Company, which moved forward with the 2nd Guards Bde. on the

* " It was difficult to get this marking out done with great precision, as our existing maps hardly did full justice to the queer irregularities in the ground east and south-east of Ginchy. These factors undoubtedly greatly increased the difficulty of keeping direction during the attack. Also, I think, no one at the time realized that the German strong point to the south-east of Ginchy enfiladed our attack—it appeared from our maps to be in a hollow, whereas it was on a slight eminence." Extract from a note supplied by Lieut.-Colonel Brough, C.R.E., Guards Division.

right of the attack, carried out the tasks allotted to it, completing the wiring and digging of some strong points designed to secure the right flank of the brigade, which, it will be remembered, was in the air throughout the day's fighting.* The 75th Field Company, which accompanied the 1st Guards Bde., was not quite so successful, as one of its parties went astray and did not complete the task assigned to it.†

On the 25th of September the R.E. dispositions were identical with those on the 15th, except that, as the Guards were attacking from a more regular and defined line, it was found possible to dig some assembly trenches and thus to enable the infantry to start the attack to better advantage. The 55th Field Company, which was attached to the 3rd Guards Bde. on the left of the divisional front, was kept fully occupied in wiring the refused flank and in the construction of strong points in depth. Its work was carried out with complete success, and some of the wire which it put out was found to be still in position when the division returned to this part of the line in November. When darkness set in, on the 25th, every available sapper and pioneer was sent forward to assist in digging the new line and in improving the communications.

(13) WORK OF THE DIVISIONAL ARTILLERY ON THE SOMME.

The Guards Divisional Artillery arrived at Sailly-le-Sec in the area of the XIV Corps on the 1st of September, and, on the 5th and 6th, relieved the artillery of the 24th Division in the line.‡ It formed part of the group of guns covering

---

* These strong points subsequently proved of great assistance to the troops of the 20th Division who relieved the Guards.

† This divergence from its allotted route was partly due to the fact that an officer who was entrusted with the duty of reconnaissance was wounded. *See* W.D., 75th Field Co., R.E., September, 1916.

‡ Brig.-General Evans, C.R.A., Guards Division, took over the command of the artillery in the sector at 6 p.m. on the 6th of September. *See* W.D., C.R.A., Guards Division, September, 1916. The D.A.C. had assumed the control of the big ammunition dump at Méaulte on the 5th. *See* W.D., D.A.C., September, 1916.

the left sector of the XIV Corps front,* its batteries being in positions in the neighbourhood of Bernafay Wood and Trônes Wood and south of Montauban.

In the evening of the 6th of September a report, which subsequently turned out to be incorrect, was received stating that the enemy had retaken Leuze Wood and all batteries immediately opened on their S.O.S. lines. Alarmist reports and rumours of this kind were not infrequent at this time, and the divisional Artillery was kept fully occupied during its first few days in the line. The enemy's gunners, too, were not idle, and their fire was heavy and extremely accurate.

On the 8th of September orders were issued for the attack on Ginchy.† For this operation the artillery covering the 16th Division was divided into two groups each of four brigades. The 74th and 76th Bdes., R.F.A., were in the right group commanded by Lieut.-Colonel McCarthy, 6th divisional Artillery. The 61st and 75th Bdes., R.F.A., under the command of Lieut.-Colonel F. A. Buzzard, Guards divisional Artillery, formed the left group.

The attack of the infantry of the 16th Division on Ginchy was launched at 4.45 p.m. on the 9th of September. Half of the 18-pdrs. fired in the covering barrage and the other half in the standing barrage, while the howitzers were used to keep certain selected areas—such as the orchards in Ginchy—under fire.‡

After the capture of Ginchy the British gunners were

---

* Then held by the 16th Division.

† *See* W.D., C.R.A., Guards Division, App. 6. During the morning of the 8th of September the wagon lines of the 75th Bde., R.F.A., were shelled by a 15-cm. gun. Some damage was done. A German shell exploded in a gun-pit of C/76, killing 4 men of the gun detachment.

‡ The 48th Infantry Bde. which captured Ginchy expressed great satisfaction with the artillery support that it received. *See* W.D., 61st Bde., R.F.A., September, 1916.

On the 13th of September the following letter of appreciation from Major-General Hickie, G.O.C. the 16th Division, was received by the C.R.A., Guards Division :—" If it is possible later on we should be glad if you could make known to the officers and men of the Guards Artillery that the 16th Division will always remember their three days together. Among the officers and men who took part in the assault I hear nothing but praise of the accuracy and volume of your fire."
See W.D., C.R.A., Guards Division, App. 33A.

kept very busy as the Germans, it will be remembered, made persistent counter-attacks in order to regain the village.* On the night of the 9th–10th of September the 3rd Guards Bde. relieved the 47th and 48th Infantry Bdes., in the line,† and consequently the Guards divisional Artillery was once again supporting its own infantry.‡

Orders for the resumption of the attack were issued on the 12th of September. The right artillery group (74th and 75th Bdes., R.F.A., and a brigade of the 6th divisional Artillery under the command of Lieut.-Colonel Bethell) was ordered to support the attack of the Guards brigade on the right, while the left group (61st and 76th Bdes., R.F.A., and a brigade of the 6th divisional Artillery commanded by Lieut.-Colonel Buzzard) was to support the Guards on the left.§ The 18-pdr. batteries of the 74th and 76th Bdes., R.F.A., had orders to move forward after the " blue line " was taken, when they were to be at the disposal of the infantry brigade commanders.‖

Before the infantry attack was launched on the 15th of September the batteries had not only fired a preparatory bombardment for three days and nights, but had also selected, built and, in some cases, actually moved to, more forward positions.¶

On the 15th of September the field guns provided the creeping and standing barrages, while the howitzers fired on selected points in the enemy's lines. Throughout the day the guns were handled with great boldness and enter-

---

* From noon on the 9th of September until noon on the 10th the 18-pdr. batteries of the 75th Bde., R.F.A., fired nearly 6,000 rounds and the howitzer battery 833 rounds. *See* W.D., 75th Bde., R.F.A., September, 1916.

It is not surprising to hear that the D.A.C., which was now located at Carnoy, had some difficulty in supplying all the demands for ammunition. W.D., D.A.C., September, 1916.

† *See* p. 148.

‡ On the 11th of September Major Hovil (A/75) assumed the command of the 75th Bde., R.F.A., as Lieut.-Colonel Bethell took over the command of a newly formed artillery group.

§ *See* p. 146.

‖ *See* W.D., C.R.A., Guards Division, App. 24.

¶ *See* W.D's., C.R.A., Guards Division, and 75th Bde., R.F.A., September, 1916.

prise. During the afternoon first the 18-pdrs. of the 76th Bde., R.F.A., and then those of the 74th Bde., R.F.A., went into action well forward on the western side of Ginchy. They had, however, to return to their group commanders later in the day when it was definitely clear that the infantry could make no farther progress.*

The infantry attack of the 3rd Guards Bde. and the 61st Infantry Bde. on the 16th of September was covered by a portion of the artillery which fired a standing barrage,† but, owing to the difficulties encountered by the battalions of the former brigade in forming up for, and its consequent lateness in starting upon, the attack it appears to have derived little, if any, benefit from the artillery support.

After the relief of the Guards Division on the night of the 16th–17th of September, the divisional Artillery supported an attack by the 59th Infantry Bde. (20th Division) on the 17th.‡

From this date onwards preparations were steadily put in hand for the next general advance on the front of the XIV Corps—an advance which was destined to be delayed by bad weather. The batteries of the divisional Artillery were employed in systematic wire-cutting, in harassing the enemy's communications, and in moving forward their guns. Some of the guns got stuck in the mud for hours together, and the strain upon the *personnel* of the artillery during these days was very great. Roads, such as they were, were often blocked by broken down lorries and transport, so that the task of the D.A.C., which was now supplying ammunition to no less than six artillery brigades, was no light one. Nevertheless, by the 21st of September, the batteries in new positions began the work of registration in cooperation with the R.A.F.§

The grouping and the tasks of the divisional Artillery for the battle on the 25th of September were practically the same as for that on the 15th. But the batteries were

---

* *See* W.D., C.R.A., Guards Division, September, 1916.
† *See* W.D., 61st Bde., R.F.A., September, 1916.
‡ *See ib.*
§ *See* W.D., C.R.A., Guards Division, September, 1916.

now in positions in front of Guillemont and Ginchy and round Trônes Wood.

On the 25th, all went well with the infantry attack, and there is little to record from the artillery point of view, except the by no means invariable information that the infantry was " highly satisfied with the covering barrage." *

From the 25th of September to the end of the month the divisional Artillery was constantly employed. It cooperated with the infantry of the XV Corps in the capture of Gueudecourt and then again moved forward its guns. When the infantry of the Guards Division was withdrawn from the line, the divisional Artillery remained and covered the front of the 56th Division, its battery commanders being busily engaged in reconnoitring new gun positions on the Flers line for a subsequent advance upon le Transloy. But the operations on this part of the front were for the time being at an end.

Some idea of the work performed by the gunners of the Guards Division on the Somme may be gathered when it is recorded that the D.A.C. handled 275,000 rounds during the month of September, and that the 18-pdrs. of the 75th Bde., R.F.A., fired 40,000 and its howitzers 6,000 rounds between the 6th and the 30th of the month.†

* *See* W.D., 75th Bde., R.F.A., September, 1916.

† *See* W.D's., D.A.C., and 75th Bde., R.F.A., September, 1916. The camp of the D.A.C. was severely bombed by the enemy's aeroplanes on the 27th and 28th of September. No. 3 Section was located near the road at Carnoy and the headlights of passing lorries undoubtedly drew the attention of the German observers to the spot. Over 100 horses of the Guards Division were killed and wounded in these attacks.

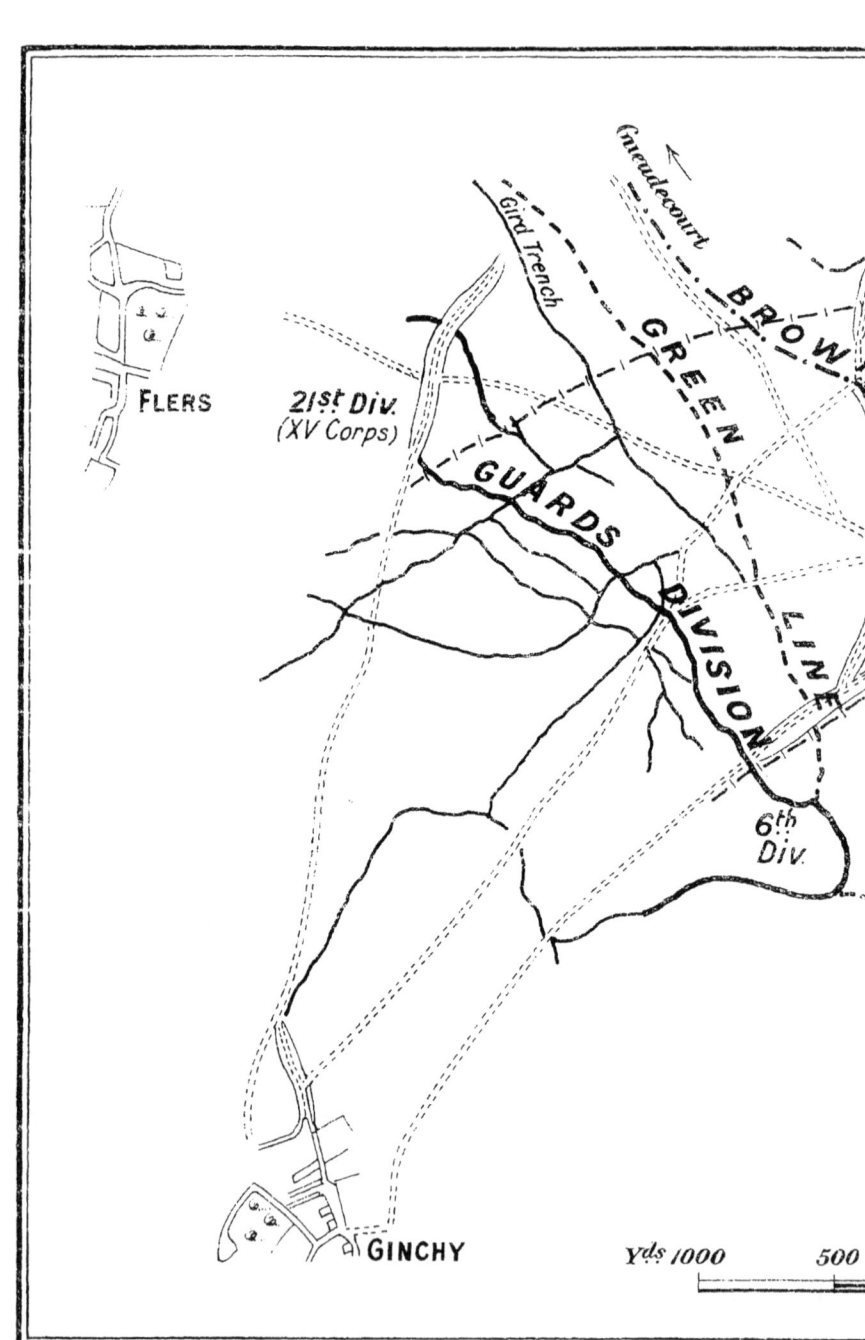

GUARDS DIVISION
Operations, Sept. 25, 1916

British Line before attack ─────
1st Objective ....
2nd ,,
3rd ,,
Divisional Boundaries ....
Trenches ....

LESBŒUFS
le Transloy
Rainy Trench
MORVAL

Scale 1000 2000 Yds

CHAPTER VII

THE WINTER ON THE SOMME, 1916-1917—THE GERMAN RETREAT TO THE HINDENBURG LINE, 14TH OF MARCH TO 5TH OF APRIL, 1917.

(1) THE GUARDS IN THE TRAINING AREA—PREPARATIONS FOR THE WINTER—WORK OF THE DIVISIONAL R.E. AND 4TH BN. COLDSTREAM GUARDS (PIONEERS) IN THE DEVASTATED AREA.

ON leaving the battle front the infantry of the Guards Division was given a period of training, and, in despite of the bad weather which prevailed throughout the month of October, a great deal of useful work was accomplished. In addition to the usual steady drill, and musketry, Lewis-gun and bombing practice,* the troops did a certain amount of route marching and tactical exercises in the field, while staff rides were held for the benefit of the officers. Although a speedy return to open warfare was scarcely anticipated by the Guards after their recent experiences in the Somme operations, the necessity for the division being fully prepared for any eventuality was not lost sight of by Major-General Feilding and his staff. During this period of training a number of non-commissioned officers belonging to the New Zealand Division were attached to each of the Guards battalions in order to obtain an insight into the Guards methods of discipline and drill, the value of which was becoming more and more apparent as the war proceeded.

While the division was out of the line the Major-General

---

* During October the 3rd Guards Bde. lost 7 men accidentally wounded at bombing and trench-mortar practices.

held several parades for the presentation of medal ribbons, and, on the 1st of November, the Guards were honoured with a visit from H.R.H. the Duke of Connaught, Colonel of the Grenadier Guards, who was accompanied by Colonel Sir Henry Streatfeild, Lieut.-Colonel commanding the same regiment. His Royal Highness held an inspection of the Division in a field between Dromesnil and Fresneville,* and all officers and other ranks, who had been decorated for gallantry since the beginnning of the war, were especially paraded, and addressed by him.†

Preparations for the coming winter were now busily pushed forward by the Administrative Staff. Warm clothing was issued to the troops and such arrangements as were possible were made for their welfare in the light of the experience gained in the two preceding winters.

A general overhaul of the transport was carried out, temporary workshops for the repair of vehicles being established in the divisional area as the nearest Ordnance workshops were at Abbeville. The Veterinary Section made a thorough inspection of all the animals in the division, as a result of which it was found necessary to evacuate many of the horses—the strain upon the horses during the Somme operations had been particularly severe. A veterinary inspection of the artillery horse lines at Carnoy in November, where the approach to the water troughs was found to be knee-deep in mud, led to the adoption by all the mounted units of the division of special precautions against necrosis

---

* The troops present on this occasion were :—The 1st, 2nd and 3rd Guards Bdes., with their machine-gun companies and trench-mortar batteries; the 76th Field Company, R.E.; Nos. 3, 4 and 9 Field Ambulances, R.A.M.C.; and detachments of the divisional Train and Supply Column—a force of about 10,000 men.

† *See* "History of the Welsh Guards," pp. 130, 131. Early in the New Year, the 23rd of February, 1917, General Lyautey, who was then the French Minister of War, visited divisional headquarters and inspected the 3rd Guards Bde. at Ville. In February the division was visited by two officers belonging to H.M.S. *Courageous*, who spent a night in the trenches. Later on, just before the Guards left the Somme area, on the 15th of May, H.M. the King of the Belgians inspected the 2nd Guards Bde. On this occasion, for the first time in the history of the battalion, its kilted pipers preceded the 2nd Bn. Irish Guards on parade.

and mud fever during the winter months; but, even so, the casualties among horses were heavy.

Although the majority of the Guards infantry remained in the training area until the second week of November, the R.E. and the 4th Bn. Coldstream Guards (Pioneers) were not so fortunate. In the devastated area occupied by the XIV Corps there was so much reconstruction work to be done that all available labour had to be employed. Defence lines had to be laid out and dug, roads had to be constructed and repaired, huts and horse-standings had to be erected. On the 6th of October, therefore, the 4th Bn. Coldstream Guards (Pioneers) was ordered forward and the 55th and 75th Field Companies, R.E., soon followed the battalion.*

The Pioneers were chiefly employed in making a corduroy road from Bernafay Wood to Trônes Wood; in cutting the necessary timber and filling in the shell-holes and craters; and in loading and unloading wagons. The Field Companies, R.E., worked on the erection of huts in the infantry camps which were being formed along the Montauban—Carnoy road.

On the 6th of November the 4th Bn. Coldstream Guards (Pioneers) returned to the division and two of the infantry battalions were sent forward to work on the roads.

* "The unfortunate Pioneers and two and a half Field Companies were soon hauled back by the corps for road-making, etc. They had a poor time of it. On my return from leave I found that my command had dwindled to half a Field Company. I had great difficulty in locating and visiting the other R.E. and the Pioneers. They had been largely kept hanging about waiting for materials. I determined never again to let them go up alone, as they were neither properly looked after nor worked; and much valuable time was wasted which should have been devoted to training. This is a subject upon which all C.R.E.'s of divisions are eloquent!" Extract from a note supplied by Lieut.-Colonel Brough, C.R.E., Guards Division.

(2) THE GUARDS RELIEVE THE 17TH DIVISION IN THE LINE, 13TH OF NOVEMBER—METHOD OF HOLDING THE FRONT—RELIEF OF THE GUARDS BY THE 5TH AUSTRALIAN DIVISION, 21ST OF NOVEMBER.

The Guards relieved the 17th Division in the left sector of the XIV Corps front on the 13th of November, divisional headquarters being established in Bernafay Wood the following day. For tactical purposes the three Guards brigades were now divided into two groups which carried out their own reliefs. The right group was composed of the 1st Guards Bde., together with the 1st Bn. Coldstream Guards * and the 2nd Bn. Irish Guards; the left group consisted of the 3rd Guards Bde., to which were attached the 3rd Bn. Grenadier Guards and the 1st Bn. Scots Guards. By the institution of this system the troops could count upon occupying the same front, support or reserve trenches in turn, as the various battalions always remained in the same sectors of the divisional front; whilst one brigade headquarters, one machine-gun company and one trench-mortar battery were held in reserve, available for reliefs which were regularly carried out by means of a roster.

The front taken over by the Guards ran along the spur of high ground lying east of Lesbœufs on the right and Gueudecourt on the left.† Although the front trenches were

* On the 12th of November Lieut.-Colonel G. B. S. Follett replaced Lieut.-Colonel R. B. J. Crawford in the command of the 2nd Bn. Coldstream Guards, the latter succeeding Lieut.-Colonel J. Campbell, who left the division to command an infantry bde., in the command of the 3rd Bn. of the same regiment. Major E. B. Gregge-Hopwood succeeded Lieut.-Colonel Follett in the command of the 1st Bn. Coldstream Guards. Lieut.-Colonel Follett was wounded towards the end of November and Captain L. M. Gibbs was in command of the 2nd Bn. Coldstream Guards from the 25th of that month until the 7th of March, when Lieut.-Colonel Follett reassumed the command.

† In front of Lesbœufs it was much the same line as the Guards had left at the end of September. After the capture of the Combles—Morval—Lesbœufs—Gueudecourt line (25th–28th of September) Sir Douglas Haig had intended to push forward at once against the enemy's system of defences covering the villages of le Transloy and Beaulencourt and the town of Bapaume. A necessary preliminary to an attack upon these positions was the capture of the spur lying between le Transloy

fairly deep, there were no communication trenches, and the journey over the open across the devastated area from the reserve line was a lengthy and laborious process which severely tried the physical endurance of all ranks.* There was a desperate shortage of duck-boards, trench grids and other R.E. stores; but, nevertheless, the Guards battalions, assisted by the Field Companies, R.E., did much useful work on the defences and communications before they were relieved in the line by the 5th Australian Division, although the rain which fell steadily during their last days in this sector of the line did much to destroy what they had accomplished.

The relief began on the 21st of November, and, on its completion, the Guards Division was withdrawn to the area round Méaulte preparatory to relieving the French farther to the south. Except for a certain amount of hostile artillery fire, this short period in the line was uneventful—the weather and the state of the ground made any further infantry action impossible on this part of the Somme front.†

and Lesbœufs and the high ground round Sailly-Saillisel. The unfavourable weather throughout October, which converted the whole battle area into a morass, greatly interfered with operations, but, nevertheless, the French succeeded in capturing Sailly-Saillisel, and the British had reached the crest of the le Transloy Spur by the end of the first week in November. See " Sir Douglas Haig's Despatches," pp. 47, 48.

* " There were no communication trenches and, in that windy waste of dead weed and wreckage, no landmarks to guide the eye. Trench equipment was utterly lacking, and every stick and strand had to be man-handled up from Ginchy. . . . It was a test, were one needed, that proved all ranks to the uttermost. The heroism that endures for a day or a week at high tension is a small thing beside that habit of mind which can hold fast to manner, justice, honour and a show of kindliness and toleration, in despite of physical misery and the slow passage of bleak and indistinguishable days." See " The Irish Guards in the Great War," vol. i. pp. 193, 194. Cf. " The Grenadier Guards in the Great War," vol. ii. p. 152.

† The casualties reported in the division during the period (13th–21st of November) amounted to 8 officers and 257 other ranks.

(3) The Guards relieve the French at Sailly-Saillisel, 4th of December—Bad condition of the new Front—Work of the Guards in the Line—Their Relief by the 20th Division, 1st of January, 1917.

The relief by the Guards of the IX French Corps was safely accomplished by the 4th of December, on which day divisional headquarters was established in deep dug-outs at Arrow Head Copse a little to the south-west of Guillemont.* On the 7th, the Division took over some more of the line on the right from the 39th French Division, and the Guards sector of the front then ran from the eastern and north-eastern outskirts of Sailly-Saillisel on the right to a point behind the Morval—le Transloy road about one and a half miles north-east of Morval. The possession of the high ground at Sailly-Saillisel was of the utmost importance to the defence of the divisional area, as it commanded the whole of the Combles valley. A defensive flank was formed, therefore, with machine guns disposed in depth from the village of Sailly-Saillisel to Mouchoir Copse. From this flank excellent observation could be obtained over the enemy's positions and the British trenches could be drained into his line.

But during the winter months of 1916–1917 on the Somme there was little to be feared from the enemy. Rain and snow made the activities of the Germans a matter of secondary importance, and, bad as were the conditions on the British side of the line, those on the German side were probably worse.

On the front of the Guards Division the line was held as a series of posts—" islands " in the mud †—about 20 yards

---

* The taking over of this sector of the line was a somewhat complicated proceeding, especially for the divisional Signal Company, as the French signal system was very different from the British. There was, too, considerable congestion in the French camps behind the line, most of which were in an unfinished condition. The bad weather of course added to the difficulties of the situation.

† " Two days in and two days out of the trenches became the routine till the end of the month, and by degrees the ' islands ' were made habitable." *See* " The Grenadier Guards in the Great War," vol. ii. p. 156.

apart, and reliefs had to be conducted over the open, although, in places, the enemy's posts were not more than 40 yards distant. So terrible was the condition of the ground that men often sank up to their thighs in the mud and had to be dug out.* The area in rear of the front line was little better.† The rest camps—although the sight of the blazing braziers at Bronfay and Malzhorn Farm camps became very welcome to the exhausted men who at last succeeded in finding their way down to them from the line—were seas of mud, while the state of the wagon lines of the divisional Train at Carnoy was so appalling that horse-drawn sledges had to be used to get the forage from the road to the horses.‡

The distances to the front trenches were very great, the

---

* " Unless the men in the trenches, already worn out with mud-wrestling to get there, kept moving like hens on hot plates, they sank and stuck. (' It is funny, maybe, to talk about now, that mud-larking of ours; but to sink, sink, sink, in the dark and you not sure whether they saw ye or could hear you, puts the wind up a man worse than anything under Heaven. Fear? Fear is not the word. 'Twas the Somme that broke our hearts. Back, knees, loins, across your chest—you were dragged to pieces, dragging your own carcase out of the mud.')" See " The Irish Guards in the Great War," vol. ii. p. 117.

† At the beginning of December, 1916, " Works " battalions were formed in the divisions in the Somme area for the purpose of keeping the existing roads in a state of repair, the Labour battalions being unable to cope with the situation without additional help. These Works battalions worked under the chief engineers of corps and had the necessary technical advice regarding road making and repair given to them by the corps roads officers. The hours of work were very long, but the work itself was usually outside the shelled area, and so the *personnel* of the battalions, composed chiefly of non-commissioned officers and men who had had considerable war service, had a chance of resting their nerves after the hard fighting of the summer and autumn. In the Guards Division the *personnel* of the Works Battalion was found equally from every battalion, except the 4th Bn. Coldstream Guards (Pioneers), and had a total strength of between 500 and 600. It was organized in four companies, and was commanded by Major G. J. Edwards, 4th Bn. Coldstream Guards, who had under him a second-in-command, an adjutant and 12 company officers. Accommodation was found for the battalion for the first month in a hutted camp near Carnoy. It was then moved to dug-outs in Maurepas ravine, and then to a camp between Bernafay and Trônes Woods. It was disbanded in April, 1917. During its 4½ months' existence, 1,300 other ranks passed through the battalion.

‡ Nearly 1,000 animals had to be evacuated from the division during November and December.

roads when the Guards arrived in the area were well-nigh impassable, and the going across country over the shell-torn battle-field was most exhausting.

The R.E., Pioneeers and infantry all worked with tireless energy to improve the line and the communications in rear. The three existing communication trenches had finally to be abandoned and duck-board tracks were laid down.* In the front line the coils of French wire were replaced by barbed wire; intermediate and reserve lines of defence were sited and laid out by the R.E.; † dug-outs were made; ‡ huts were erected in the back areas; and roads and tracks were constructed, repaired and maintained so far as was humanly possible." §

* The task of repairing and maintaining the communication trenches was entrusted to the 4th Bn. Coldstream Guards (Pioneers). It was found impossible to keep them open as any kind of drainage was out of the question among the shell-holes, and so the Pioneers were told to lay down duck-walks. "They soon proved themselves adepts at this work, and the supply of trench grids reviving, we quickly had a net-work of duck-walks, leading all over the front area." Extract from note supplied by Lieut.-Colonel Brough, C.R.E., Guards Division.

† The R.E. were largely concentrated on the construction of an intermediate line, which was to be the main line of resistance in the event of a big attack. This line was selected by the G.S.O.1 and the C.R.E. It was wired (with gaps) throughout, certain of the most important points in the trench system being dug to full depth and revetted. Machine-gun positions on the flank were selected, and the general scheme of flank protection settled in conjunction with the divisions on the right and left.

‡ "We had a tunnelling company allotted to us, and decided at once that front line mining was useless. So we started deep dug-outs for our battalion and brigade headquarters in the valley facing north from Haie Wood. . . . These dug-outs were a great success, as may be gathered from the fact that at least three divisions claimed *they* had made them!" Extract from note supplied by Lieut.-Colonel Brough, C.R.E., Guards Division.

§ The care of the important road from Combles leading to Haie Wood and the front line was entrusted to the 4th Bn. Coldstream Guards (Pioneers) and the task of keeping it in repair was a very onerous one. It was so much cut up by the incessant passage of lorries and wagons taking up ammunition for the artillery and R.E. stores that Major-General Feilding felt bound to tell the corps commander that it was out of the question to keep it in a state of good repair. He pointed out that the road was the main approach to the front line, and that, if it were shelled by the enemy's artillery, the approaches to, and exits from, Combles might easily be blocked. He suggested an extension of the Decauville railway line to relieve the traffic pressure

RATIONS BY LIGHT RAILWAY

At the beginning of December the divisional railhead was moved to Plateau, south of Carnoy, which was far enough forward to make it possible to dispense with the Supply Column, and, as the Decauville railway line to Combles ran past this spot, a special siding was erected for divisional purposes. The French provided the necessary rolling stock, and, from the 16th of December onwards, rations were divided into platoon portions at railhead and then sent up to Combles for the troops in the line. Fuel and water were also conveyed by the same train which left the siding at noon daily. In consequence, too, of this use of the light railways, the horses and vehicles of the divisional Train became available for the carriage of road material in the forward area.*

Throughout December, although the visibility was bad, the artillery on both sides was fairly active. The Guards divisional Artillery, which relieved the French gunners early in the month, carried out a regular programme of " shoots " on the enemy's trenches and communications. The German artillery usually took up the challenge and most of the casualties at this time were due to shell fire.†

On the 1st of January, 1917, the relief of the Guards by the 20th Division began, and, on its completion, the

---

on the road. *See* W.D., Guards Division, App. 1228. During the time the Guards were in this sector of the line the Germans shelled Morval with fair persistency, but, owing no doubt to the bad weather which prevented air reconnaissance, they did not discover the main traffic route.

* The 17th Division lent the Guards 40 wagons and teams, and, when these were no longer available, the 29th Division came to the rescue with 23 wagons and teams.

† On the 20th of December A/76 and C/76 were heavily shelled, but only one man was slightly wounded. At Christmas—which was celebrated by all units in the division as enjoyably as the unpleasant conditions permitted—a series of special artillery bombardments was arranged in order that the enemy should clearly understand that no kind of fraternization would be tolerated. A few Germans who wandered into the line bore eloquent testimony to the loss and damage caused on their side of the line by the British artillery. The casualties in the Guards Division during this tour of duty in the line appear to have amounted to 9 officers and 355 other ranks, exclusive of those evacuated for sickness. Considering the weather conditions and the state of the line, the amount of sickness was surprisingly small.

division was concentrated in the Méaulte—Corbie—Ville area with its headquarters at Corbie.*

(4) WORK OF THE DIVISIONAL ARTILLERY DURING THE MONTHS OF OCTOBER AND NOVEMBER, 1916.

When the infantry of the Guards Division was withdrawn from the line at the end of September, the artillery remained in the battle area. The battery positions of all four brigades, R.F.A., were in the vicinity of Trônes Wood, Bernafay Wood and Guillemont, and north-east and south-east of Ginchy. The D.A.C. was still located at Maricourt.

A succession of infantry attacks during the month of October gradually pushed forward the line of the XIV Corps towards the crest of the spur of high ground which overlooked le Transloy from the west and south-west and gave observation over the country beyond. These operations, in which the 4th, 6th, 8th, 20th and 56th Divisions all took part, provided continuous employment for the gunners,† but the almost incessant wet weather made their work very difficult. Ammunition had often to be brought up to the gun positions on pack horses as no wheeled vehicles could be drawn through the mud, and the conditions of life for the *personnel* of the batteries were deplorable.

By the 10th of October the 18-pdr. batteries of the 76th Bde., R.F.A., had advanced and were in action between Gueudecourt and Lesbœufs. D/76 put two howitzers into the latter village and, later on, established the other two in a sunken road south of Gueudecourt. In the arduous work entailed by these moves over the heavy ground the artillery received much assistance from the *personnel* of the trench-mortar batteries, who spent the greater part of October

---

* Corbie now became the railhead. This again necessitated the employment of the Supply Column.

† The G.O.C. the 8th Division complimented the Guards divisional Artillery upon the accuracy of its barrages and the promptitude with which it responded to calls for assistance by the infantry of his division.

DIVISIONAL ARTILLERY REORGANIZED

working on gun positions, dug-outs and tracks. The 75th Bde., R.F.A., by the 12th of October, was in positions near Guillemont. There were no infantry attacks during the last ten days of October, and, consequently, there was less work for the 18-pdrs., but the howitzers, in conjunction with the corps heavy artillery, fired steadily into Beaulencourt, le Transloy, Riencourt and Villers-au-Flos.*

On the 31st of October the *personnel* of the 76th Bde., R.F.A., was withdrawn from the line for a short rest, leaving a guard over their guns.†

At the beginning of November the divisional Artillery gave effective support to the 33rd Division which carried out a minor operation. The enemy's artillery fire was very heavy about this time, but it does not appear to have been particularly well-directed. The 74th Bde., however, suffered several casualties and had one gun destroyed and two buried.

On the 11th of November the divisional Artillery, after handing over its guns and ammunition to the gunners who remained in the battle zone, went back to Méaulte where the reorganization into 6-gun 18-pdr. batteries was effected. By this arrangement the 61st Bde., R.F.A., ceased to exist, its twelve 18-pdrs. being equally divided between the 74th and 75th Bdes., each 18-pdr. battery of these brigades being thus expanded to six guns. The 76th Bde. received no fresh guns and now comprised only two 18-pdr. batteries ("A" and "B"), each of six guns. This reorganization did not affect the "D" batteries in any of

---

* Some figures are available with regard to the ammunition expended during October. The 74th Bde., R.F.A., fired 45,700 rounds from its guns and 5,985 rounds from its howitzers. The task of the D.A.C. may be judged from the fact that 126,613 rounds of gun and howitzer ammunition were supplied to the brigades. In addition to this, the Column was engaged in extensive salvage operations, sending 243,550 fired cartridge cases ; 2,860 rounds of gun ammunition ; 265,590 rounds of S.A.A. ; 2,673 rounds of Stokes mortar ammunition ; and 3,597 hand grenades back to railhead. Nearly 9,300 rounds of gun ammunition was recovered, found fit for use and re-issued.

† Casualties in the brigades during the month were not heavy. The 61st Bde., R.F.A., lost 1 officer and 8 other ranks and the 74th Bde., 1 officer and 13 other ranks.

the brigades, the armament of which still consisted of four howitzers.*

For the remainder of November the three brigades rested and trained in the Hangest area. But the D.A.C. sent a section forward again, on the 23rd of November, to work with the siege artillery in the corps line.

At the beginning of December the 75th and 76th Bdes., R.F.A., took over positions from the French artillery and formed the right group covering the Guards Division in the line. Both brigades were in action by the 6th of December north of Frégicourt and round Combles.†

The D.A.C. (less No. 3 Section) was now concentrated at Carnoy and ammunition dumps were formed at Plateau Siding and at Combles.‡

(5) THE GUARDS RELIEVE THE 8TH DIVISION BETWEEN RANCOURT AND SAILLISEL, 11TH OF JANUARY—WORK IN THE NEW SECTOR—SEVERITY OF THE WEATHER— GERMAN WITHDRAWAL ON THE ANCRE.

Almost immediately after the Guards came out of the Sailly-Saillisel sector of the front, orders were received for them to relieve the 8th Division farther to the south. This relief was completed by the 11th of January, divisional headquarters being established in dug-outs at Maurepas.

The line now taken over by the Guards Division ran along the forward slope beyond the Péronne—Bapaume road with the right just north of Rancourt and the left on the south-western outskirts of Saillisel. The German positions lay along the western edge of St. Pierre Vaast Wood, and, on the extreme right, were only about 50 yards from the British line.

---

* Lieut.-Colonel F. A. Buzzard, R.A., who had commanded the 61st Bde., R.F.A., since October, 1915, assumed the command of the 74th Bde., R.F.A., on the reorganization of the divisional Artillery.

† One battery was subsequently moved to positions near Mouchoir Copse.

‡ No. 1 Section resumed duty as S.A.A. Section for the infantry. No. 3 Section was brought up to Morlancourt about the middle of the month.

WORK IN THE NEW SECTOR

The group system * was now abandoned and the 2nd Guards Bde. took over the front with the 3rd Guards Bde. in support at Priez Farm and Maurepas.† The 1st Guards Bde. remained in reserve in the Méaulte—Ville—Maricourt area where the work of training was continued and a number of Canadian non-commissioned officers were attached for instruction.‡

When the Guards went into their new sector, they found that the position was a good one as the front line outposts just topped the Sailly-Saillisel—Rancourt ridge, and there was a fine field of view. In rear of these posts behind the ridge the troops of the 2nd Guards Bde. dug an excellent support line, and, farther back still, the 4th Bn. Coldstream Guards (Pioneers) soon completed a reserve line formed out of a series of posts which were already in existence when the division went into the line.§ The communications in the

* *See* p. 190.

† Brig.-General J. Ponsonby went on sick leave to England on the 28th of November. He did not return to the division until the 20th of March, 1917. During this period Lieut.-Colonel Lord Henry Seymour commanded the 2nd Guards Bde. Lieut.-Colonel G. C. Hamilton succeeded Lord Henry Seymour in the command of the 4th Bn. Grenadier Guards until his appointment as an instructor at the Senior Officers' School at Aldershot in April, 1917, when Captain (Brevet-Major) Viscount Gort assumed the command of the battalion.

‡ On the 27th of December, 1917, Brig.-General Pereira had relinquished the command of the 1st Guards Bde., much to the regret of all ranks in the brigade, on his appointment as G.O.C. 2nd Division. He was succeeded in the command of the 1st Guards Bde. by Brig.-General G. D. Jeffreys, whose return to the division was a popular event. Lieut.-Colonel W. H. Darell, A.A., and Q.M.G., left the divisional staff on the 23rd of December on his appointment as D.A. and Q.M.G. IV Corps. His place was taken by Lieut.-Colonel F. G. Alston, who remained with the division in this capacity until the 6th of December, 1918, when he returned to England and was succeeded by Lieut.-Colonel H. L. Aubrey Fletcher.

§ " Strangely enough these posts, though dug in shell-torn and apparently water-logged ground, remained tolerably dry, the yellow clay being fairly impervious." Extract from a note supplied by Lieut.-Colonel Brough, C.R.E., Guards Division.

A portion of a tunnelling company was still with the Guards and was employed in making deep dug-outs in the support line, which soon supplied excellent accommodation. Underground company headquarters were also made, and the 4th Bn. Coldstream Guards (Pioneers) constructed one large battalion headquarters, which was subsequently used as an advanced brigade headquarters.

sector were good, the left of the line being fed by the Combles—Sailly-Saillisel road, and the right by the Combles—Rancourt road. Both these roads required a good deal of attention and repair, but they were kept in order as far forward as possible.* There were no communication trenches, duck-board tracks leading up to the front from convenient points on the two main roads.† The R.E. set to work upon the construction of an intermediate line, and, before the bad weather, which brought all work to a standstill, set in, had completed the wiring, traced the new line in detail and mined dug-outs for the flanking machine-gun positions.‡

In view of the fact that the defences required so much work expended upon them, and in order that the troops might make themselves familiar with the new ground with as little interruption as possible from the enemy, a strictly defensive attitude was adopted by the 2nd Guards Bde. during its first week in the trenches. Then the following notice was issued from brigade headquarters with orders that it was to be thrown into the German line :—" Warning. All Germans exposing themselves after daylight to-morrow, January 19th, will be shot. By order." Just before dawn on the 19th, therefore, the warning notices were taken out by a party of the 1st Bn. Scots Guards and handed to a German officer at one of the enemy's posts. This meeting took place outside the enemy's wire, and it was observed that there were about seven men in the post, apparently well-fed and of good moral. Unfortunately, the German officer knew no English and his men were equally ignorant of the language, so the warning was translated to the officer who promised to make it known to the Germans in the vicinity. On the part of the front occupied by the 2nd Bn. Irish Guards,§

---

* The work on these roads was carried out by the 4th Bn. Coldstream Guards (Pioneers).

† A 40-cm. tramline was laid to the support line so that the provision of stores to the troops in the trenches was a comparatively easy matter.

‡ The R.E. had also plenty of work in the back area. Additional shelters were erected, a bathing establishment was fitted up near Maurepas ; brigade headquarters were rendered habitable ; Bronfay Farm was rebuilt as a recreation room, bathhouse and garage.

§ Lieut.-Colonel P. L. Reid, commanding the battalion, who

A DECLARATION OF WAR

Pte. King and one other man went out about 6.30 a.m. with the notices pinned to boards which it was intended to plant in the enemy's wire. This was successfully accomplished, but, as he was crawling away, Pte. King noticed a German behind the enemy's parapet. Several other Guardsmen, who had followed the notice bearers, immediately covered the German with their rifles and Pte. King called to him to come over the wire. After a little not unnatural hesitation, the German did as he was requested, and met Pte. King whilst other Germans looked on. As the German did not understand English, Pte. King—who had served in the Malay Police—tried him with Chinese and Malay with equal want of success. Then he handed over the warning notice with the admonition "Shoot! Pom-pom! Give it to an officer." The German seemed to grasp his meaning, and retired promptly to his own trench, where about forty of his friends were observed to crowd round him. They were oldish men, who looked tired and depressed. During this historic interview the German, whose overcoat bore the numerals "357," endeavoured to look at Pte. King's shoulder straps, but the latter was wearing a leather jerkin in order to conceal them, and so defeated the enemy's curiosity. It was noted that the German trenches were in good condition, and that the ground fell away behind them into St. Pierre Vaast Wood.*

Shortly after this declaration of war had been delivered there was a heavy fall of snow followed by a very severe frost, which put an effectual stop to all digging and revetting, and little could be done in the front area except the carrying up of materials for use when the thaw came.†

returned from hospital in October, 1916, became ill again early in January, 1917, and had to be evacuated. Major E. B. Greer succeeded him in the command.

* *See* W.D., 2nd Guards Bde., January, 1917, Apps. 32 and 38A; *cf.* "The Irish Guards in the Great War," vol. ii. pp. 126, 127.

† "We started taking up stores to the sites where they were required in case of a thaw, but even this work had to cease for we soon had enough materials on the ground for all our requirements. I estimate that the frost penetrated six feet into the ground. We tried some experiments in blowing the ground up with explosives and came to the conclusion that it was almost as slow and expensive as blasting sound rock. The great curse at this period was lack of fresh

THE WINTER ON THE SOMME, 1916–1917

There was no infantry action on the front of the Guards Division during this period, and the bad visibility limited to a great extent the work of the gunners. Nevertheless, the divisional Artillery, which relieved that of the 8th Division on the new front on the 11th, 12th and 13th of January,* in accordance with the artillery policy of the Fourth Army, maintained a regular programme of harassing fire and carried out certain special bombardments and wire-cutting operations. Some of the batteries were hampered at times by the enemy's aerial activity, and the gun positions near Haie Wood were heavily shelled on one or two occasions. On the 8th of February troops of the 17th Division on the left of the Guards carried out a minor operation and the Guards divisional Artillery cooperated in the attack firing in the creeping and standing barrages. The 3rd Guards Bde. Machine-Gun Company also assisted the operation with overhead fire.†

On the 16th of February the weather had improved and the enemy's aircraft bombed the XIV Corps ammunition dump at Plateau siding, causing a great deal of damage. The dump was set on fire early in the morning and continued burning

---

meat and vegetables. Eternal bully-beef is not good fare." Extract from a note supplied by Lieut.-Colonel Brough, C.R.E., Guards Division. The work of the divisional Signal Company on the reorganization of the communications was greatly impeded and delayed by the frost. The cold weather, too, was a source of much trouble to the machine gunners, as their guns could only be kept in working order by a free use of hot water and glycerine and the cartridge belts were frozen stiff.

* The 74th Bde., R.F.A., whose howitzer battery had been replaced by that of the 75th Bde., occupied positions near Haie Wood with one battery in front of Arderlu Wood. This brigade formed the group covering the left of the divisional line. The right group consisted of the 75th Bde., R.F.A., which had taken over the guns of the 8th divisional Artillery in positions behind Frégicourt and near Bois Douage and Arderlu Wood. In addition to these two groups, two siege batteries of 6-in. guns covered the whole of the Guards front.

The 76th Bde., R.F.A., was withdrawn from the line early in January and became an Army Bde.—its howitzer battery, however, was posted to the 74th Bde. as D/74 had been split up between D/75 and D/76 in order to bring up the number of howitzers in each of those batteries to six, the number laid down in the new artillery establishment.

† The 4th Guards Machine-Gun Company arrived at Plateau siding from England on the 23rd of March. *See* Appendix VI.

throughout the day, and divisional railhead had to be moved to Grovetown siding for two days and all road traffic had to be diverted through Bray and Suzanne. The enemy's artillery about this time became much more active, its fire being mainly directed on the front line and the Combles—Rancourt road. On the 3rd of February the positions held by the King's Company, 1st Bn. Grenadier Guards, were barraged and a half-hearted attempt was then made by the enemy's infantry to raid them. No Germans succeeded in getting near to the Grenadiers, who only suffered 4 casualties. A week later the same company drove back a hostile bombing attack without loss.*

By the 24th of February it was known that the Germans had withdrawn from Miraumont and Pys,† and the following day patrols were sent out in order to report whether there were any signs of a withdrawal opposite the Guards. These patrols were heavily fired upon before they reached the enemy's wire, but some of the 1st Bn. Irish Guards cut their way through the wire and engaged the Germans before

* On the 5th of February a German shell unluckily fell among the King's Company, wounding four non-commissioned officers. One of them, Sergeant-Major Bradbury, had both his legs blown off. " . . . it was plain to everyone, including himself, that he could not live. As he was being borne away he asked to speak to the Adjutant, Captain Pearson-Gregory, who at once came up thinking it was some personal request or last wish the dying man wanted to communicate. 'You won't forget, Sir,' said Bradbury, ' the Battalion has to find a fatigue party of a hundred men to-morrow early.' . . . His sole idea, to the very last, was to do his duty to the Battalion." *See* " The Grenadier Guards in the Great War," vol. ii. p. 164.

† The capture of Beaumont Hamel (13th–18th of November, 1916) had secured to General Gough's Army the command of the valley of the Ancre on both banks of the river at the point where it entered the German lines. In January, 1917, operations, designed for the purpose of driving the enemy from the remainder of the Beaumont Hamel spur, were recommenced and steadily proceeded with. The spur was captured on the 11th of January and the Germans were driven out of the rest of the Ancre valley south of Serre hill on the 5th of February. The next day they evacuated their positions lying between Stuff Redoubt and Grandcourt, and the troops of General Gough's Army, continuing their pressure, moved forward up the Beaucourt valley. On the 17th, the actions of Miraumont were fought which resulted in the British gaining complete command over the enemy's defences and round Pys and Miraumont. Both these villages were then evacuated by the Germans.

retiring to their own line with 1 officer and 4 men wounded.*
Four days later patrols again reconnoitred the enemy's
trenches and posts. This reconnaissance, which took place
late in the day after an attack had been made by troops of
the 29th Division on Palz trench at Saillisel,† found the
Germans in strength and fully prepared to defend themselves.

(6) Extension of the Divisional Front—German withdrawal to the Hindenburg Line—Pursuit by
the Guards—Difficulties of the Advance—The
Guards ordered to consolidate their new
positions.

In the first week of March the front of the Guards Division
was extended to the left, the 3rd Guards Bde. relieving a
brigade of the 29th Division as far northward as Sailly-
Saillisel. The XIV Corps had now only two divisions in the
line—the Guards on the right and the 20th Division on the
left.‡

A general withdrawal of the German Armies to the
Hindenburg Line had been anticipated for some time past
by the Intelligence Branch of the British General Staff.§
The marked increase in the volume of hostile artillery fire,
therefore, which began early in March and grew in intensity
as the days went by, was interpreted by the Guards as a
sign that the enemy's retirement from that particular sector
of the line was timed to take place in the near future—his
gunners were clearly firing away their surplus ammunition

---

* *See* " The Irish Guards in the Great War," vol. ii. pp. 209, 210.

† The divisional Artillery and the machine-gun company attached
to the 2nd Guards Bde. assisted in this attack. The trench in question
was captured by the troops of the 29th Division, but subsequently
half of it had to be abandoned owing to the severity of the enemy's
artillery fire.

‡ About this date some of the guns were withdrawn on this part of
the line—the artillery left to cover the whole of the XIV Corps front
consisting of three army brigades, the Guards divisional Artillery
and one brigade of the 29th divisional Artillery.

§ *See* " Sir Douglas Haig's Despatches," p. 71.

THE GERMANS BEGIN TO WITHDRAW 205

preparatory to moving back their guns.* The vigilance of the watch maintained upon the enemy's trenches was redoubled, and all preparations were made by Major-General Feilding and his staff to enable the pursuit of the enemy to be taken up at a moment's notice. The method of advance to be adopted by the infantry was settled; forward artillery positions were reconnoitred; and dumps of the R.E. and other stores necessary for an advance were formed and placed as near as possible to the front.†

Patrol encounters now became frequent, and fires could be observed behind the enemy's lines. On the night of the 13th of March, however, when the Germans actually began their withdrawal opposite the Guards Division, nothing unusual was noticed, and it was not until the afternoon of the next day, when the enemy began firing at his own forward trenches, that the departure of the German infantry from its front line positions was discovered.‡

At dusk that evening, the 14th of March, the Guards battalions in the front line § pushed forward and took

---

* " Not till towards mid-March did the much-written-of German ' crack ' affect their chilly world. The C.O.'s of the Battalions conferred at Brigade Headquarters on the 13th to discuss the eventuality, and in the middle of it the Major-General came in and announced there was good reason to think that the retirement in front of them would begin that night." See " The Irish Guards in the Great War," vol. ii. p. 131.

† *E.g.* material for repair of roads; artillery bridges; posts, notice boards and tapes for marking tracks; ropes, buckets and windlasses for wells; crowbars and explosives; tools of all kinds.

‡ It is difficult to decide definitely who actually first entered the German line and found it empty. Captain D. H. Brand is credited with having walked along the enemy's trench on the edge of St. Pierre Vaast Wood and found it empty. No mention is made of his having been accompanied by anyone else. *See* W.D., 1st Bn. Scots Guards, March, 1917. The 75th Bde., R.F.A., states in its diary that Second-Lieutenant Cropper of D/75, who was acting as F.O.O., entered the German trench at 2 p.m. on the 14th of March with an infantry patrol and at once reported the enemy's withdrawal. The 74th Bde., R.F.A., reported that a " F.O.O. went into the wood with an infantry officer." *See* W.D's. 75th and 74th Bdes., R.F.A., March, 1917.

§ In the right sector of the divisional front (2nd Guards Bde.) were the 1st Bn. Scots Guards and 1st Bn. Coldstream Guards, on the right and left respectively; in the left sector (1st Guards Bde.) the 1st Bn. Irish Guards on the right and the 2nd Bn. Coldstream Guards on the left were holding the line.

possession of the German front posts and trenches. On the right of the line patrols of the 1st Bn. Scots Guards, which were sent on into St. Pierre Vaast Wood, had some skirmishing with the enemy and suffered several casualties, but otherwise there appears to have been little or no opposition to this—the first stage of the advance.

As the gunners had already settled upon their new positions, they were able to take forward their guns without delay, and thus during the next few days it was possible for the infantry to push forward the outpost line with the support of the artillery.* But the advance was by no means a rapid one. The local opposition of the skilfully posted German rearguards and the heavy fire of the enemy's guns, combined with the difficult nature of the country, made it necessary for the troops to advance with great caution—the whole movement was carried out with the precision of the drill-book, with perfect discipline and with steady persistency.

At 7 a.m. on the 15th of March the 1st Bn. Scots Guards advanced into St. Pierre Vaast Wood, keeping touch with troops of the 8th Division on its right and with the 2nd Bn. Irish Guards, which had relieved the 1st Bn. Coldstream Guards, on its left. The Scots Guards met with no opposition, but the advance of the 2nd Bn. Irish Guards was checked by the enemy's long range machine-gun and artillery fire, which also considerably interfered with the movements of the 1st Battalion of the same regiment in the vicinity of Sailly-Saillisel.† However, at nightfall, the whole of the

---

* The Guards divisional Artillery, as a matter of fact, although some of its guns were moved forward to positions on the reverse slope of the Rancourt-Saillisel ridge, was unable to do much shooting as the advance progressed. On the 17th of March all firing upon villages had to be stopped as the exact whereabouts of the infantry was uncertain. On this day, however, the 74th Bde., R.F.A., found a good target—firing upon a party of Germans engaged upon the demolition of dug-outs in the trenches west of St. Martin's Wood. The gunners proceeded to reconnoitre the route forward through Rancourt and St. Pierre Vaast Wood, and selected advanced positions, but, on the 19th, they were ordered to stand fast.

† *See* " The Irish Guards in the Great War," vol. ii. p. 133, *cf.* also *ib.*, vol. i. pp. 211, 212. On the 3rd of March Lieut.-Colonel R. C. McCalmont had relinquished the command of the 1st Bn. Irish Guards on his being appointed to the command of an infantry bde. The

German front and support systems were in the possession of the Guards Division.

On the 16th, the 1st Bn. Scots Guards occupied the north-eastern portion of St. Pierre Vaast Wood and was relieved in the outpost line that evening by the 3rd Bn. Grenadier Guards. The 2nd Bn. Irish Guards also made progress during the day, as did the 1st Bn. Irish Guards and the 2nd Bn. Coldstream Guards on the front of the 1st Guards Bde. farther to the left. But the fire of the enemy's artillery and snipers effectively prevented the Guards from getting to grips with the retreating Germans, and on their left the troops of the 20th Division experienced even greater difficulty in moving forward.

On the 17th, the infantry of the two Guards brigades was for the most part out of touch with the enemy, except with his snipers, who kept up a continuous fire from Government Farm and Le Mesnil.*

The next day the 3rd Guards Bde. relieved the 2nd Guards Bde. in the outpost line, and, early in the morning, the XIV Corps cavalry passed through the infantry. The divisional Signal Company then established a visual station half-way between Saillisel and Le Mesnil, and reports soon began to come through from the cavalry, which, during the day, reached the line Le Mesnil—Lechelle—Etricourt.† All these villages were stated to be clear of the enemy. The whole

---

command of the battalion devolved upon Major the Honble. H. R. Alexander until the arrival of Major C. E. A. S. Rocke in May.

* *See* "The Irish Guards in the Great War," vol. ii. p. 134. The German retreat was undoubtedly conducted with great skill. "One cannot say that we caused them to leave one position an hour before they intended. They inflicted upon us a considerable number of casualties . . . they left little or nothing behind." But of course it must be remembered that the task of the (German) Regimental officers was an easy one, however difficult it may have been for the staff. Given time there is no difficulty in withdrawing battalions from trenches by night, for a few snipers and machine gunners, knowing the ground, and retreating from trench to trench, can hang up an advance indefinitely unless the troops advancing have strong reserves and are prepared for heavy losses.

† The divisional Signal Company was now commanded by Major L. G. Phillips who succeeded Captain W. E. Pain in December, 1916, on the latter's promotion.

of the German trench system lying between le Transloy and Bapaume was now in British hands and the few hostile guns which were still in action were firing at very long range.

On the 19th of March the 1st and 3rd Guards Bdes., which were holding the outpost line, were ordered to send out advanced guards in conjunction with the 8th Division to the line le Mesnil—Manancourt—Nurlu, but they were not to cross the Tortille river until the troops of the 8th Division had secured possession of Nurlu. The high ground in the neighbourhood of this last-mentioned village was held by the enemy and the 1st Bn. Grenadier Guards, which was the leading battalion of the 3rd Guards Bde., was compelled to halt west of the river on the outskirts of Vaux Wood and Hennois Wood. On the left of the divisional front the 2nd Bn. Grenadier Guards, which met with but slight opposition, carried forward the line of the 1st Guards Bde. to St. Martin's Wood—le Mesnil where it was in touch with troops of the 20th Division. By this time the divisional Signal Company had succeeded in establishing a visual station at le Mesnil, and the cavalry, which was now in front of Lechelle, Bus and Ytres, was in touch with the enemy's mounted patrols and snipers.*

On the 20th of March the 8th Division occupied Nurlu and the 3rd Guards Bde. was able to enter Manancourt. The following day the 1st Bn. Grenadier Guards was relieved by the 1st Bn. Welsh Guards † in the brigade outpost line which ran from a point about half a mile north-west of Nurlu to Manancourt. Here touch was maintained with the 1st Guards Bde., whose line extended in a north-westerly direction to le Mesnil.

The Guards were now ordered to consolidate their positions

---

* On the 19th of March the Guards battalions were practically out of touch with the German infantry. Their opinion of the assistance given to them by the cavalry is worth recording :—" The cavalry on our front usually withdraws at night and seldom reports anything which our infantry patrols have not discovered several hours previously." *See* W.D., 2nd Bn. Grenadier Guards, March, 1917.

† The 1st Bn. Welsh Guards was now under the command of Lieut.-Colonel G. C. Douglas Gordon, Lieut.-Colonel W. Murray-Threipland having been obliged to relinquish the command owing to ill-health in December, 1916.

as, although the enemy was still retreating,* no farther advance was deemed to be practicable until more guns and supplies could be brought forward, and this was out of the question until the roads could be cleared of obstructions and repaired.† The Germans had done their work of destruction systematically and with great thoroughness. Craters and felled trees blocked most of the roads which led eastward; the walls of all the houses in the villages and farms had been blown in; mines and "booby traps" of various kinds had been placed in every likely and unlikely position. During the advance work on communications was carried on with the greatest energy. But the difficulties in the way of speedy reconstruction were enormous. The thaw, following so long and hard a frost, had converted the country into a quagmire, and the urgent traffic, which it was absolutely necessary to send forward, cut up the remains of the roads and made the work of repairing them all the more difficult.

The divisional R.E. performed invaluable services in "mine-sweeping," ‡ and, with the assistance of the infantry, set to work upon road-clearing and bridge-making from the moment the advance began. The enemy's trenches and dug-outs were searched for "booby traps." § Charges were removed from places prepared for demolition. Roads and

* Equancourt, Metz and Gouzeaucourt could be seen in flames.

† The casualties incurred during the advance were mostly caused by the enemy's artillery fire at the outset. The chief sufferers were the 1st and 2nd Guards Bdes. The casualties in the former brigade during March amounted to 2 officers and 84 other ranks; in the latter brigade, to 3 officers and 86 other ranks, killed or wounded.

‡ "Fortunately we had considered the possibility of 'booby traps,' and I sent forward R.E. parties with the advanced guards to reconnoitre for them. We discovered quite a number of simple traps in cellars and dug-outs." Extract from a note supplied by Lieut.-Colonel Brough, C.R.E., Guards Division.

§ No traps were discovered until Vaux Wood was reached. Several dug-outs in this wood and Hennois Wood were found prepared for demolition in the ordinary way. At Manancourt was found in a cellar a mine which a footstep upon a loose floor-board would have exploded. In another dug-out the danger spot was discovered owing to the third step down to it being a very little lower than the second. Bombs left on a track in Vaux Wood were adjusted so as to go off at the slightest touch. "Explosive rum jars" were found in a good many dug-outs.

tracks were reconnoitred for mines and snares, and cleared of the felled trees which generally lay across them. Craters were filled in.* A floating bridge was repaired for the passage of pack transport across the Canal du Nord near Manancourt, where an arch of masonry in the existing bridge had been destroyed by the enemy leaving a gap of 90 feet at road level. The water supply was also steadily carried forward as there was some fear that the wells in the new area might have been tampered with by the enemy.†

By the 23rd–24th of March (on which days the 1st and 3rd Guards Bdes. were relieved respectively by troops of the 20th and 8th Divisions) a main line of defence had been dug and a piquet line wired along the front held by the Guards.

The infantry of the division, with the R.E. and Pioneers, was now withdrawn from the line, and set to work on the repair of the communications in rear. The divisional Artillery went back to Morlancourt, where it was given some weeks' training before it was sent north into the area of the Second Army.‡ The D.A.C. remained at Maricourt and was employed mainly in the salving of ammunition. The Guards Machine-Gun Regiment, including the 4th Machine-Gun Company, which joined the division on the 23rd of March, and the *personnel* of the Trench-Mortar Batteries, was concentrated at le Transloy for work on the communications.

(7) RECONSTRUCTION WORK DONE BY THE DIVISION IN THE DEVASTATED AREA—CONCENTRATION IN THE HEILLY AREA PREPARATORY TO MOVING TO FLANDERS.

From the 24th of March to the 6th of May the R.E. and the bulk of the infantry of the Guards Division were engaged in the laborious work of pushing forward the broad-gauge railway lines from Trônes Wood to Rocquigny and from

---

* By the 23rd of March the road from Saillisel to Hennois Wood and thence on to Manancourt was fit for the passage of field artillery.

† All the wells at Etricourt were destroyed by the enemy. Samples of water appear to have been taken from other wells, but there is no record of any poisoned water having been discovered.

‡ *See* p. 219.

Plateau to Ham and Péronne.* The R.E. also carried out an extension of the 60-cm. light railway from Haie Wood up to the Sailly-Saillisel—le Transloy road where a small but very useful railhead was temporarily opened. The restoration of the roads, however, was probably the most formidable of the tasks undertaken by the division. The first road to be tackled was that leading from Combles through Frégicourt and Sailly-Saillisel to le Transloy. Two Field Companies, R.E., two infantry battalions and the 4th Bn. Coldstream Guards (Pioneers), with a large number of D.A.C. wagons, succeeded in making it fit for traffic in four days and subsequently widened it to its full width and drained it.† The roads from Ginchy through Lesbœufs to le Transloy, and from Manancourt through le Mesnil to Rocquigny, were also repaired and reconstructed by the Guards Division.‡ While this work was in progress one

* The work on the railways brought the Guards into touch with the 1st Bn. Canadian Railway Troops, whose commanding officer was loud in his appreciation of the spirit with which officers, non-commissioned officers and men carried out the work assigned to them. *See* " History of the Welsh Guards," p. 146 ; *cf.* " The Irish Guards in the Great War," vol. ii. pp. 135, 136.

† " It was a formidable task as the road had been heavily punished by the artillery fire of both sides and various trench systems had been dug across it. However . . . we transferred the remains of Sailly-Saillisel into the numerous shell-holes and obstacles and got traffic going in about four days." Extract from a note supplied by Lieut.-Colonel Brough, C.R.E., Guards Division.

‡ The nature of the work on the roads may be gathered from the following instructions issued with regard to the repair of the road leading from Lesbœufs to le Transloy :—All mud was to be scraped off down to the old road surface which was not to be damaged. Drains were to be dug at the sides of the road—these drains were to be 6 feet clear of the sides of the road wherever possible. The width of the roadway was to be 18 feet—there were to be box drains under the roadway if it was considered necessary. Shell-holes were to be pumped dry and cleared of mud, and were then to be filled with material from the ruined houses —timber below and 6 ins. of broken brick on the top. There was to be a top layer of timber across the road which was to be carefully hand-packed. Big shell-holes might be bridged by portable wooden bridges as a temporary measure for the immediate assistance of transport. *See* W.D., 76th Field Company, R.E., April, 1917. In connexion with these instructions the following description of the state of the road through le Transloy is of interest :—" The *débris* of houses was several feet deep in places. Outside the village the road ran through a cutting

Lewis gun per company was detailed to protect the working parties from attack by hostile aircraft, but, as a general rule, the weather throughout this period was unfavourable for flying and the Guards appear to have been little troubled by the enemy's aviators. They worked with their customary steadiness and vigour, and the manner in which they set about their task earned for them a special word of praise from the Commander-in-Chief when he met Major-General Feilding in Péronne during the course of the month.*

About the middle of April the 4th Bn. Coldstream Guards (Pioneers) was withdrawn from the devastated area for a well-deserved period of rest and training before it was sent north into the area of the Second Army.†

The 4th Guards Machine-Gun Company, after being given a fortnight's training at Bronfay, was attached to the 40th Division, and, on the 5th of May, covered a raid carried out by the 120th Infantry Bde. in the line between Villers Plouich and Beaucamp. The company then returned to Bronfay.‡

By this date the units of the Guards Division were

which had been one of our heavy artillery targets throughout the winter. No sign of the old road surface was to be seen, but it was anticipated that, on the removal of the mud, a lot of the old surface would be revealed intact, having been protected by the large quantity of earth thrown on it from the sides of the cutting. This proved to be so, the road surface coming to light at a varying depth of 2 to 5 feet of mud. The depth of the mud and the depth of the cutting involved five or more throws with the hand shovel during the task of clearing. There were also the usual difficulties with transport control and turning and passing in a narrow space. As far as possible, the road was made full width right along, no attempt being made to carry a rough track forward in advance."

* *See* W.D., Guards Division, App. 188, April, 1917. Earlier in the month the Major-General had issued an order reminding commanding officers that it was an old-established custom in the Guards for officers to take off their coats and work with their men. *See ib.*, App. 187.

† The Pioneers reached Bailleul on the 15th of May. *See* p. 218. The divisional Artillery, and the headquarters of the divisional Train, had preceded them. Lieut.-Colonel H. Davies succeeded Lieut.-Colonel J. C. L. Black in the command of the Train on the 1st of May, on the latter's appointment as A.D. of S. and T., Malta.

‡ The company lost one of its guns, knocked out by a German shell, but had no casualties among its *personnel*.

MUSKETRY TRAINING

beginning to concentrate in the Morlancourt area, preparatory to leaving the Somme front. The Arras offensive was now drawing to a conclusion and the Flanders offensive was about to begin.* The Guards were to go north with the XIV Corps which was to form part of the Second Army.

Divisional headquarters was established at Heilly and the troops spent the remainder of the month of May in billets in the neighbouring villages. As the surrounding country was closely cultivated and the crops were growing, training on an extensive scale was impracticable; but commanding officers were able to give some useful instruction to their young officers in the art of leading men in open warfare, and company commanders had an opportunity of exercising their companies and preparing them for the coming operations. Especial attention at this time was paid in the Guards Division to musketry training, for the Arras offensive had made it only too clear that the long months of trench warfare had resulted in a lamentable falling off in the old skill of the British infantry with the rifle.†

Brigade and battalion athletic competitions, boxing contests and recreations of all kinds marked this period out of the line. The weather was fine and all ranks in the division keenly appreciated their return to civilization after the long winter months spent as road-menders, scavengers and railway engineers in the devastated area.

At the end of May the Guards were moved by train to the area of the Second Army. Before their departure for Flanders the Fourth Army Commander, under whom they had now served for nine months, sent a message to Major-

---

* The Arras offensive lasted from the 9th of April to the 15th of May, but the Guards Division had no share in it. *See* p. 217.

† " By this time specialization had run its course through our armies till the latest platoon organization acknowledged but one section that was known as a 'rifle' section. The others, although behung with the ancient and honourable weapons of their trade, were Bomb, Lewis-gun, and Rifle (Sniper) Sections. But the Battle of Arras had proved what angry Company Commanders had been saying for months past—that infantry lived or died by their knowledge of the rifle. These Somme officers were accordingly told that most of their time should be given to platoon-training, fire direction and musketry."
See " The Irish Guards in the Great War," vol. ii. p. 138.

General Feilding in which he expressed his appreciation of the work done by the Guards in battle and in the holding and organizing of the line. He made particular allusion to the road and railway construction accomplished by the division since the German retreat.*

* *See* W.D., Guards Division, App. 242, May, 1917.

CHAPTER VIII

THE FLANDERS OFFENSIVE, 1917—THE BATTLE OF PILCKEM RIDGE, 31ST OF JULY.

(1) THE ALLIED INITIATIVE ON THE WESTERN FRONT—THE SPRING OFFENSIVE, 1917.

THROUGHOUT 1917 the Allies held the initiative on the Western Front and the record of the year's fighting is a heavy one, especially for the British Army—units of which were engaged upon offensive operations almost continuously from the end of January to the beginning of December. The great French attack in the spring, however, proved a disappointment. Too high hopes had been placed by British and French statesmen upon the ambitious scheme planned by General Nivelle * to break through the enemy's defensive system on the Aisne, and, when his attempt collapsed early in May, the inevitable disillusionment was all the greater. The heavy losses, too, incurred by the French Army, which were much exaggerated at the time, and the feeling that someone had blundered, had a very bad effect not only upon public opinion in France but also upon the

---

* General Nivelle, who had won much distinction at Verdun in the autumn of 1916, replaced General Joffre in the command of the French Army in December of the same year. In February, 1917, he was given supreme control of the coming Allied offensive. The curious and rather complicated story of the Nivelle episode is discussed at great length in "Sir Douglas Haig's Command," vol. i. It is unnecessary to deal with it here. It is not surprising that the confident assurance of the new French Commander-in-Chief of his ability to end the war by means of a single great coup should have appealed to " the politicians"—they were living in dread of the repetition of another "wearing-out" battle, such as the Somme, and were incapable of appreciating the military difficulties which made the success of the Nivelle plan improbable to say the least of it.

moral of the French Army.* This subject is not one into which it is necessary to enter here, but, nevertheless, it should not be forgotten by students of military history, because it was owing to the shaken moral of the French troops after the failure of the Nivelle offensive that the brunt of the fighting during the remainder of the year had to be borne by the British Army—fighting which, putting aside entirely the needs and interests of the Western Allies themselves, was absolutely essential if assistance was to be given to the Russian and Italian Armies.†

The British Army, as has already been related,‡ began to push forward on the Ancre early in January, and the steady pressure maintained on this front, which was originally intended to prepare the way for the renewal of the Allied advance on the Somme,§ undoubtedly hastened the German retreat to the Hindenburg Line. This withdrawal by the enemy necessitated a considerable modification in the scheme of operations as originally planned by the British Commander-in-Chief. It was decided that the British Army should

---

* "Before the offensive was stopped . . . the French Army suffered from disillusionment. The troops had gone into battle with extravagant hopes—believing that this was the last effort in the war, and that victory and peace were coming swiftly. When, within a day or two, these hopes vanished, the effect on the military moral was bad." *See* "Sir Douglas Haig's Command," vol. i. p. 331. Even before the offensive on the Aisne began, the moral of certain units in the French Army had been none too good owing largely to a "pacifist" campaign among the troops. General Nivelle thought so seriously of this movement that he had addressed a memorandum on the subject to the French Government. This memorandum is printed in "Sir Douglas Haig's Command," vol. i. pp. 254–257.

† The Abdication of the Tsar took place in the middle of March, 1917, but the Provisional Government which then came into power continued to carry on the war, and until its overthrow by the Bolsheviks it was clearly the duty, as well as to the interest, of the Western Allies to do their utmost to assist the operations of the Russian Army. The Italians began their offensive in June, but they could hardly have been expected to embark upon it had both the French and British decided to remain completely inactive throughout the summer.

‡ *See* p. 203.

§ *See* "Sir Douglas Haig's Command," vol. i. p. 259, where General Joffre's and Sir Douglas Haig's plans for 1917 are discussed. *Cf.* also "From Private to Field-Marshal," by Field-Marshal Sir William Robertson, pp. 284, 285.

attack on the Arras front and Sir Douglas Haig proposed as a preliminary operation to capture the Vimy ridge, pointing out the importance of securing this high ground as a protection for his left flank. General Nivelle for some reason, which so far has not been satisfactorily explained, was opposed to this course of action. Sir Douglas Haig, however, refused to give way and the successful capture of the ridge by the Canadians early in April and the value of its possession during the critical days of the great German offensive in March, 1918, amply justified his insistence in this controversy.

In the operations which are comprised in the battle of Arras, the Guards Division took no part. This offensive of the Third Army, commanded by General Allenby, was at first attended with brilliant success, but it led to no strategic results—a comparative failure which was almost inevitable in view of the ill-success of the French offensive on the Aisne.* After the French Government had finally decided to bring General Nivelle's operations to an end early in May, the question arose whether the British Army was to continue a "wearing-out" battle on the Arras front in conjunction with the French farther south, or whether its efforts should be directed to the Flanders front. In the end it was decided at a conference held in Paris on the 4th and 5th of May, that, in view of the inability of the French to carry out a further offensive on a large scale, the best results would be obtained by transferring the British offensive to the north—the representations of the British naval authorities as to the paramount importance of driving the Germans from the Belgian coast line in view of the depredations of their submarine warfare being a powerful argument in favour of an attack on this part of the front.

While, therefore, the activities of the Third Army in the

* *See* "Sir Douglas Haig's Command," vol. i. p. 260. It would be a mistake to suppose, however, that the enemy did not suffer severely in the Arras offensive. On the British front alone, in less than one month's fighting, in addition to his other casualties, he lost 19,500 prisoners, including over 400 officers, 257 guns (including 98 heavy guns), 484 machine guns, 227 trench mortars and immense quantities of war material. *See* "Sir Douglas Haig's Despatches," p. 140.

Arras area were maintained on a small scale with the object of deceiving the enemy as to the region in which the new attack was to be delivered,* instructions were given to General Sir Herbert Plumer, commanding the Second Army, to proceed at once with the necessary preparations for an attack on the Messines—Wytschaete ridge, the capture of which was to form the first stage in the Flanders operations.

(2) THE OPENING OF THE SUMMER CAMPAIGN IN FLANDERS—RÔLE OF THE GUARDS DIVISIONAL ARTILLERY AND OTHER UNITS OF THE DIVISION IN THE BATTLE OF MESSINES, 7TH OF JUNE.

The summer offensive in Flanders was successfully opened on the 7th of June by the Second Army which captured in a single day's fighting the Messines—Wytschaete ridge by means of a perfectly planned and thoroughly well executed operation. The infantry of the Guards Division, which had been concentrated at the beginning of June in the Wardrecques—Renescure area,† was held in readiness during this attack, but was not called upon to take any active part in the fighting. The divisional Artillery, however, and the 4th Bn. Coldstream Guards (Pioneers) were employed in the operations both before and during the battle and some account of their share in the victory must be given, therefore, in these pages. The 4th Bn. Coldstream Guards (Pioneers), which was sent northward in advance of the division, reached Bailleul on the 15th of May and moved at once to Locre, where it came under the orders of the IX Corps which

* " The required effect was to be attained by a careful selection of important objectives of a limited nature, deliberate preparation of attack, concentration of artillery and economy of infantry. Importance was to be given to these operations by combining them with feint attacks, and by the adoption of various measures and devices to extend the apparent front of attack." *See* " Sir Douglas Haig's Despatches," p. 101.

† Divisional headquarters was at Renescure ; the 1st Guards Bde. at Renescure and along the Arques—Cassel road ; the 2nd Guards Bde. at Wardrecques ; the 3rd Guards Bde. at Campagne and Ecques-le-Biberou ; the S.A.A. Section D.A.C. at Arques ; and the 4th Guards Bde. Machine-Gun Company at Arques.

WORK OF THE PIONEERS

was holding the centre of the Second Army front facing Wytschaete.

The battalion was immediately set to work upon the tasks of widening roads, laying pipe lines for water, and loading and unloading lorries containing battle stores. Most of this work had to be done during the hours of darkness as Mount Kemmel and the roads east of Lindenhoek and Wulverghem were exposed to the enemy's artillery observation and subject to heavy bombardment. The Coldstream, however, were fortunate in having but few casualties, and by dint of hard work succeeded in finishing their tasks by the 6th of June when they rejoined the Guards Division, billets being found for them at Arques.

The divisional Artillery, with the headquarters company of the Train, but without the S.A.A. section of the D.A.C., upon its arrival in Flanders went first to Renescure, but moved to Strazeele on the 22nd of May. Four days later its mobile wagon lines were established at Dranoutre under the orders of the C.R.A., 25th Division. This division was the left division of the II Anzac Corps which was on the right of the fighting line, and its task on the 7th of June was to advance from a point north of Ploegsteert Wood to Messines.* The 74th and 75th Bdes., R.F.A., were now formed into " N " artillery group under the command of Lieut.-Colonel Bethell, and were added to the four other groups which covered that portion of the front.

The necessary work for the bringing up of ammunition and for the construction and improvement of gun positions north of Wulverghem on either side of the Wytschaete road was begun on the 25th of May under a heavy hostile artillery fire, which caused some casualties and a certain amount of destruction of material in the wagon lines.† By the 1st of

* See W.D., 25th Divisional Artillery, May, 1917.
† On the 27th of May the ammunition dumps of the New Zealand Division along the Wulverghem road were heavily shelled by the enemy and a S.A.A. dump was exploded, causing temporarily a great congestion of traffic. A Guards D.A.C. convoy sustained 10 casualties and lost 20 animals on this occasion, but the officer in charge and his non-commissioned officers displayed commendable coolness and courage in dealing with the situation. During the last three days of May the

June, however, all the guns were in position and the next few days were occupied in registration. During this period most of the battery positions in the area were systematically bombarded by the German gunners, and the *personnel* of the Guards divisional Artillery—especially of the 74th Bde., R.F.A.—suffered fairly heavily, while no fewer than four battery ammunition dumps, three belonging to the 75th Bde., were blown up. Group headquarters, which had been established west of Wulverghem, between the Douve river and the Lindenhoek road, was also shelled intermittently both day and night.

During the first stages of the battle on the 7th of June, " N " group fired in the standing barrages as far as the Despagne Farm line—barrages which were designed to keep all the enemy's defensive positions within 1,500 yards of the attacking infantry's line of departure under continuous fire until the creeping barrage reached them. As soon as this happened, the Guards divisional Artillery joined in the creeping barrage which advanced at a rate varying from 100 yards in 3 minutes to 100 yards in 5 minutes.*

The dust and smoke were so great during the first few hours of the battle † that the F.O.O. of " N " group could see little beyond Hill 63 on the south side of the Douve, and, even after the infantry had crossed the ridge north of Messines village and artillery observers were able to move forward to this high ground, the observation was not good, as the trees and hedges, which are a conspicuous feature of the landscape in this part of the country, greatly obscured the field of view. Several German batteries, which would have been easy targets had they been seen in time, were thus enabled to make their escape. So completely shattered, however, was the enemy's resistance during the morning

---

Guards D.A.C. issued to R.F.A. brigades over 21,000 rounds of ammunition.

* The number of rounds at the gun positions, after the explosion of the dumps, was made up to 7,800 for the 18-pdrs. and 6,600 for the howitzers. The 74th Bde., R.F.A., fired 1,000 rounds per gun on the 9th of June.

† This was, of course, largely due to the effects of the explosion of the mines under the Messines ridge.

owing to the successful explosion of the British mines that the infantry was able to carry all before it and some cavalry was sent forward. As a result of this movement, "N" group, which had had two batteries searching beyond the barrage, ceased firing at 1 p.m. But, almost immediately afterwards, Lieut.-Colonel Buzzard, who was acting as artillery liaison officer with an infantry brigade,* reported a general advance of the enemy's infantry, and the barrage was accordingly again put down. This fire was also effective in checking another attempt at a counter-attack made by the enemy from the direction of Gaapard. At 2.40 p.m. the rate of fire, which had been reduced after the collapse of the threatened counter-attacks, was again increased to cover the advance to the Oosttaverne line, and was developed into a creeping barrage at 3.10 p.m., when the Australians began their attack. Before 5.30 p.m. all the objectives had been gained and the batteries ceased firing in order to lay on their S.O.S. lines.

During the night of the 7th–8th of June no call was made on the Guards divisional Artillery, But the following day the enemy bombarded the new British line fairly heavily, and during the night of the 8th–9th, several S.O.S. calls were replied to by "N" group; no serious counter-attack, however, seems to have been attempted on the front actually covered by the group.

On the 9th and 10th of June both the 74th and 75th Bdes., R.F.A., were withdrawn from the line, and, on the 11th, reached Borre and Pradelles for a few days of well-deserved rest before concentrating at Herzeele. The D.A.C. also moved back to Borre.†

The Trench-Mortar Batteries of the Guards Division also played a useful part in the Messines operations. They were conveyed to a camp east of La Clytte on the 24th of May where

* This officer, who commanded the 74th Bde., R.F.A., acted as liaison officer with the infantry throughout the day, first with the 75th Infantry Bde. (25th Division) and then, when the 4th Australian Division went through the 25th Division to continue the attack, with the 13th Australian Bde.

† The D.A.C. issued 40,000 rounds of ammunition for the Messines operations and also managed to salve no less than 22,000 rounds.

they came under the orders of the 19th Division, IX Corps.* They were attached to the trench-mortar batteries of that division and their detachments were employed in carrying forward ammunition, in constructing emplacements and in firing upon selected points in the enemy's lines. The policy on this part of the front was not to demolish the German trenches indiscriminately, but to disorganize the enemy's defensive system by cutting the wire and destroying his machine-gun emplacements and strong points. The Guards divisional Trench Mortars (heavy and medium) carried out their work very effectively, cutting much wire in front of the German trenches in the neighbourhood of Bois Quarante and Grand Bois, as well as in shell-holes in front of the crater just north of the Vierstraat road.

The tasks assigned to the batteries were completed before zero hour on the 7th of June,† and they were moved back to Borre before the attack began.

(3) THE GUARDS TAKE OVER THE BOESINGHE SECTOR OF THE LINE PREPARATORY TO THE BRITISH OFFENSIVE ON THE YPRES FRONT.

After the arrival of the Guards Division in the area of the Second Army every available moment was utilized by Major-General Feilding and his staff to train the troops for the coming offensive in the north in which it was known that they would be employed. Tactical exercises in open warfare, which, together with steady drill, usually formed the basis of the training practised by the Guards when out of the line, for the time being were dispensed with, and the infantry was given as much practical teaching as was possible in the art of attacking established positions.‡ As many men, also, as could be received there were sent to the musketry ranges near Tilques, whilst an especial point was made of the training by the divisional Signal Company of

---

* *See* W.D., 19th Division, May–June, 1917.
† Zero hour on the 7th of June was 3.10 a.m.
‡ *See* W.D., Guards Division, June, 1917, App. 249.

twenty-eight men in each brigade to act as relay runners to supplement other means of communication in the forward battle area.*

On the 10th of June Major-General Feilding held a divisional conference at which he outlined the rôle which the Guards would be called upon to fill in the coming battle. He explained that the division would be on the left of the XIV Corps, which was to be the northern corps of the Fifth Army, and that its task would be the capture of the enemy's defensive positions east and north-east of Boesinghe.†

At this conference it was arranged that the initial attack should be carried out by the 2nd and 3rd Guards Bdes., and that the 1st Guards Bde. should be employed to exploit their success.

Two days later the 2nd Guards Bde. began its advance towards the front, and on the 15th of June relieved a brigade of the 38th Division which was holding the line east of Boesinghe. The 1st Guards Bde. also moved forward, going into bivouacs in the woods west of Woesten, and divisional

---

* These runners proved themselves of the greatest value during the operations.

† The general plan of operations for the Flanders offensive in 1917 may be summarized briefly as follows :—the Fifth Army, commanded by General Gough, which took over the greater part of the front of the Second Army on the 10th of June, was to strike eastward from Ypres in order to gain possession of the Passchendaele ridge. It was to advance on a front lying between the Zillebeke—Zandvoorde road and Boesinghe, inclusive, with four corps in the line—the II Corps (Lieut.-General Jacob), the XIX Corps (Lieut.-General Watts), the XVIII Corps (Lieut.-General Maxse), the XIV Corps (Lieut.-General Lord Cavan), from south to north. As soon as the Fifth Army had established itself firmly on the ridge, it was to move forward in an easterly and north-easterly direction, the French and Belgians coming into action to cover its left flank until the whole of the area lying to the west of the high ground between the Menin road and Clercken, just south of Dixmude, was in the hands of the Allies. The right flank of the Fifth Army was to be protected by General Plumer's Second Army operating south of Ypres. If the task assigned to General Gough's troops were speedily and successfully accomplished, the intention was for the Fifth Army to advance towards Roulers and Bruges in rear of the enemy's forces holding the Belgian coast line, while the Belgian Army was to push forward from Dixmude and General Rawlinson's Fourth Army, which was to relieve the French near Nieuport early in July, was to advance along the coast in conjunction with the Navy.

headquarters was established in "J" Camp near International Corner, west of the Poperinghe Canal. The 3rd Guards Bde. went to the Herzeele area, where it continued its training for the attack, practising the various phases of an advance in conjunction with contact aeroplanes, and paying particular attention to signal communications and medical arrangements.

The Boesinghe sector of the line in which the Guards now found themselves was situated in the low-lying ground which stretches along the bend of the Yser Canal, north and south-east of the village of Boesinghe, the canal itself forming the dividing barrier between the two hostile trench systems. The country in rear of the German defensive positions, which extended eastward to a depth of about 1,000 yards, was for the most part almost flat and much cultivated as far as Houthulst Forest, which stands on somewhat higher ground. There were no villages in the area over which the Guards were to advance with the exception of Langemarck, a small country town situated on the Ypres—Staden railway line, but the district was studded with farm houses, many of which, it was known, had been put in a state of defence by the Germans.* The enemy, too, from the Pilckem ridge, the northern extremity of the high ground which stretches north of Ypres, and also from a small detached hill lying a little to the north-west of Pilckem, had excellent

* The fullest information with regard to the topography, etc., of the country in and behind the German lines as far north as the sector opposite Boesinghe had been collected by the Second Army, which held this part of the front uninterruptedly from its formation to the beginning of this offensive. This information, derived either directly from refugee inhabitants of the district and German prisoners, or from a continuous study of air photographs, captured maps and other documents, had been carefully codified and arranged in a handy form by the General Staff (Intelligence) of the VIII Corps which occupied the Ypres front from July, 1916, to the beginning of June, 1917. The whole of this material was handed over to the Fifth Army when it took over the line. It was known that most of the farm houses in the German area were solidly built and had concrete cellars, and it was considered practically certain that these cellars had been put into a state of defence by the enemy. The extent, however, to which the enemy had been able to construct concrete block-houses, or "pill-boxes" as they came to be termed, could only be conjectured, as these erections were so skilfully sited and camouflaged that they usually defied detection from the air.

observation not only over the British trenches along the canal, but also over the defensive system round Boesinghe and Elverdinghe, and the communications in rear.

(4) Preliminary Preparations in the Front Area.

It will be seen, therefore, that the position of the Guards was not a happy one from which to launch an offensive—for, in addition to the fact that the enemy could see all the preparations for the attack in progress, the canal bed, which had a surface of about 70 feet of soft and tenacious mud into which a man sank like a stone, and a narrow, shallow stream of water flowing down the middle, was a formidable obstacle —so formidable, indeed, that neither side had made any serious attempt to cross it during the war.

The 38th Division during its occupation of the sector in a time of comparative tranquillity had done its best to improve the trenches, and had expended a vast amount of hard work along a very wide frontage; but of course this did not mean that the preparations necessary for an offensive on a large scale were at all complete or satisfactory when the Guards took over the line. The front trenches along the canal bank were in good condition and a reserve line some 300 to 400 yards in rear was also in fairly good order. There was, however, no support line, and of the four communication trenches between the reserve and front lines, two were out of use and badly damaged. These four communication trenches were at once re-aligned and renovated by the 76th Field Company, R.E., assisted by the 2nd Guards Bde. At the same time, the two long communication trenches, by means of which the reserve line was reached from the country in rear, were put into a better state of repair by the 4th Bn. Coldstream Guards (Pioneers) and linked up with two of the communication trenches leading forward from the reserve line. Connexion with the two other communication trenches was secured by means of overland tracks which were carefully marked out with screw pickets and plain wire. In this way four distinct lines of approach to the canal front were made available for the troops—and these various routes were carried back, cleared and marked through the woods behind the line as far as the road running north and south through International Corner.*

A farm house just north of Elverdinghe Château was fixed upon for the battle headquarters of the division and converted into a veritable fortress by the R.E. The existing battalion headquarters in the front line—one in a cellar in Boesinghe village, a most unpleasant locality, the other in a cellar in a ruined farm house situated on the southern of the two main communication trenches—were both unsuitable command posts during active operations. A little to the east of the farm house, however, the Tunnelling Company,† after desperate efforts, succeeded in finding a pocket of blue clay into which were sunk a shaft and a series of chambers which were made into a combined headquarters for the two brigades destined to carry out the attack, while four new shelters were put up for battalion headquarters in the reserve line. Suitable sites for R.E. dumps in the forward area were selected and filled with the necessary implements and material. But, in order to supply accommodation in close proximity to the front for the stores which would be required for the bridging of the canal and to ensure their safety from hostile artillery fire as many as nineteen chambers ‡ were tunnelled in the canal bank, these chambers being so constructed that they could be broken open from the eastern side, thus enabling the bridging material to be

---

* Of course some of these tracks were already in existence, but the majority of them had to be re-aligned and all the signposts had to be replaced in order to suit the requirements of the new scheme. The greater part of this important work was carried out by the 4th Bn. Coldstream Guards (Pioneers) under the direction of the C.R.E. The battalion worked mainly during the nights and was constantly under shell fire as the grounds of Boesinghe Château formed a favourite target for the enemy's gunners. Its camp, too, near International Corner was often shelled and the battalion was certainly fortunate in not losing more than 1 officer and 31 other ranks during June.

† One and a half Tunnelling Companies were still with the Guards Division.

‡ Only one out of these nineteen chambers proved unserviceable, although several of them contained water.

lifted direct on to the canal. On the right flank of the division, in order to make it possible to carry forward the old road which ran eastward from Boesinghe with as little delay as possible after the troops had crossed the canal, arrangements were made by the Tunnelling Company to blow up the bank of the canal so as to give readier access for the pontoons.* Throughout the course of these various engineering and tunnelling operations the working parties of the Guards Division were harassed incessantly by the enemy's artillery fire—much of which was attributed by the troops, and probably with justice, to the feverish activity in railway construction which was deemed necessary in this offensive. The whole, or at any rate by far the larger part, of this work on the railways was of course carried on in full view of the enemy, and must have made him amply aware—if, indeed, he required any such additional enlightenment—that an attack on an imposing scale was being rapidly staged.†

In addition to the strenuous work in the forward area the actual training for the attack was continued. The troops who were to carry out the initial assault were given as much practical instruction as was possible in the details of the operation which lay before them.

A short length of a stream which ran through the wooded country in the divisional area was selected and converted, under the superintendence of the C.R.E.,‡ into an exact

---

* *See* p. 252.

† The gunners indignantly complained that the unremitting work of the broad gauge railway line, which many competent observers considered was already quite far enough forward for all possible requirements early in June, drew the enemy's fire on to areas in which they fondly imagined they were constructing new gun positions unknown to the enemy. The miles of 60-cm. track which were laid down were of no particular assistance in the preparations before the battle, but might no doubt have been useful had the Fifth Army carried all before it on the 31st of July. " Prevision and provision," as an eminent General on the Western Front was never tired of explaining to his *entourage*, are necessary in the mounting of a great offensive—however inconvenient they may make it for those concerned in the actual business of preparation.

‡ Lieut.-Colonel A. Brough was responsible for the initiation and the carrying out of most of the R.E. preparations for the attack; but he did not remain to see the final results of his work, as he was appointed

model of the Yser Canal, in the crossing of which the assault was constantly rehearsed. Close to divisional headquarters a large sand model was erected of the whole of the area over which the XIV Corps was to operate. This model, which was laid out to scale and showed the enemy's positions together with the natural and artificial features of the country, proved most useful both to officers and other ranks. It gave a good idea of the ground which would have to be traversed, thus enabling the leaders to decide upon, and then to explain to their followers, the best tactics for the overcoming of the various obstacles in the course of the advance.*

(5) THE PROBLEM OF THE CROSSING OF THE YSER CANAL.

Over and above all the other matters in connexion with the coming operations which called for his attention, the outstanding problem which confronted Major-General Feilding was how best to convey his troops across the Yser Canal. The successful conduct of the advance—indeed, the possibility of any advance at all—on the Boesinghe front clearly depended upon the rapidity and precision with which this initial and exceedingly difficult movement could be carried out. Several suggestions for crossing the canal were put forward and considered, but the first plan which seemed really practicable was an ingenious one recommended by the Belgians. By their advice a number of mats about a yard in width and somewhat longer than the canal at its broadest point were constructed out of strong canvas, reinforced with a backing of wire netting and small wooden slats at close intervals. A demonstration on the Poperinghe Canal proved that these mats when rolled up could be carried with tolerable ease and could be unrolled by two men as they went forward. It was found, too, that the mats did not sink much in the

D.D.G.T. at G.H.Q. on the 10th of July. He was succeeded as C.R.E., Guards Division, by Lieut.-Colonel E. F. W. Lees.

* See "The Irish Guards in the Great War," vol. ii. p. 157. The excellent air photographs and maps, which were plentifully supplied by the General Staff (Intelligence) XIV Corps, were also of the greatest assistance to all ranks.

MATS AND BRIDGES

mud and that a rope taken forward as a hand rail served to mark the position of the mat when submerged under water.*

But although this demonstration, and their actual employment in one or two raiding expeditions across the canal, showed that use could be made of the mats when there was comparatively little water in the canal, it was obvious that it would be unwise entirely to rely upon them—for, in the event of heavy rain, the water level in the canal would be certain to rise with great rapidity. Some light, single file, bridges, therefore, made of wooden piers with a foundation of petrol tins and joined together by trench grids, were also constructed by the R.E., and carefully stored in the chambers under the canal bank to which allusion has already been made.†

---

* No less than 500 men successfully passed over the Poperinghe Canal during this demonstration. Two companies of the 4th Bn. Coldstream Guards (Pioneers) were given special training in the putting down of these mats. They were also instructed in the art of laying down the light bridges which were also made for the crossing of the canal.

† *See* p. 226. By about the 23rd of July the bridging preparations for the crossing of the canal were nearly ready. In each chamber under the bank were stored a petrol tin bridge, 5 wooden foot-bridges for infantry, and a quantity of tools, pickets and other necessary stores. Behind each tunnel were 9 mats and repairing materials. A heavier petrol tin bridge was placed in the interval between each tunnel. The conveyance of all these stores to the front line taxed the energies of large carrying parties nightly for the best part of a week. As much as possible was brought up during the daytime, but the heavier loads could only be handled under cover of the darkness, for the enemy's artillery fire not only killed, wounded and scattered the carriers, but it also destroyed material which could only be replaced with difficulty. The R.E. guides did splendid work in getting parties forward through the German barrages, and in collecting men and stores when they had been scattered. " During the last fortnight the company has marched an average of 160 miles per man in addition to daily work. A good portion of this has been with heavy loads and all in shelled areas. The company has been in contact with ' windy ' working parties, and though R.E. casualties have been small, many casualties in carrying parties have been seen. The company is generally worn out and in need of a rest, but its moral remains good." *See* W.D., 76th Field Company, R.E., July, 1917. It should be noted that the " windy " working parties to which reference is made were not supplied by the Guards Division.

(6) Reconnaissance Work by the Troops in the Line.

During the early days of its sojourn in the line the 2nd Guards Bde. did some excellent patrol work, which was of material assistance to the divisional staff when drawing up the operation plans for the offensive.

Throughout the month of June the enemy's artillery and flying force were active in firing and bombing in the area behind the line and left the troops in the front trenches in tolerable peace. The German infantry, too, during this period was quiet and unenterprising.

As soon as they took over the Boesinghe sector, consequently, the Guards availed themselves of the opportunity and lost no time in making a full reconnaissance of the German wire and trenches. It became the practice of the battalions of the 2nd Guards Bde. to indulge in from 5 to 10 minutes' rifle fire each night in order to cover the passage of the canal by their patrols, and it soon became evident from the reports of these patrols that the trenches in the enemy's front system of defence were generally, if not invariably, unoccupied during the hours of darkness.

On the night of the 25th of June, therefore, the 1st Bn. Scots Guards sent a large party of men across the canal in order to test the value of the mats with which by this time they had been provided. The mats, which were in charge of a small party of R.E., proved a great success. The Scots Guards remained about two hours in the enemy's front line trenches without even seeing a German, and reported that the wire was damaged and that the trenches were in bad condition. They also brought back the information that the small stream known as the Yper Lea was dry in many places, whilst in others it was pitted with shell-holes which were full of water and unfordable.

Before the end of June the 1st Guards Bde. took over the line, while the 2nd Guards Bde. withdrew to Herzeele for training,* and the 3rd Guards Bde. moved up into immediate reserve in the woods round Woesten.

* The losses of the 2nd Guards Bde. whilst in the line during this period were 1 officer and 121 other ranks. A practice attack carried

A HOSTILE RAID

The 1st Guards Bde. was as active in patrolling as had been the 2nd Guards Bde. On the 2nd of July two parties of the 2nd Bn. Grenadier Guards crossed the Yser Canal near the ruins of the railway bridge, and found the German front line trenches deserted. They were attacked, however, by some of the enemy's bombers who came up from the support line, and also fired upon, before they withdrew. A few days later the 2nd Bn. Coldstream Guards sent two patrols into the German trenches. They came upon one of the enemy's posts and after a short fight returned with one wounded prisoner.*

This continuous activity on the part of the Guards at last had the effect of stirring up a spirit of retaliation among the Germans and in the early morning of the 14th of July a hostile raid took place. At 1.50 a.m., when it was still very dark, the enemy put down a heavy box barrage round the right of the 1st Guards Bde. front, cutting off the two right platoons of the 1st Bn. Irish Guards. Three-quarters of an hour later a party of about 50 Germans attempted to rush this portion of the line, but was met by such vigorous rifle and machine-gun fire that the majority of the attackers turned back. A few of the more daring spirits, however, made their way into a trench just north of the railway line, and, although one of them was captured, the others managed to make their escape.† Shortly after this episode, the 2nd

out by the brigade at Herzeele was witnessed by H.M. The King, H.R.H. The Prince of Wales, Sir Hubert Gough and Lord Cavan.

* The capture of this prisoner and the discovery of some German documents in a dug-out identified the presence of the 228th Regiment in the line opposite the Guards and of the 49th Reserve Division north of the Ypres—Staden railway line, with the 23rd Reserve Division on its left—information which confirmed the enemy's order of battle as already given in the XIV Corps Intelligence reports.

† Considering the intensity of the box barrage, the front line casualties of the Irish Guards were extremely light: the companies in the support line, which was subjected to a shrapnel bombardment, suffered more severely. See "The Irish Guards in the Great War," vol. i. pp. 221–223. Just about this time the 1st Bn. Irish Guards was singularly unfortunate with regard to casualties. On the 11th of July, Lieut.-Colonel C. A. Rocke, who had succeeded Major the Honble. H. R. Alexander in the command of the battalion earlier in the month, was injured by a fall in the trenches. Major R. V. Pollok from the 2nd Bn. then assumed the command of the 1st Bn. On the 12th of

and 3rd Guards Bdes. took over the line in anticipation of the coming attack, while the 1st Guards Bde. went back to the Herzeele area for further training.

(7) Plan of attack by the Guards Division.

While the preparations in the front area were being pushed forward with as much rapidity as possible, the details of the forthcoming operations were being carefully elaborated by Major-General Feilding and his staff.

At a conference, held on the 18th of June at divisional headquarters, the brigadiers of the 2nd and 3rd Guards Bdes. submitted their plans of attack, and the general scheme for the advance of the division was explained by the Major-General. The 2nd Guards Bde. on the right of the divisional front with the 38th Division on its right, and the 3rd Guards Bde. on the left, with a division of the First French Army * on its left—each brigade, attacking on a front of two battalions—were to assault the first objective, a line running a little north-east of Wood 15 and thence in a southerly direction just west of General's Farm and Palissade Farm across the Ypres—Staden railway.† As soon as this line had been carried, the supporting companies of the battalions which had made the initial attack were to advance and seize the "black line," just east of the Pilckem—Het Sas road.‡ When this objective had been secured, the remaining two battalions of each brigade were to push forward and to capture a line on the eastern side of the road which ran from Kortekeer Cabaret to Pilckem,§ which formed the third objective.

The task assigned to the 1st Guards Bde., the exact extent of which was not definitely decided upon until early

---

July the battalion transport was heavily shelled and all four company quartermaster-sergeants became casualties: later, on the evening of the same day, the transport officer was gassed.

 * The First French Army relieved the Belgians north of the Guards Division in the early days of July.
 † Known as the "blue line." *See* Map facing p. 254.
 ‡ *See* Map facing p. 254.
 § Known as the "green line." *See* Map facing p. 254.

in July, was to exploit the successes gained by the other two Guards brigades. This entailed first the forcing of the passage of the Steenbeek—a stream which in fine weather was not a formidable obstacle, but which was apt to be speedily flooded if there were much rain—and secondly, the consolidation of a defensive position on its eastern side with the left battalion of the brigade linked up with the French at a point a little to the east of Colonel's Farm.* In the event of a complete collapse of the enemy's resistance, the brigade was to push forward without delay to a line east of Langemarck and Wijdendrift.

(8) WORK OF THE DIVISIONAL ARTILLERY, TRENCH MORTARS AND MACHINE GUNS ON THE DIVISIONAL FRONT IN THE PRELIMINARY BOMBARDMENTS.

The artillery bombardment of the German defences before the battles of Ypres, 1917, began on the 16th of July.† On the front held by the Guards Division the field artillery

* *See* Map facing p. 254.
† Sir Douglas Haig in his final Despatch, dated the 21st of March, 1919, states that the third Ypres was an artillery battle—" an intense struggle for artillery supremacy " between the opposing armies. " By dint of reducing his artillery strength on other parts of the Western front, and by bringing guns from the East, the enemy definitely challenged the predominance of our artillery. In this battle, therefore, the proportion of our artillery to infantry strength was particularly large. In the opening attack on the 31st July our artillery *personnel* amounted to over 80 per cent. of the infantry engaged in the principal attack on our front, and our total expenditure of artillery ammunition on this day exceeded 23,000 tons." *See* " Sir Douglas Haig's Despatches," pp. 332, 333. It might possibly be argued that the increase of the German artillery on the Flanders front in the summer of 1917 to which Sir Douglas Haig alludes was a direct consequence of the British concentration in that area, and that it might have been a wiser policy on our part, had it been possible, to have mounted our offensive less elaborately with less advertisement and more of the element of surprise. At the time many of those most familiar with the salient were doubtful whether an artillery preparation on the scale adopted on the Somme and at Arras would be equally successful in the Ypres area. They knew that the water was very near to the surface throughout the greater part of the district and they were convinced that the ground would be ploughed up by the gun fire to such an extent that the progress of the infantry would be immensely impeded and tanks rendered useless.

was divided into two groups, the Guards divisional Artillery together with the Fifth Army Bde., R.H.A., under the command of Lieut.-Colonel A. B. Bethell,* forming the left group for the support of the 3rd Guards Bde., while the group supporting the 2nd Guards Bde. was composed of batteries belonging to the 29th Division.†

As has been already stated,‡ no villages lay in the path of the projected advance of the Guards Division, and in rear of the German trench line which formed the first objective there was no organized system of trenches until the defensive positions east of Wijdendrift were reached. Consequently, in the preliminary bombardment, the heavy artillery and the 4·5 howitzers—apart from counter-battery work—were required to fire upon the numerous fortified woods, farms and concrete block-houses, all of which were likely to prove serious obstacles to the advancing infantry. The rôle of the field artillery was to assist in the cutting of wire; to keep the enemy's defences, which had been damaged or demolished by the heavies, under intermittent fire by day and night; to search areas for parties of the enemy who might be occupying defensive positions in shell-holes or in the open; to co-operate when required in concerted bombardments; and to cover the raiding parties into the enemy's lines. To the trench mortars was given the task of cutting the enemy's

---

* As Lieut.-Colonel Bethell was in command of the group, the command of the 75th Bde., R.F.A., devolved upon Major R. Hovil throughout the duration of the battle. On the 23rd of July Lieut.-Colonel F. A. Buzzard, commanding the 74th Bde., R.F.A., was wounded; he was succeeded in the command of the brigade by Major C. E. Vickery.

† Of the Guards divisional Artillery only the 74th Bde. went into action with the division when it took over the line in June. Its batteries relieved a brigade of the 38th divisional Artillery in gun positions near Elverdinghe, White Hope Corner, Bluet Farm and Zuydschoote. The guns were employed in the usual routine shooting associated with trench warfare. The *personnel* was further employed, however, in preparing new positions for the coming offensive—a task which was shared by parties sent up by the 75th Bde. The men of the D.A.C. worked on the construction of observation posts. On the 11th of July the 75th Bde. began to move into action, and, on the 13th, its batteries covered the front while those of the 74th Bde. took up their battle positions.

‡ *See* p. 224.

THE COMING OF "MUSTARD" GAS

wire and of destroying the strong points in his forward trenches.* On the day the bombardment began, sixteen 2-in. mortars started upon the work of destruction, and a day or two later, three 9·45-in., one super 9·45-in. and two 6-in. mortars were also brought into action.† The Guards Machine-Gun Companies throughout the preliminary bombardment worked in effective conjunction with the gunners—their overhead harassing fire being an important adjunct to the artillery preparation.‡

An unpleasant, but inevitable, effect of the opening of the British bombardment was an immediate increase in the activity of the enemy's artillery, his guns being mainly employed in searching for the British batteries and in shelling with gas the back areas. It was about this time that the Germans first made use of " mustard " gas, which, in addition to producing in its victims some of the usual symptoms of gas poisoning, raised painful blisters on the skin, even through the clothing. So many casualties were occasioned by this new kind of " frightfulness " during the days of preparation for the offensive that a special warning was issued by the Fifth Army as to the nature of the gas, its effects and the precautions to be used against it.§

---

* The Trench-Mortar Batteries of the Guards Division, in spite of the assistance rendered by the *personnel* of the batteries of the 29th and 56th Divisions, had a difficult task in constructing their emplacements and bringing up their ammunition. The latter was delivered as far as Bluet Farm, 1,000 yards east of Elverdinghe, by the D.A.C., and then was conveyed by trench tramway to Boesinghe Château where carrying parties awaited it. On the 17th of July, however, the explosion of an ammunition dump damaged the tramline and subsequently the shells had to be man-handled all the way from the " X " line (*see* Map facing p. 254). Some idea of the amount of work required may be gathered from the fact that during the bombardment which preceded the offensive over 5,200 rounds of trench-mortar ammunition were fired on the Guards divisional front. All artillery *personnel* were given 8 hours' rest in every 24 hours. See W.D., Guards Divisional Artillery, App. 8, July, 1917.

† The two last-mentioned types of mortar were used for the first time during this bombardment and the results achieved by their fire are reported as having been extremely satisfactory.

‡ *See* W.D., 4th Guards Bde. Machine-Gun Company, July, 1917.

§ *See* W.D., Guards Division, Apps. 355 and 393, July, 1917. When good discipline was maintained and the proper precautions taken, it was easy to exaggerate the dangers of " mustard " gas. On the 17th of

(9) Postponement of the Ypres offensive—Further raids by the Guards.

The opening of the offensive had been fixed for the 25th of July, but the British counter-battery work proved so effective that the Germans were compelled to withdraw many of their guns, and it thus became necessary to bring fire to bear upon them in their new positions before the infantry attack could be safely launched.* This led to the postponement of the battle for three days. Then, unfortunately, the visibility became extremely bad, and the French gunners insisted upon being allowed a little more time for their preparations, with the result that zero day had to be put off until the 31st of July.

In view of this change of plans, Major-General Feilding decided to give the two attacking brigades a few days' rest, and so, on the 26th of July, the 1st Guards Bde. took over the whole of the divisional front, occupying the line with one battalion—the 3rd Bn. Coldstream Guards.

Before their withdrawal, however, the 2nd and 3rd Guards Bdes. had been very active in their raids across the Yser Canal. On the night of the 19th–20th of July the whole of the enemy's front line defences opposite the Guards Division was raided by the 2nd Bn. Irish Guards on the right and the 4th Bn. Grenadier Guards on the left. This attack was carried out without any artillery support. Mats were placed over the canal bed by parties of the 4th Bn. Coldstream Guards (Pioneers), but it was found that the water had risen a good deal so that only a part of the passage could be bridged in this way. On the right, some of the Irish Guards had to wade with the water up to their arm-pits, but they succeeded in making their way into the enemy's trenches. They found them deserted and much damaged

---

July the camp of No. 1 Section of the Guards D.A.C. between Elverdinghe and Zommerbloem was heavily bombarded with gas shell. All ranks behaved with great coolness. The transport animals—90 in all—were fitted with their respirators and then led quietly away, the section sustaining no casualties whatever. See W.D., Guards Division, App. 360, July, 1917.

* See " Sir Douglas Haig's Despatches," p. 112.

by the bombardment. Another party belonging to the same battalion effected the passage of the canal, although two men were nearly drowned, and had a bombing encounter with a party of Germans. The remaining Irish raiders found it impossible to get through the mud and water, and had to abandon the attempt.

Four parties of Grenadiers after much difficulty were successful in crossing the canal a little to the north of the Pont de Boesinghe, and found the enemy on the alert. One party had a fairly stiff fight before it could make its way into the German trenches, and an enveloping movement by the enemy, who seemed to be in considerable strength, eventually caused the raiders to retire to their own line—their withdrawal being admirably covered by the rifle fire of the men of the 4th Bn. Coldstream Guards (Pioneers) who were in charge of the mats.*

On the night of the 22nd–23rd of July patrols of the 3rd Bn. Grenadier Guards reported that the canal in the neighbourhood of the railway line was easy to cross, but that farther to the north the water was much deeper. They met with no opposition from the enemy. The following night, however, raiders from the 1st Bn. Coldstream Guards had a sharp fight with the Germans and suffered several casualties.†

The various experiences of these raiding parties and the ominous reports as to the increase of water in the canal did not lessen the anxieties of Major-General Feilding and his staff, for although it was tolerably clear by this time that the enemy was not holding his front line trenches in any strength, it was yet equally clear that his troops were fairly on the alert, and that, in the event of the water rising to any appreciable extent, the passage of the canal must inevitably be a lengthy and costly operation.

The effect, too, of the enemy's artillery fire on the front

---

* *See* W.D., 3rd Guards Bde., July, 1917.

† Two German deserters surrendered on the 24th of July. They enlarged upon the effectiveness of the British bombardment and stated that no rations had reached the enemy's troops in the front line trenches for five days.

trenches, in retaliation for the British bombardment, during this period of waiting, showed only too clearly what heavy losses the crossing of the canal might entail.*

(10) The crossing of the Yser Canal, 27th of July.

The anxieties of those responsible for the crossing of the Yser Canal by the Guards Division were unexpectedly laid to rest by the action of the enemy. In the early hours of the morning of the 27th of July two wounded men belonging to the 38th Division were observed on the bank of the canal opposite the Guards front and were brought into the British lines without any sign of life being observed in the enemy's trenches.† A report was also received at divisional headquarters, before 9 a.m. the same day, from an R.F.C. observer stating that there were few if any Germans west of the Steenbeek, at any rate in the sector of the line facing the Guards Division.

Upon receipt of this important information Major-General Feilding made up his mind to attempt the crossing of the Yser Canal in broad daylight and with no preliminary artillery bombardment or covering fire. He sent at once for Lieut.-Colonel Crawford, commanding the 3rd Bn. Coldstream Guards whose battalion, it will be remembered, was holding the divisional front, and told him to cross the canal and then to send forward strong patrols as far as the line, Baboon support trench—Artillery Wood, the object being to secure as good a defensive position as possible on

---

* The casualties in the line were heavy. The 1st Bn. Scots Guards, for example, which took over the 3rd Guards Bde. front on the 22nd of July, lost 5 officers and 200 other ranks in less than four days—the majority of the casualties being due to gas. Two days before, the 1st Bn. Coldstream Guards had the misfortune to lose its third commanding officer, Lieut.-Colonel E. B. Gregge-Hopwood. He was killed together with his second in command, Major S. Burton, by the same shell when going on a tour of inspection after taking over the line. The command of the battalion devolved on Major J. C. Brand. Lieut.-Colonel Gregge-Hopwood was an officer of exceptional ability and experience, and his death was a severe loss to the division.

† See " The Grenadier Guards in the Great War," vol. ii. p. 201.

THE 3RD COLDSTREAM CROSS THE CANAL

the eastern side of the canal.* At about 5.20 in the afternoon, therefore, four patrols of the 3rd Bn. Coldstream Guards crossed the canal on mats, and, finding the German front trenches completely deserted, quietly continued to feel their way forward, while four other patrols followed in immediate support. A few of the enemy were either killed or captured by the leading patrols as they advanced, while those which followed unearthed a few more Germans hiding in dug-outs south of the Ypres—Staden railway line.†

The Coldstream patrols eventually reached a line, Wood 14—south of Bois Farm—Baboon reserve trench—south-west edge of Artillery Wood—Ypres-Staden railway line, and were in touch with troops of the 38th Division in Canal avenue on their right and with the French on their left.‡ By this time, however, the Germans were beginning to concentrate, and the Guards outposts were subjected to a good deal of machine-gun and rifle fire. The Coldstream, therefore, set to work to dig a trench in rear of the position which they had gained, and, as soon as this had been completed, two companies were stationed in the new front line and one company in the new support trench, while the remaining company stayed just east of the canal.

After darkness had set in, the French decided to retire,

---

* An explanation for the unexpectedly easy crossing of the canal which followed is contained in the XIV Corps Intelligence Summary. It appears that when the British aircraft went over the enemy's lines in the early morning of the 27th of July the Germans took shelter in their dug-outs. This accounted for the air report that the enemy had deserted his positions. Opposite the Guards Division the German front was thinly held because sounds of tunnelling had been heard on the canal bank and the enemy, after his unpleasant experience at Messines, was fearful of mines—moreover, a portion of the line was really destitute of defenders as a company of the 226th R.I. Regt. (49th Reserve Division) had retired without orders owing to the severity of the British artillery bombardment. A similar retirement took place opposite the French farther north, but the 23rd Reserve Division, which was holding the front opposite the 38th Division, was in strength and showed little disposition to give ground. *See* Intelligence Summary, No. 47, XIV Corps, July, 1917.

† The total captures amounted to 2 officers and 42 other ranks.

‡ The French troops on the left crossed the Yser Canal about the same time as the Guards and troops of the 38th Division, whose line already lay on the far side of the canal, moved forward.

while the troops of the 38th Division found themselves unable to maintain their hold on the new positions which they had secured. These retrograde movements on both sides of them made it necessary for the Coldstream to throw back two defensive flanks. Throughout the night of the 27th–28th of July, the battalion worked hard to improve its position and its patrols were very active; * the enemy, however, made no attempt at a counter-attack, and the new line was more or less firmly consolidated by daybreak on the 28th. By 5 a.m., too, the 4th Bn. Coldstream Guards (Pioneers) had succeeded, notwithstanding the vigorous shelling of the canal bank by the enemy's artillery, in placing fourteen bridges of various kinds across the canal, twelve of which remained available for troops from this time onwards until the offensive was launched on the 31st of July.

With the return of daylight the French reappeared on the scene, returning to their position at Wood 14. This relieved any anxiety about the left flank, but on the right it was deemed advisable to maintain the defensive flank from Artillery Wood along the railway line and Canal avenue to the junction of the Yser Canal and the Yper Lea.

Although it was soon apparent that the enemy was in some strength in Cariboo avenue and Artillery Wood, the 28th of July passed tolerably quietly in the new line, and the 1st Bn. Irish Guards, consequently, was able to take over without much difficulty the portion of the front between Douteuse House and Wood 14. The Germans, indeed, appear to have been under the impression for some time during the day that the Guards had retired, for most of the enemy's men who were captured on the 28th were on their way to take up their old positions.† In the evening—by

---

* The Coldstream were in constant touch with the enemy throughout the night and captured 1 officer and 20 other ranks, besides killing or wounding a number of Germans.

† This may have been the impression among the troops in the area immediately behind the forward trench system, but the situation must have been known farther in rear as a German wireless message was intercepted during the day ordering a counter-attack to drive back the Guards across the canal. "Point 195" was given as the spot

which time the new positions held by the Guards had no doubt been more or less accurately located by hostile aeroplane observers—the enemy's artillery became much more aggressive, both the advanced line held by the 1st Guards Bde. and also the canal front being heavily shelled.* The Germans also attempted to make a counter-attack from the direction of Artillery Wood and the Ypres—Staden railway line, but, although they were in some force, they were quickly dispersed and driven back by artillery and machine-gun fire.†

During the night of the 28th–29th of July the 1st Bn. Irish Guards, whose patrols were particularly active, seized a German block-house in front of Bois Farm, capturing a machine gun, and killing or taking prisoner most of its garrison. Throughout the 29th the enemy's artillery maintained a persistent bombardment on the Guards front, but in spite of this, about dusk that day, the battalions of the 2nd and 3rd Guards Bdes., which were to carry out the attack on the 31st, successfully relieved the 3rd Bn. Coldstream Guards and the 1st Bn. Irish Guards in the front line.‡

---

for the concentration for this attack. This point was identified on one of the enemy's maps as the junction of Canal avenue and Cable support trench. The Guards line was accordingly strengthened at this point and machine guns and Lewis guns placed in suitable positions to cover the defence.

* Half of the 76th Field Company, R.E., with an infantry carrying party, which was going forward with wire for the new line, was caught in the enemy's barrage near the canal. Most of the carriers were dispersed and the few sappers who made their way to the forward area had only enough wire with them to cover 120 yards. In the early morning of the 29th of July, however, men belonging to the same Field Company managed to lay a heavy footbridge across the canal at Hunter Street, just south-west of Pont de Boesinghe, and thence marked out a track with tape and pickets to the new front line. During the night of the 29th–30th of July another attempt was made to carry forward wire and other material for the construction of strong points in Baboon reserve trench; but the 55th Field Company, R.E., which was employed on this attempt was no luckier than the 76th Company, being checked by a heavy hostile barrage.

† This was the counter-attack to which allusion was made in the captured wireless message. *See* note on p. 240.

‡ The XIV Corps commander sent a special message of congratulation to Brig.-General Jeffreys, commanding the 1st Guards Bde. :—
" Although there are much bigger things ahead of you I do congratulate

The advance of the Guards on the 27th of July, combined with this relief and the ant-like activity in rear of the British lines, no doubt made it plain to the German observers that the long expected offensive was at last about to be launched, and the enemy's guns were continuously active during the night of the 29th of July and throughout the whole of the following day. The front line, the canal bank, Boesinghe and the district in rear of that village were systematically bombarded.* Nevertheless, the movement of troops to their appointed positions went forward with tolerable smoothness even during the light of day, and, once dusk had set in, the actual concentration of the Guards battalions in their forming up positions for the attack was carried out with rapidity and with perfect precision.†

By 1 a.m. on the 31st of July the leading battalions of the 2nd and 3rd Guards Bdes. were all east of the canal and were ready to advance from a line a little in rear of the forward positions which had been held by the Guards Division since the 27th of July. The remaining two battalions of each brigade were stationed in the old front line and the "X" line, while the troops of the 1st Guards Bde. were in a position of readiness north of Cardoen and Roussel Farms, behind Elverdinghe. The officers were all dressed and equipped like their men, and each brigade was accompanied by its trench mortars and a proportion of the guns belonging to its machine-gun companies.

your brigade most heartily on your achievements of the past few days. I believe the successful crossing of the canal will prove the salvation of hundreds of gallant Guardsmen." See W.D., 1st Guards Bde., App. 7, July, 1917.

* On the extreme right of the front of the Guards Division the 1st Bn. Scots Guards lost about 76 men, and one of the enemy's shells struck Bn. headquarters, unfortunately wounding Lieut.-Colonel Romilly, the commanding officer. Captain Hugh Ross took over the command of the battalion.

† The comparative immunity with which all the troops reached their places was largely due to the fact that the artillery carried out a gas bombardment of the enemy's gun positions from about 10 p.m. on the night of the 30th which lasted almost to the time when the advance was due to begin. This successful bombardment appears to have been suggested by Brig.-General J. Ponsonby, commanding the 2nd Guards Bde. See W.D., Guards Division, App., Report of the 2nd Guards Bde., July, 1917.

THE ATTACK LAUNCHED

(11) Artillery and Machine-gun Barrage, 31st of July.

Much time and attention were given to the artillery arrangements for the 31st of July—for, in view of the enemy's great strength in this arm and the almost uninterrupted observation which his gunners had over the battle area, it was recognized that unless the fullest protection were afforded to the infantry the task of the attacking troops might be too onerous a one—even for the Guards. In the artillery programme, as finally drawn up, it was arranged that the advance of the Guards brigades should be covered by a creeping barrage, provided by six brigades, R.F.A., and that this barrage should be moved forward at an average rate of 100 yards in 4 minutes. The fire of the field artillery was also to be supplemented by a machine-gun barrage supplied by the 2nd, 3rd and 4th Guards and the 88th Machine-Gun Companies—each company being represented by two sections of its guns.

In addition to the creeping barrage, the attacking troops were to be further protected by means of a standing barrage, provided by the heavy artillery of the XIV Corps, which was to be lifted eastward in advance of the creeping barrage. These artillery plans had been settled before the advance across the Yser Canal on the 27th of July took place; but, except that the barrage on the front of the Guards Division and the 1st French Division had to be timed to come down a little later and a little farther forward than had been arranged, the programme required no alteration.

(12) Advance of the Guards to their first Objective,
31st of July.

The early hours of the 31st of July were dull and overcast, but no rain fell, and, at 3.50 a.m. zero hour, the artillery barrage came down in front of the 38th Division, and the attacking troops of that division moved forward. The enemy immediately began to shell the line of the Guards Division, but not with much severity, and thirty-four minutes later, when the advance of the 38th Division had reached the level of the Guards front, the British barrage was extended northward and the leading troops of the 2nd and 3rd Guards Bdes. dashed forward to the attack.

The advance began on the extreme right of the line of the 2nd Guards Bde. as the right flank battalion—the 1st Bn. Scots Guards—had to keep in touch with the troops of the 38th Division. The Scots Guards met with but little resistance from the enemy and reached their first objective without much difficulty. The 2nd Bn. Irish Guards, on the left of the Scots Guards, had an even easier task as they made their way to the " blue line " within a quarter of an hour from the beginning of the attack, having encountered no opposition of any kind. The two battalions set to work at once to consolidate the new front, linking up with the 16th R.W. Fusiliers (38th Division) on their right. During this work of consolidation the Scots Guards suffered a good many casualties from the fire of a machine gun in Artillery Wood, the presence of which had not been discovered during the advance. It took some little time to clear the enemy out of the wood, but the task was successfully carried out and the new position made tenable.

Meanwhile, on the left of the Guards advance, the 3rd Guards Bde. with the 1st Bn. Grenadier Guards on the right and the 1st Bn. Welsh Guards on the left, had also reached the line of the first objectives.

The actual advance of these two battalions was carried out with little fighting, but the Grenadiers had had several casualties, including one company commander, before they moved forward to the attack. The Germans held out for some time in block-houses in Wood 15, but the Welsh Guards by means of a vigorous bombing attack eventually drove them out of their strongholds. Both the battalions of the 3rd Guards Bde. arrived on their new line at the appointed time, having killed, wounded or captured about 150 of the enemy. A perfect cooperation with the French on the left flank was a feature of this advance which largely contributed to its complete success.

A HARD TASK FOR THE IRISH GUARDS

(13) ADVANCE TO THE SECOND OBJECTIVE.

Soon after 5 a.m. the 2nd Guards Bde. continued its advance to the second objective. This was carried out, as arranged, by the supporting companies of the two battalions which had made the original attack. The Scots Guards again met with but slight opposition, the only resistance which at all delayed their progress coming from a few of the enemy's machine gunners posted in shell-holes. The Irish Guards had a much harder task.* They encountered a very heavy enfilade machine-gun fire from the direction of Hey Wood, the enemy being quick to take advantage of a break in the British barrage on this part of the front. But, in spite of the determined character of the defence, the Irish Guards succeeded in reaching the "black line" by 6 a.m., having captured 4 machine guns and 2 trench mortars during their advance, and killed or wounded a good many of the enemy.†

The supporting companies of the leading battalions of the 3rd Guards Bde. had not so far to advance in order to reach their second objective as had those of the 2nd Guards Bde., and they gained the "black line" with comparative ease, the fire of some German machine guns, which proved troublesome on the right flank of the Grenadiers, being quickly silenced by a few rounds from a trench mortar.

* The 49th Reserve Division, which had been holding this sector of the enemy's line with the 226th R.I. Regt. on the 27th of July (see note, p. 239), had been relieved by the 31st by the 111th Division, a much more formidable formation consisting of the 73rd (Hanoverian) Fusilier Regt., and the 78th and 164th Regts. The colonel and adjutant of the first mentioned regiment—whose men wear the word "Gibraltar" on the left sleeve in memory of the regiment's share when in British service in the capture of that fortress—were taken prisoners by the Irish Guards during their advance to the "black line."

† Lieut.-Colonel E. B. Greer, commanding the 2nd Bn. Irish Guards, was unfortunately killed during the advance. His death was a great loss to his battalion. He had proved himself an inspiring and most capable commanding officer, and was very popular with all ranks. The command of the battalion temporarily devolved upon Captain Gunston as Major Ferguson, the second in command, was in regimental reserve, and Captain Alexander, the senior company officer, was out in advance with his company.

Meanwhile, the four reserve battalions of the 2nd and 3rd Guards Bdes., detailed for the capture of the third line of objectives, had crossed the canal in rear of the attacking battalions of their respective brigades and were following the advance in close support. They moved forward in artillery formation and their losses from shell fire were surprisingly light in view of the severity of the hostile artillery barrage through which they had to pass just east of the canal.*

(14) ADVANCE TO THE THIRD OBJECTIVE.

At 7.15 a.m. the supporting battalions of the 2nd and 3rd Guards Bdes., which had been deployed behind the " black line," moved forward to the attack under the cover of the barrage. On the right of the 2nd Guards Bde. the 3rd Bn. Grenadier Guards, which had already assisted the 1st Bn. Scots Guards in the capture of the second objective, found its advance much impeded by machine-gun fire from the German block-houses along the Ypres—Staden railway line. In order to overcome the enemy's opposition on this flank, which was also hindering the advance of the 38th Division, it was found necessary to extend and to reinforce the right company of the battalion, and then to support its attack with covering fire from the left flank. This manœuvre was entirely successful ; the German block-house, which had been the most serious obstacle to the attacking force, was captured ; † and, by 8 a.m., the Grenadiers were in possession of their objective and in touch with the 1st Bn. Coldstream Guards on their left. They were also in a position to give further assistance to the troops of the 38th Division on their right, for they drove back the enemy from Vulcan Crossing and brought fire to bear on his machine guns, which were in action east of that point.

* The 3rd Bn. Grenadier Guards, for instance, which did not leave its trenches west of the canal until 5 a.m., effected the crossing of the canal without a single casualty, although the passage was a somewhat lengthy one owing to so many of the bridges having been broken. *See* " The Grenadier Guards in the Great War," vol. ii. p. 211.

† Three officers and 52 other ranks together with 4 machine guns were taken by the Grenadiers in this block-house.

THE THIRD OBJECTIVE SECURED

On the left of the Grenadiers, the 1st Bn. Coldstream Guards, one of whose companies had already been of great assistance to the Irish Guards in the capture of their second objective, reached its new line without much trouble, although it had to extend its left to support the right flank battalion of the 3rd Guards Bde. which had been temporarily checked in Abri Wood. The Coldstream captured a good many prisoners and several machine guns during their advance, as well as a 4·2 gun which they found in a concrete pit on reaching their objective. The 4th Bn. Grenadier Guards, on the right of the 3rd Guards Bde. front, was less fortunate than the battalions of the 2nd Guards Bde., inasmuch as it came under heavy hostile machine-gun fire from Abri Wood whilst in the act of deploying for the attack. The Grenadiers, however, with the assistance of a smoke barrage, succeeded in outflanking these machine-gun positions, the majority of their defenders surrendering before the bombing parties reached them. The battalion then pushed forward rapidly and, after carrying Fourche Farm and Captain's Farm, arrived upon the line of its objective at the scheduled time, where the work of consolidation was at once put in hand.*
The battalion captured 3 trench mortars near Abri Farm in the course of this attack.†

The 2nd Bn. Scots Guards, which attacked on the extreme left of the divisional front in close touch with the 201st French Regiment, met with but slight opposition and gained its objective without difficulty. On its left, however, the French advance was checked for some time by the Germans in Colonel's Farm, and consequently, until late in the afternoon when this farm was at last captured, the Scots Guards had to throw back a defensive flank on the left of their line. At Major's Farm they captured 2 field guns and about

---

* A company of the 1st Bn. Grenadier Guards which had been placed under Lord Gort's orders assisted in the work of consolidation. By 2 p.m. the whole of the 4th Battalion's new defences " were complete and efficiently wired." *See* " The Grenadier Guards in the Great War," vol. ii. p. 225.

† The Grenadiers paid a high tribute to the effectiveness of the creeping barrage, which was so accurate on their part of the front that the leading troops were able to keep within 60 yards of it. *See* W.D., 4th Bn. Grenadier Guards, July, 1917.

50 prisoners, but the majority of the latter had to be sent to the rear through the French lines as men for escorts could not be spared *—an unsatisfactory way of ensuring that the final total of prisoners taken should tally with a battalion's returns.

(15) ADVANCE TO THE FOURTH OBJECTIVE.

By 8 a.m., consequently, as a result of these successive attacks by the 2nd and 3rd Guards Bdes.—attacks which had been conducted with perfect precision and punctually to time—the whole of its third line of objectives was in the possession of the Guards Division, while touch was maintained with the troops on each flank.

It was now the turn of the 1st Guards Bde. to carry on the advance. Its task, as has already been stated,† was to seize the crossings of the Steenbeek and then to consolidate a line beyond the valley in which that stream lies; it was also to wheel half left on the western side of the Steenbeek in order to secure a line facing north for the purpose of linking up with the French on the left.

The two battalions of the 1st Guards Bde. detailed for the attack—the 2nd Bn. Grenadier Guards on the right and the 2nd Bn. Coldstream Guards on the left ‡—reached the "green line" shortly after it had been secured. They had begun their advance as early as 4 a.m. and had crossed the Yser Canal by 6 a.m. Their advance was made in such good time that the company commanders were able to avail themselves of gaps in the German barrage and so succeeded in bringing their men through it with but few casualties.§

---

* The 3rd Guards Bde. reported the capture of 102 prisoners—a total which included men from the 73rd and 76th R.I. Regts. and from the Fusilier Regt. of the Guard.

† *See* p. 233.

‡ The two remaining battalions of the brigade—the 3rd Bn. Coldstream Guards and the 1st Bn. Irish Guards—were in divisional reserve.

§ "The Battalion (2nd Bn. Grenadier Guards) advanced in very good order, the intervals and distances being kept with great precision. Lieut.-Colonel de Crespigny, finding that he was gaining on the time allotted to him, and noticing that the German barrage was irregular, gave orders that commanders of platoons might use their discretion, and halt occasionally in shell-holes, in order to avoid any zones which

But by about 8.50 a.m., when the 1st Guards Bde. began its attack upon the final objective, the enemy's resistance had stiffened in a noticeable degree, and the heavy rifle and machine-gun fire, directed principally from the farm houses and block-houses west of the Steenbeek, proved extremely troublesome, especially to the 2nd Bn. Grenadier Guards on the right of the line. The difficulties of the Grenadiers were made still greater owing to the fact that the troops of the 38th Division on their right were not ready to move forward at the hour arranged for the attack. This delayed them considerably, as the advance of their right company was checked and it thus lost the shelter afforded by the covering barrage. The Grenadiers, nevertheless, contrived by the skilful employment of their Lewis-gun and rifle fire to gain ground on the right which enabled them to form a defensive flank along the Ypres—Staden railway line until the advance of the 17th Bn. R.W. Fusiliers (38th Division) made the situation secure. The Grenadiers then pushed forward with great gallantry in the face of a vigorous artillery and machine-gun defence which caused many casualties. On the right, the fire of the enemy's machine guns in the village of Langemarck and beyond the Langemarck—Wijdendrift road proved so deadly that the right half of the battalion was forced to dig in about 80 yards west of the Steenbeek, thus just failing to reach its actual objective, but in a position, nevertheless, from which it had a good field of fire. On the left, the leading company, which was reinforced by the left support company, pressed on with great determination, and, after seizing Signal and Ruisseau Farms,* forced the passage of the Steenbeek and established itself on a line about 60 yards from the eastern bank of the stream. By 9.30 a.m. the 2nd Bn. Grenadier Guards, therefore, was in possession of the greater part of its objective.

appeared to be receiving particular attention from the German artillery. The enemy was continually shortening his range, and there is no doubt that, by avoiding the shelling as necessity demanded, many casualties were avoided." *See* " The Grenadier Guards in the Great War," vol. ii. pp. 228, 229.

* Thirty prisoners were captured in these farms including a battalion commander and other officers.

Meanwhile, on the left of the 1st Guards Bde. front, the 2nd Bn. Coldstream Guards had succeeded in making the difficult wheel to the left and in gaining the line of the objective facing northward. The battalion had sustained a good many casualties before it began its attack, but had met with little serious resistance as it advanced. It was unable to gain touch with the French until late in the afternoon after the capture of Colonel's Farm.

(16) ORGANIZATION OF THE NEW LINE, RELIEFS, ETC.

Before 10 a.m., therefore, on the 31st of July, the Guards had succeeded in capturing all their objectives except on the frontage of one company on the extreme right of the line. By this time, however, the enemy had clearly been reinforced and was in such strength beyond the Langemarck—Wijdendrift road and in Langemarck that any farther advance was out of the question. It was decided, therefore, to consolidate the new positions as effectively as possible. The machine-gun defence was quickly organized. On the front held by the 2nd Bn. Coldstream Guards the four guns which had accompanied the battalion in the attack were soon distributed in positions that had previously been agreed upon and proved of the greatest value in the defence of the captured line. The machine gunners with the 2nd Bn. Grenadier Guards placed two of their guns in position to cover Vulcan Crossing,* and the machine guns which had accompanied the 2nd and 3rd Guards Bdes. in the advance were also distributed for the protection of the work of consolidation.

In the afternoon the organization of the new line was so complete that it was found possible to withdraw some of the battalions in occupation of rear positions in the captured area. Accordingly, the 2nd Bn. Irish Guards relieved the 1st Bn. Scots Guards and was relieved in its turn at dusk by the 3rd Bn. Grenadier Guards and the 1st Bn. Coldstream

* The machine gunners with the 2nd Bn. Grenadier Guards had had greater difficulties with which to contend than those who went with the Coldstream—one of their guns with its entire team had been destroyed by a German shell. *See* "The Grenadier Guards in the Great War," vol. ii. p. 232.

FURTHER SUCCESS OF THE 2ND COLDSTREAM

Guards. These two battalions in depth then held the 2nd Guards Bde. sector in rear of the final objective. On the left of the divisional front, in the 3rd Guards Bde. sector, the 1st and 4th Bns. Grenadier Guards relieved the 2nd Bn. Scots Guards and the 1st Bn. Welsh Guards.

No incident of importance occurred in the new front line for the remainder of the day, although the enemy's artillery fire increased considerably, and German snipers were unpleasantly active along the entire front—their fire unhappily being instrumental in putting several officers of the 2nd Bn. Coldstream Guards out of action.

In the evening a French attack upon Kortekeer Cabaret ended in failure, and, at about 9 p.m., a German artillery barrage was put down in rear of the British front positions. A counter-attack was anticipated, but did not take place. The situation of the troops in the battle area, however, was becoming uncomfortable from another cause. The rain which had been threatening all day began to fall in torrents soon after dark and speedily converted the country into a quagmire, rendering the conditions of life in the trenches more unpleasant than ever. But, in despite of the deluge, the 2nd Bn. Coldstream Guards managed during the night of the 31st of July–1st of August to improve its position considerably by the capture and consolidation of Sentier and Pinson Farms.

(17) WORK OF THE DIVISIONAL R.E. AND 4TH BN. COLDSTREAM GUARDS (PIONEERS), ETC., 31ST OF JULY.

No account of the operations on the 31st of July would be in any way complete without some description of the wonderful work accomplished in rear of the advance by the Field Companies, R.E., and the 4th Bn. Coldstream Guards (Pioneers), the 183rd Tunnelling Company, and the R.A.M.C. The prompt manner in which communications were opened up in the captured area and the expedition with which the battle-field was cleared of wounded were alike deserving of the highest praise. Ten minutes after zero hour the 75th Field Company, R.E., moved forward from Elverdinghe and at once set to work to place two pontoons in position across the Yser Canal—one due west of the Bois de Crapouillots, the other at Pont de Boesinghe—and, as early as 5 a.m. the 4th Bn. Coldstream Guards (Pioneers) was busily employed clearing the road between White Hope Corner and Boesinghe as well as the western approaches to the canal. With the object of lessening as far as possible the manual labour, the 183rd Tunnelling Company blew up the banks on both sides of the canal,* but, as a matter of fact, the craters formed by the explosion rather increased than minimized the difficulties of laying the pontoons. The enemy's artillery barrage also proved troublesome; it caused a good deal of delay and was responsible, especially in the earlier hours of the morning, for numerous casualties among the R.E. and Pioneers. About 8 a.m., however, the German bombardment of the canal became less intense, and, by dint of unremitting labour, the pontoon bridge at Pont de Boesinghe was ready for wheeled transport at 2.15 p.m. The bridge west of the Bois de Crapouillots, to which the approach was over marshy ground was not ready until the evening, and then, as a result of the heavy rain, was soon unfit for anything except pack transport.† But in the meantime artillery bridges had been thrown across the Yper Lea and access to the forward area was consequently rendered much easier.

The repair and reconstruction of the communications in the area behind the old front line, made necessary owing to the work of destruction carried out by the enemy's artillery fire, called for incessant labour throughout the day. The trench tramway from White Hope Corner to Boesinghe had been torn up in many places, but, by 4 p.m., it had been repaired by the 75th Field Company, R.E., and was in running order. The double track, which ran from Boesinghe

* Arrangements for blowing up the banks of the canal had been made beforehand. *See* p. 227.
† Pack animals were waiting to move forward long before the pontoon bridges were ready to carry them and so, in order to avoid delay and overcrowding near the canal, bridges constructed out of several layers of mats mounted on petrol tins, were hurriedly put together, on which the animals were safely conveyed across the canal.

Château to the canal and which had only been completed about ten days previously by the *personnel* of the trench-mortar batteries, had also been much knocked about; but it was repaired in the course of the day and utilized for the forward transport of S.A.A. and artillery ammunition.*

On the eastern side of the canal the 55th and 76th Field Companies, R.E., each provided two parties of sappers who with tape and pickets traced forward no less than four tracks to the near vicinity of the line of the final objective. Almost the whole of this work was carried out under heavy shell fire which caused several casualties, and in the forward area the enemy's snipers and machine gunners also proved very troublesome.

The tasks of the R.E. were not confined, however, to the organization of the lines of communication. The 55th and 76th Field Companies each sent forward two sections with a carrying party of 100 Guardsmen to wire the line of the third objective, and also two sections with 80 carriers to do the same work in front of the final objective. The former task was performed without much difficulty under cover of the mist in the course of the afternoon, although on the extreme left the work had to be delayed until late in the evening owing to the slow progress of the French on that flank. The wiring of the forward line was a much less easy undertaking. It was not possible to begin the work until darkness had set in and then, unfortunately, the working parties were caught in the German barrage about 9 p.m.† and dispersed with numerous casualties. In this area, therefore, the wiring of the line had to be postponed for the time being.

(18) Advance of the Divisional Artillery, 31st of July.

The forward movement of the divisional Artillery began about 8 a.m. on the 31st of July, and the 74th Bde., R.F.A.,

* The ammunition was carried across the canal by hand and also by means of an aerial rope-way. Four rope-ways, each capable of carrying 300 lbs. weight, had been constructed beforehand by the R.E. and were quickly put in position by the 75th Field Company.

† See p. 251.

was in action near Gouvy Farm on the " X " line before 10.30 a.m., where its new gun positions were heavily shelled.* At first there was some difficulty in supplying the batteries with ammunition, but this difficulty was soon overcome by the D.A.C., which quickly established forward dumps east of Elverdinghe and subsequently on the eastern side of the canal.

During the night of the 31st of July–1st of August the brigade, R.H.A., which was attached to the Guards Division, crossed the canal and went into action in a position in rear of Wood 15 and Artillery Wood, while the 4th Guards Machine-Gun Company, which had moved forward as soon as the line of the first objective had been taken, established itself on the eastern side of Abri Wood from which position it was able to supply covering barrage fire in response to S.O.S. calls.

(19) RESULTS OF THE DAY'S FIGHTING ON THE FRONT OF THE FIFTH ARMY—SHARE OF THE GUARDS DIVISION IN THE GENERAL ADVANCE.

In a congratulatory message to his Army issued on the 2nd of August, 1917, General Gough stated that the enemy had been driven " from the whole of his front system on a front of about 8 miles, and that the British and French troops were firmly established in or beyond the German second line on a front of 7 miles." †

---

* " At zero plus 5 hours on the 31st July after firing its creeper, the Brigade moved forward to positions just north of ' X ' line and south of the canal, headquarters being in the ' X ' line. Positions were occupied without a check. One 5·9 shell fell into a group of officers at A/74's position, killing the adjutant, medical officer, and three subalterns of A/74, and grievously wounding the captain and another subaltern of A/74." Extract from Lieut.-Colonel Vickery's Diary. The casualties in this brigade during its sojourn in the Boesinghe area up to the 31st of July had been 2 officers wounded, and 12 other ranks killed and 21 wounded, while 4 other ranks were wounded and about 40 horses destroyed in the wagon lines.

† *See* W.D., Guards Division, August, 1917. " Over 6,100 prisoners, including 133 officers, were captured by us in this battle. In addition to our gains in prisoners and ground we also captured some 25 guns, while a further number of prisoners and guns were taken by our Allies." *See* " Sir Douglas Haig's Despatches," p. 116.

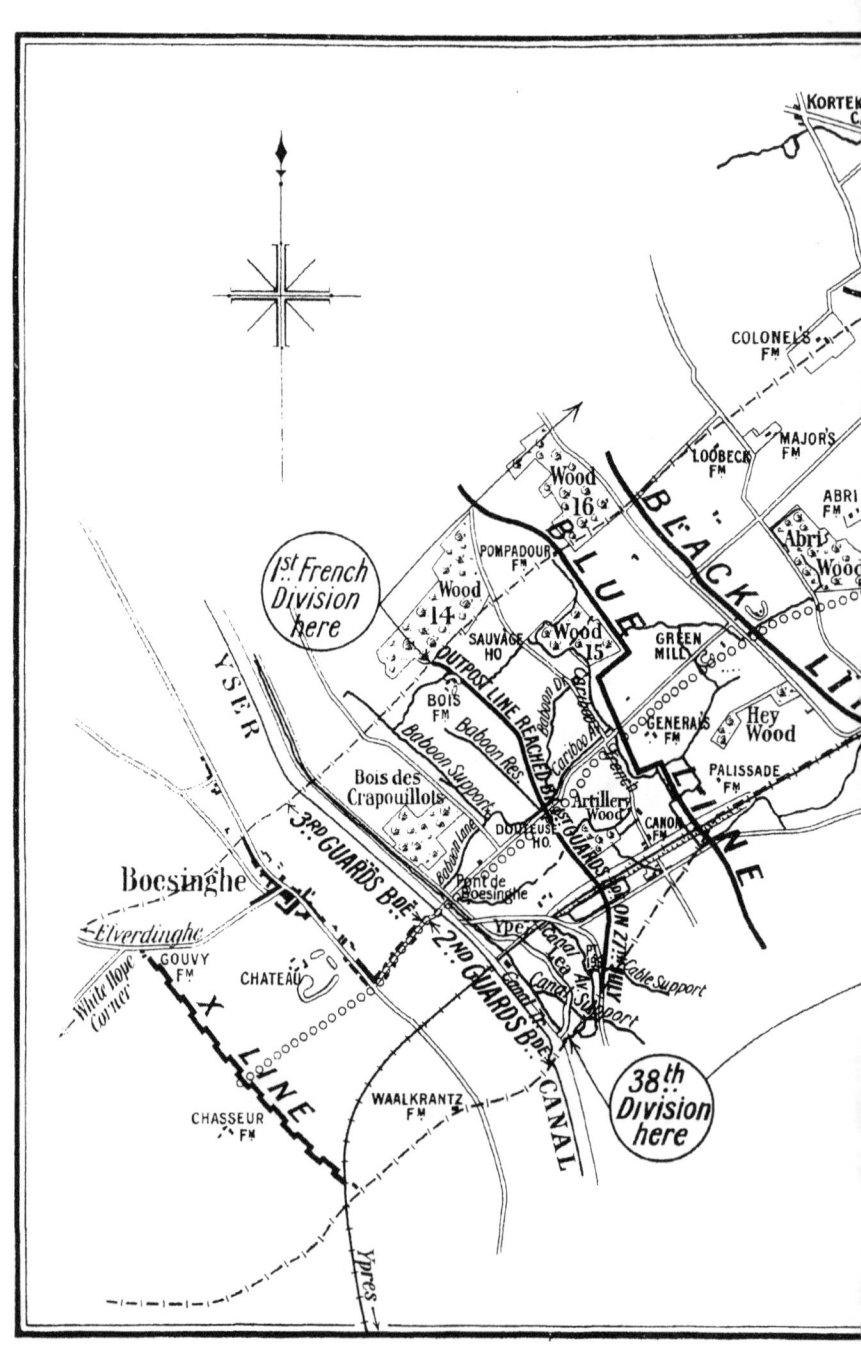

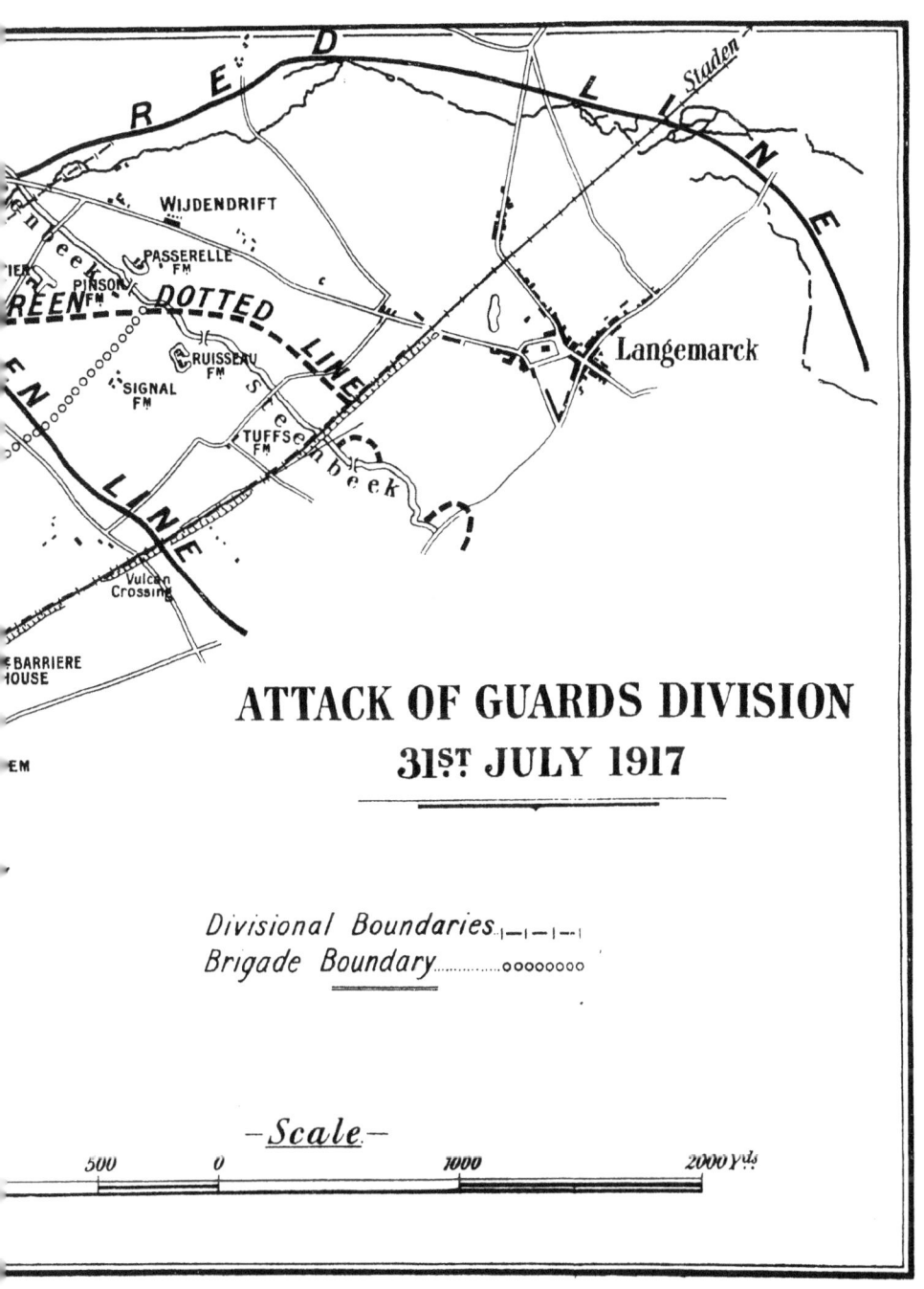

ATTACK OF GUARDS DIVISION
31ST JULY 1917

A GREAT ACHIEVEMENT

The share of the Guards in the fighting on the 31st of July is one of which all ranks in the division were justly proud.* Its troops carried out almost in its entirety the task assigned to them. They drove back the enemy to a depth of $2\frac{1}{2}$ miles on a front of about 1,500 yards. They captured 15 officers and 617 other ranks, and inflicted serious losses on the Germans both in men and material. All arms in the division behaved throughout the day with the utmost gallantry and devotion to duty, and the whole operation from beginning to end was conducted with perfect coolness and admirable skill. The leading of the officers was only equalled by the steady discipline of the men. No more fitting tribute to the work of his troops can be given than the words used by Major-General Feilding in a message which he issued to the division when circulating the corps commander's congratulations † :—

"I cannot find words to express my own thanks to all ranks for their splendid services. From all sources I hear that the artillery barrage was excellent, while the work of the R.E., Pioneers and carrying parties was indefatigable throughout. The infantry carried on the great traditions of the Brigade of Guards. Finally, the clearing of the battle-field by the R.A.M.C. was beyond reproach."

* The evacuation by the enemy of his front line system on the 27th of July, which enabled the Guards to cross the Yser Canal without opposition, was undoubtedly a stroke of luck that materially aided them in carrying out their task with so much success, but it should not be forgotten that it was owing to the prompt decision of Major-General Feilding and the admirable manner in which the 3rd Bn. Coldstream Guards carried out his orders to advance that the opportunity was not lost.

† The XIV Corps commander expressed his gratitude to all who served under him in the following terms :—" The Corps Commander thanks every officer and man in the XIV Corps for their splendid efforts to-day. R.E., the Field and Heavy Artillery share the chief honours of an advance of $2\frac{1}{2}$ miles. Labour Companies and all sorts of transport drivers deserve the fullest recognition also, for the way they have stuck to their job under harassing fire." *See* W.D., Guards Division, App. 404, August, 1917.

CHAPTER IX

THE FLANDERS OFFENSIVE, 1917 (*continued*)—THE CROSSING OF THE BROEMBEEK, 9TH OF OCTOBER—SUMMARY OF THE WORK DONE BY THE GUARDS DIVISION IN THE BATTLES OF YPRES, 1917.

(1) HOLDING THE LINE—RELIEF OF THE GUARDS BY THE 29TH DIVISION, 7TH OF AUGUST.

FROM the evening of the 31st of July the rain fell almost without cessation for four days and nights. The country which in the area occupied by the Guards Division was nowhere much above sea level, was soon converted into a bog, the Steenbeek and its tributaries overflowing their banks and pouring their waters into the shell-holes and open ditches and drains. The situation of the troops in the line became miserable in the extreme. " The men were standing up to their knees in water. Every shell-hole was a pond and the going had become terrible. It was found that the only way to keep the men going was to dig a new trench at dusk and dawn each day; this trench remained dry for a short time and the digging of it gave the men exercise. Wiring and consolidation on a large scale were out of the question. The difficulties were intensified owing to the fact that all the trenches were on a forward slope which, in spite of the rain and mist, the enemy could observe, and shelled continuously day and night." *

Any continuation of active operations in such weather conditions was clearly out of the question, and the main problem which had to be faced by Major-General Feilding and his staff was how best to preserve the health and moral

* *See* W.D., Guards Division, App., Report of the 1st Guards Bde., August, 1917.

of the troops. Forty-eight hours in the line was as much as human endurance could stand, and so, consequently, for the remainder of the sojourn of the Guards on this part of the front frequent reliefs were carried out between battalions and brigades. The result of this policy proved satisfactory, inasmuch as during this period the division had a lower percentage of sick than any other division engaged in the operations.*

Luckily the rain fell with equal persistence on the enemy's side of the line and his infantry, except for the snipers along the Langemarck—Wijdendrift road, displayed but few signs of life. An attempt, however, by the Germans to regain some of their lost territory in spite of the rain and the bad state of the ground was always a contingency which had to be borne in mind and guarded against, and, in the evening of the 1st of August, it appeared more than likely that a counter-attack on a large scale was about to be launched on the Guards front. A report reached the 1st Guards Bde. headquarters about 6 p.m. stating that the troops of the 38th Division on the immediate right of the brigade had been driven out of their forward positions by a severe artillery bombardment. The 1st Bn. Irish Guards—the battalion in support of the right of the line—at once formed a defensive flank linking up its new positions with the front line held by the 2nd Bn. Grenadier Guards. The enemy's infantry, however, made no offensive movement, and, after darkness set in, the 38th Division was able to reoccupy its forward trenches. But, as the situation still appeared uncertain and the S.O.S. signal was repeatedly observed on the other side of the Ypres—Staden railway line, the 1st Guards Bde. maintained its defensive flank throughout the night—a precaution which, as a matter of fact, proved unnecessary,

* *See* W.D., Guards Division, App. 421, August, 1917. At a divisional conference held on the 9th of August, it was stated that only one straggler had appeared at the divisional stragglers' post since the 31st of July, and that there was even some doubt as to whether this individual was a genuine straggler. It was also stated at this same conference that in the course of the seven previous days seven letters written by officers of the division had been opened by the censor and found to contain information which should not have been given.

as no counter-attack was attempted. The next day passed more or less uneventfully, but, in the afternoon on the 3rd of August, the French succeeded in capturing Kortekeer Cabaret and the enemy's trenches running south-east of it. The 2nd Bn. Irish Guards, which was holding the left of the divisional front, was at once ordered to push forward a post north of Sentier Farm in order to link up its defences with the French main line of resistance which now ran from Kortekeer Cabaret to Colonel's Farm. After this, no further incident of any importance occurred before the 7th of August, when the Guards were relieved by the 29th Division.

(2) IN REST BILLETS IN THE PROVEN—HERZEELE AREA.

When the infantry of the Guards Division was withdrawn from the line, one company of the 4th Bn. Coldstream Guards (Pioneers) was left behind in order to carry out the task of patrolling the Decauville railway, which by this time had been extended as far as the Yser Canal, while the 55th Field Company, R.E., also remained in the forward area, being employed upon road construction east of the canal.*

On handing over the command of the front area, Major-General Feilding established his headquarters at Proven and the three Guards brigades were billetted in the Proven—Herzeele area in which officers and men were provided with tolerably comfortable quarters, and where, as is customary with British troops, they managed to enjoy the present, forgetful alike of all they had been through and of what the future still had in store for them.† But all the units in the division were undoubtedly in great need of rest and refitment. They had been in active employment since the

* On the 12th of August the 76th Field Company, R.E., was recalled to the line to work on the roads east of Boesinghe and in the Pilckem area, being relieved later on in the month by the 75th Field Company.

† " We amused ourselves well enough at Herzeele, and had cricket matches and . . . our Transport Officer . . . produced a wonderful and most realistic Wild West Show, and we entertained all the women and children of Herzeele, who seemed much impressed." *See* " Reminiscences of a Grenadier," by E. R. M. Fryer, p. 163.

beginning of July—first, engaged in the arduous and trying work entailed in the mounting of a great offensive, then, in the actual attack, and finally, engulfed in the Flanders bog. All ranks were thoroughly tired out, while the gaps in the battalions caused by the battle losses had to be filled up.* The work of reorganization, however, proceeded apace, and, in a comparatively short period of time, the various units were reorganized and re-equipped, the new drafts had been absorbed into their respective units and the work of training was in full swing—that marvellous piece of military mechanism represented by the Brigade of Guards was again ready for further service in the line. Those who witnessed the special parade held, by the request of General Anthoine, commanding the First French Army, at which he presented decorations to numerous officers and other ranks as a fitting commemoration of the perfect cooperation between his troops and the Guards on the 31st of July, could see no falling off in the general turn out and soldierly bearing of the troops who marched past the representative of France.

(3) Work of the Divisional Artillery during the month of August.

The divisional Artillery was kept in the line when the infantry was withdrawn and was in action throughout the remainder of August. Notwithstanding the low visibility caused by the rain and mist, the batteries were employed almost continuously in bringing harassing fire to bear on the area lying between Wijdendrift and the Broembeek stream. Much difficulty was experienced in moving forward the guns owing to the water-logged state of the ground and it was not until the 8th of August that the 75th Bde., R.F.A., was in a position to open fire from Baboon support trench near the ruins of the mill. The same day A/74, which had established itself in a position in rear of the Bois des Crapouillots, was relieved by the 84th Battery, R.F.A.

On the 11th of August the left group of guns on the XIV

* For the casualties in the Guards Division during the Ypres offensive, *see* p. 287.

Corps front, which included the Guards divisional Artillery, took part in a barrage in support of a slight advance made on the right of the 29th Division, and the following day it was employed in covering an attack made by a brigade of the same division on Passerelle Farm. On the 16th of August the 20th Division, XIV Corps, captured Langemarck, and the same day the 29th Division, advancing from the line which its troops had taken over from the Guards, drove the enemy out of his trenches east of Wijdendrift,* and advanced as far as the Broembeek. The Guards divisional Artillery covered this latter attack, and, later in the same day, effectively assisted in the repulse of several hostile counter-attacks. Three days later, on the 19th of August, the 74th Bde., R.F.A., succeeded in getting forward two batteries to the vicinity of General's Farm, but the following day the whole of the back area as far as Boesinghe was shelled so heavily by the enemy's artillery that it was found impossible to bring forward any more batteries. On the 21st, however, a battery of the 74th Bde. succeeded in relieving the 84th Battery. From this date onwards to the end of the month the batteries both of the 74th Bde. and also of the 75th Bde. were subjected to a persistent bombardment from the enemy's guns in Houthulst Forest and on the high ground in the neighbourhood of Poelcappelle. Fortunately, there were few casualties among the *personnel* of the batteries, but considerable damage was done to the guns, dug-outs and battery positions.†

It soon became quite evident that the positions of some of the guns—notably of C/74 and D/74—were under the direct observation of the German gunners,‡ and orders were

---

* The 2nd Guards Bde. was held in readiness to go to the assistance of the 29th Division, but its help was not required.

† On the 24th of August the howitzer battery of the 75th Bde. was put out of action, 3 howitzers being practically destroyed. One section, however, managed to open fire again three days later.

‡ "The Hun seems to shoot when and where he likes, our heavies don't seem to be able to find him." *See* W.D., 74th Bde., R.F.A., August, 1917. It may be noted that throughout the Flanders offensive "the German guns were firing at extreme range" and that they considerably outranged all types of the British artillery "from the 77-mm. field-gun with a range of 11,000 yards as compared with the 6,200

consequently given to the battery commanders not to fire except in response to the S.O.S. signal. When the Guards Division again took over the line, the C.R.A. of the division resumed command of the left artillery of the corps, and, early in September, as will be narrated later on, he gave orders for the battery positions to be moved farther from the canal.

(4) Return of the Guards Division to the Line, 27th of August.

On the night of the 27th of August in pouring rain the Guards relieved the 29th Division in the line, the 3rd Guards Bde. taking over the front which now ran from the Ypres—Staden railway line westward through Japan House over the Langemarck—Koekuit road, and thence in a northerly direction to a bridgehead on the Broembeek stream at Ney cross-roads. East of this point the main line of defence ran south of the Broembeek, but there were advanced posts in Ney Wood, and also in Ney Copse where the left flank of the division was in touch with the French.

No sooner were they back in the line than the Guards set to work to improve the tactical position in which they found themselves. The weather about this period became a little finer, and, although the ground was still very wet and muddy, the opportunity was seized by the troops of the 3rd Guards Bde. to enlarge the bridgeheads all along their front, thus materially strengthening the defensive position and securing a better starting line for the next attack.*

The task which now lay before the Guards was the crossing of the Broembeek and an advance into Houthulst

---

yards of our 18-pdr. at this time, to the 15-in. naval gun with a range of at least 35,000 yards." *See* " Sir Douglas Haig's Command," vol. i. p. 373.

* The incessant activity of the enemy's bombing aeroplanes, especially at night-time, was a source of great annoyance at this period in the operations not only to the troops in the front line, but also in the camps in rear. A proportion of the available machine guns had to be detailed for anti-aircraft defence.

Forest. In view of the marshy ground along its banks and the swollen size of the stream the passage of the Broembeek in full view of the enemy presented considerable difficulty. There was, however, plenty of time to make all the necessary arrangements, and nothing was left to chance. A careful reconnaissance of the Broembeek was carried out by the R.E. at the beginning of September, who reported that near Ney Wood access to the stream was greatly impeded owing to a stretch of boggy ground, and that south of Lannes Copse the water channel was so seriously blocked that the flooding of the surrounding country was inevitable if there were any further rainfall. The width of the water in the stream also varied considerably—in some places it was only about 8 feet wide whilst in others the surface covered by the water amounted to 20 feet. The water was from 2 to 3 feet deep and below it there was a bed of thick mud, while the banks on both sides of the stream were broken and damaged by shell-holes. There was a partially destroyed brick bridge near Ney cross-roads and a ruined culvert just west of Ney Wood.*

Major-General Feilding's original intention had been to secure the line of the Broembeek by means of a " peaceful penetration," his hope being that the enemy would find himself forced to withdraw from his advanced positions as the Guards gradually pushed forward their posts on its northern bank. But, in spite of the activities of the 3rd Guards Bde., it was soon clear that it would not be possible to drive back the Germans without a definite operation, and, at a divisional conference held on the 4th of September, it was decided that the 2nd Guards Bde. should carry by assault the line of the Broembeek and then consolidate a new line beyond its farther bank to serve as a starting point for the troops of the 29th Division, who were to carry forward the advance.†

* See W.D., Guards Division, App. 482, September, 1917.
† See W.D., Guards Division, App. 468, September, 1917.

THE IRISH GUARDS v. WURTEMBURGERS

(5) Fighting on the Broembeek.

This attack would doubtless have been carried out had not the aggressive action of the enemy made it necessary to cancel the order given to the 2nd Guards Bde.*

On the 10th of September the 1st Guards Bde., which had relieved the 3rd Guards Bde. a few days earlier, was holding the line. Very early in the morning a party of about 30 Germans belonging to the 65th R.I. Regt. (208th Division) succeeded in creeping round an advanced post held by the French in Ney Copse, and bombed it from the rear. The enemy was speedily driven back,† but, emboldened by this temporary success, the Germans raided the British advanced posts in Ney Wood at 3 a.m. the following morning. They managed to take possession of two of them and were not ejected from them for some little time.

On the evening of the 12th of September the relief of the 1st Guards Bde. by the 2nd Guards Bde. was begun and by midnight the 2nd Bn. Irish Guards had taken over the left sector of the front from the 3rd Bn. Coldstream Guards, the line of advanced posts in this area at this time running from the south-east corner of Ney Wood to Ney Copse. At 2.40 a.m. in the morning of the 13th the German gunners put down a heavy barrage on these posts, lifting it some twenty minutes later on to the southern bank of the Broembeek and the country south-west of it. A body of about 200 Wurtemburg storm troops—most of them clad in armour—then attempted to rush the whole line of posts. Their attack was checked for a time by the rapid fire of the Irish Guardsmen, but the defenders who had survived the bombardment were so few in number that finally they were compelled to withdraw to shell-holes in rear of the posts—a small party hastily collected by an officer alone being able to hold on to its original position in Ney Copse. Patrols were

---

* On the 22nd of September Brig.-General B. N. Sergison-Brooke had taken over command of the 2nd Guards Bde., Brig.-General J. Ponsonby having been appointed to command the 40th Division.

† A party of the 3rd Bn. Coldstream Guards, which was holding an advanced post on the extreme left of the Guards' front, suffered several casualties in this affair.

at once sent forward from the main line of resistance to try and clear up the situation. The withdrawal of the party in Ney Copse was satisfactorily covered, but Ney Wood was found to be held in strength by the enemy. It was then decided to bring back the isolated post, which still remained north of the Broembeek at Ney cross-roads, to the southern bank of the stream. This movement was carried out without much opposition from the Germans, and the line held by the Irish Guards then ran from Panther trench parallel with the Broembeek to a point due south of Ney Copse where it was linked up with the French.* The enemy in Ney Wood made no attempt to cross the Broembeek either on the 14th or 15th of September, but, at 4 a.m. in the morning of the 16th, his gunners put down a heavy barrage along the whole of the XIV Corps front. This may have been the preliminary bombardment intended to cover an organized counter-attack by the German infantry on the line of the Broembeek, but, if any such operation were actually contemplated, the prompt and vigorous reply of the British artillery to the S.O.S. call effectually checked it and no infantry attack took place.

During this artillery duel a few Irish Guardsmen—the survivors of a platoon which had been in occupation of two posts near the northern edge of Ney Copse, but who had not been able to withdraw with their comrades on the 13th—gallantly fought their way back to the British line.† They stated that a strong force of the enemy had endeavoured to surround them earlier in the morning, and that many of these Germans had been killed or wounded by the fire of the British guns.

In the course of the afternoon of the 16th the artillery fire died down, and in the evening the 2nd Bn. Irish Guards was relieved in the line—its four days' tour of duty having

---

* The S.O.S. line was altered so as to ensure the defence of the line of the Broembeek, and, on the night of the 14th of September, an artillery barrage was put down on this line in order to search the ground north of the stream. The following day a special shoot was carried out by the heavy guns upon the German block-houses in Ney Wood and the little copse immediately to the east of it.

† For a picturesque account of the doings of this little band, see "The Irish Guards in the Great War," vol. ii. pp. 166–168.

cost the battalion 3 officers and 166 other ranks killed, wounded or missing.

(6) RELIEF OF THE GUARDS BY THE 29TH DIVISION, 21ST OF SEPTEMBER.

On the 20th of September the Second and Fifth Armies once more resumed the offensive.* As a result of the fine weather earlier in the month, the ground had dried to some extent and it was considered possible for the infantry to move forward, while the improvement in the visibility enabled the artillery and the airmen once again to carry out effectively their share in the operations. From this time onwards, too, for the remainder of the Ypres offensive, the objectives given to the attacking troops were kept well within the range of the protecting guns, with the result that, although progress was slower, it became surer. Captured positions were carefully consolidated before the next step forward was undertaken, and the enemy's counter-attacks, which up to this period in the battle had been such a disconcerting feature in this offensive, especially on the southern front of the Fifth Army, were thus either nipped in the bud or beaten back with heavy losses to the attacking troops.†

* The battle front entrusted to General Plumer's Army had been extended northward and its left flank now lay between Westhoek and the Ypres—Roulers railway line, the I Australian Corps and the V Corps replacing the II and XIX Corps of the Fifth Army in this area. The Menin road sector of the front on which the Germans had hitherto successfully resisted the British advance was thus in the centre of the line of the Second Army's advance. "By this change the tasks of carrying out the capture of the much contested Menin road sector and of dealing with the German batteries that could bring flanking fire to bear on it from other areas were placed in the same hands." *See* "Sir Douglas Haig's Command," vol. i. p. 375.

† "The direction from which counter-attacks might be expected were carefully plotted out beforehand, and arrangements made to deal with them promptly and decisively. Our final objectives in each successive attack were shallow, but they were reached and held. The expected counter-attacks were invariably broken up, and the very shallowness of each separate advance not only reduced greatly the number of our casualties but enabled the next step forward to be taken with the least possible delay. The progress made in the fortnight September 20th to October 4th is some indication of what might have

The Guards were not called upon to take an active part in the fighting on the 20th of September, the share of the XIV Corps on that day being confined to a slight advance made by the troops of the 20th Division on their right—an advance which marked the northern limit of the British attack. In order, however, to enable the artillery to place a creeping barrage as near as possible to the Ypres—Staden railway line for the protection of this advance, the forward posts of the 3rd Bn. Grenadier Guards along the railway were evacuated before zero hour on the 21st of September. They were occupied again as soon as the attack had been launched in time for some of the more ardent Grenadiers to accompany the 10th Bn. K.R.R.C. to its first objective.

During the evening of the 21st of September the relief of the Guards by the 29th Division was begun, and upon its completion the three Guards brigades once again found themselves in the Herzeele—Proven area.

Except for the skirmishing on the banks of the Broembeek, the Guards had had little fighting during this tour of duty in the line, but their casualties, nevertheless, amounted to 30 officers and 760 other ranks, the majority of which were due to the incessant bombardments of the line and to the vigorous bombing of the camps and communications in rear by the enemy's aeroplanes.*

The infantry of the division, as usual, had worked very

---

been accomplished had it been possible to continue the same methodical tactics over a longer period." *See* " Sir Douglas Haig's Command," vol. i. p. 376.

* During one raid made by German aircraft the horse lines of the 75th and 76th Field Companies, R.E., were bombed, 60 animals being killed or wounded. During a similar raid on the 12th of September the camp of the D.A.C. was attacked, the casualties including 37 men and 96 animals. On the 4th of September a German aeroplane dropped bombs on the camp near Elverdinghe occupied by a company of the 3rd Bn. Grenadier Guards and caused 30 casualties. On the 12th of September the 2nd Bn. Irish Guards was caught by 12 low-flying German aeroplanes on its way to the trenches and lost 20 men and some of its transport. These are only examples to show the activity of the enemy's aircraft during the Ypres offensive, when the British Air Force undoubtedly was superior to the German. The command of the air can never be so great as to secure complete immunity from attack.

hard in improving and reconstructing the line and in spite of—or perhaps by reason of—the loss of the advanced posts north of the Broembeek, the position handed over to the 29th Division was a more satisfactory defensive system than that which the Guards had taken over. It was certainly a more suitable line for the purposes of a fresh advance.

The R.E. of the division and the 4th Battalion Coldstream Guards (Pioneers) had also been busily employed in the upkeep and development of the four new routes leading eastward, and, by the time the Guards left the front, these tracks, which were built on piers wherever the marshy condition of the ground made it necessary, had been carried forward to the front line trenches. In addition to the work on communications, much time and labour were devoted to the wiring of support and reserve lines of defence, to the camouflaging of new gun positions and to the screening of roads in places where they were more than usually exposed to the enemy's observation. The accommodation available in the various camps in rear was also considerably enlarged and improved.

(7) Work of the Divisional Artillery during the month of September.

The divisional Artillery came out of the line for a short but well-earned rest at the same time as the infantry. All its batteries, especially those of the 74th Bde.,* had suffered severely, the casualties in men and guns during the early days of September, when the rear battery positions were still in the neighbourhood of the canal, having been heavy. By the 12th of September, however, the whole of the guns of the 74th Bde. had been moved forward and were in positions

* The 74th Bde., R.F.A., fired 30,000 rounds during the month of September. It lost 3 officers and 32 other ranks casualties, and had 6 guns and 5 howitzers put out of action. During the night of the 17th of September a German 17-in. shell dropped close to C/74, burying a gun and its detachment without causing a casualty. This same battery again suffered severely on the 30th of September, but continued in action throughout the day. *See* W.D., 74th Bde., R.F.A., September, 1917.

round General's Farm, while those of the 75th Bde. were still farther forward in positions near the Ypres—Staden railway line.

Throughout the 19th of September, and the night of the 19th-20th, the guns of the Guards Division took part in the gas bombardment of the German lines which preceded the attack by the 20th Division on the 20th of September. They fired, too, in the creeping barrage which covered the right of the assaulting troops, and were in action continuously for 42 hours, during by far the greater part of which time they were subjected to a fierce retaliatory fire from the enemy's artillery. It was a trying ordeal throughout which all ranks carried out their duties with the greatest coolness and courage.

Early in September a change had been made in the *personnel* of the D.A.C., when 160 men of the 7th Bn. British West Indian Regiment arrived to replace gunners in the Column. The D.A.C. remained in the front area when the brigades, R.F.A., went out of the line and its men were employed in salvage work and in the collecting of material for the construction of winter horse-standings. At the end of the month they began the task of carrying up ammunition to forward battery positions in the valley of the Steenbeek preparatory to the resumption of the offensive by the division.

(8) PREPARATIONS FOR THE RESUMPTION OF THE OFFENSIVE.

The general British advance, which had been resumed on the 20th of September, was continued on the 26th of September and again on the 4th of October. The results of both these days' fighting were eminently satisfactory. Steady progress was made all along the line and the enemy's losses were extremely heavy, especially in the fighting on the 4th of October.* The German defence was clearly weakening,

* On the 4th of October the German Higher Command, alarmed by the British successes on the 20th and 26th of September (*see* " My War Memories, 1914–1918," by General Ludendorff, vol. ii. p. 488 *et seq.*) decided to reinforce its troops in the front line trenches and still further to increase the depth of its defensive system by employing

and the British troops had now reached the important line of high ground which stretches from Reutel and the spur of hilly country north of Poelcappelle to Broodseinde. Although admittedly it was getting late in the season, the British Commander-in-Chief hoped that, if the weather remained fine, he would still be able to strike northward and to carry out the operations in the coastal area which had been one of the main objects of the offensive. He decided, consequently, to renew the advance on the 9th of October, with the intention of gaining possession of the remainder of the ridge between Passchendaele and Poelcappelle.

The task allotted to the Guards Division in this operation was to advance across the Broembeek and then to push forward to the southern edge of Houthulst Forest, working in conjunction with the 29th Division astride the Ypres— Staden railway line on the right and the French on the left. Major-General Feilding decided to repeat his policy of the 31st of July and to carry out the attack with two brigades in the line—the 1st Guards Bde. on the right, the 2nd Guards Bde. on the left. The former, starting from Panther and Leopard trenches, was to cross the Broembeek and to advance on either side of the Koekuit road past Vee Bend to its final objective on the outskirts of Houthulst Forest. The latter was to move forward from the line Panther trench— Craonne Farm, and, after crossing the Broembeek, was to advance through Ney Wood and Gruyterszale Farm to Louvois Farm and to seize the line of the road which ran westward from Les Cinq Chemins.

The advance was planned in three stages, the two leading

divisions actually in the second line for the carrying out of immediate local counter-attacks. This " unheard-of expenditure of force," as Ludendorff described it, proved a complete failure from the German point of view. It led to the most conspicuous British success during the whole course of the Ypres offensive. " As a result of the thickening of the German front line, the tale of prisoners taken by us rose nearly to 5,000, while the massing of German divisions close up to the fighting line led to an appalling slaughter by our guns. The enemy, as Ludendorff admits, only came through the battle with enormous loss and with the knowledge that he had not yet found the remedy for our system of attack." *See* " Sir Douglas Haig's Command," vol. i. pp. 377, 378.

battalions in each brigade being made responsible for the capture of the first two lines of objectives and the remaining battalions being instructed to pass through them in order to seize the final objectives.*

On the 5th of October the 3rd Guards Bde., with the 4th Bn. Grenadier Guards and the 2nd Bn. Scots Guards in the front line, took over the battle front, and the preparations for the attack were pushed forward with great energy. But the time available was all too short in comparison with the work which had to be done. There were no battle stores at the forward dumps; there was an insufficient supply of mats and bridging material for the crossing of the Broembeek; and the communications in the forward area were in a state of dilapidation. During the three nights before the attack was timed to take place the R.E. and the 4th Bn. Coldstream Guards (Pioneers) succeeded in carrying forward 355 mats, 180 infantry bridges, wiring stores sufficient for 3,000 yards of entanglement and a supply of trench grids piles, tools and other materials without which the consolidation of a new defensive position would have been impossible. The infantry of the 3rd Guards Bde., too, worked hard upon the improvement of tracks, and in the construction of assembly positions and battle headquarters,† but unfortunately the weather which had broken again on the 4th of October was wet and the rain destroyed the new trenches almost as soon as they were dug. The elements, as usual, appeared to be on the side of the enemy.

On the evening of the 7th of October the 1st and 2nd

---

* It was decided that platoons should go into action with 32 men. All *personnel* surplus to this establishment were formed into a Guards Reinforcement Battalion, which was placed under the command of Major Sir V. A. F. Mackenzie, Bart.

† "Brigadier-General Lord Henry Seymour, who had to hold the original line for the two days before the attack, placed the 4th Battalion Grenadiers and the 2nd Battalion Scots Guards in the front trenches, and these two Battalions had a strenuous time preparing accommodation for the other two Brigades, and placing mats in readiness for the crossing of the stream. The 1st Battalion Grenadiers and 1st Battalion Welsh Guards had also to work hard forming forward dumps, and dragging guns into their new position." *See* "The Grenadier Guards in the Great War," vol. ii. p. 247.

Guards Bdes. went into their respective sectors of the front, each of their leading battalions having two companies in the front line. On the right, the 2nd Bns. of the Grenadier and Coldstream Guards relieved the 4th Bn. Grenadier Guards; on the left, the 1st Bn. Scots Guards and the 2nd Bn. Irish Guards relieved the 2nd Bn. Scots Guards. The remaining battalions of the attacking brigades moved up to their respective places of assembly during the course of the following evening and had all reached their appointed positions by midnight. Throughout their advance rain fell in torrents and the conditions in the front area during the night, which was spent by the great majority of the men in muddy shell-holes, were disagreeable in the extreme. But the wretched discomfort of their situation was mitigated to some extent by the provision of rations and rum, and of hot tea which was carried up to the line in petrol tins swathed in hay.

(9) The Guards Attack, 9th of October.

The rain ceased falling soon after midnight and the weather in the early hours of the 9th of October was fine with a drying wind. Zero was at 5.30 a.m. and punctually at that hour the British artillery barrage came down, the shrapnel of the gunners being supplemented by the fire of all the divisional Trench-Mortar Batteries.* Four minutes later the leading troops began to cross the Broembeek all along the line.

On the right the men of the 2nd Bn. Grenadier Guards and the 2nd Bn. Coldstream Guards were able to do without their mats and either waded across the stream or effected its passage on fallen trees and planks and duck-boards left by the enemy. They had scarcely had time to reform on

---

* The artillery preparation for this attack was on much the same lines as that before the attack on the 31st of July. From the statements made by prisoners, and from the readiness shown by the Germans to surrender, it was evidently very effective. In view of the heavy condition of the ground the creeping barrage was timed to move forward at the slow rate of 100 yards in 8 minutes—a precaution which was found to be a wise one.

the farther bank before Germans—mainly men belonging to the 417th R.I. Regiment, which had only taken over the front about an hour before the attack began, and of the 6th Bavarian Regiment—came hurrying forward to surrender. Apparently these troops had been taken completely by surprise and were bewildered by the bombardment.

The remainder of the advance of the 1st Guards Bde. to its first objective—a line running eastward from Gruyterszale Farm just south of Koekuit towards the Ypres—Staden railway line—met with little opposition, the majority of the Germans encountered either retiring without fighting or emerging from their shell-hole defences to give themselves up. In despite of the heavy going, therefore, the line of the first objective was reached by 6 a.m. along the whole front of the brigade.

The initial difficulty of the 2nd Guards Bde. on the left was the crossing of the swamp which lay south of the Broembeek, the shell-holes in this area having been converted into a series of ponds. However, except for the fire of a machine gun in Ney Wood, which for a short time delayed the advance of the 2nd Bn. Irish Guards, the enemy made no serious attempt to contest the passage of the stream, and, when once this had been crossed on bridges, the attacking troops had no great difficulties against which to contend before reaching their first objective—a line running slightly north-west on the far side of the road leading to Lannes Farm.

The new line gained by the two brigades was at once put into a state of defence, and then, after a pause of forty-five minutes, the creeping barrage came down again and the advance was resumed by the supporting companies of the attacking battalions.

On the front of the 1st Guards Bde. some resistance was offered by a party of the enemy in occupation of block-houses near Vee Bend, but, on finding themselves outflanked by the Coldstream, these Germans—about 35 in number, with 3 machine guns—surrendered.

There was really no other organized opposition to the advancing troops on the front of either brigade before the second line of objectives was reached. This line extended

AN OPEN FLANK ON THE RIGHT

from a point a little west of the Ypres—Staden railway line westward across the Langemarck—Koekuit—Houthulst road to a point about 1,000 yards south-east of Veldhoek. The Guards were in possession of it by 8.15 a.m., and in touch with the 29th Division on their right and the French on their left. No time was now lost in carrying forward the attack to the final objectives. The supporting battalions of the two brigades, which had followed the advance in artillery formation, began to arrive in rear of the second line of objectives at about 8.30 a.m., and half an hour later had passed through the leading battalions and launched their attack, moving forward under an artillery barrage. On the extreme right of the 1st Guards Bde., at its point of junction with the Newfoundland Regiment (29th Division), the 1st Bn. Irish Guards had some hard fighting. The advance of the Newfoundlanders was not so rapid as that of the Irishmen, who, in consequence, were subjected to a good deal of machine-gun fire from their right and right rear whilst attacking Egypt House and the brickfield to the north of it which the Germans defended stoutly. They succeeded, nevertheless, in dislodging the enemy from both of these points of vantage and then pushed on to their final objective, where the front held by the right of the battalion had to be bent back west of Angle Point in order to form a defensive flank facing eastward, the exact whereabouts of the attacking troops of the 29th Division being still uncertain. This flank unfortunately was much exposed to the fire of the German snipers on the right of the divisional boundary, as well as in Cairo House in rear of the Irish Guards, and the battalion in consequence suffered a good many casualties while the work of consolidation was being carried out.*

On the left of the 1st Guards Bde., the advance of the

---

* " All four Companies [1st Bn. Irish Guards] reached the final objective mixed up together, and since their right was well in the air, by the reason of the delay of the flanking troops, they had to make a defensive flank to connect with a battalion of the next Division that came up later. It was then that they were worst-sniped from the shell-holes, and the casualties among the officers, who had to superintend the forming of the flank, were heaviest." *See* " The Irish Guards in the Great War," vol. i. pp. 239, 240.

3rd Bn. Coldstream Guards was met by fierce rifle fire from the direction of Houthulst Forest and Les Cinq Chemins, while the battalion also had to pick its way through a hostile artillery barrage placed on the area round Suez Farm. Its attack, however, was pressed forward with much vigour and the line of the final objective—which ran just north of the road leading westward from Les Cinq Chemins—was successfully reached, the resistance of the enemy in the scattered block-houses round Les Cinq Chemins being finally overcome by means of a liberal employment of rifle grenades.

The 3rd Bn. Grenadier Guards, which advanced on the right of the 2nd Guards Bde., appears to have captured its final objective—the northern side of the road leading westward from Les Cinq Chemins—without any difficulty. The Grenadiers were also successful in capturing Suez Farm which lay within the sector of the 1st Guards Bde. and the block-houses in its vicinity,* together with 2 field guns, and, on reaching their new line, their patrols at once showed great enterprise in clearing the enemy out of the block-houses and dug-outs on their front, killing a number of Germans and returning in triumph with 23 prisoners.

The 1st Bn. Coldstream Guards, on the left of the 2nd Guards Bde., met with considerable opposition from the enemy in the strong point on its left. His resistance was so obstinate that it was decided to leave the capture of this position until later in the day and to push forward to the line of the final objective. This was reached by the Coldstream about the same time as the Grenadiers.

By about 10.15 a.m., therefore, the Guards had practically completed their day's task, although the position on the extreme right of the line was not entirely satisfactory and the troops on the left flank had not secured the whole of their objective. This latter omission was made good in the course of the afternoon, as at 1.30 p.m. two platoons of the 1st Bn. Coldstream Guards with two machine guns made an organized

* This deviation by the Grenadiers into the area of the battalion on their right is explained by the fact that the battalion in question—the 3rd Bn. Coldstream Guards—lost direction to a small extent with the result that a gap occurred between it and the Grenadiers which had to be filled.

attack on the strong point and captured it, 40 Germans with a machine gun surrendering. Meanwhile, the work of consolidation which was being proceeded with all along the line was much hampered by the enemy's sniping fire from Houthulst Forest,* many officers, as usual, being picked off. During the afternoon, too, there were signs that the Germans were organizing a counter-attack, as their aeroplanes flew low over the captured line and the movement of men and transport could be observed on the southern edge of the forest. It was not until the evening, however, that a counter-attack was actually launched, and it was then delivered on the front held by the 29th Division, the troops of which were compelled slightly to draw back their line. This movement made it necessary for the 1st Bn. Irish Guards, on the right of the Guards divisional front, to withdraw its right flank on the Egypt House road in order to maintain touch with a battalion of the Hampshire Regiment on its right, but, as events turned out, the enemy made no serious attempt to regain his lost ground in this sector of the line.

On the front held by the 2nd Guards Bde. the Germans were more aggressive but even less successful, as a concentration of their troops in the neighbourhood of Panama House was dispersed by machine-gun fire and two counter-attacks launched by them against the point of junction between the 1st Bn. Coldstream Guards and the French were brought to a standstill by the prompt action of the British artillery.

(10) WORK OF THE MACHINE GUNNERS, 9TH OF OCTOBER.

During the day's fighting the Guards machine gunners accompanied the infantry in the attack, the teams handling their guns with exceptional skill and making use of every opportunity which presented itself for their employment. The 1st Guards Bde. Machine-Gun Company had eight guns well placed for the defence of the new line very soon

* On the left the Coldstream suffered some casualties from the protecting artillery barrage, which was somewhat short and seemed difficult to correct.

after it had been captured, and subsequently brought up four more guns for the further protection of the rather insecure right flank. The casualties among the machine gunners caused by the enemy's artillery fire were heavy, especially on the right of the 1st Guards Bde. One gun was lost owing to the whole of its team being put out of action, and another with three bullets through its barrel-casing was brought back by the only survivor of its team.

By 3 p.m. on the 9th of October the 2nd Guards Bde. Machine-Gun Company had no less than fifteen guns in action on the new front, as well as two others which had been captured from the enemy. The machine gunners on this part of the line found some excellent targets and did much execution among the Germans, but the great difficulty here—and indeed along the whole line—was that of supplying the guns with sufficient ammunition, the task of bringing it forward through the mud being an exceedingly onerous one.

(11) Work of the Divisional R.E. and 4th Bn. Coldstream Guards (Pioneers), 9th of October.

The carrying forward of the lines of communication to the new front over an area of marsh and water-logged shell-holes exposed to the enemy's artillery and machine-gun fire was, as usual in the Ypres offensive of 1917, a task which tested the capacity and the endurance of the R.E. and Pioneers.

On the 9th of October the 75th and 76th Field Companies, R.E., and the 4th Bn. Coldstream Guards (Pioneers) emerged with their customary success from their trying ordeal.

Two sections from each Field Company with infantry carriers followed close behind the attacking brigades with the materials necessary for wiring the new line. But the difficulties of the carriers were so great, especially in the flooded area round the Broembeek, where they also came under heavy artillery fire, that it was found impossible to lay out more than about 200 yards of wire on the left front south of Faidherbe cross-roads. The important work of

THE BRIDGING OF THE BROEMBEEK 277

taping out the tracks leading to the new front line was carried out more successfully, for, within half an hour after the capture of the final objectives, the R.E. had laid tapes to Egypt House and Louvois Farm. These were raised on posts except for the last 300 yards before reaching Egypt House—an area which was under the direct observation of the enemy's snipers. Before 10.15 a.m., too, posts connected by tape had been placed in position to mark the route on the left flank from Montmirail Farm, via Ney Farm, to Suez Farm, of which the last named was only about 200 yards in rear of the new front line. Following these taped lines, the 4th Bn. Coldstream Guards (Pioneers) proceeded steadily with the laying of the duck-board tracks, two of which were pushed beyond the Broembeek by the evening of the 9th of October, and with the carrying forward of the trench tramway line which had already been laid as far as the Wijdendrift road.*

The 55th Field Company, R.E., was mainly employed in the task of bridging the Broembeek. All the bridges which had originally spanned the stream had long ago been destroyed, but enough remained of the bridge at Ney cross-roads to make it possible to repair it sufficiently to carry 60-pdr. guns. In addition to this bridge, no less than twenty-nine crossings were made for foot traffic, one of which had to be carried on piles above the swamp for a distance of nearly 70 yards. In the area farther in rear the infantry of the 3rd Guards Bde. was busily occupied in stocking the battle dumps, in man-handling the field guns into more advanced positions in the valley of the Steenbeek, and in the construction of roads leading northward from Martin Mill.

The difficulty of sending back messages from the front line during the course of the attack on the 9th of October had been foreseen. The heavy condition of the ground and the length of the advance over country, which for the most part was under the direct observation of the enemy's artillery, made it clear that runners would be of little practical

* Only three companies of the battalion were available for the work in the forward area as one company was still employed on the Decauville railway track in rear.

use, and that little reliance could be placed on communication by telephone. The divisional Signal Company, consequently, issued sixty pigeons for service with the attacking troops, and practically all the birds were used and returned in safety with their messages.

(12) ATTACK BY THE 3RD GUARDS BRIGADE, 12TH OF OCTOBER.

At daybreak on the 10th of October, after a tolerably quiet night, a number of Germans were observed crawling about in the mud opposite the front held by the 3rd Bn. Coldstream Guards, and 36 of them, with 2 machine guns, surrendered as soon as fire was opened upon them. Otherwise, the day passed without much incident, and in the evening the 3rd Guards Bde. with three battalions in the front line—the 1st Bn. Grenadier Guards, the 4th Bn. Grenadier Guards and the 1st Bn. Welsh Guards from right to left—took over the divisional front.*

The British advance on the 9th of October, which had been so successful in the north where the 29th Division, the Guards Division and the French had all gained their objectives, had not been equally successful farther south, where in the all-important centre and right centre of the operations the enemy's resistance had been more determined and the attacking troops had only been able to fight their way with the greatest difficulty to the first line of their objectives. The weather, too, appeared to have declared definitely against the continuance of the offensive. The 10th of October was a pouring wet day, and the meteorological experts could hold out no prospect of any improvement. The British Commander-in-Chief, however, was still hopeful of being able to carry out his strategic plan for clearing the Flanders coast and decided, therefore, to make one more attempt to gain possession of the ridge before finally giving up the

* Since the beginning of the operation on the night of the 8th of October to the time of their relief the 1st Guards Bde. had lost 27 officers and 804 other ranks; the 2nd Guards Bde. 26 officers and 537 other ranks.

A LIMITED OBJECTIVE

enterprise.* This attack was fixed for the 12th of October, but the share in it assigned to the Guards Division was a small one, as the division was already on the high ground bordering on Houthulst Forest. The objectives given to the 3rd Guards Bde., consequently, entailed only a slight advance, mainly designed to improve the tactical position by cutting off the whole of the spur of hill stretching north-east from Veldhoek.

During the night of the 11th–12th of October the 4th Bn. Grenadier Guards † and the 1st Bn. Welsh Guards, in heavy rain, made their way forward to the line of the new objective which in this particular sector of the front lay only a few hundred yards in advance of the positions already occupied by the two Battalions. The Germans replied to this move by putting down a heavy barrage of gas shells along the Wijdendrift road and the valleys of the Steenbeek and Broembeek. This bombardment caused a good many casualties and a considerable disorganization of traffic, but it was not the prelude to any attempt by the enemy to drive the Grenadiers and Welsh Guards out of their new positions.

At zero hour—5.25 a.m.—on the 12th of October the Welsh Guards and the left company of the 4th Bn. Grenadier Guards had only to stand fast while the right company of the latter battalion was brought back to the old front line in order to be clear of the barrage put down to cover the advance of the 1st Bn. Grenadier Guards on the right. This barrage was rather ragged and the Grenadiers in consequence had some difficulty in carrying forward their attack, but, nevertheless, they succeeded in reaching their new line and at once began the work of consolidation, the company of their 4th Battalion on the left returning to the posts which it had dug during the previous night.‡

---

* See " Sir Douglas Haig's Despatches," p. 129. *Cf.* also " Sir Douglas Haig's Command," vol. i. p. 379.

† The 4th Bn. Grenadier Guards shot down one of the enemy's aeroplanes on the 11th of October. It was flying above the line at an altitude of about 300 feet and fell in flames on the edge of Houthulst Forest.

‡ The XIV Corps commander sent the following telegram to Major-General Feilding to mark his appreciation of the way in which this

Unfortunately, touch with the 17th Division, which had relieved the 29th Division on the right of the Guards, could not be obtained, although two platoons of the 2nd Bn. Scots Guards had been especially detailed to ensure the linking up of the troops of the two divisions as they advanced. These platoons were able, however, to establish themselves in the vicinity of Angle Point where they remained, although much exposed to the enemy's machine-gun and rifle fire.* There was considerable trouble on this flank until darkness set in, when the 1st Bn. Grenadier Guards, in conjunction with troops of the 51st Infantry Bde. (17th Division), drove out the Germans in occupation of the block-houses at Angle Point and Aden House.

It had been wet and cold throughout the entire day on the 12th of October, and the conditions in the front line were so bad that it was judged expedient to relieve the 3rd Guards Bde. the following night. This relief was carried out without any unusual difficulty by the 1st Guards Bde.† whose troops on taking over the line at once set to work to patrol assiduously the southern edge of Houthulst Forest. They met with but little resistance, and there no longer appeared to be any organized German defensive system on this part of the front, although in the neighbourhood of Colbert cross-roads and Colombo House the enemy's snipers still remained very active. So far as the Guards were concerned a continuance of the attack promised great results. But, except on its northern flank, the British advance on the 12th of October had been entirely brought to a standstill by the rain. The operations had to be broken off, therefore, soon after they

---

attack was carried out :—" Well done, everybody—wonderful performance in awful conditions—hearty congratulations and thanks to you and all your troops."

* The reason for this failure to maintain touch with the 17th Division was due apparently to the fact that the observer in the contact aeroplane, which accompanied the attack, did not discover that in their advance the troops of the 17th Division, owing to a slight loss of direction, had reached their objective rather farther to the right than was anticipated and so had left a gap between them and the Guards.

† The casualty returns of the 3rd Guards Bde. during the first fortnight of October show a loss of 19 officers and 725 other ranks, the 1st Bn. Grenadier Guards and the 2nd Bn. Scots Guards sustaining more than half the casualties.

had been begun, and the great attempt to drive the enemy from the coast of Flanders had to be abandoned. Henceforward the fighting in the Ypres offensive was carried on in order to secure as good tactical positions as were possible for the winter months, and to occupy the attention of the enemy while the surprise attack in the Cambrai area was in course of preparation.*

(13) Relief of the Guards by the 35th Division, 17th of October.

For the remainder of their sojourn in this part of the line the Guards were only called upon to improve the defensive organization of the new front, and to maintain the communications in rear. Neither of these tasks was an easy or agreeable one. The enemy's artillery continually bombarded the whole countryside. The rain fell incessantly, and the Steenbeek and the Broembeek, especially the latter stream, poured their waters over their broken banks until the greater part of the divisional area was under water. The mud and squalor were indescribable, but the routes to the forward area were always kept open. The duckboard tracks were steadily pushed northward, a trestle bridge 80 feet in length was carried over the Broembeek swamp, two dumps were established at no great distance from the front line trenches, and, by the 17th of October when the 35th Division began the relief of the Guards, the divisional sector had assumed the characteristics normal in trench warfare. In view of the recent acquisition of the country and the deplorable weather conditions, the achievement was one of which all ranks were justly proud. On its relief the infantry of the Guards Division, with the exception of the 4th Bn. Coldstream Guards (Pioneers) and one of the Field Companies, R.E., which remained behind in the XIV Corps area to work on roads, railways and camps until the 8th of November, was moved by rail to the Eperlecques area, divisional headquarters being established at Esquelbecq.

* See p. 291.

(14) Work of the Divisional Artillery during the month of October.

The 74th and 75th Bdes., R.F.A., on their return to the line at the beginning of October, were employed in support of the attack of the 29th Division on the 4th of that month.* For the operations on the 9th, they formed part of a group of guns under the command of the C.R.A., 20th Division. By dint of an enormous amount of labour, most of the guns of the two brigades were got forward in order to cover the advance of the Guards. The batteries of the 74th Bde. fired from positions about 500 yards north of Abri Wood, and those of the 75th Bde. from positions in the valley of the Steenbeek on the right of Ruisseau Farm. The howitzers were farther forward on the northern side of the Wijdendrift road, but, so great was the difficulty of moving them over the heavy ground, that one section of each battery stuck in the mud and could not be brought up in time to take part in the engagement. The task of supplying the guns was also a laborious and anxious one as all the ammunition had to be carried forward by pack.

The creeping barrage on the 9th of October was most effective and its slow rate of progress was found entirely satisfactory by the infantry. After the objectives had been captured, the gunners were called upon to fire fairly often in response to S.O.S. calls, and this, together with the firing of practice barrages, kept them constantly employed.

On the 12th of October the 75th Bde. formed part of the right group of guns which covered the advance of the 3rd Guards Bde., but the work of the artillery on this day was not particularly exacting.

When the Guards Division left the line, its artillery remained, and there was a rearrangement in the grouping of the guns along this sector of the front which a few days later came under the command of the C.R.A., Guards Division. The 74th and 75th Bdes., as a result of this rearrangement, returned to the left group, and, on the 20th

---

* *See* p. 268.

of October, the former brigade took over the guns of the 152nd Bde., R.F.A., in muddy positions in the valley of the Steenbeek near Tuff's Farm. That day, and the day following, the two Brigades took part in area bombardments and a special gas bombardment preparatory to an attack delivered on the 22nd of October by the 35th Division in cooperation with the French. This attack resulted in a slight tactical improvement in the line.

Another forty-eight hours' bombardment of the enemy's positions began on the 24th of October in preparation for yet another advance. The batteries of the 74th Bde. were by this time in new positions on the Broembeek, which were served by a light railway. The problem of the ammunition supply, therefore, was much simplified and the pack-horses could be reduced to ten for each battery. Observation, at any rate in the direction of Passchendaele and Westroosebeke, was also considerably improved.

The attack on the 26th of October was on the right of the front held by the 35th Division, and the Guards divisional Artillery was not called upon to any great extent. The following day, however, its gunners supported an attack delivered by the French, and, on the 28th, and again on the 30th, they joined in the barrage fire that covered further operations on the right flank in which progress was made towards Poelcappelle and Passchendaele.

Altogether the month of October was a hard one for the artillery. In the 74th Bde. alone the casualties amounted to 11 officers and 68 other ranks, while 10 guns had to be sent to the rear for repairs, 5 others being repaired in the battery positions.* Throughout the month, too, all ranks were compelled to live and to fight in appalling conditions due to the continuous rain and cold. The wagon lines were invariably in a sea of mud and many of the drivers suffered from trench feet.

* In the course of the Ypres offensive this Bde., R.F.A., fired 250,000 rounds and had 33 guns knocked out, exclusive of 16 which were knocked out and repaired *in situ* by the battery artificers.

(15) WORK OF THE R.A.M.C. ON THE DIVISIONAL FRONT DURING THE YPRES OFFENSIVE.

Allusion has already been made to Major-General Feilding's tribute to the admirable work done by the officers and men of the R.A.M.C. on the 31st of July.* During the trying weather in which the remainder of the operations was carried out, the work of the R.A.M.C. was arduous in the extreme, and the organization by means of which the Corps coped with its difficulties was worthy of the highest praise.† For the advance on the 9th of October bearer posts for the collection of the wounded were established at Ruisseau Farm, Sentier Farm and Wijdendrift. The first-named farm was at the head of the trench tramway by which all stretcher cases were sent down to the advanced dressing-station at Green Mill. From there transit to the XIV Corps main dressing station at Solferino Farm, a few miles south-east of Elverdinghe, was by the Decauville railway line as there were no roads available for motor ambulances east of the Yser Canal. Walking wounded were directed down the duck-board tracks to Boesinghe Château, where tea and food were supplied to them before they went on to the corps collecting post.

All these arrangements worked well during the course of the attack, but, when the final objectives had been reached on the 9th of October, and the regimental aid posts of the four leading battalions were moved forward to Louvois Farm and Egypt House, the journey to the rear became a very long and trying one for the stretcher bearers. Their numbers, too, were quite inadequate for the purpose. With the assistance, however, of German prisoners the evacuation of the wounded was effected without any great delay, and, except for some more or less unavoidable irregularities in the running of the Decauville trains during the afternoon, the arrangements made by the A.D.M.S. worked satisfactorily. On the days following the attack the incessant rain and the heavy condition of the ground made the work of the stretcher

* *See* p. 255.
† *See* W.D., Guards Division, App. A.D.M.S. Report, October, 1917.

bearers still more arduous, while the task of clearing the wounded from Egypt House was an exceedingly dangerous one owing to the activity of the enemy's snipers. The number of bearers available also became still more reduced as during the heavy gas bombardment on the night of the 11th of October about 50 R.A.M.C. bearers became casualties. Henceforward no reliefs were possible, and, consequently, from this date until the Guards left the line all bearers were obliged to continue working in the forward area. From noon on the 8th of October to the 17th of October the R.A.M.C. evacuated over 1,800 stretcher cases and lost 6 officers and 83 other ranks in so doing.

(16) CASUALTIES SUFFERED BY THE GUARDS DURING THE OFFENSIVE.

It is by no means an easy matter to set down exactly the casualties of the Guards Division, or indeed of any division, in a series of offensive operations extending over a considerable period of time such as the Ypres offensive in 1917. The reasons for this difficulty are, first, that in some cases the returns are missing or incomplete, and secondly, that the units engaged in the different phases of the battle did not invariably send in returns covering the same periods of time. After the fighting on the 31st of July, for instance, some units when compiling the lists of their casualties included in their returns the losses sustained during the days of preparation before the attack, whereas others merely stated their losses during the actual engagement. The casualties among the attacking troops that day were naturally severe, but were not so heavy as might have been expected in view of the extent of the advance and the strength of the enemy's defensive organization. The 1st Guards Bde. lost 21 officers and 608 other ranks between zero hour on the 31st of July and the 3rd of August, when it was relieved in the line. Nearly three-quarters of these casualties were sustained by the 2nd Bn. Grenadier Guards and the 2nd Bn. Coldstream Guards and the machine-gun sections which accompanied them in their attack on the final objective.

The losses of the 2nd Guards Bde., for the period the 26th of July to midnight on the 31st of July, are reported as having been 29 officers and 826 other ranks, the battalions which suffered most severely being the 1st Bn. Scots Guards and the 2nd Bn. Irish Guards. The casualties in the 3rd Guards Bde. during the actual day's fighting on the 31st of July were returned as 12 officers and 319 other ranks.* But, in estimating the losses suffered by the division in this offensive, the casualties during the strenuous weeks of preparation for the attack should also be included—these losses, between the 1st of July and zero hour on the 31st, are stated to have amounted to 18 officers and 600 other ranks killed, wounded, gassed or missing.

In the fighting between the 9th and 15th of October the casualties of the division amounted to 24 officers killed and 56 wounded; 399 other ranks killed, 1,621 wounded and 164 missing—the total losses being returned as 2,264.†

(17) SUMMARY OF THE WORK DONE BY THE DIVISION IN THE BATTLES OF YPRES, 1917.

During the Ypres offensive the Guards Division carried forward the British line for a distance of about 6,000 yards, advancing from the Yser Canal to the outskirts of Houthulst Forest. Its task in comparison with that of some of the other divisions farther south may not have been so difficult or exacting, but its troops never failed to achieve their purpose and their success was due alike to the admirable organization of each enterprise by its staff, to the splendid discipline and courage of its artillery and infantry, and to the strenuous and unremitting exertions of its R.E. and pioneers who, notwithstanding heavy casualties and the appalling condition of the ground, never relaxed their efforts in the

---

* It will be observed that these returns do not include the divisional Artillery or divisional units other than the infantry. References have been made to the losses sustained by the gunners and R.E. in the preceding narrative, although it has not been possible to give the total figures.

† *See* W.D., " Q " Branch, Guards Division, 16th October, 1917.

THE ACHIEVEMENT OF THE GUARDS DIVISION

development and maintenance of the communications without which any continuance of the advance after the 31st of July would have been out of the question. The division lost during the course of the operations 303 officers and 7,898 other ranks. It inflicted very heavy losses on the enemy and captured 28 officers and 1,152 other ranks.* These officers and men came from no less than thirteen German divisions which were either immediately opposed to the Guards or which were stationed in neighbouring sectors of the line and employed for the purpose of counter-attacks on the divisional front.† In addition to these divisions, it is known that four other German divisions were used to resist the Guards Division and the divisions operating on its right.‡ In view of the number of divisions used by the enemy on this part of the front during the four months in which the Guards were in the line, there would appear to be no exaggeration in the estimate made at the time that the Guards Division and the 29th Division between them put out of action no less than six German divisions.

The pauses in the battle caused by the bad weather and the stubborn defence of the enemy farther south which delayed the northern advance of the British Army, and also the fact that the great majority of the enemy's gun positions were a long way in rear, naturally prevented any sensational captures of war material by the Guards, and they did well in securing 3 field guns, 1 howitzer, 31 machine guns and 9 trench mortars. The great achievements of the Guards Division was fully recognized by the Commander-in-Chief who, at a parade held at Inglinghem on the 25th of October, personally thanked Major-General Feilding and his troops for their brilliant services during the offensive. A few days

---

* These figures do not include wounded prisoners who were able to walk.

† The 6th Bavarian Division, the 18th, 26th, 27th, 208th and 227th Infantry Divisions, the 23rd, 26th, 49th and 111th Reserve Infantry Divisions; and the 3rd Gde. Division and the 187th and 240th Divisions.

‡ The 2nd Gde. Reserve Division, the 79th Reserve Division, and the 204th and 214th Divisions. *See* W.D., Guards Division, Report of Operations, October, 1917.

previously H.R.H. the Duke of Connaught had paid the division an informal visit, and he afterwards sent to the Major-General a special message of congratulation. The Fifth Army commander and the XIV Corps commander acknowledged in glowing terms their appreciation of the gallant behaviour and magnificent discipline displayed by the division whilst under their command, and General Nollet, commanding the French XXXVI Corps, also recorded in writing his appreciation of its services.* But the message

* The following telegram was received by Major-General Feilding from General Sir H. Gough when the Guards Division left the Fifth Army :—" During their five months in the Fifth Army the Guards Division have set an example to all and maintained the high standard one expects from them—their admirable work when holding the line and their complete success in the battles of July 31st and October 9th and 12th have been of the greatest value to the Army as a whole and also to our French Allies by whose side they fought—in bidding good-bye to the division I should like all ranks to know how grateful I am for all they have done during the third battle of Ypres."

Lord Cavan wrote as follows to Major-General Feilding :—" I am sure that all Guardsmen will understand that it is difficult for me, as a Guardsman of 32 years completed service, and at the same time a commander of other divisions, to express as fully as my heart dictates, my appreciation of the performance of the Guards Division. . . . I need not say that the success in battle of the division is the dearest and sincerest wish of my heart. I think it is literally true that the division has never had what used to be called in South Africa an ' unfortunate incident '—more than that—it has never failed to perform its allotted task. In this last battle of Flanders the Guards Division have captured almost exactly 6,000 yards of fortified positions in depth. Details of its captures, of prisoners and material, I leave to your staff to compute. Those are only material results. The true results are—1. That the Guards Division has done its duty to its Colonel-in-Chief—His Majesty the King. 2. That its traditions are on a higher plane, if possible, than they have ever been. 3. That it inspires the confidence of the Commander-in-Chief and the army commander to whom it may belong. Lastly, it has never failed its corps commander, and I thank you all with a sincerity that must be obvious for the grit, determination, and valour that you have shown and the steadfast maintenance of our greatest traditions."

General Nollet, in forwarding to Major-General Feilding the brevets of some officers and men whose names he had cited in an order of the XXXVI Corps and certain *Croix de Guerre* for distribution by the Major-General, said :—" Je souhaite que ces croix perpetuent en eux le souvenir des liens d'affectueuse amitié et de confiance reciproque qui se sont noués entre eux et leurs camarades du 36m Corps au cours des heures de combat vecues côte à côte." He also paid a special tribute to the perfect satisfaction given to him by the British liaison officers.

which gave the most satisfaction to all ranks of the Brigade of Guards was the following letter addressed to Major-General Feilding by Colonel Clive Wigram on behalf of His Majesty the King :—

" DEAR FEILDING,
" Lord Cavan has informed the King of the doings of the Guards Division in the recent offensive. His Majesty has read with admiration and satisfaction the story of their splendid achievements, and the King heartily congratulates you and the division on all that has been accomplished in spite of the most unfavourable conditions of weather and mud.

" As Colonel-in-Chief of the Guards His Majesty is proud to think that there has been imposed upon the division no task that has not been successfully fulfilled. The King has no doubt that after a well-earned rest, rebuilt and re-equipped, the division will distinguish itself in the future as it has distinguished itself in the past, and His Majesty sends you all his best wishes.
" Yours sincerely,
" CLIVE WIGRAM."
"Buckingham Palace, 17th October, 1917."

(18) CHANGES IN THE COMMANDS AND ON THE STAFF OF THE DIVISION DURING THE COURSE OF THE YPRES OFFENSIVE.

Two important changes in the brigade commands occurred while the Guards Division was engaged in the third battle of Ypres. Towards the end of August Brig.-General J. Ponsonby left the division on his appointment to the command of the 40th Division. His departure was universally regretted, for no more popular commander ever existed. He was succeeded in the command of the 2nd Guards Bde. by Brig.-General B. N. Sergison-Brooke, whose appointment gave the greatest satisfaction to all ranks.* On the 22nd of September Brig.-General G. D. Jeffreys, another experienced commander who could ill be spared, left the Division in order to assume the command of the 19th Division. Lieut.-Colonel C. R. C.

* See " Reminiscences of a Grenadier," p. 163.

de Crespigny was appointed to command the 1st Guards Bde. in his place, and remained in that position until the end of the war. Major G. E. C. Rasch succeeded Lieut.-Colonel de Crespigny in the command of the 2nd Bn. Grenadier Guards. On the 5th of September Lieut.-Colonel C. P. Heywood, G.S.O.1, proceeded to England on his appointment as an instructor of the Staff Course at Cambridge, and his place was taken by Lieut.-Colonel the Honble. A. G. A. Hore-Ruthven, who previously had been G.S.O.1 of the 62nd Division.

Various changes in the commands of battalions, to which allusion has not already been made in the notes to the narrative, took place about this time. Early in October Major Longueville succeeded Lieut.-Colonel R. B. Crawford in the command of the 3rd Bn. Coldstream Guards, and a little previously Lieut.-Colonel R. Tempest, who was appointed to command the 43rd Infantry Bde., had been succeeded in the command of the 1st Bn. Scots Guards by Major M. Romer. On the 18th of October Lieut.-Colonel R. Skeffington-Smyth returned to England and Major G. J. Edwards took his place as commanding officer of the 4th Bn. Coldstream Guards (Pioneers).

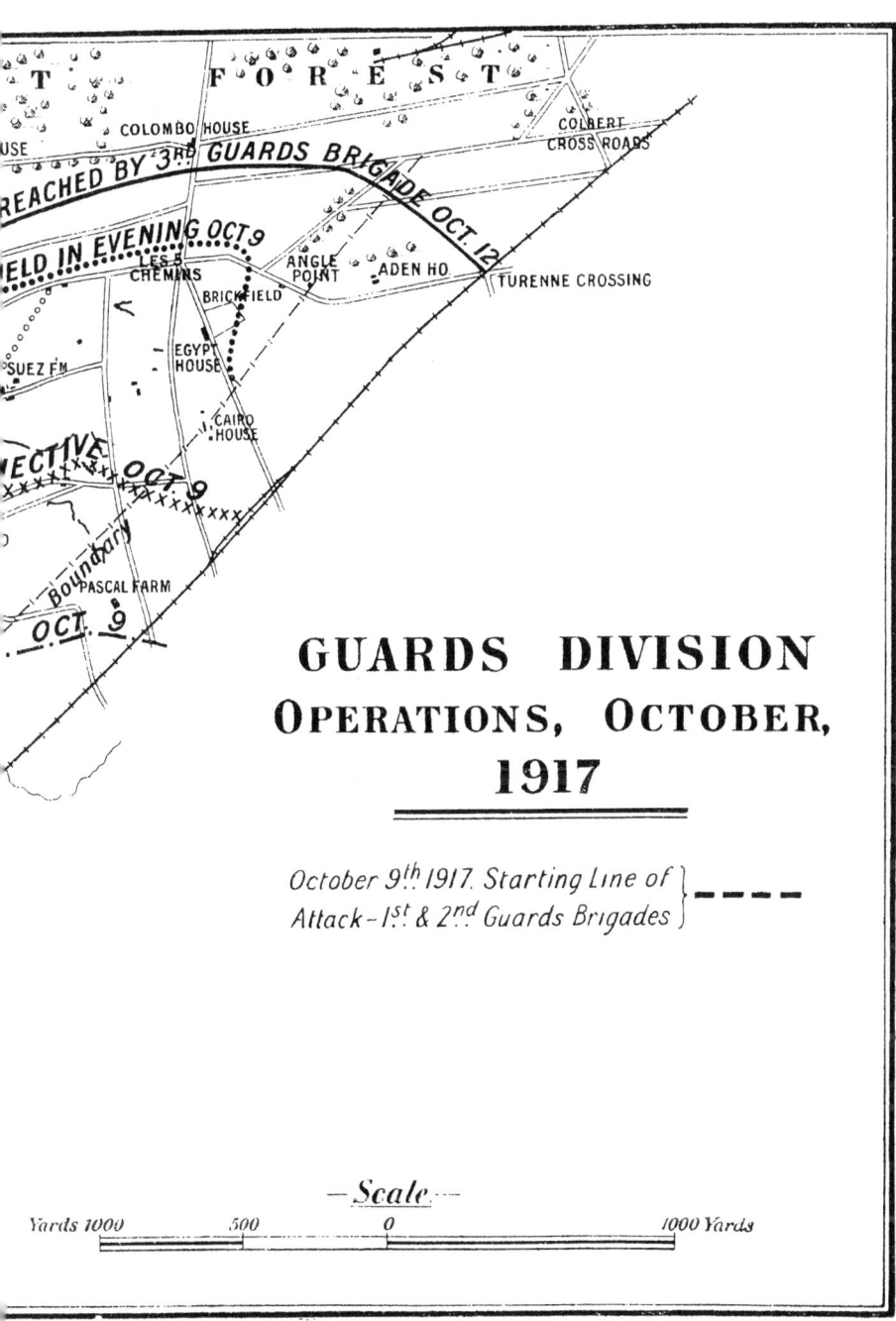

CHAPTER X

THE CAMBRAI OPERATIONS, 1917—THE ATTACK ON FONTAINE-NOTRE-DAME BY THE 2ND GUARDS BRIGADE, 27TH OF NOVEMBER.

(1) THE REASONS FOR THE CAMBRAI OFFENSIVE.

As to the political reasons which prompted the British Commander-in-Chief to carry out the attack in the Cambrai area in November, 1917, it is unnecessary to deal at any length in this book. The attack in its main features had been planned some months beforehand because it was considered that this front was " the most suitable for the surprise operations in contemplation. The ground there was, on the whole, favourable for the employment of tanks which were to play an important part in the enterprise, and facilities existed for the concealment of the necessary preparations for the attack." * The actual decision, however, to put the plan into execution at this particular date was influenced very largely by the belief that a sudden and unexpected blow on the Western Front, on which the enemy's power of resistance had already been put to a severe strain by the Flanders offensive, would be of assistance to the Italians by preventing the dispatch of German troops from France to exploit the great victory which the Central Powers had gained at Caporetto.† Nevertheless, with the limited number of troops at his disposal, it was clear to Sir Douglas Haig that, unless he was able to take the enemy completely by surprise,

---

* See " Sir Douglas Haig's Despatches," p. 151.

† The attack on the Cambrai front " was started in some part to help Italy after Caporetto, though planned months before ; it was continued in some part for the same cause after the initial success had ended." See " Sir Douglas Haig's Command, 1915–1918," p. 386.

he would be unable to achieve the object which he had in view. His intention was to break through the Hindenburg Line between the Canal de l'Escaut and the Canal du Nord. If this task were carried out quickly and successfully, he hoped to be able to exploit his victory, and, by pushing forward his cavalry before the Germans had had time to bring up their reserves to cover the advance of his infantry on to the high ground to the west of Cambrai, the possession of which would enable him to turn the enemy's defences to the north.*

The whole success of the operation, therefore, depended upon secrecy and expedition. The secret was well kept and there is no doubt that the attack at Cambrai took the Germans completely by surprise.† Had the actual conduct of the battle been equally successful, there is no reason to suppose that the operation, as originally planned by the British Commander-in-Chief, might not have led to large results. Whether or not it was wise to continue the offensive after its initial success had ended in comparative failure and the enemy had had time to reorganize his defence is a matter which will be discussed later on.

(2) THE GUARDS DIVISION MOVES SOUTH—SCOPE OF THE PROPOSED OPERATIONS IN FRONT OF CAMBRAI EXPLAINED TO MAJOR-GENERAL FEILDING—OPENING OF THE ATTACK, 20TH OF NOVEMBER—THE GUARDS MOVE INTO THE BATTLE ZONE—RELIEF OF THE 51ST DIVISION IN THE LINE BY THE 1ST AND 3RD GUARDS BRIGADES.

The Guards Division had only been in rest billets in the Second Army area for about three weeks when orders were received for it to move southward. No intimation was given, however, as to the destination of the division or as to the reasons which made the move necessary, and there was in consequence a good deal of speculation—most of it very

* See "Sir Douglas Haig's Command, 1915–1918," vol. i. pp. 390, 391.
† See "My War Memories, 1914–1918," by General Ludendorff, vol. ii. p. 494.

CAMBRAI PLANS EXPLAINED

wide of the mark—amongst officers and men as to the fate that was in store for them.* The move by route march was begun on the 9th of November, and, by the 12th, the division (less artillery) was concentrated in the neighbourhood of St. Pol, where it ceased to be in G.H.Q. Reserve and came under the orders of the V Corps. Meanwhile, the divisional Artillery, moving under orders issued direct to its commander by the First Army, had arrived in the Aubigny area, where it once more came under the orders of the Guards Division.

On the 11th of November the B.G.G.S. of the V Corps paid a visit to Major-General Feilding and explained to him privately the scope of the coming attack by the Third Army on the Cambrai front and the general plan of operations. The object of the offensive was to break through the Hindenburg Line on a front of about 10,000 yards between Gonnelieu and Havrincourt. This task was to be carried out by two Corps—the III Corps on the right and the IV Corps on the left. The two Corps were to attack simultaneously without any preliminary artillery bombardment, but the infantry was to be supported by a large number of tanks. The III Corps was to seize the Bonavis—Lateau Wood spur and the crossings of the Canal de l'Escaut at Masnières and Marcoing, thus forming a defensive flank, while the IV Corps was to storm the Havrincourt—Flesquières ridge and to advance northward in order to capture the high ground on which Bourlon Wood and the village of Fontaine-Notre-Dame were situated. Once this high ground was captured, it was confidently anticipated that the continuance of the advance towards the Sensée river would turn the whole of the German defensive positions to the north.

The scheme of operations entailed a rapid exploitation by the cavalry of any success obtained by the infantry and tanks, and orders had consequently been given to the Cavalry Corps, less the 1st Cavalry Division, to be ready to pass through

* " One knows from the record of the 1st Battalion (Irish Guards) that the whole Division now on the move were prepared for and given to believe anything—even that they might be dispatched to Italy, to retrieve October's disaster of Caporetto." *See* " The Irish Guards in the Great War," vol. ii. p. 175.

the infantry in order to isolate Cambrai and to seize the high ground to the east and north-east of that town as well as the crossings of the Canal de la Sensée east of Paillencourt. The successful carrying out of this manœuvre would have the effect of cutting off the enemy's troops within the Quéant salient. The 1st Cavalry Division, which was attached to the IV Corps, was to assist in the capture of Bourlon village, and then to secure the crossings of the Canal de la Sensée west of Paillencourt.

The V Corps was being held in readiness to support the attack, but its actual task would naturally depend upon the measure of success obtained by the other two Corps, and all that the B.G.G.S. could tell Major-General Feilding was that its three divisions—the 40th Division, the Guards Division and the 59th Division—were to approach the area of operations in the order named. On the 15th of November the V Corps Commander (Lieut.-General Sir E. Fanshawe) saw Major-General Feilding and Major-General J. Ponsonby, commanding the 40th Division, and confirmed the information already given to them by his B.G.G.S. He also strongly emphasized the importance of the maintenance of the most rigid secrecy with regard to the forthcoming offensive. Major-General Feilding then called a meeting of his brigadiers and commanding officers, and, after explaining to them the plan of operations and the urgency of keeping the secret, instructed them to spread the rumour among their troops that the division was on its way south to relieve the French and that, owing to the scarcity of transport caused by rolling stock and motor vehicles having been sent to Italy, much baggage would have to be left behind at St. Pol. This rumour was generally believed, and the mobility of the division was much increased. Every opportunity was also taken to practise the troops in open warfare schemes, while the Guards Reinforcement Battalion was reformed with the battle surplus from each battalion, the division adhering to its usual fighting strength of thirty-two men in a platoon. On the 16th of November Major-General Feilding saw General Sir Julian Byng, commanding the Third Army, who told him definitely that the Guards Division would be held in readiness to move forward in the event of Bourlon Wood being captured by the IV Corps, in which case the Division would pass through the gap in the enemy's defences and would attack north in rear of the German front line in conjunction with the 40th Division.* By the 17th of November the whole of the infantry of the Guards Division had reached the vicinity of Le Cauroy, and, at 11 p.m. on the 19th, after two fatiguing night marches along roads congested with traffic, the division was billetted round Achiet-le-Petit and Gomiecourt.

On the 20th of November, at 6 a.m., the attack of the III and IV Corps on a front of about six miles from east of Gonnelieu to the Canal du Nord opposite Hermies was launched in a mist of drizzling rain. It was at first attended with extraordinary success. The enemy's line was broken on a comparatively broad front and several thousand prisoners, as well as many guns and much material, were captured at a cost of but few casualties to the attacking troops.† At the end of the day's fighting, however, the situation was not particularly satisfactory, so far at any rate as the contemplated scheme of exploitation was concerned. Bourlon Wood had not been reached; a decided check had been experienced in front of Flesquières; the enemy's troops in Mœuvres and north of the area of attack showed no sign of withdrawing; and the British cavalry had failed to make use of its fleeting opportunity to push through the German lines and to isolate Cambrai.‡ But in despite of this partial

* In view of subsequent events it is interesting to note that the Third Army commander assured the Major-General on this occasion that the Guards Division would not be employed in the offensive unless Bourlon Wood were captured the first day of the attack. In the event of the failure of the IV Corps to capture the wood, he told the Major-General that there was no intention of continuing the operation and that the plan was to withdraw to a line through Flesquières.

† "At the end of the first day of the attack, three German systems of defence had been broken through to a depth of some four and a half miles on a wide front, and over 5,000 prisoners had already been brought in. But for the wrecking of the bridge at Masnières and the check at Flesquières, still greater results might have been attained." *See* "Sir Douglas Haig's Despatches, 1915–1918," p. 157.

‡ "Strong bodies of cavalry assembled behind the triumphant leading infantry divisions failed, even on this occasion, to overcome

success, the British Commander-in-Chief considered that the results which had been obtained were sufficient to justify him in continuing the offensive—and this, although he had failed to gain possession of the all-important Bourlon—Fontaine-Notre-Dame ridge and could no longer count upon the advantage of surprise. The attack, consequently, was resumed on the 21st of November. On the morning of this day an order was received for the Guards Division to move at short notice to the Beaumetz-les-Cambrai area, but in the course of the afternoon the destination of the division was altered to Barastre. Buses were supplied by the corps for the conveyance of the infantry, but, as they were late in arriving and as by this time the route was blocked with every kind of traffic, the journey was a long and tedious one. The 1st and 3rd Guards Bdes. did not actually reach their billets in the new area until 4 a.m. and 9 a.m. respectively, on the 22nd of November. The battalions of the 2nd Guards Bde. which, with the exception of the 3rd Bn. Grenadier Guards, elected to march, reached their new quarters somewhat earlier. The men were tired out, and the remainder of the 22nd was spent by the troops in getting as much rest as the weather and the limited accommodation would permit. Divisional headquarters was established at Haplincourt and the artillery was billetted at Lechelle.

The 23rd of November was a trying day for Major-General Feilding and for his staff, as well as for the fighting troops of the division for whom it was " a day full of orders—countermanded orders—new orders—and lack of orders." * The previous evening the division had been ordered to move forward early in the morning of the 23rd to the Beaumetz—Doignies—Lebucquière area, and by 10 a.m. the 1st Guards Bde. was at Doignies, the 3rd Guards

the last line of resistance, weak though it was, which barred the way to the flanks and rear of their opponents. The English cavalry squadrons were not able to conquer the German defence, with the help of their tanks, and proved unequal to decorating their standards with that victory for which they had striven so honourably and so often." *See* " Out of my Life," by Marshal von Hindenburg, p. 291.

* *See* W.D., 2nd Bn. Grenadier Guards, November, 1917.

Bde. at Beaumetz and the 2nd Guards Bde. at Lebucquière. The division now came under the orders of the IV Corps (Lieut.-General Sir C. L. Woollcombe), but divisional headquarters was still at Haplincourt. About midday Major-General Feilding received a telegram from the IV Corps stating that the Guards might be called upon to relieve the 51st Division in the line that night,* but the telegram contained no intimation as to the whereabouts of the headquarters of the 51st Division and its brigades. It was not until 2 p.m. that this necessary information could be obtained from the IV Corps. The brigadiers of the 1st and 3rd Guards Bdes. then started off to get in touch with the brigades which they were to relieve, but, as the locations supplied by the IV Corps turned out to be incorrect, they were for a long time unsuccessful in their quest. It was, indeed, more by good luck than by good management that by about 6 p.m. they succeeded in finding the advanced headquarters of the 51st Division at Flesquières. They then discovered that the staff of that division had received no instructions as to the relief by the Guards and was, as a matter of fact, arranging its own divisional relief. Meanwhile, the G.S.O.1 of the Guards Division had gone to the headquarters of the IV Corps where, at 2 p.m., he received at last a definite order for the Guards to relieve the 51st Division that night.

Major-General Feilding then ordered the 1st and 3rd Guards Bdes., in the order named, to move forward, and, as their brigadiers had not yet rejoined their troops, he instructed the two brigades to await their arrival at Lock No. 5 on the Canal du Nord.

The 2nd Guards Bde. was ordered to remain at Lebucquière for the night and to advance to Ribécourt via Metz and Trescault the following morning (24th of November) starting at 7 a.m. The divisional Artillery, which had been ordered by the IV Corps to move from Lechelle to Haplincourt on

---

* At 8.30 a.m. on the morning of the 23rd of November Major-General Feilding had asked the IV Corps whether his division was to be employed to relieve any division in the line and had been told that it was " most unlikely."

the 23rd, and the R.E. Companies, also received orders to move forward on the morning of the 24th, the former to the south-west corner of Havrincourt Wood, the latter to Trescault. Meanwhile, later in the evening on the 23rd of November, the brigadiers of the 1st and 3rd Guards Bdes. had rejoined their respective brigades, and, during the night of the 23rd–24th, the relief of the leading brigade of the 51st Division had been effected by the 1st Guards Bde.— the 2nd Bn. Grenadier Guards reaching Graincourt about midnight, where it replaced the 9th Bn. Royal Scots. The incoming battalion had to borrow the Lewis guns of the Royal Scots as none of its own transport had got forward beyond Hermies.

The line taken over by the 1st Guards Bde. stretched from a point south-east of Cantaing to the south-east of Bourlon Wood—a distance of approximately 4,400 yards. This front was held by three battalions in line—the 2nd Bn. Grenadier Guards on the right, the 1st Bn. Irish Guards in the centre, the 3rd Bn. Coldstream Guards on the left. The 2nd Bn. Coldstream Guards remained in support at La Justice, east of Graincourt, where also brigade headquarters was established. The 1st Guards Bde. Machine-Gun Company was obliged to take over the guns which were already in position as its own guns, together with all the brigade transport, were blocked on the line of route. Four of these guns were in position on the southern edge of Bourlon Wood and four others were in support farther south beyond the Bapaume—Cambrai road. The 3rd Guards Bde. was assembled in support round Flesquières, one of its battalions being pushed forward in divisional reserve to the south-west of La Justice.

Fortunately for all concerned the night was a quiet one, for the relief was an arduous and difficult undertaking. In order to carry it out the two Guards brigades had to cover a distance of over fifteen miles, more than half of this distance having to be traversed in the dark over entirely unknown and very heavy country. In addition to which, it must be borne in mind that the 51st Division was not expecting to be relieved by another division and had consequently

THE GUARDS IN THE LINE AGAIN

made none of the usual preparations—nor, indeed, was its staff aware of the exact positions occupied by its leading troops. The successful accomplishment of the relief, therefore, in such circumstances, was a feat of skill and endurance which reflected the greatest credit on all ranks.

At 10 a.m. on the 24th of November, Major-General Feilding took over the command of the sector of the line between Cantaing and the south-east corner of Bourlon Wood with his advanced headquarters at Flesquières and his rear headquarters at Trescault. The 2nd Guards Bde. was moved up to Ribécourt during the course of the day and the divisional Artillery was also brought forward into a position of readiness to go into action as soon as darkness set in so as to supplement the four brigades R.A., which already covered this portion of the front.*

(8) Results of the Fighting between the 21st and 24th of November.

In order to understand the situation in which the Guards Division now found itself, it is necessary to pause in the narrative in order to set down as shortly as possible the course of the battle on this portion of the front subsequent to the initial attack on the 20th of November.

The 51st Division had made its original assault from the British line in the neighbourhood of Trescault, and, after storming the Hindenburg Line, had crossed the valley and attacked Flesquières ridge and village. Here the enemy had offered a strenuous resistance and it was not until the morning of the 21st that the village was captured. The 51st Division had then pushed forward, in conjunction with the 62nd Division on its left, towards Fontaine-Notre-Dame and Bourlon. These two divisions succeeded in capturing Anneux, while the 6th Division, on the right of

---

* The front of the division was supported by four brigades R.F.A. These were reinforced on the night of the 24th–25th of November by the two brigades Guards divisional Artillery. It should be mentioned that all guns were in the open and under direct observation of the enemy holding the high ground about Fontaine-Notre-Dame.

the 51st Division, drove the Germans out of Cantaing. Later on the same day the 51st Division took Fontaine, and the 62nd Division, after heavy fighting, gained a footing in Bourlon Wood.

No further attack was made by the British on the 22nd of November, but the Germans made a vigorous counter-attack which resulted in their regaining possession of Fontaine during the course of the afternoon—an achievement which was destined to have a deciding effect upon the subsequent operations.* The next morning the 51st Division, supported by tanks, made an attempt to regain Fontaine, but, although some of the tanks succeeded in making their way into the village, no real progress was made and the locality remained in the enemy's hands. During the course of the same day, however, the 40th Division, which had relieved the 62nd Division, on the left of the 51st Division, after desperate fighting, entered Bourlon village, and, although its troops were unable to remain there, they succeeded in despite of various German counter-attacks in retaining a somewhat precarious hold of the south-western portion of Bourlon Wood throughout the night of the 23rd–24th of November.

(4) THE 3RD GUARDS BRIGADE SENT TO THE ASSISTANCE OF THE 40TH DIVISION—THE 2ND BN. SCOTS GUARDS AND THE 4TH BN. GRENADIER GUARDS IN ACTION IN BOURLON WOOD AND SOUTH-EAST OF IT, 25TH OF NOVEMBER.

Although the enemy shelled Cantaing and the Bapaume—Cambrai road intermittently throughout the day, the 24th

* This counter-attack was mainly carried out by troops of the 107th Infantry Division which had been entrained on the Eastern Front about the middle of November and which, luckily for the Germans, was beginning to arrive in the Cambrai area just at this time. General Ludendorff is of the opinion that the success on the 22nd of November materially altered the situation in favour of the Germans, and it was after the recapture of Fontaine that the plan to take the British attack in flank was decided upon. *See* " My War Memories, 1914–1918," vol. ii. p. 496.

of November passed comparatively quietly on the front held by the 1st Guards Bde. The various battalions in the line, which was held by a series of posts, sent out numerous patrols which gained touch with the 6th Division west of Noyelles-sur-l'Escaut, and ascertained that the Germans were in considerable strength at Fontaine.

On the left of the sector occupied by the Guards, however, the situation of the 40th Division in Bourlon Wood towards nightfall became distinctly critical. In the morning the enemy had launched two counter-attacks and had succeeded in strengthening his hold of the high ground. Throughout the day the troops of the 40th Division had offered a stout resistance to his farther advance, but the division had now been in action continuously for two days and it was clear that, unless it could be reinforced by fresh troops, it would be impossible for it to maintain its position in Bourlon Wood. In the evening, therefore, the 3rd Guards Bde. was placed at the disposal of the G.O.C., the 40th Division.

The 2nd Bn. Scots Guards was at once moved forward in support of the 119th Infantry Bde. At 8.30 p.m. a message reached the battalion from this brigade stating that, in consequence of repeated German counter-attacks, the position on the right of the 40th Division was critical. Upon receipt of this information the 2nd Bn. Scots Guards continued its advance with as much expedition as was possible, and soon after 10 p.m. reached Anneux Chapel. Meanwhile, the 1st Guards Bde. Machine-Gun Company had moved some of its guns in order to strengthen the threatened flank of its own brigade. The night was very dark, and the inevitable confusion was increased owing to the activity of the enemy's machine gunners, who were exceedingly well posted on the high ground in the centre of Bourlon Wood. But all difficulties were overcome and the Scots Guards were successful in linking up the refused flank of the 1st Guards Bde. on their right with mixed units of the 119th Infantry Bde. on their left. As soon as this task had been accomplished, the battalion sent out patrols to endeavour to locate the exact line held by the Germans preparatory to the attack which it was proposed to launch at dawn. Although the members of the first of these patrols were all either killed or wounded, the positions occupied by the enemy were eventually located.

Early in the morning on the 25th of November the 2nd Bn. Scots Guards, with three companies in the line, in cooperation with some reorganized units of the 40th Division on its left, assaulted the German line. The Germans were in considerable strength, fully on the alert and well provided with machine guns, but, although they offered a vigorous resistance, the attacking force drove them back and established the British line on the highest ground in Bourlon Wood. So satisfactory, presumably, were considered the results of this attack, that the Scots Guards were called upon to carry out another advance, the object of which was to force the remaining Germans off the north-eastern shoulder of the hill. At 2 p.m., consequently, the battalion again moved forward, but, although it made some progress,* the attack was on far too small a scale, and had too little weight behind it, to make it possible for the Scots Guards to effect their purpose.

Meanwhile, during the course of the same day, another battalion of the 3rd Guards Bde.—the 4th Bn. Grenadier Guards—had become involved in the fighting on this part of the front. This battalion, which advanced to the La Justice area during the night of the 24th–25th of November, was also sent to the assistance of the 119th Infantry Bde. In the morning on the 25th it was ordered to move forward in order to occupy some trenches south-east of Bourlon Wood,† and, at about 11.30 a.m., this advance was begun. The line of route through Graincourt to Anneux was under the direct observation of the German gunners and the battalion was subjected to very heavy shell fire. The Grenadiers, however, moving forward in platoons at 200 yards' interval, maintained

---

* The company on the right, after gaining some valuable ground, was forced by the intensity of the enemy's machine-gun fire to dig in. It drove back several German counter-attacks, and held its ground, although all its officers were put out of action. During the day's fighting the battalion suffered heavy casualties from the enemy's machine-gun and rifle fire.

† These trenches were marked on the map, but were found not to be in existence. *See* Guards Divisional Narrative.

their traditional steadiness and discipline.* Luckily, the casualties were less severe than might have been expected owing very largely to the fact that when the enemy's barrage was at its heaviest a violent hailstorm came down and hid the advancing troops from sight. The battalion eventually succeeded in reaching the southern edge of Bourlon Wood, where three companies dug themselves in with their entrenching tools, while the remaining company remained in support under cover in Anneux.

After nightfall on the 25th the 62nd Division relieved the 40th Division in the line, and the 2nd Bn. Scots Guards was replaced by troops belonging to the 186th Infantry Bde. The Scots Guards then withdrew into support to a position in the south-eastern portion of Bourlon Wood about 400 yards in rear of the front line, while the 4th Bn. Grenadier Guards moved forward into the wood and took up a position on their left. The two battalions remained in these positions until the evening of the 26th of November when they were both relieved, the 2nd Bn. Scots Guards moving back to Flesquières and the 4th Bn. Grenadier Guards to the south-eastern corner of Bourlon Wood, where it came under the orders of the 2nd Guards Bde.†

* The battalion " had to advance in full view of the Germans, who at once put down a heavy barrage in front of it. With the utmost coolness and steadiness the 4th Battalion advanced through this barrage as if it was on parade, and earned special praise from General Ponsonby." *See* " The Grenadier Guards in the Great War," 1914–1918, vol. ii. pp. 271, 272.

† In appreciation of the good service performed by the Guards during these two days, the following message was received from Major-General Ponsonby, commanding the 40th Division :—

" I wish to express on behalf of my division my sincere thanks for the support given us on the 24th and 25th of November, by the battalions of the Guards Division placed at my disposal for the defence of Bourlon Wood—namely, the 2nd Scots Guards and the 4th Grenadier Guards.

" I would like to bring to notice particularly the 2nd Scots Guards, who throughout the period prevented the enemy from breaking through the right flank of the position, and assisted in repelling at least two of the enemy's counter-attacks.

" I enclose extracts from the report of the Brig.-General commanding 119th Infantry Brigade :

"'The 2nd Scots Guards reinforced the firing line which had become very thin early in the morning of 25th of November and

(5) THE DECISION FOR THE GUARDS TO ATTACK FONTAINE-NOTRE-DAME—MAJOR-GENERAL FEILDING'S OBJECTIONS TO THE ATTACK OVERRULED.

The fighting on their left during the 25th of November did not much affect the battalions which were holding the front of the 1st Guards Bde., but this period of comparative peace was not to be of long duration for, in the afternoon of that day, Major-General Feilding received a visit from the B.G.G.S. of the IV Corps, who informed him that the Guards Division would be called upon to participate in an attack on Bourlon Wood at an early date. In view of what Sir Julian Byng had himself told him,* and taking into account the results so far achieved after four days' fighting, the Major-General felt very strongly that such an attack delivered from the line occupied by the Guards, in addition to being a costly undertaking, could not be carried out successfully. The wood, which was situated on a ridge running east and west, was the most commanding feature in the landscape for miles round. It crowned a conical shaped hill a little to the east of which on its southern slope lay the

---

remained in action till they came under the orders of the 186th Brigade' —62nd Division—' on the night 26–27 November.

"'All ranks behaved with the utmost gallantry, and assisted to repel two German counter-attacks at least, in addition to continual enemy pressure.

"'They inspired all with great confidence.

"'The 4th Grenadier Guards came under my command in the afternoon of the 25th inst. To reach a position of readiness they had to cross the open in artillery formation for a great distance under enemy observation and were heavily shelled in so doing.

"'They were as steady as on parade.

"'The 3rd Coldstream Guards, on the initiative of their commanding officer, materially assisted to readjust my broken right flank by reinforcements of men and machine guns, on night of the 24th inst. at a very critical period. By so doing they were instrumental in carrying out an important readjustment of the line.'

"To the above-mentioned units I wish to express my gratitude!"

In circulating the above message the G.O.C., Guards Division, "hoped that it would be kept as a record of a difficult piece of work most creditably performed." *See* W.D., Guards Division, December, 1917, App. 616.

* *See* p. 294.

THE IMPORTANCE OF BOURLON WOOD

undemolished village of Fontaine-Notre-Dame held by the enemy. South of the Bourlon ridge the country to the east of the Hindenburg Line as far south as the Flesquières ridge is of a considerably lower elevation, so that the villages of Graincourt-lez-Havrincourt, Anneux and Cantaing lay in a basin surrounded on three sides by hills.

The possession of the ridge on which Bourlon Wood stood was as essential to the enemy, therefore, as it was to the British.* It was clear that he would continue to defend it to the last man.† It was equally clear that he had reinforced

---

* See " Sir Douglas Haig's Despatches, 1915–1918," p. 159.

† In his Cambrai Despatch Sir Douglas Haig, in explaining his decision to continue the offensive and to attempt to secure possession of the Bourlon ridge, states that there were signs that the enemy was preparing for a retirement. " Craters had been formed at road junctions, and troops could be seen ready to move east." He admits that his own troops were tired out and that the enemy's reinforcements were coming up, but he was so much impressed with the great results which would follow the capture of the ridge that he felt justified in making the attempt. " It was to be remembered . . . that the hostile reinforcements coming up at this stage could at first be no more than enough to replace the enemy's losses ; and although the right of our advance had definitely been stayed, the enemy had not yet developed such strength about Bourlon as it seemed might not be overcome by the numbers at my disposal. . . . An additional and very important argument in favour of proceeding with my attack was supplied by the situation in Italy, upon which a continuance of pressure on the Cambrai front might reasonably be expected to exercise an important effect, no matter what measure of success attended my efforts. Moreover, two divisions previously under orders for Italy had on this day been placed at my disposal, and with this accession of strength the prospect of securing Bourlon seemed good." See " Sir Douglas Haig's Despatches, 1915–1918," pp. 159, 160. In their interesting but somewhat uncritical account of Sir Douglas Haig's conduct of the campaign on the Western Front, Mr. G. A. B. Dewar and Lieut.-Colonel J. H. Boraston defend the policy of the British Commander-in-Chief in continuing the operations at Cambrai after the failure of the original plan of exploitation which they insist—and rightly insist—was the main purpose of the battle. In discussing the operations, however, they appear to forget that the majority of the troops at Cambrai had only just emerged from the ordeal of the third battle of Ypres, where there was certainly no sign " of hoarding our resources," nor was there ever any question of our being able to give the enemy " a knock-out blow " at Cambrai. Even had the exploitation been fully successful in compelling the Germans to retire from that town and their positions to the north of it, it would still have been impossible at that season of the year and with the troops at his disposal for Sir Douglas Haig

his line since the opening of the battle and that his defence was becoming better organized each day. On the 21st and 22nd of November there had been comparatively little hostile artillery and machine-gun fire, as the majority of the German guns and machine guns in this sector of the line had been captured on the first day of the offensive; but, from the 23rd onwards, the enemy's artillery fire had increased in volume whilst his machine-gun defence had daily become more and more vigorous. The British Intelligence reports stated that the majority of the German guns which were now coming into action were north of Bourlon Wood, and on the high ground south and west of Cambrai. They were placed, therefore, in positions from which they could fire upon troops attacking the Bourlon ridge in front, in rear and also on the flank. If, then, the capture of this ridge could not be effected during the first days of the offensive when the enemy's defensive system was entirely disorganized and his troops in retreat, how much less easy would it be to drive him out of the wood and off the hill when he was fully prepared for the attack and had a plentiful supply of guns ? *

So profoundly convinced was Major-General Feilding that in the circumstances the proposed attack on Bourlon Wood and Fontaine-Notre-Dame was a dangerous and impracticable undertaking for which there could be no kind of justification, that he at once requested that a conference

to press his strategic advantage. It is all very well for Mr. Dewar and Lieut.-Colonel Boraston to condemn "the policy of small and 'perfect' operations without strategic aim . . . as about the most cold-blooded and diabolic in war," but the battle of Cambrai, even had it achieved its purpose, was really nothing else. Had the British Commander-in-Chief, therefore, decided to break off the engagement after the first day's fighting and drawn back his line along the main Flesquières ridge, it would have been a perfectly justifiable tactical move which most practical soldiers with experience in the war would have commended—which no one in his senses could have described as a "pottering game of *grignotage*." *Cf.* "Sir Douglas Haig's Command, 1915–1918," vol. i. p. 403.

* In addition to the reasons which have already been mentioned against the attack, possession of the Bourlon ridge would not *ipso facto* have rendered secure the line which the Third Army was then holding unless the high ground just south-east of Cambrai were also captured, for the enemy's guns in that area not only commanded the country to the west as far as Flesquières, but also the Bourlon ridge itself.

might be held in order that he might explain to the IV Corps commander his objections to the attack.*

A conference was accordingly held the following morning at the headquarters of the 62nd Division at Havrincourt. Major-General Feilding handed in a written appreciation of the situation,† in which he set out very fully the reasons which made him believe that the proposed operations must inevitably end in failure. He pointed out that his division was being ordered to make an attack into a small salient from a salient, and that his troops as they advanced would be exposed to the enemy's artillery fire from three sides. He also drew the attention of the corps commander to the fact that he only had six fresh battalions available for the operation, namely, the 2nd Guards Bde. and two battalions of the 3rd Guards Bde. Instead, therefore, of the isolated attack on the Bourlon ridge, he advocated either an attack which should include the capture of the high ground south-east of Cambrai as well as the Bourlon ridge, or the making of the Flesquières ridge the main line of defence and the consequent withdrawal of the British front to render such a line secure.

The corps commander, after listening to the Major-General's arguments, stated that he could give no decision, that the matter must be referred to the Third Army commander, whose arrival he was expecting. The Major-General then suggested that it might be well to consider the details of the proposed attack on the Bourlon ridge in case it were decided to proceed with it, but, as the corps commander was unprovided with any plan, or artillery programme, or objectives, or divisional boundaries, it was

* In view of eventualities, the Major-General took the precaution of pointing out to the B.G.G.S. that the Guards were holding a long line, and that, if the attack were to take place, they would be called upon to advance across a stretch of country in full view of the enemy's gunners and to capture an undemolished village which would be stoutly defended. He requested, therefore, that Fontaine-Notre-Dame should be subjected to an intense bombardment by all the heavy artillery available. The B.G.G.S. assured him that this bombardment should be carried out.

† *See* W.D., Guards Division, No. 2707/202/G.

impossible to make any arrangements, with the result that much valuable time was lost.

The Third Army commander arrived about 11 a.m., and, notwithstanding the Major-General's objections, decided that the attack as originally contemplated was to take place. It was settled, therefore, that on the 27th of November the Guards were to seize Fontaine-Notre-Dame, while the 62nd Division * was to complete the capture of Bourlon Wood, and to attack the eastern end of Bourlon village. The 6th Division, on the right of the Guards, was ordered to take over ground as far north as the road junction north of Cantaing in order that the wide frontage held by the Guards might be somewhat reduced. As soon as the Third Army commander had given his decision for the attack on the Bourlon ridge to take place, Major-General Feilding hurried back to his own headquarters, where his brigadiers were awaiting his arrival, and a plan for the operation on the following day was hurriedly drawn up, the unenviable task of capturing Fontaine-Notre-Dame being entrusted to the 2nd Guards Bde., which, it will be remembered, lay in reserve at Ribécourt.†

(6) The 2nd Guards Brigade takes over the line preparatory to the attack on Fontaine-Notre-Dame.

At 2.30 p.m. on the 26th of November, when the order for the attack on Fontaine-Notre-Dame the following day reached the 2nd Guards Bde., the brigade was already advancing in order to relieve the 1st Guards Bde. in the line.‡

* Commanded by Major-General W. P. Braithwaite.

† During the course of the afternoon of this day (the 26th of November) the artillery bombardment of Fontaine-Notre-Dame, for which Major-General Feilding had asked, was carried out by the IV Corps; but, as only two batteries and one section of 6-in. howitzers were employed, it was quite ineffective.

‡ " As far as the 2nd Guards Brigade was concerned, their Brigadier was not told of the intended attack on Bourlon till the afternoon of the 26th; the C.O.'s of battalions not till four o'clock, and Company Commanders not till midnight of that date. No one engaged had seen the ground before, or knew anything about the enemy's dispositions. Their instructions ran that they were to work with the 186th Brigade on their left ' with the object of gaining the whole of Bourlon Wood,

ARRIVAL OF THE 2ND GUARDS BDE.

Its battalions, therefore, had first to carry out the relief and then to move into their respective positions of assembly for the attack—a double task which complicated an already difficult situation. The weather, too, made matters still more unpleasant as it snowed persistently during the night, and the ground was terribly heavy. The troops, who had already been compelled to lie out in the open for two nights and were drenched to the skin, had to endure, therefore, a particularly trying ordeal on the eve of the battle.

The brigade, after encountering a heavy hostile barrage on the Bapaume—Cambrai road and the southern edge of Bourlon Wood,* reached its allotted positions on the Guards divisional front about 1 a.m. on the 27th of November. Its arrival released the 2nd Bn. Scots Guards,† which, as already stated, withdrew to the neighbourhood of Flesquières, and also the 4th Bn. Grenadier Guards, the other battalion which had assisted the 40th Division. This latter battalion remained in support positions in the south-eastern portion of Bourlon Wood with orders to occupy the front line as soon as the attacking battalions had vacated it, while the 1st Bn. Welsh Guards was brought up early in the morning of the 27th of November to the sunken road between La Justice and Graincourt, where it came under the orders of the Brigadier commanding the 2nd Guards Bde.

(7) HURRIED ARRANGEMENTS FOR THE ATTACK.

The only order issued by the IV Corps for the attack on the Bourlon position by the Guards Division and the 62nd Division stated that the object of the operation was to gain

La Fontaine and the high ground behind it.' As a matter of fact, they were to be brought up in the dark through utterly unknown surroundings; given a compass bearing, and despatched at dawn into a dense wood on a front of seven hundred yards, to reach an objective a thousand yards ahead." *See* " The Irish Guards in the Great War," by Rudyard Kipling, vol. ii. p. 178.

* The 2nd Bn. Irish Guards sustained 40 casualties as a result of this barrage.

† This battalion lost 5 officers and 91 other ranks between the 24th of November and this date.

all the ground on the ridge "from which the enemy can observe our batteries," and to take the village of Bourlon. The allotted objectives were for the Guards Division, Fontaine-Notre-Dame, and, for the 62nd Division, Bourlon. The attack was to be covered by a barrage supplied by the artillery of the two divisions, and the heavy artillery, and the artillery of the 36th Division were also to render such assistance as might be directed by the B.G.G.S., R.A., of the corps. Three dismounted regiments of the 2nd Cavalry Division were placed at the disposal of the G.O.C. the 62nd Division, while the artillery of the same cavalry division was placed under Major-General Feilding's orders.* Tanks, fourteen of which belonging to "F" Bn. were to assist the Guards attack,† were also detailed to cooperate with the infantry of each division.‡

On the front of the Guards Division the attack was to be covered by a creeping barrage fired by six brigades, R.F.A., the pace of the barrage throughout being fixed at 100 yards in 5 minutes with a pause of half an hour on the first objective—a line running through the cross-roads in the middle of Fontaine-Notre-Dame, thence to the railway line about 200 yards west of the station, thence approximately along the railway line and the northern edge of Bourlon Wood. It was proposed to make this line the main line of defence in the event of the attack proving successful.

The second and final objective was the railway station at Fontaine-Notre-Dame together with the eastern outskirts of that village. Here it was intended to form an outpost line with strong points on the two main roads leading eastward from the village.

A heavy standing barrage was to be placed on La Folie Wood throughout the attack, as well as on all the approaches to Fontaine-Notre-Dame, while the D.M.G.O., Guards Division, was ordered to arrange for a machine-gun barrage

* As a matter of fact this brigade, R.H.A., arrived too late upon the scene of action to take any part in the bombardment.

† Twelve of these tanks were in position with the troops of the 2nd Guards Bde. at 5 a.m. on the 27th of November. The other two broke down on their way to the front line.

‡ *See* IV Corps Operation Order, No. 328.

on the ground beyond the second objective by the guns belonging to the 3rd, 4th and 11th Bde. Machine-Gun Companies. Four guns of the 7th Motor Machine-Gun Company, were also placed on the spur of high ground just north-west of Cantaing in order to sweep with fire the eastern exits of Fontaine-Notre-Dame.

(8) Attack by the 2nd Guards Brigade upon Fontaine-Notre-Dame.

Punctually at zero hour, 6.20 a.m. on the 27th of November, the artillery barrage came down and the Guards went forward to the attack *—the 3rd Bn. Grenadier Guards on the right, the 1st Bn. Coldstream Guards in the centre, the 2nd Bn. Irish Guards on the left.

The Grenadiers, advancing along both sides of the Bapaume—Cambrai road, were to assault Fontaine-Notre-Dame; the Coldstream, extending fan-wise from their starting point, were to seize the railway line from the northern edge of that village to the eastern edge of Bourlon Wood, their task being to gain possession of the south-eastern slope of the ridge; while, farther up the same slope, the Irish Guards were to force their way through the eastern portion of Bourlon Wood and to gain touch with the troops of the 186th Infantry Bde. on their left.

The remaining battalion of the 2nd Guards Bde., the 1st Bn. Scots Guards, which was holding a trench line of about 1,000 yards to the south of Fontaine-Notre-Dame, was made responsible for the protection of the right flank of the attack, with orders to push forward a company and a machine gun along the sunken road which led northward to the southern side of the village as soon as the first objective had been taken.†

---

* The tanks were late in crossing the line, but some of them caught up the infantry during the advance.

† The reason why this battalion was especially instructed to make use of this sunken road was that in previous attacks troops crossing the open country in this area had been wiped out by machine-gun fire from La Folie Wood. *See* Narrative of Operations by the 2nd Guards Bde., 27th of November, 1917.

Almost immediately after leaving their trenches the Grenadiers encountered very heavy machine-gun fire, which came mainly from the direction of La Folie Wood. The two companies advancing south of the Bapaume—Cambrai road suffered severely from this enfilade fire, and, before they had reached the shelter of the houses on the outskirts of Fontaine-Notre-Dame all their officers and non-commissioned officers had been put out of action with the exception of one non-commissioned officer who, with six determined men, fought his way forward as far as the village church, where the party joined up with the other two companies of the Battalion. These companies, assisted by some tanks, had already reached their first objective after hard fighting. It was now 7.15 a.m. and the situation, so far as the Grenadiers were concerned, was far from satisfactory. Their first objective had, indeed, been most gallantly carried and the greater part of Fontaine-Notre-Dame was once again in British hands. But parties of Germans were still holding out in two derelict tanks, and in some trenches just south of the village, while the cost of the attack had been far too great for the strength of the attacking force. Two of the companies engaged had practically ceased to exist, and the casualties in the other two companies had been severe.

On the left of the Grenadiers the enemy almost at once gave ground as the Coldstream advanced.* But after going forward for about 200 yards the left company of the attacking force, which was badly enfiladed by machine-gun fire from the high ground in Bourlon Wood, unfortunately swung too much to the left, and so lost touch temporarily with the centre company. The advance of this latter company was checked by the determined resistance of a party of Germans posted in a quarry just outside Fontaine-Notre-Dame. Here it lost all its officers, with the exception of its

* The Coldstream complained that the artillery barrage was feeble and erratic, and also that the four tanks, detailed to cooperate with them, were late in arriving and of no practical assistance to them until they had reached their final objective. In justice to the gunners it should be borne in mind that all the arrangements for this attack were so much hurried and so incomplete that no time was given them to make their preparations or to carry out any preliminary registration

commander, and most of its non-commissioned officers, but, nothing daunted, the company pressed on, and, bombing its way along a trench, eventually succeeded in rushing the quarry from a flank capturing 3 machine guns and about 200 prisoners, in addition to killing 40 of the enemy with the bayonet. It then advanced to its first objective, to which line, however, only about 50 men of the company on the left succeeded in making their way. Meanwhile, the company on the right had made more rapid progress. After driving the Germans from their trenches on the west of Fontaine-Notre-Dame, it entered the northern side of the village at 7.30 a.m. and chased the enemy as far as the railway line at the point of the bayonet, capturing many prisoners, 2 field guns and 2 machine guns. Having gained touch with the Grenadiers on their right, the Coldstream at once sent forward patrols, but their situation was little more satisfactory than that of the Grenadiers. The battalion had carried out its allotted task with great dash and determination, but the casualties in its ranks had been so great that it was found impossible to fill up a gap of about 300 yards between its right flank and the Grenadiers, and there was also a considerable gap between its own centre company and the company on the left. It was, moreover, now exposed to a heavy and incessant machine-gun fire from the high ground north of the railway line as well as from the enemy's trenches east of Fontaine-Notre-Dame.

On the left of the attack the Irish Guards also had a difficult task. Their left company was checked by machine-gun fire from a German strong point on the front of the 186th Infantry Bde., but the other attacking companies, in despite of a particularly stout resistance on the part of the enemy, succeeded in reaching their objective, capturing a considerable number of prisoners on their way. Here they gained touch with the Coldstream on their right and with the 2/5th West Riding Regiment (186th Infantry Bde.) on their left. But, as in the case of the other attacking troops, the Irishmen were in no enviable position. The line which they had gained was being violently shelled, and, in addition to this, it was found that the enemy was still in possession of a strong point on the high ground in the centre of the wood, and was also in great strength along the railway line to the north. The battalion had suffered many casualties in the advance and it was impossible to fill up a gap which separated it from the troops on its left flank. In these circumstances there appeared to be only one thing to do, and the commanding officer ordered his men to dig themselves in, with their left flank refused. While the Irish Guards were endeavouring, therefore, to consolidate a line just outside the north-east edge of Bourlon Wood, the Grenadiers and Coldstream, at about 7.45 a.m. sent forward parties to capture the second line of objectives. The Grenadiers reached their objective, the eastern edge of Fontaine-Notre-Dame, without much difficulty; but the small party which had been left astride the Bapaume—Cambrai road was about this time driven back by a German counter-attack, and, although the men gallantly returned to the attack, and, with the assistance of two tanks, regained the lost ground, their casualties, due to the enemy's intense machine-gun fire, were too heavy for them to do anything more than to consolidate their position.*

Had the 1st Bn. Scots Guards, on the right of the Grenadiers, been able to gain touch with them, the situation might possibly have been somewhat improved. But, although a company of Scots Guards, about 7 a.m., made a great effort to proceed up the sunken road towards Fontaine-Notre-Dame, it was unable to get within about 150 yards from the southern outskirts of the village, and the patrols which were sent forward failed to reach the Grenadiers. The enemy's machine-gun fire from the houses in the southern portion of the village cost this company all its officers and half its entire strength, but, nevertheless, the remaining men, ably handled by a sergeant, successfully beat off a German counter-attack.

* The tanks went forward to put down the machine-gun fire, but were forced to withdraw on account of the effectiveness of the enemy's fire. The S.m.K. (armour piercing ammunition) used by the Germans was very powerful. It is said to have gone through brick walls as if they were made of paper. *See* Narrative of the Operations of the 2nd Guards Bde., 27th of November, 1917.

GERMAN COUNTER-ATTACK

The Coldstream, on the left of the Grenadiers, were able to seize the railway station where, besides capturing or killing about 50 Germans, they took a field gun. Their success, however, was only of a temporary nature, as they were speedily shelled out of their new position, and, although the officer commanding the party, after collecting a few more men, returned and again succeeded in capturing the objective, the position was found to be untenable.

(9) WITHDRAWAL OF THE 2ND GUARDS BRIGADE TO THE BRITISH FRONT LINE.

By about 8.80 a.m., therefore, although the troops of the 2nd Guards Bde. had reached their final objectives on the greater part of the line, the attacking force was so weak numerically that it was obvious that it could not maintain its hold of the ground which it had captured so gallantly unless it could be reinforced without delay. The enemy's counter-attacks from the north and east were developing in strength, in addition to which Fontaine-Notre-Dame still contained many Germans, for neither the Grenadiers nor the Coldstream were in sufficient strength to carry out the task of clearing up the village. The Coldstream, indeed, had been allotted so extensive a front that it had only been possible to detail one platoon for this all-important work—a force which, casualties apart, was entirely insufficient for the purpose. As a result, runners were sniped at from the houses, and prisoners broke away from their escorts to join their comrades who were still lurking in the half-ruined houses and cellars.

As soon as this state of affairs was reported to Brig.-General Sergison-Brooke, he ordered the 4th Bn. Grenadier Guards to move forward, one company in support of the 3rd Bn. Grenadier Guards, two companies in support of the 1st Bn. Coldstream Guards and the remaining company to watch the left flank of the 2nd Bn. Irish Guards. At the same time, he sent a telephone message to divisional headquarters asking that the 1st Bn. Welsh Guards might be sent forward and placed under his orders. This request was immediately complied with.

Unfortunately, however, not one of these movements could be carried out in time to improve the situation. The enemy, in considerable strength, working down the railway cutting from a northerly direction, fell upon the isolated remnants of the company on the left flank of the Coldstream and drove them in, only 1 officer and 15 men managing to find their way back to the old line.

This German success had the additional effect of rendering still more precarious the position of the Irish Guards. Threatened on their left flank by the Germans who had remained in the wood and who by this time had been reinforced, and with the enemy penetrating through the gap created by the withdrawal of the Coldstream on their right, the Irish Guards were now practically cut off from the 186th Infantry Bde. on their left * and the remainder of the 2nd Guards Bde. on their right. They had no chance of breaking off the action as there was a heavy hostile barrage on the ground in rear of them, while the enemy, covered by the fire of his field guns, pressed forward to the attack all along their thinly-held line. It was only with the greatest difficulty and at a great cost, that the Irish Guards succeeded in extricating themselves from their extremely awkward situation; but, by about 2 p.m., 1 officer and 79 other ranks had found their way back to their old line and were in touch with the troops on their flanks. At the close of the day the battalion was 117 strong.†

Meanwhile, the remnants of the 3rd Bn. Grenadier Guards

---

* The advance of the 186th Infantry Bde. had been slower than that of the Guards, but its troops are reported to have " practically reached all their objectives " during the course of the afternoon. *See* W.D., 62nd Division, November, 1917. Subsequently, they were forced back on their left flank as the result of repeated counter-attacks. By the evening the left battalion of the brigade was back on the high ground in Bourlon Wood more or less in the positions from which it had advanced to the attack, facing north-west. Its right battalion was in touch with the left battalion of the Guards. The 187th Infantry Bde., which had attacked on the left of the 186th, after making its way half-way through Bourlon, had also been forced to withdraw.

† *See* " The Irish Guards in the Great War," vol. ii. pp. 180, 181.

and the 1st Bn. Coldstream Guards were also vigorously counter-attacked, and they, too, were in great danger of being cut off and surrounded by the enemy. The Germans advanced in strength through Fontaine-Notre-Dame, and also along the Bapaume—Cambrai road where all that remained to stop their progress was a post of Grenadiers, the strength of which had been reduced to half a dozen men. Any further attempt to remain on the line of the final objectives was clearly out of the question, and the Grenadiers, after informing the Coldstream of their intention, withdrew westward to their old trenches, but not before they had temporarily checked the onrushing Germans by well-directed machine-gun and rifle fire.

The Coldstream, after doing their best to destroy with bombs the 2 captured field guns, also made good their retirement. The brigade was then ordered to hold its original line as it was deemed useless to occupy the old German line which afforded no field of fire and the wire of which was of course on the western side.

The brigade and the 4th Bn. Grenadier Guards were relieved during the night by the 1st Bn. Grenadier Guards, the 1st Bn. Welsh Guards and two companies of the 2nd Bn. Coldstream Guards. The shattered battalions of the 2nd Guards Bde. were withdrawn into support positions round La Justice, and the 4th Bn. Grenadier Guards moved to Flesquières.

(10) Work of the 2nd Guards Brigade Machine-Gun Company during the Fighting, 27th of November.

The work of the machine gunners throughout the course of the engagement on the 27th of November was extremely arduous from the beginning to the end of the day.* One gun was utilized to fire on La Folie Wood from the front occupied by the 1st Bn. Scots Guards; and another gun, the whole of the team of which became casualties, was

* *See* W.D., 2nd Guards Bde. Machine-Gun Company, November, 1917.

carried forward with the attacking company of the same battalion, which advanced up the sunken road.* The two gun teams, which attacked in conjunction with the Grenadiers, got well forward to a position in the main street of Fontaine-Notre-Dame and brought their guns into action in rear of a barricade after the Germans had been bombed out of the adjacent houses. When the attacking force was obliged to withdraw, these machine guns were fired from a position near the factory and did much execution among the enemy's troops as they came back into the village. The four gun teams, which accompanied the 1st Bn. Coldstream Guards, reached the railway cutting with the centre attacking company, but were unable to find a good field of fire and so could play no important part in the fighting. The officer in command of the two gun teams which acted in cooperation with the company on the right flank of the Irish Guards was killed; his guns were reported to have been in action at the north-eastern corner of Bourlon Wood, but no more was heard of them. The officer in command of the two teams on the left flank of the Irish Guards was also killed, and there was little opportunity for his gunners until the time came for the withdrawal when they played an effective part in covering the extreme left of the Guards line.

(11) COMMENTS ON THE ENGAGEMENT OF THE 27TH OF NOVEMBER.

The losses suffered by the 2nd Guards Bde. in the abortive attack upon Fontaine-Notre-Dame were naturally very severe. The total casualties returned for the period from the 26th to the 28th of November amounted to 38 officers and 1,043 other ranks of whom 9 officers and 481 other ranks were reported as missing.†

* *See* p. 314.
† A great many of the wounded among these casualties were brought back with the aid of German prisoners. Most of those reported missing were either killed or severely wounded during the final counter-attack. The 2nd Guards Bde. took over 600 prisoners during the course of the fighting, but many of these escaped on their way to the rear

When such heavy losses occur in a comparatively small and unsuccessful action, the question naturally must be asked whether the operation as planned was a feasible one—in this case, whether the 2nd Guards Bde. could have achieved success. There can be little doubt that all that Major-General Feilding said in opposition to the proposed attack on the Bourlon ridge, was amply borne out by the day's fighting on the 27th of November, and that the higher authorities completely under-estimated the difficulties of the task which they were setting the Guards Division and the 62nd Division. They were so anxious to obtain possession of the all-important high ground that they failed to realize that a task, which it had been proved impossible of attainment when the enemy had been taken by surprise, could not be achieved by means of a minor attack seven days later, when he had reorganized his defences and brought up reinforcements. The limited scope of the operation of course made the task of the attackers all the more difficult, because the fire of the enemy's guns was concentrated upon a small area of country and the advancing troops were under direct observation almost from the moment they left their trenches. But, in addition to the failure to appreciate the strength of the enemy's positions, the higher authorities called upon the Guards to attack upon a front which previous experience should have taught them was far too wide. When the division was called upon to assault Fontaine-Notre-Dame, it will be remembered that it was occupying a front about 3,500 yards in length, but, when its final objectives were reached by the 2nd Guards Bde. on the 27th of November,

---

owing to the lack of men for their escort. In addition to the casualties in the 2nd Guards Bde., the 1st Guards Bde., whilst holding the line previous to the attack, lost 5 officers and 51 other ranks, and the 2nd Bn. Scots Guards and the 4th Bn. Grenadier Guards, which were involved in the fighting on the 26th of November, lost 12 officers and 169 other ranks between the 25th and 28th of November.

The medical arrangements in the forward area worked well, although on the 27th of November, it was found impossible to clear the battlefield after the withdrawal to the original front line until after darkness had set in. The clearance of the wounded from the main divisional dressing station at Flesquières was much hindered owing to lack of cars.

this line was increased to 5,300 yards *—a front wholly beyond a division's capacity to hold after a hard day's fighting in the face of a determined and more powerful hostile force plentifully supplied with machine guns and artillery of all types. Over and above this serious blemish in the plan of operations, however, it must not be forgotten that all the arrangements for the attack were hurried and incomplete. After Major-General Feilding's return from the conference at IV Corps headquarters on the 26th of November there was barely time for the necessary orders for the attack to be written; neither the officers nor the non-commissioned officers of the attacking battalions could be given any opportunity of seeing by daylight the assembly positions or the ground over which they were to advance †; the artillery arrangements were wholly inadequate; the preliminary bombardment by the heavy guns, which was essential to success in an attack upon a fortified village where the element of surprise was lacking, was quite ineffective, there was no neutralizing fire on the enemy's batteries and strong points (such as La Folie Wood) during the course of the engagement, and the barrage covering the attack was not dense enough to protect the advancing troops from the enemy's machine-gun fire. It is highly questionable whether a local attack, arranged in such a haphazard and casual manner, against a position of such strength as the Bourlon ridge could have been successful, even if it had been possible to utilize twice the number of men available; but the task of the assaulting troops on the 27th of November was rendered still more difficult owing to the fact—unknown of course to the Third Army commander—that the Germans were themselves planning a counter-attack for the same day. The fierce attacks from north-east of Bourlon Wood and Fontaine-Notre-Dame, which finally drove back the remnants of the 2nd Guards Bde., were delivered by no less

* In Flanders on July 31st the line held by the Guards Division at the beginning of the offensive was about 1,600 yards in length, and when the troops had reached their objectives this frontage had only been increased by 300 yards.

† Even air photographs of the ground to be attacked were not available.

THE GUARDS LEAVE THE LINE 321

than four German battalions supported by heavy artillery fire, while the enemy had still three more regiments in reserve.*

In the circumstances, therefore, the results of the day's fighting reflected no discredit upon the Guards Division. Its officers and men went through the ordeal with their customary discipline and courage. If they did not actually win success, they gave their lives ungrudgingly to achieve it. Their failure was nothing of which to be ashamed. The pity of it was that so many brave men were sacrificed in vain.

(12) RELIEF OF THE GUARDS BY THE 59TH DIVISION.

About 4 p.m. on the 27th of November the IV Corps informed Major-General Feilding that the Guards were to be relieved by the 59th Division, but, as two of the brigades of this Division had a considerable distance to come in order to reach the front line, the relief could not be carried out in its entirety that night. The 2nd Guards Bde., therefore, was moved to Ribécourt and the 3rd Guards Bde. (less one battalion in Flesquières) to Trescault, while the 1st Guards Bde. (less one battalion, the 2nd Bn. Coldstream Guards) marched from Ribécourt to Metz-en-Couture on its relief by a brigade of the 59th Division. Luckily, the enemy's artillery was not particularly active during the night of the 27th–28th of November, and these various movements were effected without much difficulty.

The 28th of November was also a tolerably quiet day, although the enemy bombarded the valley south of Bourlon Wood with great persistency. During the following night the remaining infantry of the Guards Division in and north of Flesquières were relieved by troops of the incoming 59th Division, and, at 10 a.m. on the 29th, Major-General Feilding handed over the command of the sector to the G.O.C. of that division. The 3rd and 4th Guards Bde. Machine-Gun

* *See* prisoners' statements, Narrative of Operations by the 2nd Guards Bde., 27th of November, 1917.

Companies remained in Flesquières under the orders of the 59th Division.

By about 6 p.m. on the 29th of November divisional headquarters had been established at Neuville; the 1st Guards Bde. was concentrated in Metz; the 2nd Guards Bde. in Ruyaulcourt and Bertincourt, and the 3rd Guards Bde. in Trescault.

END OF VOL. I.

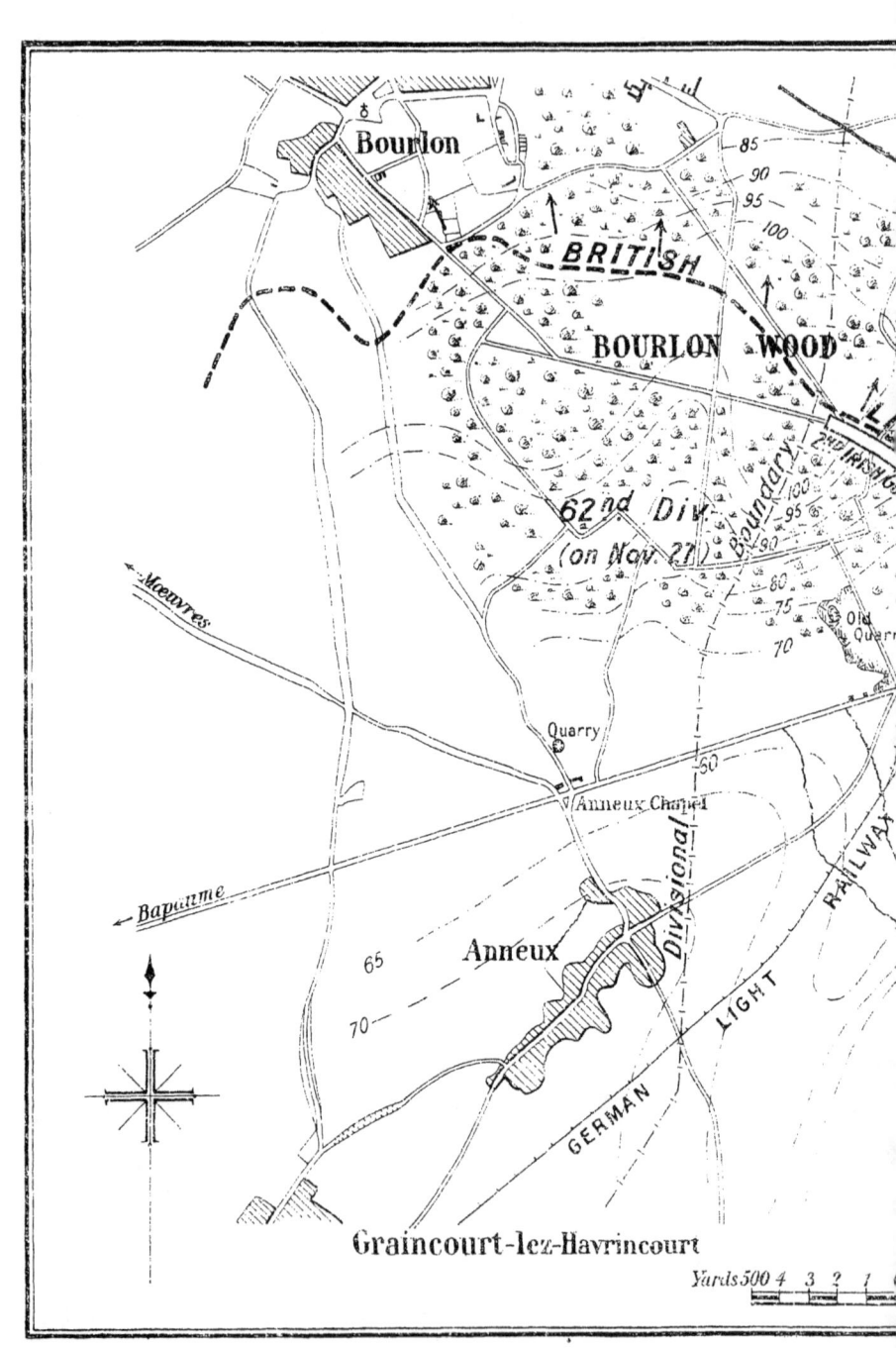

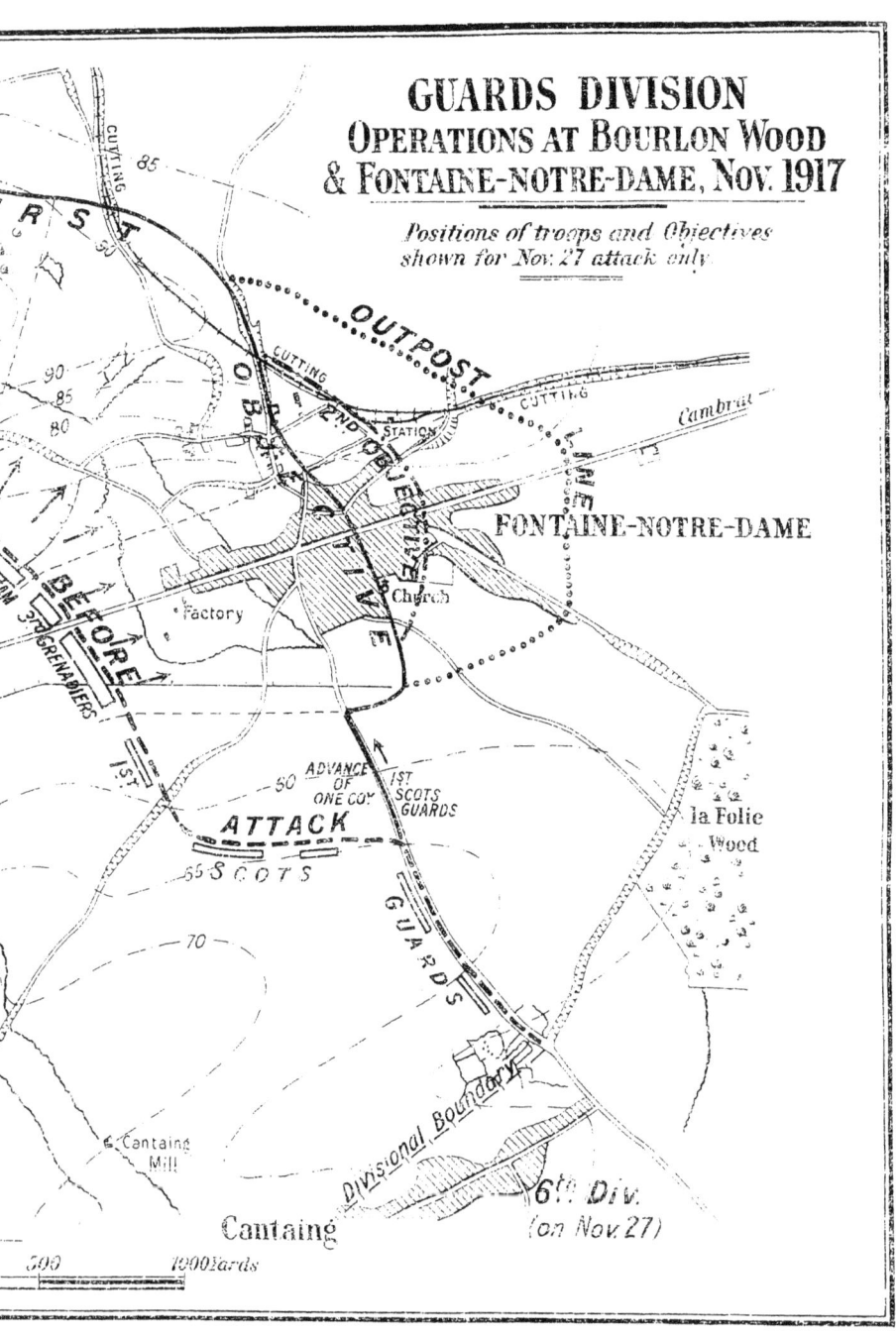

www.ingramcontent.com/pod-product-compliance
Lightning Source LLC
Chambersburg PA
CBHW061930220426
43662CB00012B/1856

HISTORY OF THE GUARDS DIVISION IN THE GREAT WAR, 1915–1918

Vol. I

All rights reserved